P9-DUJ-996

AN INVESTMENT

IN KNOWLEDGE ALWAYS

B FRANKLIN

GIFT of THE

John
Templeton
Foundation

in HONOR of THE

Benjamin
Franklin
TERCENTENARY

1706 - 2006

INTEREST

PAYS THE BEST

Page Talbott EDITOR

Richard S. Dunn and John C. Van Horne CONSULTING EDITORS

Rosalind Remer EXECUTIVE DIRECTOR, BENJAMIN FRANKLIN TERCENTENARY

Walter Isaacson INTRODUCTION

Edmund S. Morgan AFTERWORD

ESSAYS BY Ellen R. Cohn, James N. Green, E. Philip Krider, Emma J. Lapsansky-Werner,

J. A. Leo Lemay, Robert Middlekauff, Billy G. Smith, and Page Talbott

PHOTOGRAPHY BY Peter Harholdt

BENJAMIN

Franklin

IN SEARCH OF A BETTER WORLD

Yale University Press NEW HAVEN AND LONDON

To the late Edward C. Carter II, former librarian of the American Philosophical Society

Published with assistance from the Benjamin Franklin Tercentenary.

Designed by Sonia L. Shannon
Set in Bulmer type by BW&A Books, Inc.
Printed in Italy by EuroGrafica SpA.

Library of Congress Cataloging-in-Publication Data
Benjamin Franklin : in search of a better world / Page Talbott, editor ; Richard S. Dunn and John C. Van Horne, consulting editors ; introduction by Walter Isaacson ; afterword by Edmund S. Morgan ; photography by Peter Harholdt.
    p. cm.
   "Essays by Ellen R. Cohn, James N. Green, E. Philip Krider, Emma J. Lapsansky-Werner, J. A. Leo Lemay, Robert Middlekauff, Billy G. Smith, and Page Talbott."
   Includes bibliographical references and index.
   ISBN 0-300-10799-4 (alk. paper)
   1. Franklin, Benjamin, 1706–1790—Exhibitions. 2. Franklin, Benjamin, 1706–1790—Anniversaries, etc.—Exhibitions. 3. Statesmen—United States—Exhibitions. 4. Scientists—United States—Exhibitions. 5. Inventors—United States—Exhibitions. 6. Printers—United States—Exhibitions. I. Talbott, Page. II. Dunn, Richard S. III. Van Horne, John C.
   E302.6.F8B485 2005
   973.3'092—dc22   2005005185

A catalogue record for this book is available from the British Library.

The paper in this book meets the guidelines for permanence and durability of the Committee on Production Guidelines for Book Longevity of the Council on Library Resources.

10 9 8 7 6 5 4 3 2 1

Benjamin Franklin Tercentenary Commission

French Honorary Committee

Under the High Patronage of Jacques Chirac, *President of the French Republic*

Co-Chairman Howard H. Leach, *United States Ambassador to France*

Co-Chairman Jean-David Levitte, *Ambassador of France to the United States*

Pierre Arizzoli-Clémentel, *Director, National Museum of Versailles*

François d'Aubert, *Minister Delegate for Research*

Etienne–Emile Baulieu, *President, Academy of Sciences, Emeritus Honorary Professor at the Collège de France*

Jean-René Bernard, *President, France-Amériques Association*

Michel Besson, *National President, France/US Associations*

Chatel de Brancion, *Regent of the Daughters of the American Revolution, Rochambeau Chapter*

Bertrand Delanoë, *Mayor of Paris*

Renaud Donnedieu de Vabres, *Minister for Culture and Communication*

Jacques Friedmann, *President, Conseil d'Orientation, Quai Branly*

Michel Garcin, *President, France-America Foundation*

Paul Girod, *Chairman, Senate France-USA Friendship Group*

Jean-Noël Jeanneney, *President, Bibliothèque Nationale de France*

Jean-Marc Leri, *Director, Musée Carnavalet*

Christine Malphettes, *State Regent, Rochambeau Chapter, Daughters of the American Revolution*

Maurice Marchand-Tonel, *President, French-American Chamber of Commerce*

Thierry de Montbrial, *Director, French Institute for International Relations (IFRI)*

Hélie de Noailles, *President, Sons of the American Revolution*

Laurence Paye-Jeanneney, *General Director, Conservatoire National des Arts et Métiers*

Axel Poniatowski, *Chairman, National Assembly France-USA Friendship Group*

Pierre Rosenberg, *Member of the French Academy*

Pierre Taittinger, *Mayor of the 16th district in Paris (Passy)*

Daniel Thoulouze, *Director for Scientific and Technical Culture, CNAM, and Director, Musée des Arts et Métiers*

Lenders to the Exhibition

Institutions

American Philosophical Society, Philadelphia

Atwater Kent Museum, Philadelphia

Bakken Library and Museum of Electricity, Minneapolis

Bartram's Garden, Philadelphia

Bostonian Society

Carnegie Museum of Art, Pittsburgh

Château de Versailles, France

Cheekwood Museum of Art, Nashville, Tennessee

CIGNA Museum and Art Collection, Philadelphia

The College of Optometrists (British Optical Association Museum), London

College of Physicians of Philadelphia

Colonial Williamsburg Foundation

Columbia University Archives, New York

Didier Aaron et Cie, Paris

Diplomatic Reception Rooms, U.S. Department of State, Washington, D.C.

Franklin and Marshall College, Lancaster, Pennsylvania

The Franklin Institute, Philadelphia

Harvard University Portrait Collection, Cambridge, Massachusetts

Historical Society of Pennsylvania, Philadelphia

The Huntington Library, San Marino, California

Independence National Historical Park, Philadelphia

Library Company of Philadelphia

Library of Congress, Washington, D.C.

Masonic Library and Museum of Pennsylvania, Philadelphia

Metropolitan Museum of Art, New York,

Musée Carnavelet, Paris

Musée National de la Coopération Franco-américaine, Château de
   Blérancourt, France

Musée du Grand Orient de France, Paris

National Archives and Records Administration, College Park, Maryland

National Museum of American History, Smithsonian Institution, Washington, D.C.

National Museum of Health and Medicine, Smithsonian Institution, Washington, D.C.

National Portrait Gallery, London

National Portrait Gallery, Smithsonian Institution, Washington, D.C.

Natural History Museum, London

New York Public Library

New York State Library, Albany

The New-York Historical Society

Pennsylvania Academy of the Fine Arts, Philadelphia

Pennsylvania Hospital, Philadelphia

Philadelphia Museum of Art

Rosenbach Museum and Library, Philadelphia

Scottish National Portrait Gallery, Edinburgh

State Museum of Pennsylvania, Harrisburg

Sterling and Francine Clark Art Institute, Williamstown, Massachusetts

Transylvania University, Lexington, Kentucky

U.S. Naval Academy Museum, Annapolis, Maryland

University of Pennsylvania Archives and Records Center, Philadelphia

University of Pennsylvania Art Collection, Philadelphia

Valley Forge National Historical Park, Pennsylvania

Walter J. and Leonore Annenberg Rare Book and Manuscript Library, University of Pennsylvania

Winterthur Museum, Garden and Library, Delaware

Yale University Library, New Haven, Connecticut

Individuals

Leonore Annenberg

Melissa Clemmer

Roy Goodman

Mr. and Mrs. Joseph H. Hennage (Gift to the Colonial Williamsburg Foundation)

Benjamin Franklin Kahn

Stuart E. Karu

Noah Katz

Set Momjian

Mr. and Mrs. Benjamin Franklin Pepper (on loan to the Contributionship Companies)

Rosalind Remer

Jay T. Snider

Robert Staples and Barbara Charles

Jay Robert Stiefel

Robert Sullivan

Page Talbott

S. Robert Teitelman

Nicola Twilley

Theodore E. Wiederseim

Michael Zinman

Contents

Board of Directors' Preface

Benjamin Franklin, the oldest and one of the greatest of our founding fathers, is inextricably associated with Philadelphia, making the city the natural focal point for the celebrations of the three hundredth anniversary of his birth. Starting in 2005, Philadelphia will be the center of national and international celebrations that include an extraordinary exhibition, *Benjamin Franklin: In Search of a Better World*—to which this book is a companion—an ongoing Web site and database, commissioned artworks, and performances. But this upcoming two-year, multinational celebration, involving hundreds of organizations and thousands of individuals, did not just happen. The Benjamin Franklin Tercentenary came into being only after several institutions joined to lay the groundwork and organize the celebration with funding from The Pew Charitable Trusts that gave the effort its vital early momentum.

The prime movers were two far-sighted Philadelphians, Dennis Wint, president of The Franklin Institute, and the late Edward C. Carter II, librarian of the American Philosophical Society, who understood the national and international ramifications of Franklin's three hundredth anniversary and set about to create a celebration worthy of the occasion. Their first tentative conversations in 2000 led to invitations to representatives of the Library Company of Philadelphia, the Philadelphia Museum of Art, and the University of Pennsylvania to join the discussions, and the five institutions that now make up the Tercentenary began to shape the project.

The first task was to find leadership for the project and to secure additional grants to fund our ambitious plans. Conover Hunt joined the project as executive director in 2002 and during her eighteen months at the helm the Tercentenary secured passage of the federal legislation creating the Benjamin Franklin Tercentenary Commission, identified potential host institutions for the exhibition, hired Staples and Charles as the exhibition designers, and began the arduous task of fundraising. We are in Ms. Hunt's debt for her dedicated work on behalf of the Tercentenary. Page Talbott, who was first engaged as chief curator for the exhibition and now also serves as associate director of the Benjamin Franklin Tercentenary, is an independent curator with decades of experience who has brought imagination and energy to our project. When Ted Carter, to whom this book is affectionately dedicated, died suddenly in October 2002, the Tercentenary lost not only a dear friend but also the imaginative thinker who conceived the outline of the exhibition. Many times since then we have deeply regretted that we can no longer rely on Ted for creative ways to deal with our myriad challenges.

In the spring of 2004, Rosalind Remer, a historian and former director of planning and programming for the National Constitution Center in Philadelphia, became executive director. She quickly established herself as a superlative organizer and fundraiser with impeccable instincts. Within nine months of Dr. Remer's arrival we had reached our fundraising goals, ensuring that the ambitious international celebration we had envisioned would take place. In those same nine months Dr. Remer and Dr. Talbott—a truly dynamic duo— negotiated the arrangements with exhibition venues around the country and abroad, completed the outlines of the exhibition, prepared this companion volume, began to lay the groundwork for a variety of innovative public programs, and forged relations with scores of partner institutions and organizations.

From Franklin's tercentenary year in 2006 through early 2008, the Benjamin Franklin Tercentenary's programs will, in their spirit, originality, depth, and diversity, form an inspiring international commemoration of Benjamin Franklin's three hundredth birthday. The centerpiece of the commemoration is the international traveling exhibition *Benjamin Franklin: In Search of a Better World*. The exhibition, an engaging and seamless blend of art, history, science, and material culture, features Franklin's original possessions, including many items never publicly displayed, as well as iconic works of art and rare documents. In particular, we are proud to have five key original founding documents in America's history: the 1754 Albany Plan, the Declaration of Independence, the Treaty of Amity and Commerce with France, the Treaty of Paris ending the American Revolution, and the U.S. Constitution, all of which Franklin signed. The exhibition also features some forty hands-on, interactive devices that enable visitors to explore Franklin's eighteenth-century world using twenty-first-century technology. The exhibition is scheduled to travel to five museums across the United States; portions will then cross the Atlantic for display in Paris.

In addition to the exhibition, the Tercentenary is charged with creating, coordinating, and promoting programming about Franklin. Tercentenary staff have worked with historical, cultural, and scientific institutions and associations to create programs that explore Franklin in his historical context and are inspired by his values, interests, and achievements. Programs include lesson plans, lectures, and symposia; a play on Franklin's life to be performed at Franklin and Marshall College; a symphony commissioned by the Philadelphia Orchestra; a piece of chamber music commissioned by the American Philosophical Society to be performed at the society's meetings in Philadelphia, San Francisco, and Paris; a revival of *Franklin Court*, a ballet by the Pennsylvania Ballet; exhibitions on Franklin and his contemporaries at the American Philosophical Society, the Library Company of Philadelphia, the Philadelphia Museum of Art, and the University of Pennsylvania; partnership programs with the Free Library of Philadelphia, which will mount two exhibitions and sponsor a citywide reading program centered on Franklin; a puppet theater featuring three hundred Franklin heads; the flying of three hundred kites on Benjamin Franklin Parkway in Philadelphia; a parade re-creating Franklin's arrival in his adopted city, and much more. Although the Philadelphia region is at the core of these Franklin-related programs, the Tercentenary has worked with the exhibition's host museums to replicate many of these programs in their cities. The Tercentenary's French partners plan major celebrations to close out the last segment of the exhibition's tour while the Tercentenary's English partners, led by 36 Craven Street (Franklin's London home), are coordinating Franklin-related exhibitions and programs.

In the codicil to his final will and testament, Franklin expressed his hope that his legacy would extend at least two hundred years. In that spirit, three of the Tercentenary's projects, in particular, will remain long after the Tercentenary celebrations as lasting resources. Our Web site, www.benfranklin300.org, will be maintained as a host for lesson plans, scholarly essays, facts and timelines, links, and an interactive almanac, which will translate the best of our exhibition for the Web. The Web site will continue to host the Frankliniana Database, the first of its kind to represent a comprehensive overview of the material culture of an American founder in an accessible format that will never lose its currency. Anyone anywhere will be able to reference hundreds of images and artifacts associated with Franklin and his world. Finally, the Tercentenary undertook a program of conservation of hundreds of the artifacts in the exhibition, and these rare items have now been stabilized for years to come.

Richard S. Dunn, *Co-Executive Officer, American Philosophical Society*
Dennis Wint, *President, The Franklin Institute*
John C. Van Horne, *Director, Library Company of Philadelphia*
Gail Harrity, *Chief Operating Officer, Philadelphia Museum of Art*
Leslie Laird Kruhly, *Secretary, University of Pennsylvania*

Foreword

ROSALIND REMER AND PAGE TALBOTT

It is difficult to write about Franklin without compulsively quoting him. After all, the man who wrote his own epitaph—years before it was needed—was keenly aware of the power of a few well-chosen words. In a maxim from his first *Poor Richard's Almanack* of 1733, he appears to have predicted in just a few words the path of his global career and the role that his brilliance would play in it: "A fine genius in his own country, is like gold in the mine." Gold and genius are valued the world over, and for Franklin, genius was inextricably linked to usefulness, a trait he particularly prized. He undertook all he did in order to be useful—to himself and to society—and he had no inclination to lie hidden like unmined gold, deep in the colonial hills. His genius, in a sense, lay in being useful, as both Walter Isaacson and Billy Smith suggest in two of this book's essays, and his usefulness was, in turn, an expression of his genius.

When Franklin retired from his printing business in 1748 he became freer to act in the public arena, and, more important, he was able to expand his usefulness abroad, becoming a global citizen through his scientific and diplomatic achievements. Perhaps it was inevitable that genius like his would seek out other countries. He had lived his adult life in an increasingly cosmopolitan Philadelphia, a city where, in the words of Billy Smith, "most residents, directly or indirectly, depended on commerce with people scattered throughout the Atlantic World." Despite Philadelphians' familiarity with the world beyond the banks of the Delaware River, Europeans remained relatively unfamiliar with Americans. This lack of awareness may have enhanced their appreciation of Franklin's achievements and character abroad, for when viewed by his European contemporaries, he represented a kind of native genius from the new world, unalloyed by rank and privilege.

At the same time his long years in London and Paris made him vulnerable to American suspicions that he was not American enough, or that his genius had become tainted by proximity to courts and kings. This paradox is what has made Franklin so interesting in the intervening years—and so open to frequent reassessment by biographers—but it has also made his character somewhat elusive. Americans feel that they know Franklin well, and Leo Lemay's essay in this volume serves to reacquaint readers with many of the aspects of Franklin's life story that Franklin himself chose to emphasize in his *Autobiography*. Yet an understanding of his genius and a sense of his relevance today can also be seen in a global context, as other contributors in this book suggest. Franklin's experiences abroad, for example, may have been pivotal in changing his position on slavery, as Emma Lapsansky-Werner suggests. And his printing activities at the press he set up at Passy were not, as has been previously believed, simply a way of amusing himself, but integral to his serious diplomatic mission, as Ellen Cohn's fresh perspective shows. Franklin believed that the official documents produced on his press would serve to enhance America's reputation among the French.

James Green's essay on Franklin as printer and publisher shows that throughout his career, Franklin sought to expand his reach, whether across the Atlantic or throughout the British North American colonies. In Robert Middlekauff's essay, we learn that before he became a revolutionary Franklin viewed the British Empire as the perfect vehicle for spreading liberty, and his efforts as colonial agent in London were devoted to keeping that vehicle well oiled. Franklin's experiments in electricity, discussed by Philip Krider, opened the door for scientific discourse with scientists working in Europe. According to Page Talbott, Franklin's extraordinarily energetic consumption of everything from fine china to furniture and fabric in London and Paris was intended to make his Philadelphia home cosmopolitan, reflecting his experiences abroad. And the afterword by Edmund Morgan takes up the question of Franklin's pragmatism and how it affected his transformation from Briton to American.

The Benjamin Franklin Tercentenary has undertaken to commemorate and celebrate Franklin, amid centuries of widespread, unflagging fascination with him, largely generated by the power of his *Autobiography*. From the time of its initial publication in France in 1791, Franklin's *Autobiography* was a global enterprise, more widely read than any other memoir, never out of print, and enjoyed in translation by readers of almost forty languages. For many, the *Autobiography* is the only source of information about Franklin, but it is merely one element in the richly textured story of the man who was Benjamin Franklin, a story the Tercentenary wishes to tell through its exhibition and programs.

This volume, both as companion to the exhibition and on its own, is intended to take readers beyond the *Autobiography* into the many scenes of Franklin's life in America and abroad. It is our hope that these essays will draw readers into the cultures of which Franklin was a part: domestic life, science, international politics, and social and political reform. We cannot think of better guides to Franklin and his world than the scholars who contributed to this volume, and we hope that readers—and visitors to the exhibition—will find in our commemorative efforts a fresh way to appreciate this complex and fascinating figure.

We would like to offer thanks to our friends and families, who, in "lending" us to this multiyear project, have allowed Benjamin Franklin to enter their homes and lives in ways they may never have expected. We extend our special gratitude to James Green, Franklin, Alice, Daniel, Paul, and Wendy Remer; and to Jim, Jody, Alex, Katie, and Adam Gould, Bud Talbott, and Josephine Large Talbott, to whose memory "Benjamin Franklin at Home" is dedicated.

Introduction

What Benjamin Franklin Means for Our Times

WALTER ISAACSON

What leadership lessons can we learn from our founders? What qualities and personality traits make a leader great? There is not, I think, one answer. What made the era of the founders so successful was that there was a group of leaders who each had different talents and who together complemented one another.

It was critical to have someone like George Washington, who was revered by all and could command authority. We also needed men like John Adams and his cousin Samuel, who were unflinching and unbending and uncompromising in pursuit of principle. Then, too, we needed bright young philosophers like Thomas Jefferson and James Madison.

But equally important, the aborning nation needed a Benjamin Franklin: someone who was sage yet sensible and very pragmatic, who could bring people together and calm their passions, who could understand that it was possible to uphold core values while also seeking to find common ground with others.

Indeed, these are the traits, I think, that account for Franklin's recurring popularity in times of social discord and strife. He enjoyed a brief vogue, for example, during the Depression, when Carl Van Doren wrote the masterful biography of his life and I. Bernard Cohen exalted the practical and pragmatic nature of his science. And as Franklin nears his three hundredth birthday, after a decade of rising divisiveness in politics and the media, almost a dozen new books celebrate him as a voice of reason and moderation.

Each new age can relate to him because, more than any other, he is the founding father who winks at us. Washington's colleagues found it hard to imagine touching the austere general on the shoulder, and we would find the idea even more unthinkable today. Jefferson and Adams are just as intimidating. But Ben Franklin, that ambitious urban entrepreneur, seems made of flesh rather than marble; addressable by nickname, he turns to us from history's stage with eyes that twinkle from behind those new-fangled spectacles. He speaks to us, through his letters and hoaxes and autobiography, not with orotund rhetoric but with a chattiness and clever irony that is very contemporary, sometimes unnervingly so. We see his reflection in our own time, which can be a bit disconcerting.

Franklin helped invent the type of a middle-class meritocracy that informs the American dream today. Jefferson's idea of a meritocracy, expressed in his founding documents for the University of Virginia, was to take the cream of naturally talented young men and elevate them from the masses to become part of a new "natural aristocracy." But Franklin, though he loved young Jefferson, had a less elitist ideal. In his document launching the academy that became the University of Pennsylvania, he talked of helping all "aspiring" and "diligent" young men (alas, not women) from any stratum or of any natural endowment, for he felt that society was helped by elevating people from all levels who strove to improve themselves.

He believed in a new political order in which rights and power would be based not on the happenstance of heritage but on merit, virtue, and hard work. He rose up the social ladder from runaway apprentice to royal dinner guest in a way that would become quintessentially American. Yet in doing so he resolutely resisted, as a matter of principle—sometimes to a fur-capped extreme—aristocratic pretensions. More than almost any other founder (certainly more than Washington and Adams) he held firm to a fundamental faith that the New World should avoid replicating the hierarchies of the Old. His aversion to elitism and his faith in a new order built on the virtues of common people are among his most lasting legacies.

Indeed, the roots of much of what distinguishes the nation can be found in Franklin: Its cracker-barrel humor and wisdom. Its technological ingenuity. Its pluralistic tolerance. Its ability to weave together individualism and community cooperation. Its philosophical pragmatism. Its celebration of meritocratic mobility. The idealistic streak ingrained in its foreign policy. And the Main Street (or Market Street) virtues that serve as the foundation for its civic values. Franklin was egalitarian in what became the American sense: he approved

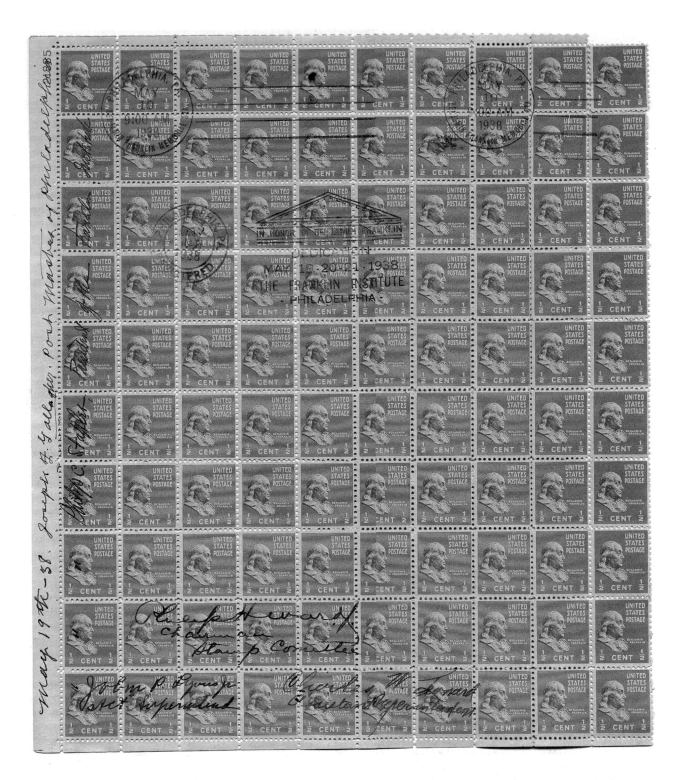

of individuals making their way to wealth through diligence and talent but opposed giving special privileges to people based on birth.

The way he built his own media empire foreshadowed the strategies of media tycoons today. He had a printing press, so he decided he needed something to print, such as a newspaper or a magazine or *Poor Richard's Almanack*. Next he franchised his operations up and down America with relatives and former apprentices, and then he created the first media distribution system, the colonial postal service, to tie them together.

At the height of his success, Franklin did something unusual. He stepped back from his businesses to devote himself to philanthropy, community projects, and civic works. His mother, back in Boston, disapproved of his lack of focus on his earthly calling. She was a good Calvinist Puritan who believed in the doctrine of salvation through God's grace alone. Her son, on the other hand, had rejected this doctrine and espoused instead the covenant of works. He believed that salvation came through good works, that the only religious doctrine he could be sure of was that if God loved all his creatures then the best way to serve God was to serve your fellow men. He explained this in a letter to his mother, which ended with the wonderful line "I would rather have it said, '*He lived usefully*,' than, '*He died rich*.'"

Fig. 1.2 (opposite) Red Grooms, Dr. Franklin's Profile, 1982. In this modern caricature, Grooms captures the whimsical attitude of Franklin as many people imagine him today: a wise old man in his trademark spectacles.

Fig. 1.3 (above) Attributed to Samuel Skillin, Portrait bust of Benjamin Franklin, ca. 1777–85. Skillin, a member of a well-known Philadelphia woodcarving family, drew on the appeal of the popular French image of Franklin in his fur cap, as it appeared in the widely circulated 1777 Cochin-Saint-Aubin print (fig. 1.24).

Fig. 1.4 Figurine of Benjamin Franklin seated among books and scientific objects, mid-nineteenth century.

When it came time for a declaration to be written explaining why the colonies had asserted their independence, the Continental Congress appointed a committee to draft it—perhaps the last time Congress created a good committee. It included, among others, Thomas Jefferson, Benjamin Franklin, and John Adams.

They were clear, in their first sentence, about the purpose of the declaration. "A decent respect to the opinions of mankind" required the signers to explain their actions. It was, in short, a propaganda document or, to put it more politely, a piece of public diplomacy designed to enlist others to their cause.

Jefferson wrote the first draft and sent it down Market Street to Franklin. He had begun his famous second paragraph with the words, "We hold these truths to be sacred." Franklin took his heavy black printer's pen—you can see the rough draft in the Library of Congress—crossed out sacred, and made it: "We hold these truths to be self-evident." His point was that our rights come from rationality and reason and depend on the consent of the governed, not the dictates or dogmas of a particular religion.

Jefferson went on to say that by virtue of their equal creation people are endowed with certain inalienable rights. Here we see the probable influence of that old Massachusetts Puritan John Adams. The committee added the phrase "endowed by their Creator." The final sentence became a perfect balance of fealty to divine providence tempered with an understanding that our rights are guaranteed by the consent of the governed.

Fig. 1.7 William Overend Geller after André-Edouard, Baron Jolly, Franklin at the Court of France, *1853. This frequently reproduced print portrays Franklin at Versailles in 1778, when he, along with the other American Commissioners for Peace, was presented to Louis XVI a few days after the Treaty of Amity was signed.*

Americans have long struggled to come to grips with the role of religion and divine providence in our politics and society. But our founders were sensible enough to realize that whatever each of us believes about the place of religion in public life—whether the words "under God" should appear in the Pledge of Allegiance or the Ten Commandments be displayed in public buildings —invocations of the Lord should be used to unite rather than divide us.

In order to transform a document into a nation, America had to enlist France on its side in the Revolution. (Even back then, the French were a bit of a handful.) So Congress sent old Dr. Franklin, then in his seventies, to woo them. He wrote wonderful memos explaining why joining the American cause was in the interest of France, but then he did something unusual. He began appealing to France's ideals as well. He built a press at his house on the outskirts of Paris, and there he printed the Declaration of Independence and other inspiring documents to show the French that the Americans were fighting for the

Fig. 1.8 Abbé Jean Richard Claude de Saint-Non after Jean-Honoré Fragonard, Le Docteur Francklin couronné par la Liberté, *1778. Franklin visited Saint-Non's home, where the artist made this print to demonstrate the process of aquatint. Depicting Franklin's bust resting on the hemisphere containing the New World and crowned with roses by Liberty, the picture uses the scroll (a reference to the constitutions of the colonies) to salute Franklin's service as legislator as well as liberator.*

ideal of liberty and against tyranny, sentiments that were welling up in France as well.

Franklin realized that it was the appeal of America's ideals that would win the United States support in the world. He realized that ideas had power—and that this power would prove even stronger than weapons.

He even realized that the French had read Rousseau, perhaps once too often, and thought of America as a romantic wilderness filled with forest philosophers and natural men. And so Franklin, a man of Boston, Philadelphia, and London who had barely even seen the wilderness, dressed up for his meetings at Versailles and went to hug Voltaire on the steps of the Académie Royale wearing not a ceremonial wig and robe but a fur cap and frontier frockcoat.

It worked. No American in history has so wowed the French. The women started wearing their hair in what was called *le coiffure à la Franklin,* done up to look like a fur cap, and sporting little medallions with cameos of Franklin on them. This so amused—or annoyed—King Louis that when a woman in his court persisted in dressing this way and talking of Franklin's natural virtues, he had a porcelain chamber pot made for her with a Franklin medallion embossed inside of it.

The complex interplay among various facets of Franklin's character—his ingenuity and unreflective wisdom, his Protestant ethic divorced from dogma, the principles he held to and those on which he was willing to compromise—means that each new look at him reflects and refracts the nation's changing values. He has been vilified in romantic periods and lionized in entrepreneurial ones. Each era appraises him anew, and in doing so reveals some aspect of itself.

Franklin has a particular resonance in twenty-first-century America. A successful publisher and consummate networker with an inventive curiosity, he would have felt right at home in the information revolution, and his unabashed striving to be part of an upwardly mobile meritocracy made him, in the social critic David Brooks' phrase, "our founding Yuppie." We can easily imagine having a beer with him after work, showing him how to use a Palm Pilot, sharing the business plan for a new venture, or discussing Bill Clinton's foibles and George Bush's foreign policy. He would laugh at the latest joke about a priest and a rabbi, or the one about the farmer's daughter. We would admire both his earnestness and his self-aware irony. And we would relate to the way he tried to balance, sometimes uneasily, a pursuit of reputation, wealth, earthly virtues, and spiritual values.

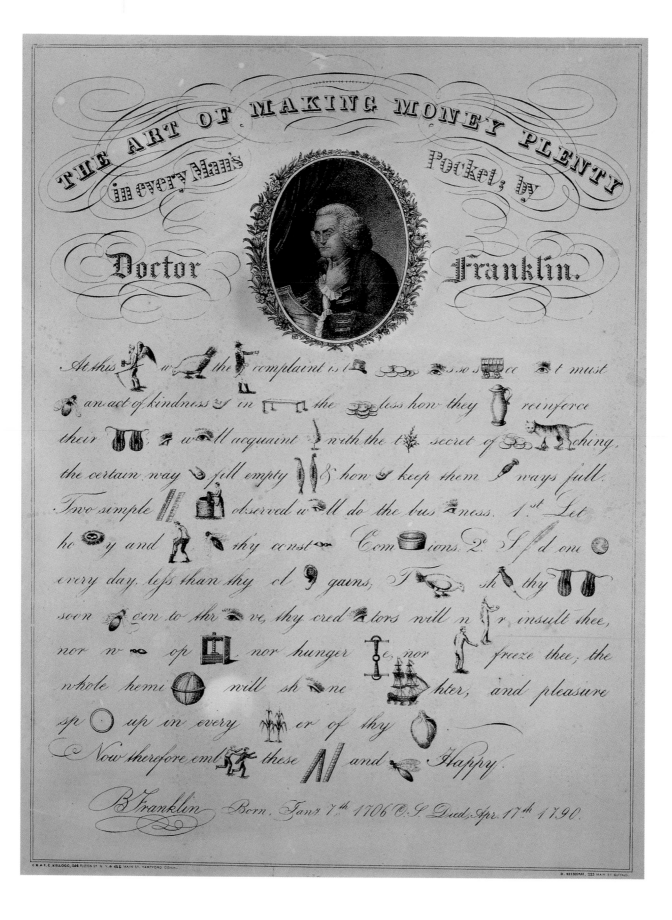

THE ART OF MAKING MONEY PLENTY
in every Man's Pocket, by
Doctor Franklin.

Fig. 1.12 (Opposite) The Art of Making Money Plenty in every Man's Pocket; by Doctor Franklin, *ca. 1847. This humorous rendition of Franklin's teachings has been a popular souvenir since it was first published in 1791.*

Fig. 1.13 Benjamin West, Benjamin Franklin Drawing Electricity from the Sky, *ca. 1816. In his day England's most celebrated painter, Benjamin West first met Franklin in Philadelphia, years before he painted this dramatic image. The small portrait was a study for a larger painting, never completed, intended for Pennsylvania Hospital.*

Some who see the reflection of Franklin in the world today fret about our shallowness of soul and spiritual complacency, which seem to permeate our culture of materialism. They say that he teaches us how to live a practical and pecuniary life, but not an exalted one. Others, seeing the same reflection, admire the basic middle-class values and democratic sentiments that now seem under assault from elitists, radicals, reactionaries, and other bashers of the bourgeoisie. They look upon Franklin as an exemplar of the personal character and civic virtue that is too often missing in modern America.

Much of the admiration is warranted, and so too are some of the qualms.

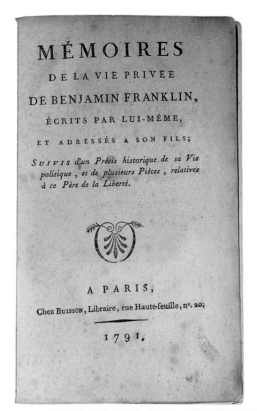

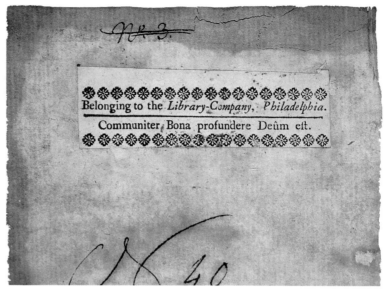

Fig. 1.15 Bookplate of the Library Company of Philadelphia, ca. 1740. This bookplate, designed and printed by Benjamin Franklin, includes the Library Company's motto, "Communiter Bona profundere Deûm est," which translates freely as: "To pour forth benefits for the common good is divine."

Fig. 1.14 Title page of Jacques Gibelin, trans., Mémoires de la vie privée De Benjamin Franklin, écrits par lui-méme, *1791. This first published version of Franklin's* Autobiography, *translated into French from his manuscript by Jacques Gibelin, covered the first twenty-five years of his life. This edition is important not only as the first French printing of the* Autobiography *but also because it established the validity of textual variants in later editions and translations.*

But the lessons of Franklin's life are more complex than those usually drawn by either his fans or his foes. Both sides too often confuse him with the striving pilgrim he portrayed in his autobiography. They mistake his genial moral maxims for the fundamental faiths that motivated his actions. But his morality was built on a sincere belief in the value of leading a virtuous life, serving the country he loved, and hoping to achieve salvation through good works. This led him to make the link between private and civic virtue, and to suspect, based on the meager evidence he could muster about God's will, that these earthly virtues were linked to heavenly ones as well. As he put it in the motto for the library he founded, "to pour forth benefits for the common good is divine."

In contrast to the views of contemporaries such as Jonathan Edwards, who believed that men were sinners in the hands of an angry God whose salvation could come through grace alone, Franklin's outlook might seem somewhat complacent. In some ways it was, but it was also genuine.

Franklin represents one side of a national dichotomy that has existed since the days when he and Edwards stood as contrasting cultural figures. On one side are those, like Edwards and the Mather family, who believed in an anointed elect and salvation through grace. They tended to have religious fervor, a sense of social class and hierarchy, and an appreciation of exalted values over earthly ones. On the other side were the Franklins, who believed in salvation through works, whose religion was benevolent and tolerant, and who were unabashedly striving and upwardly mobile.

Out of this grew many related divides in the American character, and Franklin represents one side: pragmatism versus romanticism, practical benevolence versus moral crusading. He was on the side of religious tolerance rather than evangelical faith. The side of social mobility rather than an established elite. The side of middle-class virtues rather than aristocratic aspirations.

Whichever view we take, it is useful to engage anew with Franklin, for in doing so we are grappling with a fundamental issue: how can we live a life that is useful, virtuous, worthy, moral, and spiritually meaningful? For that matter, which of these attributes is most important? These are questions just as vital for a self-satisfied age as they were for a revolutionary one.

During his lifetime, Franklin contributed to the building fund of every church in Philadelphia. And at one point, when the people of Philadelphia were trying to raise money for a hall for visiting preachers, he wrote the fundraisers' prospectus. Even if the Mufti of Constantinople, he said, were to come here to preach Muhammad to us and teach us Islam, we should offer him a pulpit, we should be open and listen, for we might learn something. And on his deathbed, he was the largest individual contributor to the Mikveh Israel synagogue, the first synagogue built in Philadelphia. So at his funeral, instead of just his minister accompanying his casket to the grave, all the ministers, preachers, and priests of Philadelphia, along with the rabbi of the Jews, linked arms and marched with him to his burial place.

Franklin did not embody every transcendent, poetic ideal, but he did embody the most practical and useful ones. That was his goal, and a worthy one it was. The most important of these ideals, which he held from the age of twenty-one when he first gathered his Junto, was a faith in the wisdom of the common citizen that was manifest in an appreciation for the possibilities of democracy. It was a noble ideal, transcendent and poetic in its own way.

And it turned out to be, as history has proven, practical and useful as well.

Fig. 1.16 Quart whisky flask with portrait of Benjamin Franklin, ca. 1820–38. This is one of four glass flasks with Franklin's portrait made at the Kensington Glass Works. On the shoulder of the flask is the often used motto "ERIPUIT COELO FULMEN, SCEPTRUMQUE TYRANNIS." During his lifetime and afterward, Franklin's face appeared on countless decorative souvenir objects, ranging from buttons to curtain tiebacks to ceramics to jewelry.

Fig. 1.17 "Oraison Funèbre de M. Franklin par L'Abbé Fauchet," in Le Panthéon des philantropes, ou, L'école de la révolution; almanach . . . , [1792]. *Franklin was mourned widely in France as a statesman and philosophe. The author and orator the comte de Mirabeau announced Franklin's death to the members of the National Assembly, who agreed by acclamation to wear mourning bands for three days and send a letter of condolence to the U.S. Congress. Speeches in Franklin's honor were given by politicians, printers, Masons, and clergy. In the Halle-aux-Blés in Paris the abbé Fauchet addressed an audience of more than three thousand mourners on July 21, 1790. A Catholic priest and member of the National Assembly, Fauchet praised the Protestant free thinker and advocated religious tolerance and political freedom.*

Chapter 1

The Life of Benjamin Franklin

J. A. LEO LEMAY

Benjamin Franklin, printer, writer, inventor, entrepreneur, natural philosopher, politician, and statesman, was born in Boston on January 6, 1705/6, and
baptized in the Congregational Old South Church that day (fig. 1.1).[1] He was
the youngest son and the ninth of eleven children of Josiah and Abiah Franklin. Josiah, a tallow chandler and soap maker who emigrated from England in
1683 to improve his finances and practice his Puritan faith, had seven children
by a previous marriage. Abiah was the daughter of Peter Folger, schoolmaster
and surveyor of Nantucket.

Franklin's father intended for him to become a minister and so sent him
to the Boston Grammar School, which offered the traditional Latin education
(fig. 1.2). After one year (apparently 1713–14), Josiah reconsidered, perhaps
because he could hardly afford it, and the next year sent Benjamin to a school
that taught English and mathematics. In his *Autobiography* Franklin included
an ignominious anecdote about himself as "a Leader among the Boys": in order to build a wharf where he and his friends could fish, they stole stones from
workmen building a house. The boys were discovered and "corrected by our
Fathers."[2] It is surprising that Franklin would write about his discreditable act,
but a revealing honesty characterizes the *Autobiography*. This may be one reason why he seems so much more human and approachable than younger contemporaries like George Washington, John Adams, and Thomas Jefferson.

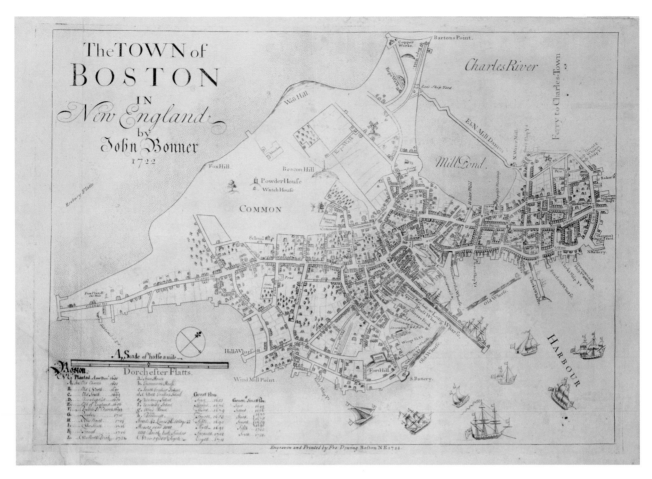

Fig. 1.1 (Above) John Bonner, The Town of Boston in New England, *1722. Franklin's childhood home was on Milk Street, which lies near the lower center of this map, the oldest printed map of Boston and the first printed town plan in the United States.*

Fig. 1.2 The First King's Chapel in the Boston Grammar (Latin) School, ca. 1810. Boston Latin School, where Franklin briefly studied in 1713–14, is the oldest public school in America in continuous existence. It was founded by the town of Boston on April 23, 1635, antedating Harvard College by more than a year.

THE FIRST KING'S CHAPEL.[1]

At about age nine or ten Franklin began working for his father, but he disliked the trade and wished to become a sailor. In 1718 Josiah apprenticed the twelve-year-old Franklin to his twenty-one-year-old brother James, who had just opened a printing shop in Boston. Since Franklin loved to read and write, the printing business seemed like a good choice. And with the little money he made as an apprentice, Franklin bought books (fig. 1.3). After purchasing an odd volume of Joseph Addison and Richard Steele's *Spectator,* he decided to improve his writing skills by imitating the essays (fig. 1.4). Franklin's description of his study habits in his autobiography reveals the ambition, hard

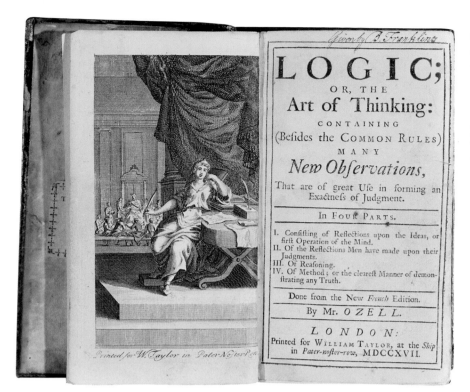

work, perseverance, and self-discipline that remained fundamental characteristics. He would read a *Spectator* essay, make notes on it, and some weeks later use the notes to write an essay on the topic. Finding his diction less exact and suggestive than the original, he practiced writing the essay as poetry, which forced him to search for synonyms with sounds and rhythms that matched the verse form. He later concluded that the effort improved his diction. To master method, he jumbled up his notes, put them aside for months, rearranged them in the best possible order, and then rewrote the essay. When he compared his version with the original, he would sometimes find that he had been "lucky enough to improve the Method or the Language." [3]

From friends who were bookseller's apprentices, the young Franklin borrowed books: "Often I sat up in my Room reading the greatest Part of the Night when the Book was borrow'd in the Evening and to be return'd early in the Morning." He became a vegetarian in part to save money so he could buy more books. [4]

In 1721 James Franklin started the *New-England Courant,* America's earliest antiestablishment newspaper. The following year, at age sixteen, Benjamin wrote the first essay series in American literature. He adopted the persona of Silence Dogood, a middle-aged widow of a country minister: "But being still a Boy, and suspecting that my Brother would object to printing any Thing of

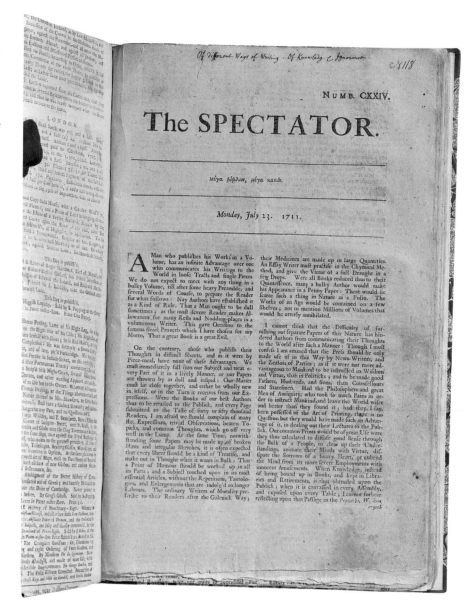

mine in his Paper if he knew it to be mine, I contriv'd to disguise my Hand and
writing an anonymous Paper I put it in at Night under the Door of the Printing-House." In the Silence Dogood essays, he mocked the Reverend Cotton
Mather (fig. 1.5) and Boston's secular authorities, criticized Harvard College,
ridiculed New England's funeral elegies, and proposed projects to do good.
Franklin's humor, sexual suggestiveness ("Women are the prime Cause of a
great many Male Enormities"), protofeminism (Dogood is the first notable
feminine persona in American literature), and egalitarianism all made their
first appearance in the Silence Dogood essays.[5]

Later, in 1723, Franklin contributed essays and skits to the *Courant*, revealing bold political and religious thinking. He also created the first interesting slave persona ("Dingo") in American literature.[6] Franklin's colloquial style, developed in part by imitating the *New-England Courant* writers, reflected a populist aesthetic.

In Silence Dogood, the teenager revealed the wry self-awareness that characterized the man throughout his life. When Silence fancied herself "a Queen from the Fourteenth to the Eighteenth Year of my Age," who "govern'd the

Fig. 1.5 Peter Pelham, Cottonus Matherus *(portrait print of Cotton Mather), 1727. Based on his own painting, Pelham's portrait of Mather is the first mezzotint made in the colonies. Despite having mocked Mather in the Silence Dogood letters, Franklin was influenced by Mather's* Essays to Do Good *(1710) and by his support of smallpox inoculation.*

World all the Time of my being govern'd by my Master," King Franklin, the apprentice, was doing the same, recognizing the absurdity of his daydream, and spoofing himself.[7]

Throughout his youth, Franklin demonstrated ambition, self-discipline, cockiness, and intellectual curiosity. His worst qualities were pride, occasional disregard for the rights of others, and rebelliousness. He became an excellent printer and demonstrated the ingeniousness that would serve him well not only in his printing career but later in science and technology. Books, which he read for both knowledge and delight, were the key to his self-education. By age seventeen, he had become one of America's best writers.

In the summer of 1722 and again in the early winter of 1723, James was imprisoned for criticizing the authorities in the *New-England Courant*. Dur-

Fig. 1.6 Nathaniel Emmons, Portrait of Samuel Sewall, 1728. Sewall served as judge of the superior court of Massachusetts (1692–1728) and as chief justice for the last ten years. He was one of the three judges of the Salem witchcraft trials; later, in 1705, he published an apology for his part in them. His diary offers considerable insight into the man and his period.

ing these periods, Franklin took charge of the *Courant* and gave Chief Justice Samuel Sewall (fig. 1.6) and other "Rulers some Rubs in it." Yet despite their similar political and journalistic talents, the brothers often quarreled. At seventeen, Franklin was sometimes "saucy and Provoking," and when James, who "was otherwise not an ill-natur'd Man," lost his temper, he would beat his apprentice.[8] Franklin ran away.

Looking for work, Franklin sailed to New York, but the only printer in the city needed no additional help. He told Franklin that the Philadelphia printer, Andrew Bradford, had recently lost his principal hand and might need another. So Franklin sailed to Perth Amboy, New Jersey, walked the fifty miles across New Jersey to Burlington, sailed and rowed down the Delaware River to Philadelphia, and arrived in the city on a Sunday morning, October 6, 1723, with one Dutch dollar and about a shilling in copper. "The latter I gave the People of the Boat for my Passage, who at first refus'd it on Account of my Rowing; but I insisted on their taking it." Revealing both an interest in psychology and an ironic amusement at himself, Franklin added, "a Man being sometimes more generous when he has but a little Money than when he has plenty, perhaps thro' Fear of being thought to have but little."[9]

When he came to write his autobiography, Franklin noted that he was "the more particular in this Description of my Journey, and shall be so of my first Entry into that City, that you may in your Mind compare such unlikely Beginning with the Figure I have since made there." He meticulously described his first walk in Philadelphia, emphasizing his "awkward ridiculous Appearance" and the unfamiliarity of Philadelphia's customs. This archetypal passage of initiation is the best-known embodiment of the American Dream and a touchstone of American literature, echoed by Charles Brockden Brown, Nathaniel Hawthorne, Henry James, and F. Scott Fitzgerald, among others.[10]

Andrew Bradford could offer Franklin only part-time work, but a new printer, Samuel Keimer, had just opened a shop. Franklin went to work for him and made friends with a group of young men who loved literature, one of whom, James Ralph, became a particularly close companion. Seven months later, befriended by Pennsylvania's governor, Sir William Keith, who promised to give him the public printing, Benjamin returned to Boston to ask his father for a loan to start a printing shop, but Josiah Franklin was in debt and had to refuse his youngest son's request. In Philadelphia, Keith pledged to lend Franklin the money to buy the press and types but suggested he go to London to make the purchases and arrange for supplies from the stationers, booksellers, and printers. At the time Franklin was courting Deborah Read, his landlady's daughter, and they planned to marry, but her mother insisted they wait until Franklin's return. With Ralph, he sailed for London on November 5, 1724, by chance on the same ship as Thomas Denham, a Quaker merchant, who would soon become an important figure in Franklin's life.

In London, Franklin learned that Governor Keith had deceived him and had "no Credit to give."[11] Without money or prospects, Franklin found work at Samuel Palmer's printing shop, where in February 1724/5, he set in type the third edition of William Wollaston's *Religion of Nature Delineated* and wrote an irreligious rejoinder, *A Dissertation on Liberty and Necessity, Pleasure and Pain.* With no publisher, no author, and no bookseller listed, the pamphlet was archetypal clandestine literature and won its author notoriety among London libertines, including William Lyons, who had spent six months in jail for expressing similar freethinking views. Through Lyons, Franklin met Bernard Mandeville, author of the *Fable of the Bees* (1714, revised and expanded 1723), which, according to a Middlesex grand jury, denigrated virtue and religion.[12]

Meanwhile, Franklin supported his impractical friend James Ralph. After Ralph took a job in the country, Franklin became friendly with Ralph's mistress and attempted "familiarities," which she rejected. Again, as with his admission of stealing the workmen's stones as a boy, Franklin showed himself surprisingly honest about his "errata."[13]

In the fall of 1725 Franklin left Palmer's for the larger printing house of John Watt; there "the Water American" gained a reputation as a wit and suggested and carried through a series of changes in the workmen's regulations.[14] In the spring of 1726 Thomas Denham encouraged Franklin to return with him to Philadelphia and work as his clerk and shopkeeper while learning the mercantile business. Franklin agreed, and they left England on July 23. In London, Franklin had demonstrated literary skill, leadership, printing ability, adaptability, and sociability.

Sailing back to America, Franklin formed a plan to guide his future conduct, beginning with the resolve "to be extremely frugal . . . till I have paid what I owe." He and Denham set up a store, but in February 1727, Franklin fell ill with pleurisy and nearly died. He recovered after two months, but by this time Denham too had become severely ill. His creditors had hired another clerk, and Franklin was out of a job. He returned to work for Samuel Keimer, now as the manager of Keimer's expanded printing shop. That fall, he formed the Junto, a group comprised mainly of young artisans, which combined sociability and self-education. The Junto met regularly on Friday nights until 1765.

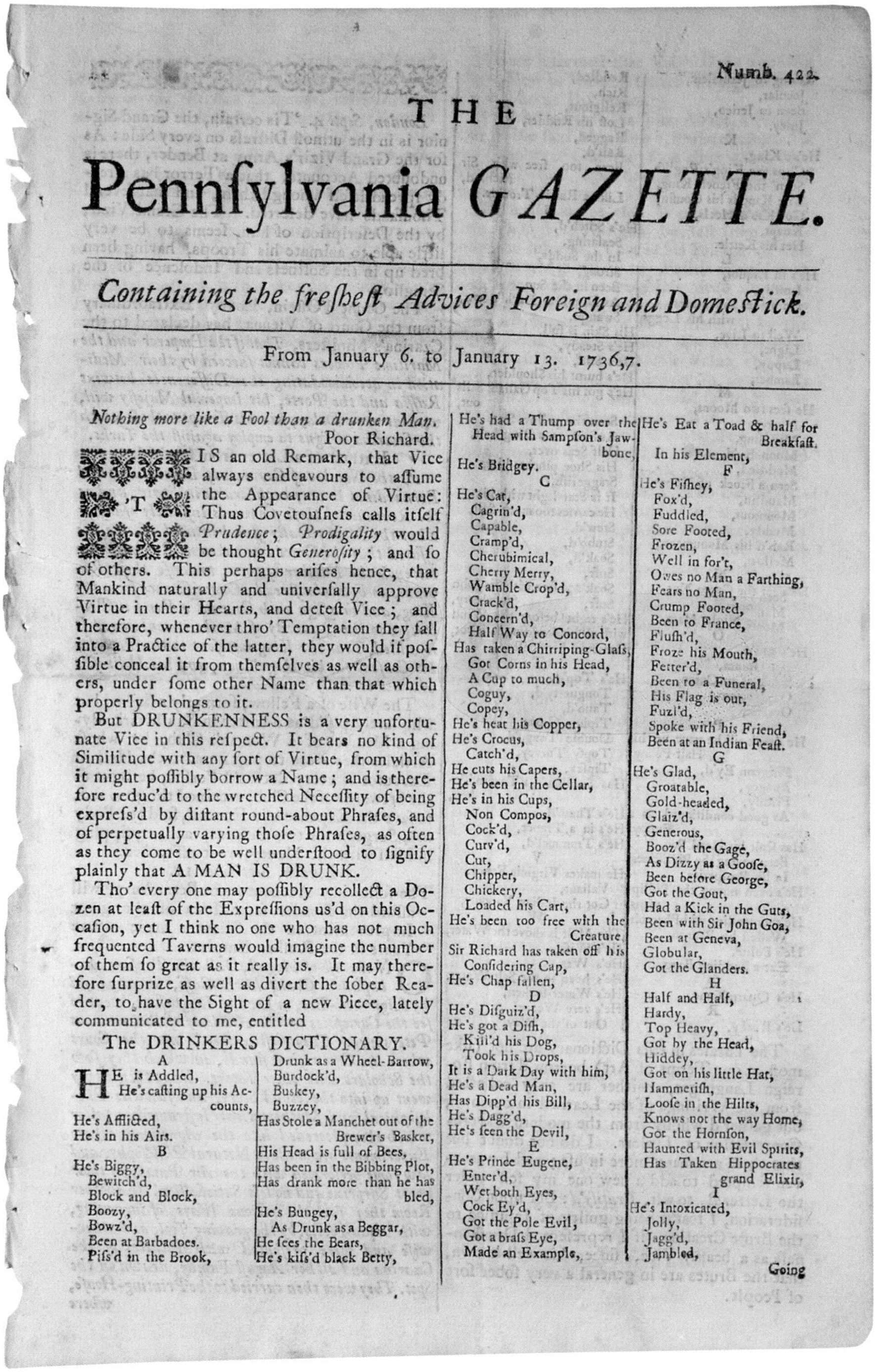
Numb. 422.

THE

Pennſylvania GAZETTE.

Containing the freſheſt Advices Foreign and Domeſtick.

From January 6. to January 13. 1736,7.

Nothing more like a Fool than a drunken Man.
Poor Richard.

'TIS an old Remark, that Vice always endeavours to aſſume the Appearance of Virtue: Thus Covetouſneſs calls itſelf *Prudence*; *Prodigality* would be thought *Generoſity*; and ſo of others. This perhaps ariſes hence, that Mankind naturally and univerſally approve Virtue in their Hearts, and deteſt Vice; and therefore, whenever thro' Temptation they fall into a Practice of the latter, they would if poſſible conceal it from themſelves as well as others, under ſome other Name than that which properly belongs to it.

But DRUNKENNESS is a very unfortunate Vice in this reſpect. It bears no kind of Similitude with any ſort of Virtue, from which it might poſſibly borrow a Name; and is therefore reduc'd to the wretched Neceſſity of being expreſs'd by diſtant round-about Phraſes, and of perpetually varying thoſe Phraſes, as often as they come to be well underſtood to ſignify plainly that A MAN IS DRUNK.

Tho' every one may poſſibly recollect a Dozen at leaſt of the Expreſſions us'd on this Occaſion, yet I think no one who has not much frequented Taverns would imagine the number of them ſo great as it really is. It may therefore ſurprize as well as divert the ſober Reader, to have the Sight of a new Piece, lately communicated to me, entitled

The DRINKERS DICTIONARY.

A

HE is Addled,
He's caſting up his Accounts,
He's Afflicted,
He's in his Airs.

B

He's Biggy,
Bewitch'd,
Block and Block,
Boozy,
Bowz'd,
Been at Barbadoes.
Piſs'd in the Brook,
Drunk as a Wheel-Barrow,
Burdock'd,
Buskey,
Buzzey,
Has Stole a Manchet out of the Brewer's Basket,
His Head is full of Bees,
Has been in the Bibbing Plot,
Has drank more than he has bled,
He's Bungey,
As Drunk as a Beggar,
He ſees the Bears,
He's kiſs'd black Betty,
He's had a Thump over the Head with Sampſon's Jawbone,
He's Bridgey.

C

He's Cat,
Cagrin'd,
Capable,
Cramp'd,
Cherubimical,
Cherry Merry,
Wamble Crop'd,
Crack'd,
Concern'd,
Half Way to Concord,
Has taken a Chirriping-Glaſs,
Got Corns in his Head,
A Cup to much,
Coguy,
Copey,
He's heat his Copper,
He's Crocus,
Catch'd,
He cuts his Capers,
He's been in the Cellar,
He's in his Cups,
Non Compos,
Cock'd,
Curv'd,
Cut,
Chipper,
Chickery,
Loaded his Cart,
He's been too free with the Creature,
Sir Richard has taken off his Conſidering Cap,
He's Chap fallen,

D

He's Diſguiz'd,
He's got a Diſh,
Kill'd his Dog,
Took his Drops,
It is a Dark Day with him,
He's a Dead Man,
Has Dipp'd his Bill,
He's Dagg'd,
He's ſeen the Devil,

E

He's Prince Eugene,
Enter'd,
Wet both Eyes,
Cock Ey'd,
Got the Pole Evil,
Got a braſs Eye,
Made an Example,
He's Eat a Toad & half for Breakfaſt.
In his Element,

F

He's Fiſhey,
Fox'd,
Fuddled,
Sore Footed,
Frozen,
Well in for't,
Owes no Man a Farthing,
Fears no Man,
Crump Footed,
Been to France,
Fluſh'd,
Froze his Mouth,
Fetter'd,
Been to a Funeral,
His Flag is out,
Fuzl'd,
Spoke with his Friend,
Been at an Indian Feaſt.

G

He's Glad,
Groatable,
Gold-headed,
Glaiz'd,
Generous,
Booz'd the Gage,
As Dizzy as a Gooſe,
Been before George,
Got the Gout,
Had a Kick in the Guts,
Been with Sir John Goa,
Been at Geneva,
Globular,
Got the Glanders.

H

Half and Half,
Hardy,
Top Heavy,
Got by the Head,
Hiddey,
Got on his little Hat,
Hammeriſh,
Looſe in the Hilts,
Knows not the way Home,
Got the Hornſon,
Haunted with Evil Spirits,
Has Taken Hippocrates grand Elixir,

I

He's Intoxicated,
Jolly,
Jagg'd,
Jambled,

Going

Fig. 1.7 Front page of the Pennsylvania Gazette, *January 6–13, 1736/37. Owned, edited, and printed by Franklin from 1729 to 1748, the* Gazette *was known for its humor and originality and had a strong influence on public opinion.*

In June 1728 Franklin and Hugh Meredith, a fellow employee of Keimer's, quit and set up their own printing shop with funds loaned by Meredith's father. That September, Franklin proposed that they start a newspaper to compete with Andrew Bradford's *American Weekly Mercury,* but Keimer, learning of the plan, advertised his own forthcoming paper, the *Pennsylvania*

Gazette, on October 1. In response, Franklin began publishing a weekly essay
series, the "Busy-Body," in Bradford's *Mercury* to popularize Bradford's paper and ensure Keimer's failure. In his eighth "Busy-Body," published March
27, 1729, the twenty-three-year-old Franklin boldly entered Pennsylvania politics. He demanded that the Pennsylvania Assembly authorize a paper currency and threatened uprisings if it did not. Bradford was out of town, but after
a few copies of the *Mercury* were printed, the essay was suppressed. Franklin,
however, continued his political campaign by publishing, on April 10, *A Modest Enquiry into the Nature and Necessity of a Paper-Currency,* the first highly
successful pamphlet from his press. Though the "Rich Men dislik'd it," the
pamphlet had the desired effect, and the legislature passed a paper currency

bill.[15] *A Modest Enquiry* showed Franklin's political daring, his populism, and, in its subtle criticism of British authorities, his Americanism.

In a reply to the "Busy-Body," Keimer on March 13, 1729, satirized Franklin as "A Fellow whose . . . Merits [are] as threadbare as his Great Coat" (confirming that Franklin was living up to the plan formed on shipboard "to be extremely frugal"). Franklin's finances were shaky, and he worked long and hard: "To show that I was not above my Business, I sometimes brought home the Paper I purchas'd at the Stores, thro' the Streets on a Wheelbarrow." He regarded work as honorable and considered artisans and other laborers the most valuable members of society. His attitudes were uncommon in eighteenth-century society, but not extraordinary. One early model was the Reverend John Wise, who wrote that "equality amongst men" was a fundamental right, and who, in a pamphlet printed by James Franklin (and perhaps set in print by Benjamin), celebrated the farmer as "the great Studd & Strength of our Country."[16]

Franklin's campaign worked, and Franklin and Meredith bought the failing *Pennsylvania Gazette* from Keimer in the fall of 1729 (fig. 1.7). Franklin immediately made it famous by publishing an editorial analyzing the controversy between Governor William Burnet and the Massachusetts Assembly that deftly criticized Burnet and the British authorities. On January 30, 1730, the Pennsylvania Assembly chose Franklin and Meredith to print its proceedings. That spring, Meredith's father found that he could not pay his bills for the printing press and types. The creditors brought suit against him, and because Hugh Meredith wanted to return to farming, Franklin borrowed money from two Junto friends to buy him out and pay off the debt.

Franklin's former fiancée, Deborah Read, had married nine months after Franklin left for London. But she soon left her husband, who was rumored to have a wife elsewhere, and returned to live with her mother. In December 1727, the husband absconded and by 1730 was thought to have died in the West Indies. Meanwhile, Franklin sired an illegitimate son, William, who was born about 1728; his mother is unknown.[17] Early in 1730 Franklin began courting Deborah again. Because they did not know whether her former husband was alive, they joined together in a common-law marriage on September 1, 1730, and took William into their home to bring up as their son. On October 20, 1732, Francis Folger Franklin was born; he died of smallpox at age four. Eleven years after the birth of Francis, Franklin's third and last child, Sarah (called Sally), was born, on August 31, 1743.

Deborah and the children attended Philadelphia's Anglican Christ Church, where both Francis Folger and Sarah were baptized and Francis was

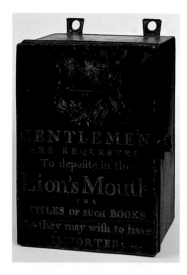

Fig. 1.9 "Lion's Mouth" box, ca. 1750. Patrons of Franklin's Library Company requested acquisitions for the library by inserting their suggestions through the lion's mouth.

Fig. 1.10 Whale oil street lamp, ca. 1800. The four-sided design, conceived by Franklin, was an improvement on the traditional globe because it was easier to clean (hence brighter) and was more economical because broken panes could be individually replaced.

buried. Though Franklin never joined the church, he paid for his family's seats and aided in the church's fundraising.

Franklin did become a Freemason. He was admitted in January 1731 and attended his first meeting in February. Three years later, on June 24, 1734, he was elected Grand Master. On that occasion, "the Proprietor, the Governor, and several other Persons of Distinction honour'd the Society" by joining the Masons for "a very elegant Entertainment" at the Tun Tavern.[18] It was a heady moment for the twenty-eight-year-old Franklin, who remained active in the Philadelphia Freemasons until 1757 and attended Masonic meetings during his travels in the colonies and later abroad (fig. 1.8).

Late in 1732, Franklin published the first in a series of almanacs titled *Poor Richard's Almanack*. (*Poor* in an almanac title signaled that it contained humor.) In a sensational preface, the compiler "Richard Saunders" (Franklin) predicted the death of Titan Leeds, who at the time wrote the best-known almanacs in the Middle Colonies. Litterateurs among Franklin's readers recognized his imitation of Jonathan Swift's 1708 Bickerstaff hoax. On the whole, Franklin's almanac differed little from others, except in its superior writing, especially in the entertaining prefaces, original sententiae, and revised and improved proverbs. *Poor Richard* had all the standard almanac features: a calendar interspersed with information concerning the time of sunrise and sunset, weather predictions, and proverbs. At the back of the calendar information appeared concerning the dates of various city, county, and colony courts, the times of the annual fairs, and the mileage between towns.

Franklin's public projects began with the Library Company of Philadelphia, which he started on July 1, 1731 (fig. 1.9). Like the Junto, it provided a means of self-education. With great self-discipline, Franklin taught himself to read German, French, Spanish, Italian, and Latin. The public-spirited Franklin also organized the Union Fire Company, Philadelphia's first, on December 7, 1736, and projected plans to clean up the environment, to reform the police, and to pave, clean, and light the streets (fig. 1.10).

As his finances improved, Franklin sponsored a series of printing partners, a way of combining idealism and practicality. With these partnerships, Franklin helped out young beginners and also, if they were successful, made money. Each venture was a gamble, and no other colonial American printer offered such partnerships to any but family members. Deborah and Franklin kept a shop, which she usually ran during the 1730s. Most printers sold stationery and the staples of the book trade: hornbooks, primers, psalters, catechisms, Bibles, grammars, arithmetics, almanacs, broadsides, and chapbooks.

Franklin the book lover gradually became a bookdealer, buying and selling not only new but also secondhand and rare books.

Franklin was elected clerk of the Pennsylvania Assembly in 1736. He was frequently bored by its proceedings, and to amuse himself he contrived mathematical "magic" squares and circles. In the simplest ones, the sums of all the numbers in a row, whether a horizontal, a perpendicular, or a diagonal, are equal.[19] He was appointed postmaster of Philadelphia in 1737, and at about that time he also became the primary wholesale paper merchant of colonial America, buying rags for the papermakers and encouraging new paper mills (fig. 1.11).

The ingenious Franklin devised a method of nature printing (that is, reproducing the complex images of actual plant leaves; see fig. 1.12) on paper currency to deter counterfeiting (1736) and experimented with fireplaces and stoves, designing his improved Pennsylvania Fire-Place by 1741 (fig. 1.13).

Fig. 1.11 (Right) Milepost. When Franklin was postmaster, he improved mail delivery on the east coast by traveling 1,600 miles inspecting post offices, measuring and marking postal routes, and using markers like this stone milepost to mark the distances from cities, such as Philadelphia. During Franklin's tenure, the post office cut mail delivery time in half with the use of relay riders, brought credit to the post, improved accounting records, expanded and standardized service, and became profitable.

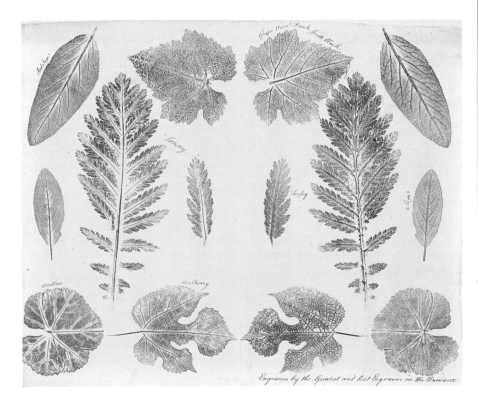

Fig. 1.12 Joseph Breintnall, Page of a book of nature prints of leaves, ca. 1731-44. Franklin's friend and fellow Junto member Breintnall inscribed this sheet of leaf prints, "Engraven by the Greatest and best Engraver in the Universe." Breintnall made these prints by inking leaves, putting them between a folded piece of paper, and putting it under the printing press. (The "best Engraver" was God.)

Fig. 1.13 James Turner after Lewis Evans, Illustration of the parts of the "Franklin Stove," from Benjamin Franklin, An Account Of the New Invented Pennsylvanian Fire-Places . . . , *1744. Franklin printed and distributed this pamphlet to promote his new stove design, which conserved fuel and improved the flow of heat into the room.*

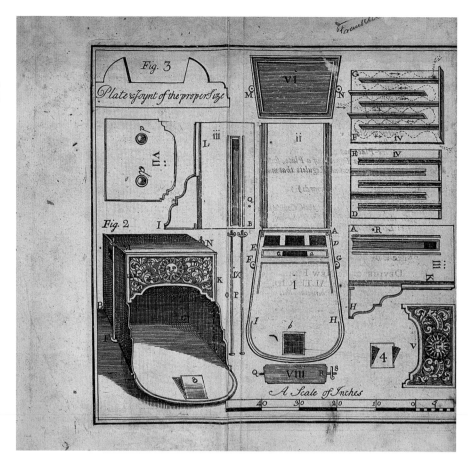

Throughout his life, he continued to tinker with improvements to heating systems. Both innovations demonstrated Franklin's extraordinary ingenuity, a trait that remained with him throughout his lifetime. Franklin wrote prolifically for the *Pennsylvania Gazette* and made it the best colonial American newspaper. Like other eighteenth-century men of letters, he circulated a number of pieces in manuscript, including "The Speech of Miss Polly Baker, before a Court of Judicature, at Connecticut near Boston in New England; where she was prosecuted the Fifth Time, for having a Bastard Child: Which influenced the Court to dispense with her Punishment, and induced one of her judges to marry her the next day." A multifaceted satire on religion, the pride of mankind, and the double standard for rich and poor and for men and women, the hoax appeared in several English newspapers and the two most popular English magazines within weeks of its first publication.

Hard work, frugality, perseverance, ingeniousness, entrepreneurial risk-taking, and attempts to do good characterized Franklin's life during the 1730s and 1740s. In 1746 he became fascinated with the new science of electricity, at that time little understood. Franklin began to form hypotheses and design experiments; the subject consumed him. He eventually decided that he needed more time for science, and took on David Hall as a printing partner. In January 1748, just as he turned forty-two, he retired from his work at the press.

Franklin ceased only his printing and bookselling activities; he continued to write for the *Pennsylvania Gazette* and *Poor Richard,* to run the post office, to collect rags for papermakers, and to sell paper to other colonial American printers. But King George's War (1740–48) interfered with his plans to pursue science. When French and Spanish ships began plundering homes along the Delaware Bay and the French with their Indian allies began attacking the frontier, the Pennsylvania Assembly, partly composed of pacifist Quakers, refused to act. In response, Franklin published a stirring pamphlet, *Plain Truth,* in late 1747, which contained the first American cartoon used in a political context (fig. 1.14). By the spring of 1748 he had formed a volunteer militia association numbering more than ten thousand men. Peace was declared late in 1748.

In 1749 Franklin conceived the idea of establishing an academy in Phila-

Non Votis, &c.

Fig. 1.14 *"The Waggoneer and Hercules"* cartoon from Plain Truth; or, Serious considerations on the present state of the city of Philadelphia, and province of Pennsylvania. By a tradesman of Philadelphia, *1747. Considered the first American political cartoon, this image representing one of Aesop's Fables was used by Franklin to urge western Pennsylvanians to defend themselves against Indian attacks. He printed two thousand copies of* Plain Truth *to publicize his efforts to organize a volunteer militia in opposition to the Quaker-dominated Assembly. For the illustration Franklin reused a woodblock, one of a set of twelve that he purchased (probably from London) to illustrate the selection of fables in his 1747 edition of the standard English speller, Thomas Dilworth's* A New Guide to the English Tongue.

delphia; he then raised funds for it, supervised its construction, and served as its first chairman of the board of trustees (fig. 1.15). The school later became the Academy and College of Philadelphia, and is now the University of Pennsylvania. With Dr. Thomas Bond, Franklin founded the Pennsylvania Hospital in 1751 and, to fund it, proposed the first matching grant (fig. 1.16). In another project, he started a fire insurance company.

Throughout this period, he pursued his research in electricity. The first electrical condenser (the Leyden jar) gave powerful shocks of electricity, but why it did so was a mystery. Franklin's theory of the separation of positive and negative electricity explained why there was a shock when the separated electrical fluids came back together. His hypotheses concerning atmospheric electricity were established when French experimenters, following his directions, proved that lightning was electrical in nature.

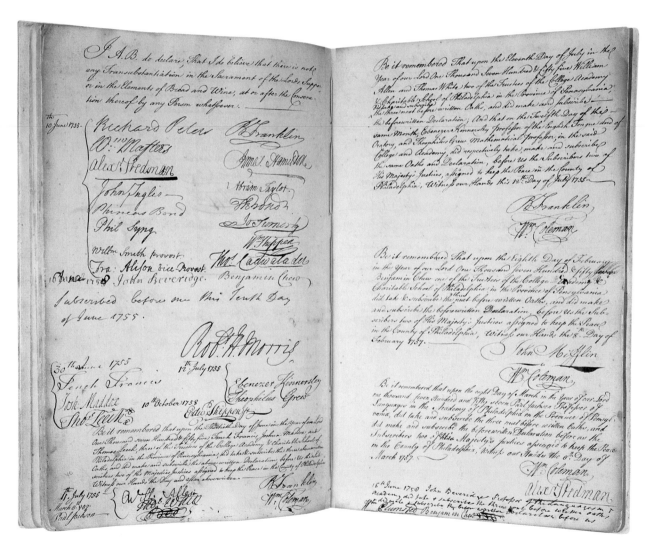

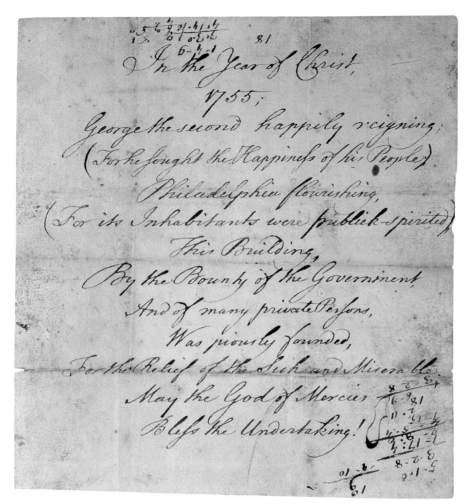

In May 1751, Franklin was elected to the Pennsylvania Assembly, and his son William succeeded him as clerk. About the same time, he wrote a bitter editorial ("Jakes on Our Tables") against the British for shipping convicts to America and followed it up a month later with a satire proposing that America ship rattlesnakes to England in return for the convicts. Later in the year he composed "Observations Concerning the Increase of Mankind, Peopling of Countries, etc," which showed that the American population was increasing exponentially. He predicted that America's population would surpass England's within a century. Circulating widely in manuscript until 1755, when it was printed, the essay became one of the fundamental documents of the American Revolution, for it contains a subtle threat that Americans would demand independence if mistreated. "Observations" roused the young John Adams to contemplate the future glory of America and influenced Adam Smith's *Wealth*

of Nations (1776) and Thomas Malthus's *Essay upon the Principle of Population* (1798; revised and expanded, 1803).[20]

Alarmed by French incursions into the Ohio Valley, Franklin wrote an editorial on May 4, 1754, urging unification of the colonies. With it, he printed a woodcut depicting a snake cut into pieces over the caption "JOIN, or DIE." The most famous American cartoon, it is the first symbol of a unified America. The same year, as a commissioner from Pennsylvania, Franklin attended a conference in Albany called by the British authorities to consider the French threat on the frontier. Journeying to the conference, he drafted a plan to unite the colonies into a union; with slight revisions, the plan was adopted by the conference on July 10, 1754 (fig. 1.17). The colonies, however, rejected the Albany Plan, in part because they thought it gave too much power to the British authorities, and the British rejected it in part because they feared that a union could lead to American independence.[21]

In December 1754 Franklin wrote to Massachusetts governor William Shirley that Englishmen had "an undoubted Right . . . not to be taxed but by their own Consent given thro' their Representatives." Replying later that month to Governor Shirley's suggestion that the colonists elect members of Parliament, Franklin said that if all the past Acts of Trade and Navigation were repealed and the colonies given "a reasonable number of Representatives," then the colonists might be satisfied. In a statement that the British authorities would have found amazing, Franklin said that Americans should have greater rights than the English because they had done the most "to enlarge Britain's empire and commerce, encrease her strength, her wealth, and the numbers of her people, at the risque of their own lives and private fortunes in new and strange countries." Franklin's Americanism struck a new note in eighteenth-century political discourse. Half a century later, James Madison wrote that Franklin's letters to Shirley "repelled with the greatest possible force, within the smallest possible compass" Britain's claim to govern America.[22]

Franklin had been appointed joint deputy postmaster general of North America in 1753 and had journeyed as far as New Hampshire and Williamsburg, Virginia, to plot the best postal routes and set up new post offices. Over the next few years he enlarged the reach of the post office north, south, and west, and made mail delivery along the major routes quicker and more frequent. He designed forms for postmasters (fig. 1.18), instituted home delivery of letters in the cities, advertised uncollected mail, created a dead-letter office, and began delivering newspapers and magazines (and charging for doing so).

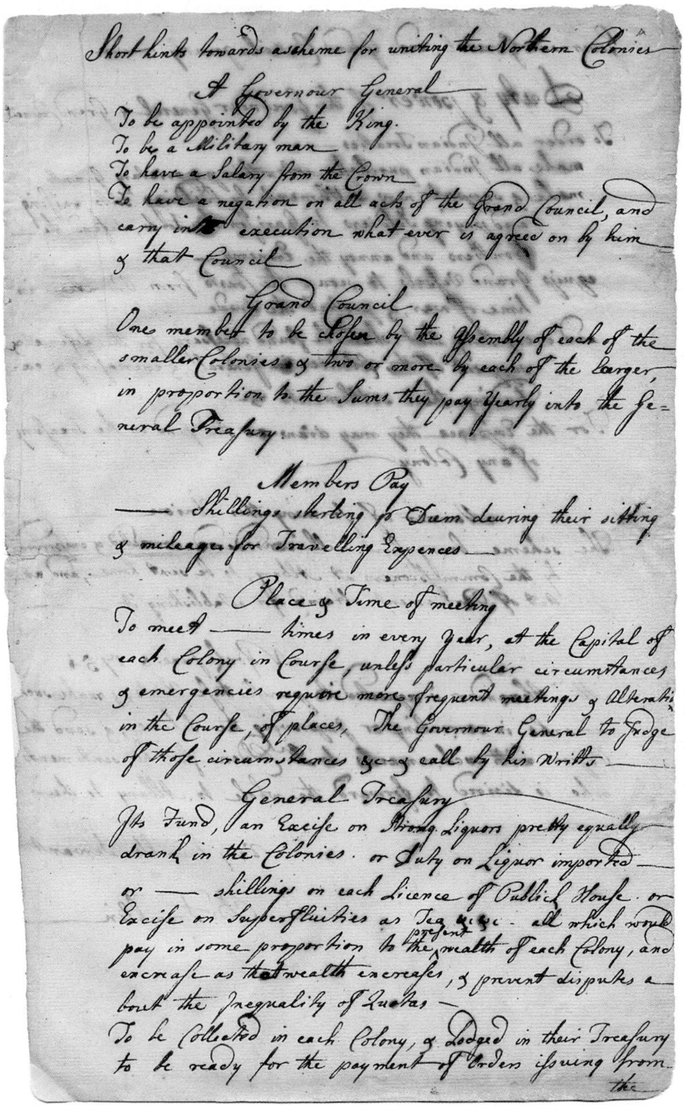

Short hints towards a scheme for uniting the Northern Colonies

A Governour General

To be appointed by the King.
To be a Military man
To have a Salary from the Crown
To have a negation on all acts of the Grand Council, and carry into execution what ever is agreed on by him & that Council

Grand Council

One member to be chosen by the Assembly of each of the smaller Colonies & two or more by each of the larger in proportion to the Sums they pay Yearly into the General Treasury.

Members Pay

—— Shillings sterling p Diem during their sitting & mileage for Travelling Expences

Place & Time of meeting

To meet —— times in every Year, at the Capital of each Colony in Course, unless particular circumstances & emergencies require more frequent meetings & Alteration in the Course of places. The Governour General to Judge of those circumstances &c & call by his Writts ——

General Treasury

Its Fund, an Excise on Strong Liquors pretty equally drank in the Colonies. or Duty on Liquor imported —— or —— shillings on each Licence of Publick House. or Excise on Superfluities as Tea &c &c. all which would pay in some proportion to the present wealth of each Colony, and encrease as that wealth encreases, & prevent disputes about the Inequality of Quotas ——
To be Collected in each Colony, & Lodged in their Treasury to be ready for the payment of Orders issuing from the

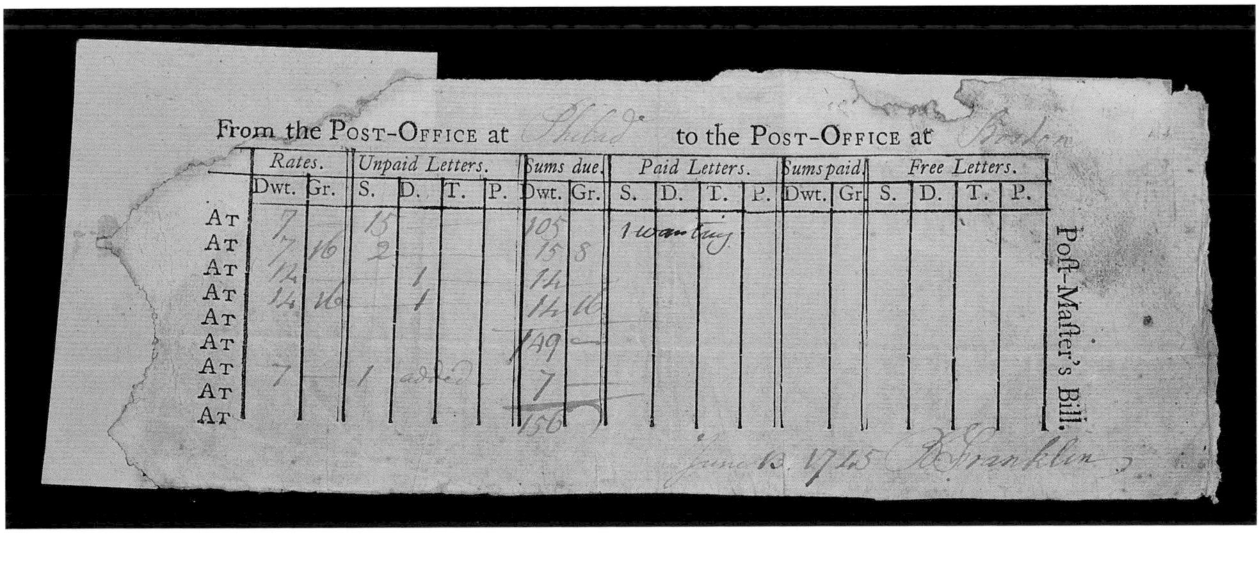

From the Post-Office at *Philad.* to the Post-Office at *Boston*

	Rates.		Unpaid Letters.				Sums due.		Paid Letters.				Sums paid.		Free Letters.			
	Dwt.	Gr.	S.	D.	T.	P.	Dwt.	Gr.	S.	D.	T.	P.	Dwt.	Gr.	S.	D.	T.	P.
At	7		15				105		1 wanting									
At	7	16	2				15	8										
At	14			1			14											
At	14	16		1			14	16										
At																		
At							149											
At	7		1	added			7											
At																		
At							156											

Post-Master's Bill.

June 13. 1745 B Franklin

Fig. 1.17 Benjamin Franklin to James Alexander and Cadwallader Colden, "Short hints towards a scheme for uniting the Northern Colonies" (Draft of the Albany Plan of Union), June 8, 1754. The Albany Plan is considered the first of America's founding documents. It provided for the union of the colonies and proposed a government with the authority to operate directly on behalf of its citizens.

Fig. 1.18 Postmaster's bill, 1745? Franklin devised a number of ways to make the post office more efficient, including pre-printing forms to standardize the postal accounting system.

He was the most entrepreneurial, efficient postmaster America ever had—and the only one under whom the post office ever made a profit.

In 1755 he even traveled to the camp of General Edward Braddock on the frontier to set up postal service. He found Braddock's advance toward the French Fort Duquesne stalled for lack of wagons and supplied them from the Pennsylvania farmers by guaranteeing payments himself. After Braddock's defeat, the French and their Indian allies ravaged the Pennsylvania frontier. Franklin was elected colonel of a Philadelphia regiment and led an expedition to the frontier, where he built forts.

After he returned to Philadelphia, Franklin once more became involved in Assembly business. Pennsylvania's proprietors—the descendants of the Penn family who ruled the colony—refused to assent to any tax bill unless it exempted their own land, and the Pennsylvania Assembly resolved to petition the British authorities. The assembly appointed Franklin as its agent to England. Fearing the ocean voyage, Deborah Franklin remained in Philadelphia.

During the passage to England, Franklin wrote the preface to *Poor Richard* for 1758; the piece became famous under the title *The Way to Wealth* (fig. 1.19). Eighteenth-century society generally scorned manual labor, but throughout the *Poor Richard* almanacs from 1733 to 1758, Franklin had celebrated work as worthy in itself and as a contribution to the welfare of society. He repeated such maxims in *The Way to Wealth:* "He that hath a Trade, hath an Estate"; "He that hath a Calling hath an Office of Profit and Honour"; and "The Borrower is a Slave to the Lender, and the Debtor to the Creditor, disdain the Chain, preserve your Freedom; and maintain your Independency: Be industrious and free; be frugal and free."[23]

The years 1748 to 1757 marked Franklin's most extraordinary intellectual achievements. He emerged as the most public-spirited citizen of Philadelphia, the most active member of the Pennsylvania Assembly, the most outspoken critic of English policies toward America, the most American of Americans, and the premier scientist of his day.

Arrived in London, Franklin met Lord Grenville, president of the Privy Council, who told him that the king in council (that is, the proceedings of official bodies such as the Privy Council [today, the Cabinet] and the Parliament, as approved by the king) was the supreme legislator of the colonies. Franklin disagreed, but he realized that it would do no good to quarrel with Grenville. He found lodgings with a widow, Margaret Stevenson, who lived on Craven Street, not far from Whitehall, seat of the British government offices

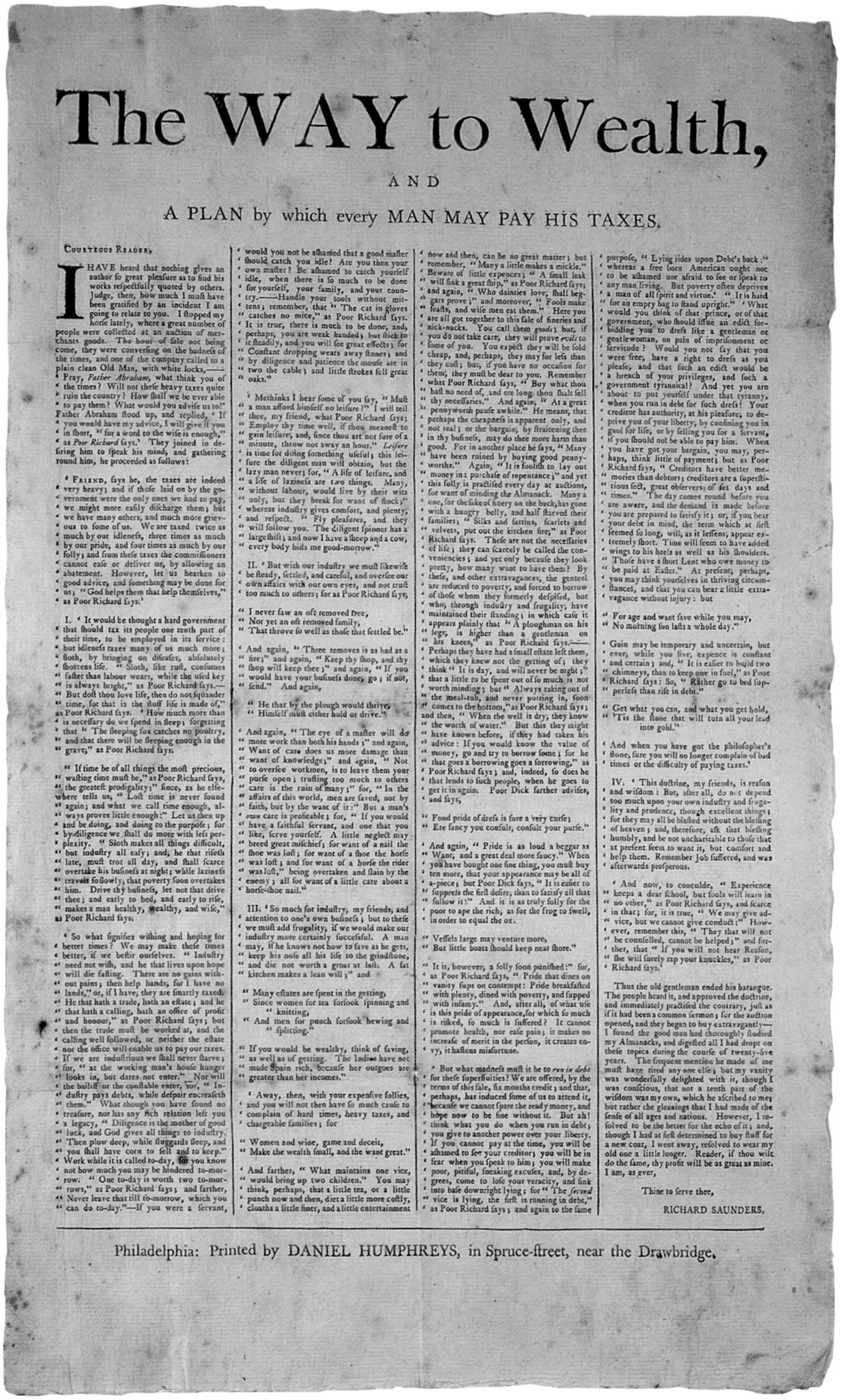

The WAY to Wealth,

AND

A PLAN by which every MAN MAY PAY HIS TAXES.

COURTEOUS READER,

I HAVE heard that nothing gives an author so great pleasure as to find his works respectfully quoted by others. Judge, then, how much I must have been gratified by an incident I am going to relate to you. I stopped my horse lately, where a great number of people were collected at an auction of merchants goods. The hour of sale not being come, they were conversing on the badness of the times, and one of the company called to a plain clean Old Man, with white locks,—'Pray, *Father Abraham,* what think you of the times? Will not these heavy taxes quite ruin the country? How shall we be ever able to pay them? What would you advise us to?' Father Abraham stood up, and replied, 'If you would have my advice, I will give it you in short, "for a word to the wise is enough," as *Poor Richard* says.' They joined in desiring him to speak his mind, and gathering round him, he proceeded as follows:

'Friends, says he, the taxes are indeed very heavy, and if those laid on by the government were the only ones we had to pay, we might more easily discharge them; but we have many others, and much more grievous to some of us. We are taxed twice as much by our idleness, three times as much by our pride, and four times as much by our folly; and from these taxes the commissioners cannot ease or deliver us, by allowing an abatement. However, let us hearken to good advice, and something may be done for us; "God helps them that help themselves," as *Poor Richard* says.

I. 'It would be thought a hard government that should tax its people one tenth part of their time, to be employed in its service; but idleness taxes many of us much more; sloth, by bringing on diseases, absolutely shortens life. "Sloth, like rust, consumes faster than labour wears, while the used key is always bright," as *Poor Richard* says.—But dost thou love life, then do not squander time, for that is the stuff life is made of," as *Poor Richard* says. "How much more than is necessary do we spend in sleep! forgetting that "The sleeping fox catches no poultry, and that there will be sleeping enough in the grave," as *Poor Richard* says.

'If time be of all things the most precious, wasting time must be," as *Poor Richard* says, "the greatest prodigality;" since, as he elsewhere tells us, "Lost time is never found again; and what we call time enough, always proves little enough." Let us then up and be doing, and doing to the purpose; so by diligence we shall do more with less perplexity. "Sloth makes all things difficult, but industry all easy; and, he that riseth late, must trot all day, and shall scarce overtake his business at night; while laziness travels so slowly, that poverty soon overtakes him. Drive thy business, let not that drive thee; and early to bed, and early to rise, makes a man healthy, wealthy, and wise," as *Poor Richard* says.

'So what signifies wishing and hoping for better times? We may make these times better, if we bestir ourselves. "Industry need not wish, and he that lives upon hope will die fasting. There are no gains without pains; then help hands, for I have no lands," or, if I have, they are smartly taxed. He that hath a trade, hath an estate; and he that hath a calling, hath an office of profit and honour, as *Poor Richard* says; but then the trade must be worked at, and the calling well followed, or neither the estate nor the office will enable us to pay our taxes. If we are industrious we shall never starve; for, "at the working man's house hunger looks in, but dares not enter." Nor will the bailiff or the constable enter, for, "Industry pays debts, while despair encreaseth them." What though you have found no treasure, nor has any rich relation left you a legacy, "Diligence is the mother of good luck, and God gives all things to industry. Then plow deep, while sluggards sleep, and you shall have corn to sell and to keep." Work while it is called to-day, for you know not how much you may be hindered to-morrow. "One to-day is worth two to-morrows," as *Poor Richard* says; and farther, "Never leave that till to-morrow, which you can do to-day."—If you were a servant, would you not be ashamed that a good master should catch you idle? Are you then your own master? Be ashamed to catch yourself idle, when there is so much to be done for yourself, your family, and your country.—Handle your tools without mittens; remember, that "The cat in gloves catches no mice," as *Poor Richard* says. It is true, there is much to be done, and, perhaps, you are weak handed; but stick to it steadily, and you will see great effects; for "Constant dropping wears away stones; and by diligence and patience the mouse ate in two the cable; and little strokes fell great oaks."

'Methinks I hear some of you say, "Must a man afford himself no leisure?"—I will tell thee, my friend, what *Poor Richard* says; "Employ thy time well, if thou meanest to gain leisure; and, since thou art not sure of a minute, throw not away an hour." *Leisure* is time for doing something useful; this leisure the diligent man will obtain, but the lazy man never; for, "A life of leisure, and a life of laziness are two things." Many, without labour, would live by their wits only, but they break for want of stock;" whereas industry gives comfort, and plenty, and respect. "Fly pleasures, and they will follow you. The diligent spinner has a large shift; and now I have a sheep and a cow, every body bids me good-morrow."

II. 'But with our industry we must likewise be steady, settled, and careful, and oversee our own affairs with our own eyes, and not trust too much to others; for as *Poor Richard* says,

'I never saw an oft removed tree,
Nor yet an oft removed family,
That throve so well as those that settled be.'

'And again, "Three removes is as bad as a fire;" and again, "Keep thy shop, and thy shop will keep thee;" and again, "If you would have your business done, go; if not, send." And again,

'He that by the plough would thrive,
Himself must either hold or drive.'

'And again, "The eye of a master will do more work than both his hands;" and again, Want of care does us more damage than want of knowledge;" and again, "Not to oversee workmen, is to leave them your purse open; trusting too much to others care is the ruin of many;" for, "In the affairs of this world, men are saved, not by faith, but by the want of it:" But a man's own care is profitable; for, "If you would have a faithful servant, and one that you like, serve yourself. A little neglect may breed great mischief; for want of a nail the shoe was lost; for want of a shoe the horse was lost; and for want of a horse the rider was lost," being overtaken and slain by the enemy; all for want of a little care about a horse-shoe nail."

III. 'So much for industry, my friends, and attention to one's own business; but to these we must add frugality, if we would make our industry more certainly successful. A man may, if he knows not how to save as he gets, keep his nose all his life to the grindstone, and die not worth a groat at last. A fat kitchen makes a lean will;" and

'Many estates are spent in the getting,
Since women for tea forsook spinning and knitting.'

'And men for punch forsook hewing and splitting.'

'If you would be wealthy, think of saving, as well as of getting. The Indies have not made Spain rich, because her outgoes are greater than her incomes.'

'Away, then, with your expensive follies, and you will not then have so much cause to complain of hard times, heavy taxes, and chargeable families; for

'Women and wine, game and deceit,
Make the wealth small, and the want great.'

'And farther, "What maintains one vice, would bring up two children. You may think, perhaps, that a little tea, or a little punch now and then, diet a little more costly, cloaths a little finer, and a little entertainment now and then, can be no great matter; but remember, "Many a little makes a mickle." Beware of little expences; "A small leak will sink a great ship," as *Poor Richard* says; and again, "Who dainties love, shall beggars prove;" and moreover, "Fools make feasts, and wise men eat them." Here you are all got together to this sale of fineries and nick-nacks. You call them *goods*; but, if you do not take care, they will prove *evils* to some of you. You expect they will be sold cheap, and, perhaps, they may for less than they cost; but, if you have no occasion for them, they must be dear to you. Remember what *Poor Richard* says, "Buy what thou hast no need of, and ere long thou shalt sell thy necessaries." And again, "At a great pennyworth pause awhile." He means, that perhaps the cheapness is apparent only, and not real; or the bargain, by straitening thee in thy business, may do thee more harm than good. For in another place he says, "Many have been ruined by buying good pennyworths." Again, "It is foolish to lay out money in purchase of repentance;" and yet this folly is practised every day at auctions, for want of minding the Almanack. Many a one, for the sake of finery on the back, has gone with a hungry belly, and half starved their families;" "Silks and sattins, scarlets and velvets, put out the kitchen fire;" as *Poor Richard* says. These are not the necessaries of life; they can scarcely be called the conveniencies; and yet only because they look pretty, how many want to have them? By these, and other extravagances, the genteel are reduced to poverty, and forced to borrow of those whom they formerly despised, but who, through industry and frugality, have maintained their standing; in which case it appears plainly that "A ploughman on his legs is higher than a gentleman on his knees," as *Poor Richard* says.—Perhaps they have had a small estate left them, which they knew not the getting of; they think "It is day, and will never be night;" that a little to be spent out of so much, is not worth minding; but "Always taking out of the meal-tub, and never putting in, soon comes to the bottom," as *Poor Richard* says; and then, "When the well is dry, they know the worth of water." But this they might have known before, if they had taken his advice: If you would know the value of money, go and try to borrow some; for he that goes a borrowing goes a sorrowing;" as *Poor Richard* says; and, indeed, so does he that lends to such people, when he goes to get it in again. *Poor Dick* farther advises, and says,

'Fond pride of dress is sure a very curse;
Ere fancy you consult, consult your purse.'

'And again, "Pride is as loud a beggar as Want, and a great deal more saucy." When you have bought one fine thing, you must buy ten more, that your appearance may be all of a-piece; but *Poor Dick* says, "It is easier to suppress the first desire, than to satisfy all that follow it." And it is as truly folly for the poor to ape the rich, as for the frog to swell, in order to equal the ox.

'Vessels large may venture more,
But little boats should keep near shore.

'It is, however, a folly soon punished;" for, as *Poor Richard* says, "Pride that dines on vanity sups on contempt: Pride breakfasted with plenty, dined with poverty, and supped with infamy." And, after all, of what use is this pride of appearance, for which so much is risked, so much is suffered? It cannot promote health, nor ease pain; it makes no increase of merit in the person, it creates envy, it hastens misfortune.

'But what madness must it be to *run in debt* for these superfluities! We are offered, by the terms of this sale, six months credit; and that, perhaps, has induced some of us to attend it, because we cannot spare the ready money, and hope now to be fine without it. But ah! think what you do when you run in debt; you give to another power over your liberty. If you cannot pay at the time, you will be ashamed to see your creditor; you will be in fear when you speak to him; you will make poor, pitiful, sneaking excuses, and, by degrees, come to lose your veracity, and sink into base downright lying; for "The *second* vice is lying, the first is running in debt," as *Poor Richard* says; and again to the same purpose, "Lying rides upon Debt's back:" whereas a free born American ought not to be ashamed nor afraid to see or speak to any man living. But poverty often deprives a man of all spirit and virtue.' "It is hard for an empty bag to stand upright." "What would you think of that prince, or of that government, who should issue an edict forbidding you to dress like a gentleman or gentlewoman, on pain of imprisonment or servitude? Would you not say that you were free, have a right to dress as you please, and that such an edict would be a breach of your privileges, and such a government tyrannical? And yet you are about to put yourself under that tyranny, when you run in debt for such dress! Your creditor has authority, at his pleasure, to deprive you of your liberty, by confining you in goal for life, or by selling you for a servant, if you should not be able to pay him. When you have got your bargain, you may, perhaps, think little of payment; but *Poor Richard* says, "Creditors have better memories than debtors; creditors are a superstitious sect, great observers of set days and times." The day comes round before you are aware, and the demand is made before you are prepared to satisfy it; or, if you bear your debt in mind, the term which at first seemed so long, will, as it lessens, appear extremely short. Time will seem to have added wings to his heels as well as his shoulders. "Those have a short Lent who owe money to be paid at Easter." At present, perhaps, you may think yourselves in thriving circumstances, and that you can bear a little extravagance without injury; but

'For age and want save while you may,
No morning sun lasts a whole day.'

'Gain may be temporary and uncertain, but ever, while you live, expence is constant and certain; and, "It is easier to build two chimneys, than to keep one in fuel," as *Poor Richard* says: So, "Rather go to bed supperless than rise in debt."

'Get what you can, and what you get hold, 'Tis the stone that will turn all your lead into gold.'

'And when you have got the philosopher's stone, sure you will no longer complain of bad times or the difficulty of paying taxes.'

IV. 'This doctrine, my friends, is reason and wisdom: But, after all, do not depend too much upon your own industry and frugality and prudence, though excellent things; for they may all be blasted without the blessing of heaven; and, therefore, ask that blessing humbly, and be not uncharitable to those that at present seem to want it, but comfort and help them. Remember Job suffered, and was afterwards prosperous.

'And now, to conclude, "Experience keeps a dear school, but fools will learn in no other," as *Poor Richard* says, and scarce in that; for, it is true, "We may give advice, but we cannot give conduct:" However, remember this, "They that will not be counselled, cannot be helped;" and farther, that "If you will not hear Reason, she will surely rap your knuckles," as *Poor Richard* says.

Thus the old gentleman ended his harangue. The people heard it, and approved the doctrine, and immediately practised the contrary, just as if it had been a common sermon; for the auction opened, and they began to buy extravagantly.—I found the good man had thoroughly studied my Almanacks, and digested all I had dropt on these topics during the course of twenty-five years. The frequent mention he made of me must have tired any one else; but my vanity was wonderfully delighted with it, though I was conscious, that not a tenth part of the wisdom was my own, which he ascribed to me; but rather the gleanings that I had made of the sense of all ages and nations. However, I resolved to be the better for the echo of it; and, though I had at first determined to buy stuff for a new coat, I went away, resolved to wear my old one a little longer. Reader, if thou wilt do the same, thy profit will be as great as mine.

I am, as ever,

Thine to serve thee,

RICHARD SAUNDERS.

Philadelphia: Printed by DANIEL HUMPHREYS, in Spruce-street, near the Drawbridge.

Fig. 1.19 Benjamin Franklin, The Way to Wealth, *ca. 1785. An early version of the most frequently reprinted of Franklin's works, consisting of proverbs culled from twenty-five years of* Poor Richard's Almanacks, *this copy of* The Way to Wealth *is the first American broadside printing.*

Fig. 1.20 Gilbert Stuart, Portrait of John Fothergill, 1781. An active Quaker and successful physician, Fothergill in 1751 recommended that Franklin's papers on electricity be published and wrote the preface to the volume; he later became one of Franklin's closest friends in London.

where Franklin expected to do business. Leading Philadelphia Quakers had recommended that he call on Peter Collinson and Dr. John Fothergill (fig. 1.20), two eminent London Quakers, for advice about how to deal with the proprietors. They suggested that he attempt to reconcile differences with the proprietors, rather than appeal directly to the British authorities. Franklin negotiated with the Penns, but they refused to allow their estates to be taxed.

Finding the British public and the authorities ignorant about and prejudiced against America, Franklin began a campaign to enlighten them. "A Defense of the Americans," published in the *London Chronicle*, May 9, 1759, has been called the major statement of Americanism in the colonial period.[24] It echoed Franklin's bitter anti-English editorial "Jakes on Our Tables" and censured the British for their excessive pride in their "regular" army troops and their condescension to the American militia.

These issues notwithstanding, the sociable Franklin soon established several circles of friends (fig. 1.21). Besides the Stevensons (his landlady and her daughter Mary, known as Polly) and their circle, he became a close friend of William Strahan, a successful London printer, and of Sir John Pringle, a physician and scientist. On Mondays he dined at the George and Vulture tavern with a group of scientists that sometimes included Captain James Cook. On Thursdays he dined at St Paul's Coffee House, with the Club of Honest Whigs, which included Richard Price, Joseph Priestley, and occasionally James Boswell. Franklin regularly attended meetings of the Royal Society (the premier scientific society), the Associates of Dr. Bray (a small philanthropic organization devoted to educating blacks), and the Society for the Encouragement of Arts, Manufactures, and Commerce. On a tour to Scotland in 1759 he met Adam Smith, the historian William Robertson, the jurist Lord Kames, and the philosopher David Hume.

Time permitting, Franklin continued his scientific interests, inventing a clock with only three wheels (1758), experimenting with an early form of air conditioning (1758), designing a damper for stoves and chimneys (1758), and gradually improving his new musical instrument, the glass armonica (1762). Franklin's scientific contributions were recognized by British universities: he received an honorary degree of Doctor of Laws from St Andrews in 1759 and a doctorate of Civil Law from Oxford in 1762.

One means that Franklin used to make the British look more favorably on American concerns was a short book, *The Interest of Great Britain Considered* (1760), that argued for the economic and strategic importance of Canada to Great Britain. It was partly responsible for persuading the British to retain Canada rather than Guadeloupe at the conclusion of the Seven Years' War (1756–63). David Hume, who judged Franklin to be a "great Man of Letters" in 1764, said in 1773 that he thought *The Interest of Great Britain Considered* was the best book written in English in the previous thirty years.[25]

Franklin's first English mission achieved partial success. On August 28, 1760, the Privy Council agreed to approve a bill taxing the proprietors' lands after Franklin personally guaranteed that the proprietary estates would be taxed with perfect equity.[26]

As the Pennsylvania agent and the best-known American in England, Franklin had become more cautious about expressing views concerning Brit-

Fig. 1.21 Attributed to Ralph Wood, Staffordshire statuette of Benjamin Franklin, ca. 1762–72. The earliest of the many Staffordshire figures of Franklin, Wood's version was created to honor him while he was living in England and is a sign of his popularity there. The medal around Franklin's neck could be the Copley award presented to him by the Royal Society in 1753.

ish injustice to America. His bitter editorials and satires against England of the early 1750s were not equaled again until 1773, when he began to abandon hope that he could lessen England's increasingly adamant actions against America. But during his first English agency, 1757 to 1762, he saw that anti-English expressions would do little good and might harm rather than improve relations between England and the colonies. Nevertheless, "A Defense of the Americans" was extraordinarily bold.

Franklin arrived back in Philadelphia on November 1, 1762. Having been an elected member of the Pennsylvania Assembly throughout his time in England, Franklin now returned to its active service as an assemblyman. In December 1763 a frontier mob known as the Paxton Boys murdered a group of Christian Indians in Lancaster. Franklin denounced the action in a pamphlet entitled *A Narrative of the Late Massacres* (January 1764). When the Paxton Boys marched on Philadelphia early in February to attack Christian Indians there, the government foundered. Franklin organized its defense, met with the mob's leaders, and persuaded them to present a list of grievances and disperse. When warfare on the frontier dwindled in late 1764, the danger to the peaceful Indians subsided.

On May 26, 1764, as news of the impending Stamp Act, which would impose a tax on newspapers, legal documents, and many other printed materials, reached the colonies, the former Speaker of the Pennsylvania Assembly resigned, and the Assembly elected Franklin as Speaker. On June 13, the Massachusetts Assembly asked the other colonial assemblies to oppose the act. On September 12, Franklin presented the request to the Pennsylvania Assembly, which promptly instructed Pennsylvania's London agent Richard Jackson to resist the proposed act and argue that only the Pennsylvania legislature had the right to impose taxes in the colony.

Before the annual Pennsylvania election in October, political opponents defamed Franklin through a number of slanderous charges: that he coveted the governorship, that he had embezzled public money while he was the Assembly's agent in England, that William Franklin's mother was a servant whom he had mistreated and buried in an unmarked grave, that he was prejudiced against the Pennsylvania Germans, and that he was an Indian lover. (The last had some truth.) The most bitterly contested Assembly election in colonial Pennsylvania began at 10 A.M. on October 2, 1764, and continued until 3 P.M. the following day. Franklin lost by eighteen votes.[27] The anti-proprietary party, however, retained its majority and appointed Franklin co-agent to England with Richard Jackson on October 26, 1764.

Fig. 1.23 "MAGNA Britannia: her
Colonies REDUC'D," designed by Benjamin Franklin, ca. 1766. Franklin had
this cartoon printed on cards and distributed them to Parliament at the debate over the repeal of the Stamp Act.
This is the only known original to have
survived, preserved by Pierre Eugène
Du Simitière. Franklin hoped that
the visual impact of the cartoon would
convey the disastrous effects on the empire from unfairly taxing the colonies: "The Moral is, that the Colonies
may be ruined, but that Britain would
thereby be maimed."

The purpose of Franklin's second mission to England was to change
Pennsylvania's proprietary government to a royal government, but British imperial politics intervened (fig. 1.22). At first, the Stamp Act took all his time.
He strenuously opposed it in essays and in letters to the London newspapers.
His efforts failed. The Stamp Act passed the Commons on February 27, 1765,
and received the royal assent in March, to take effect on November 1. Franklin, like most American opponents of the act, accepted defeat. Then, on May
30, Virginia's House of Burgesses passed the Stamp Act Resolves, denying
that Britain had the right to tax Virginians. Emboldened by the Virginia Resolves, other colonies followed suit, and local mobs threatened the stamp dis-
tributors. Because of rumors that Franklin had supported the Stamp Act, his
Philadelphia home was threatened on September 16. Deborah armed herself,
ready to fight to defend their home, but the menace fizzled out. On November
1, the day the Stamp Act was to take effect, courts throughout the colonies refused to convene. British colonial administration of the colonies collapsed.

Attempting to have the Stamp Act repealed, Franklin satirized it in a cartoon he designed about the beginning of 1766, "MAGNA Britannia: her Colonies REDUC'D" (fig. 1.23). He also attended a committee of the whole House of
Commons on February 13 to testify against the act. His answers to the members of Parliament displayed Americanism and superb political knowledge. To
the suggestion that military forces should be sent to America, he boldly asserted, "They will not find a rebellion; they may indeed make one."[28] Publi-

cation of his testimony confirmed Franklin's reputation as America's preeminent spokesman. On April 11, 1768, the Georgia Assembly appointed him its agent; on November 8, 1769, New Jersey did the same; and on October 24, 1770, the Massachusetts Assembly followed suit. He was now the agent for four colonies.

Throughout the period 1764–75, Franklin wrote a series of spirited American essays, among them the tall tale "The Grand Leap of the Whale over Niagara Falls" (published May 3, 1765), the shrewdly analytical "Causes of the American Discontents before 1768" (January 7, 1768), the satire "Rules by Which a Great Empire May Be Reduced to a Small One" (September 11, 1773), and the political hoax "An Edict by the King of Prussia" (September 22, 1773). Franklin's treasonous manuscript "Remarks on Judge Foster's Argument in Favor of the Right of Impressing Seamen," probably written about 1770, circulated clandestinely. In it Franklin wrote that George III deserved to be impressed rather than poor sailors, for "I am not satisfied of the Necessity or Utility" of the "Office of King." Though Franklin privately predicted American independence, he had proven in "Observations Concerning the Increase of Mankind" that every year brought America increasing strength. If there must be war, he believed it better to postpone it for as long as possible.[29]

Secretly, Franklin was given purloined letters in 1772 from Thomas Hutchinson and Andrew Oliver in Massachusetts. The letters, addressed to a British subminister, requested the British to use authoritarian measures in Massachusetts. Franklin sent the letters to the Massachusetts Speaker of the House, hoping that when the Boston radicals learned that Americans among them had instigated the repressions, they would be less angry with the British authorities. The correspondence, however, exacerbated the strife in Massachusetts, and the Assembly petitioned for Governor Hutchinson's and Lt. Governor Oliver's removal. In turn, Hutchinson obtained a copy of Franklin's July 7, 1773, letter urging the colonial assemblies to resolve never to "grant aids to the Crown in any General War" until the rights of Americans "are recogniz'd by the King and both Houses of Parliament." "Such a Step," he wrote, "I imagine will bring the Dispute to a Crisis; and whether our Demands are immediately comply'd with, or compulsory Means are thought of to make us Rescind them, our Ends will finally be obtain'd."[30] Hutchinson sent the copy to Lord Dartmouth, the colonial secretary, who judged it treasonable. On Dartmouth's instruction General Thomas Gage, military commander-in-chief in America, tried to obtain the original so Franklin could be prosecuted, but Gage failed.

Two Londoners were suspected of stealing the Hutchinson-Oliver letters.

They accused each other, dueled, and, after one was wounded, vowed to duel again. To prevent this, Franklin published on Christmas Day, 1773, the bold and incriminating statement, "I alone am the person who obtained and transmitted to Boston the letters in question."[31] He also forwarded to Lord Dartmouth a Massachusetts petition to remove Hutchinson and Oliver.

News of the Boston Tea Party reached London on January 20, 1774, and infuriated the British authorities. The hearing on the Massachusetts petition before the Privy Council took place in the Cockpit (the council's meeting place) on January 29. In an hour-long diatribe, the British solicitor general, Alexander Wedderburn, excoriated Franklin, demanding that he be marked and branded as a thief. Britain's major officials, many of whom Franklin knew well, sneered and snickered while he stood silent, America's scapegoat.

Two days later Franklin was dismissed as deputy postmaster general for North America. During 1774 and early 1775, even as he petitioned against the Boston Port Bill (which closed Boston's port), Franklin satirized the British government's handling of American politics while still attempting to reconcile Great Britain with the colonists. In an effort to forestall the bill, he personally guaranteed payment of the cost of the tea dumped in Boston harbor. His efforts, including his collaboration with William Pitt, earl of Chatham, in January 1775, came to nothing. He spent his last day in London with Joseph Priestley, who wrote that as Franklin read the American news which made war seem inevitable, "the tears trickled down his cheeks."[32] He left London on March 20, his second mission a complete failure. He was being prosecuted in court for his role in securing the Hutchinson-Oliver letters, and on May 13, 1775, the sheriff of Middlesex was ordered to arrest him.

While Franklin was at sea on his return from England, the battles of Lexington and Concord took place, on April 19, 1775, and started the War of American Independence. He arrived at Philadelphia on May 5, and the next day the Pennsylvania Assembly unanimously chose him as a delegate to the Second Continental Congress. His draft "Articles of Confederation," written before July 21, asserted America's sovereignty and delegated greater powers to the central government than the U.S. Constitution would do in 1787. But Congress was timorous. On July 23, John Adams reported that Franklin "does not hesitate at our boldest Measures, but rather seems to think us, too irresolute, and backward." His propagandistic writings of the period included the satiric song "The King's Own Regulars" (published November 27), which made George Washington laugh, and the hoax "Bradshaw's Epitaph" (December 14), which concluded with the words that Thomas Jefferson adopted as his personal motto, "Rebellion to Tyrants Is Obedience to God."[33]

In Congress, Franklin argued on January 16, 1776, for the union of the colonies but was defeated. Appointed a member of the commission to persuade the Canadians to join with the Americans against Britain, Franklin, though seventy years old and in ill health, undertook the arduous journey, which lasted from March 26 to May 30. But the mission failed. On his return, he served on the committee to draft the Declaration of Independence. Thomas Jefferson, chair of the committee, composed the document, though Franklin added to and revised it. Congress voted for independence on July 2, and then debated, altered, and finally adopted the Declaration on July 4, 1776.

Congress appointed Franklin and John Adams to a committee to confer with Lord Howe (Admiral Richard Howe, commander of all British Forces in America), on Staten Island. At their meeting, on September 11, 1776, Howe stated that he felt for America and would lament her fall as a brother would. Adams recorded Franklin's witty and combative reply: with "a Bow, a Smile and all the Naivetee which sometimes appeared in his conversation and is often observed in his Writings," Franklin said, "'My Lord, We will do our Utmost Endeavours, to save your Lordship that mortification.'"[34] The next month, elected a commissioner to France by the Continental Congress, he sailed from Philadelphia, on October 27, 1776.

Franklin arrived in France on December 3 and proceeded to Paris, where he met secretly with the comte de Vergennes, the French foreign minister. The American commissioners—Silas Deane (replaced by John Adams in 1778), Arthur Lee, and Franklin—formally requested French aid on January 5, 1777, and on the 13th they received a secret promise of two million livres. From Voltaire's *Lettres philosophique* (1734) and Montesquieu's *L'esprit des lois* (1748), Franklin knew that the French associated Pennsylvania and Quakerism with virtue and simplicity, and he dressed and presented himself accordingly. On February 8, he wrote his friend Emma Thompson: "Figure me . . . very plainly dress'd, wearing my thin grey strait Hair, that peeps out under my only Coiffure, a fine Fur Cap, which comes down my Forehead almost to my Spectacles. Think how this must appear among the Powder'd Heads of Paris" (fig. 1.24).[35]

John Adams testified that Franklin was idolized while in France: "His name was familiar to government and people, to kings, courtiers, nobility, clergy, and philosophers, as well as plebeians, to such a degree that there was

Fig. 1.24 Augustin de Saint-Aubin after Charles-Nicholas Cochin, Benjamin Franklin (portrait print), 1777. One of the first images of Franklin available in France, made within a few weeks of his arrival, this print referred to Franklin as the "New World Ambassador" and was reproduced on countless souvenir objects. The fur cap Franklin wore that winter attracted the attention of the French public, who associated it with a similar hat worn by the philosopher Jean-Jacques Rousseau.

Fig. 1.25 (Opposite) Marguerite Gérard after Jean-Honoré Fragonard, Au génie de Franklin (To the genius of Franklin), ca. 1778. The often-quoted statement by the French statesman and economist Anne-Robert-Jacques Turgot ("He snatched the lightning from the skies and the scepter from the tyrants") appeared as the inscription on this allegorical print epitomizing the French view of Franklin. He himself demurred that the epigram gave him more credit than he deserved, but it was frequently quoted during his years in Paris.

BENJAMIN FRANKLIN.

Né à Bofton, dans la nouvelle Angleterre le 17 Janvier 1706

Deffiné par C. N. Cochin Chevalier de l'Ordre du Roi, en 1777. et Gravé par Aug. de St. Aubin Graveur de la Bibliothéque du Roi.
Se vend à Paris chés C. N. Cochin aux Galleries du Louvre ; et chés Aug. de St. Aubin, rue des Mathurins.

scarcely a peasant or citizen, a *valet de chambre*, coachman or footman, a lady's chambermaid or a scullion in a kitchen, who was not familiar with it, and who did not consider him as a friend to human kind." The French finance minister, Anne-Robert-Jacques Turgot, composed the most famous epigram of modern times on Franklin: "Eripuit coelo fulmen, sceptrumque tyrannis" (He snatched the lightning from the skies and the scepter from the tyrants; see fig. 1.25).[36]

Early in 1777 Franklin wrote "The Sale of the Hessians," creating in the count de Schaumbergh a startlingly horrible persona: "I have learned with unspeakable pleasure the courage our troops exhibited at Trenton, and you cannot imagine my joy on being told that of the 1,950 Hessians engaged in the fight, but 345 escaped." Besides literary propaganda, Franklin used personal wit to combat the British. Lord Stormont, the British ambassador to France, frequently exaggerated American losses. When asked whether it was true that six battalions of Washington's army had surrendered, Franklin replied with a quip that made Stormont the laughingstock of Paris: "No, it is only a Stormont."[37]

News of General Burgoyne's defeat at Sarotoga in October 1777 arrived in December and spurred negotiations leading to the French alliance on February 6, 1778. On October 21, following France's decision to send a minister plenipotentiary to the United States, Congress responded by giving Franklin a similar title. As minister plenipotentiary Franklin had innumerable responsibilities. He borrowed funds from France for the expenses of Congress and for all the salaries and expenses of the other American ministers in Europe; issued letters of marque for American privateers; managed the interests of the Continental Navy overseas; oversaw the purchase and shipping of arms and other supplies for the Continental Army; negotiated for the humane treatment and exchanges of American prisoners of war; helped hundreds of escaped American prisoners; cultivated friendships with influential French intellectuals and politicians; and issued documents to American vessels to give safe passage to English ships on humanitarian or scientific missions, including a passport for Captain James Cook's expedition.

The sociable Franklin made friends among a number of French social sets. He relished the hospitality of his neighbor at Passy, Madame Brillon, to whom he addressed a multilayered bagatelle on the human condition, "The Ephemera," and the social life at the salon of Madame Helvétius, to whom he addressed the daringly flirtatious bagatelle "The Elysian Fields."[38] Though his multifarious duties precluded extensive scientific experimentation, Franklin suggested projects for others. Observing that ships used in the salt trade lasted longer than others, he conceived a method for prolonging the life of lumber by seasoning it in salt. He devised a test for the conductivity of metals. A display of the aurora borealis on December 3, 1778, prompted him to write a series of "Suppositions and Conjectures" on the phenomenon. He described his new technological device, bifocal glasses, on May 23, 1784.

In June 1781 Congress appointed Franklin, Henry Laurens, and Thomas Jefferson commissioners to negotiate peace along with John Jay and John Adams. (Jefferson declined.) Although Congress naively bound Franklin and its other representatives to "undertake Nothing" regarding a peace treaty without France's "Knowledge and Concurrence," Franklin boldly disregarded the instruction. From March to June 1782, he negotiated with the British emissary Richard Oswald. On April 19, Franklin suggested that Britain should cede Canada to the United States.[39] Had Franklin been the only commissioner, he might have been able to settle the peace then and secured Canada. But John Jay arrived in Paris on June 23 and insisted on British recognition of American independence before he would conduct formal peace negotiations, thus delaying the talks while the war at sea changed to favor the British.

On July 10, 1782, Franklin proposed to Oswald four "necessary" and four "advisable" terms for peace; in September, Oswald's new British commission effectively recognized the United States and overcame Jay's hesitation.[40] A draft of the articles for the treaty was prepared and sent to Britain. John Adams arrived in Paris on October 26 and joined the negotiations, and, on November 30, Oswald and the American commissioners signed the preliminary articles of peace. In December, when the comte de Vergennes complained of America's failure to consult the French, Franklin diplomatically admitted the impropriety, expressed gratitude to France, and asked for another loan. Vergennes assured him of a further six million livres. Franklin, Adams, and Jay signed the final treaty of peace on behalf of the United States on September 3, 1783.

While negotiations were going on in the late summer and early fall of 1783, Franklin witnessed and wrote accounts of several balloon flights. He hoped they would "pave the Way to some Discoveries in Natural Philosophy of which at present we have no Conception." When a skeptic asked, "What good is it?" Franklin replied with a wonderful defense of the possibilities that might result from pure research: "What good is a new-born baby?" While still in France conducting treaties with other nations, Franklin offered an interpretation of American culture, *Information to those who would remove to america* (February 1784). He claimed that Americans valued the worker, not the gentleman. Franklin wrote that "People do not enquire concerning a Stranger, What is he? but What can he do?" Franklin's middle-class, pragmatic attitudes echoed those he expressed throughout the *Poor Richard's Almanack* from 1733 to 1758,

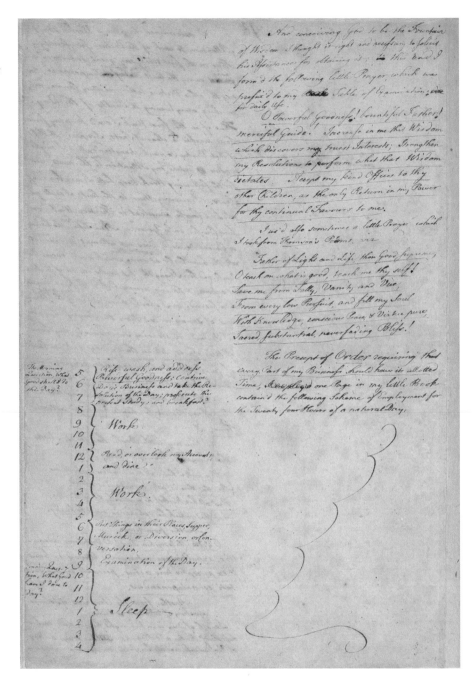

in numerous letters, in the Constitution of Pennsylvania, and in the *Autobiography* (fig. 1.26). But these opinions were revolutionary in the hierarchical society of the eighteenth century, even in America.[41]

　　Formal ratifications of the peace treaty with Great Britain were exchanged
on May 12, 1784, and the next day Franklin requested to be relieved of his post

so he could return home. On May 2, 1785, he received permission: "I shall now be free of Politicks for the Rest of my Life. Welcome again my dear Philosophical Amusements." He left Passy on July 12, in pain from a bladder stone. Nonetheless, Franklin spent most of the voyage to America writing pieces such as the maritime observations, which suggested a number of improvements for convenience, safety, and swiftness in sailing.[42]

Franklin's great diplomatic success in France was due primarily to his ability to win over the French people and ministers, especially the French foreign minister, the comte de Vergennes. As a diplomat, Franklin was eminently reasonable. He projected sympathy for the positions of others and appreciated the reasons influencing their decisions. At the same time, he inexorably defended the rights of Americans. He was helped by his reputation. Long before he came to France as a minister, he was known and respected in numerous French circles, including those of the physiocrats, the philosophes, and the scientists. He was one of only eight foreign members of the prestigious French Académie Royale. During the time in France, the sociable Franklin attended Académie meetings, as well as those of the Masonic Loge des Neuf Soeurs, and cultivated its members (fig. 1.27). Carefully, discreetly, and consistently making use of all his contacts, Franklin was the most essential and successful American diplomat of all time.

Franklin arrived at Philadelphia on September 14, 1785. Elected to the supreme executive council of Pennsylvania on October 11, he was chosen its president on the 18th, and served in that position (in effect, governor) for three years. The late 1780s also saw a final flourish of practical inventions. In January 1786 he fashioned an instrument for taking down books from high shelves; he followed this with a series of chairs: one had a seat that unfolded to become a ladder, another had a writing arm on one side (a staple feature of today's classroom chairs), and a third was a rocking chair with a fan.

From May 28 to September 17, 1787, Franklin served in the Constitutional Convention. He advocated that representation be proportional to population, but delegates from the smaller states fiercely argued for equal representation by state. On June 30, he said, "When a broad table is to be made, and the edges of planks do not fit, the artist takes a little from both and makes a good joint. In like manner here both sides must part with some of their demands, in order that they may join in some accommodating proposition." With the members divided and seemingly deadlocked on the issue, Franklin was appointed to a committee to recommend a solution. On July 3 he moved the "Great Compromise" in the committee, whereby representation was proportional in the

Fig. 1.27 Masonic sash, ca. 1782. This sash, or collar, is said to have been worn by Franklin as a "Venerable" member of the Loge des Neuf Soeurs (Lodge of the Nine Muses) in Paris.

Fig. 1.28 Joseph Sansom, Silhouette of Benjamin Franklin, ca. 1790. Local Philadelphia artist Sansom captured a hunchbacked, frail old man with this silhouette taken at the end of Franklin's life.

House of Delegates but equal by state in the Senate. The committee adopted it that day and the Constitutional Convention ratified it on July 16.[43]

Franklin asserted in Congress on August 7 and 10 that the right to vote should be extended as widely as possible. He condemned making property qualifications necessary either for the franchise or for office holding. Though the oldest member of the Constitutional Convention, he was its most egalitarian, indeed populist, voice. His closing speech was the most effective propaganda for the ratification of the constitution.[44] At age seventy, in 1776, he had been the oldest signer of the Declaration of Independence; now, age eighty-one, he was the oldest signer of the U.S. Constitution. Only Franklin signed all three of the fundamental documents of American statehood: the Declaration of Independence, the peace treaty with Great Britain, and the U.S. Constitution.

Franklin ended his service as president of the supreme executive council of Pennsylvania on October 14, 1788, terminating his career in public office. Despite suffering from gout and a bladder stone, the sociable and genial Franklin still, as of November 25, enjoyed "many comfortable Intervals, in which I forget all my Ills, and amuse myself in Reading or Writing, or in conversation with Friends, joking, laughing, and telling merry Stories" (fig. 1.28).[45]

On April 23, 1787, Franklin accepted the position of president of the Pennsylvania Society for Promoting the Abolition of Slavery, and on February 5, 1790, he signed its remonstrance against slavery addressed to John Adams, vice president, as head of the Senate, and to Frederick Augustus Muhlenberg, Speaker of the House. Adams presented the letter to the Senate on February 15, "rather with a sneer"; the senators debated it that day and decided to do nothing. On February 12, Muhlenberg presented the remonstrance to the House, where a committee was formed to deal with the issue. The committee submitted its report on March 5, and the House debated it in a committee of the whole from March 16 to 22, and on March 23, the House voted that it had no authority to interfere in the internal affairs of the states. On that same day, Franklin's final belletristic writing, less than a month before his death, parodied a speech that Georgia's congressman James Jackson had made on the necessity of slavery. In the satire, "Sidi Mehemet Ibrahim" (Franklin) defended the taking of Christian slaves in Algiers and concluded: "The doctrine that plundering and enslaving the Christians is unjust, is at best *problematical;* but that it is the interest of this state to continue the practice, is clear; therefore let the petition be rejected."[46]

"Nothing can be said to be certain except death and taxes," wrote Franklin. At age eighty-four, he died of pleurisy on April 17, 1790. He was buried at Philadelphia's Christ Church burial ground beside his wife, Deborah, and their son, Francis. In his will, he wrote that he would like "to be useful" in helping young persons starting out in business and left a thousand pounds each to the cities of Philadelphia and Boston to be lent to young artificers. As he had written in *Poor Richard* for 1737 (echoing Cotton Mather), "The noblest question in the world is, What Good may I do in it?"[47]

Fig. 2.

Chapter 2
Benjamin Franklin, Printer
JAMES N. GREEN

Benjamin Franklin was a man of many firsts: he was the founder of the first American subscription library, the first fire insurance company, the first hospital, the first learned society, Pennsylvania's first college; the list goes on. In his long career as a printer, however, he was almost always second. He published the second newspaper in Pennsylvania, and the second magazine; *Poor Richard's Almanack* had to compete with two rivals when it was first published in 1732 (fig. 2.1). Franklin was the second bookseller in town, the second postmaster, and the second government printer. The man who did all these things first was Andrew Bradford. But Franklin was not merely Bradford's successor, he was his rival. For almost twenty years Franklin and Bradford were locked in a competitive struggle, and Franklin was the underdog, the one who had to carve out a niche at the expense of the other. In all these efforts, he was not so much an innovator as an emulator and an improver.

Andrew Bradford's father, William, had been invited by the Society of Friends to set up a press in Pennsylvania in 1685; at that time he was the only printer in British North America outside Boston and Cambridge. The Friends were then the highest authority in the colony, and they directed him to print only what they approved, but soon he was printing the controversial writings of George Keith. Though approved by one faction of the Society, Keith's pamphlets were condemned by another, and so the very question of who had the

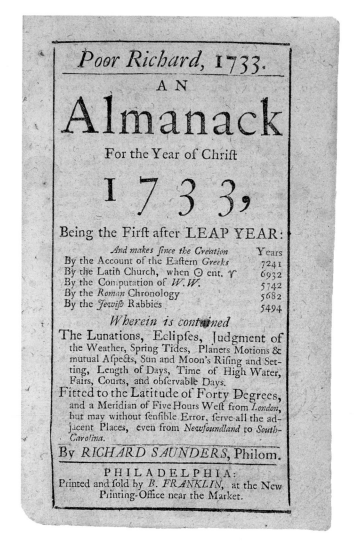

authority to approve their publication threatened schism in the Society. Bradford moved to New York in 1693 to become printer to the New York Assembly, and in that office he prospered by taking care never again to print anything
that might possibly offend anyone. Pennsylvania was without a printer as often as not until 1712, when William's son Andrew came of age and was invited
to take over the Friends' press on terms that ensured he would not repeat his
father's youthful mistakes. Thus the Bradford family had a virtual monopoly
on printing in the middle colonies, but their presses were strictly controlled
by civil and religious authorities and kept separate from the realms of commerce and politics.[1] By the time Franklin established himself as Bradford's rival in 1728, colonial authorities were no longer as preoccupied with control-

ling the press. Franklin was neither controlled nor supported by church or state; rather he was left to make his living as he saw fit, to find a niche for himself in the local ecology of print. This meant seeking out the patronage of individual consumers of print and operating his press on a strictly commercial basis. He also attempted to compete for the patronage of church and state; but because those in power were already connected with the Bradfords, he turned to those who were out of power. Thus the press was plunged into the realms of commerce and politics to a far greater extent than it had been before. To lure away Bradford's customers, Franklin made his almanac more entertaining and his newspaper more controversial. As the second bookseller he not only imported books from London, he also published books of his own choosing. As the second printer, he printed pamphlets that took issue with those published by his rival and thus began the kind of public debate in print that we now see as the fundamental role of the press. As the second printer, Franklin brought the press of Pennsylvania to life.

Franklin learned the second printer's role early in life. His older brother James and his first employer in Philadelphia, Samuel Keimer, were both upstart printers. At the age of twelve Franklin was apprenticed to James, a young printer struggling to find a place in a town already crowded with them. (fig. 2.2) In fact, Massachusetts had had more than one printer since the 1670s, but for many years there had been but one newspaper, published by the local postmaster and devoted entirely to reprinting dispatches from the London press. Since there was not enough room in each weekly half sheet to print all these dispatches, the postmaster kept carrying them over until he was thirteen months behind. In 1719 a new postmaster established a competing newspaper and employed James Franklin as printer. This newspaper turned out to be much like the first, and Franklin was soon dismissed, leaving him free to start a third paper, *The New-England Courant* (fig. 2.3). James made it completely different from the other two papers. Rather than merely replicating the London press, he included local news and essays on controversial subjects by local writers. It was not only useful but entertaining, and it engaged the other newspapers in dialogue, making them more topical—and more entertaining, too. Many young Bostonians were inspired to write by the prospect of seeing themselves in print; one of them was James's brother and apprentice, Benjamin, whose Silence Dogood essays appeared in the *Courant* in 1722.[2]

Inevitably, the *Courant* offended the authorities by "boldly reflecting on His Majesty's Government": the ministry, churches, and college. In 1723 James

Franklin was jailed and prohibited from publishing. He got around the wording of the court order by publishing under the name of his younger brother. Benjamin took advantage of this deception to escape from his apprenticeship contract, but James went to the other printers and warned them not to employ his brother. Boston's printing trade was too crowded for Benjamin, so he resolved to go to New York, where there was but one printer, William Bradford. Not that he had any idea of becoming New York's second printer. Without money or patronage there was no hope of his setting up as an independent master. His plan was simply to work for Bradford. As it turned out, Bradford had no need of a helper, but he thought his son Andrew in Philadelphia might, since his principal hand, the poet Aquila Rose, had just died.[3]

When the seventeen-year-old Benjamin Franklin made his entrance into Philadelphia in the fall of 1723, he thought that there was just one printer in town, who published a newspaper almost as dull as the Boston postmaster's had been

Fig. 2.2 James Franklin's printing press, ca. 1716–17. This press is believed to have been brought by James to Boston from London in 1716. If so, it would have been used by Benjamin Franklin while he worked for his brother.

THE
New-England Courant.

From MONDAY March 26. to MONDAY April 2. 1722.

Honour's a Sacred Tye, the Law of Kings,
The Noble Mind's Diftinguifhing Perfection,
That aids and ftrengthens Vertue where it meets her,
And Imitates her Actions where fhe is not,
It ought not to be fported with ——— Cato.

To the Author of the New-England Courant.

SIR,   *Sagadahock, March 20.*
HONOUR is a Word that Sounds big and makes a moft ravifhing Entrance into Men's Ears, while a Juft and proper Notion of it, is miftaken by moft, and the Rules and Meafures of it, are comply'd with but by few.

Hence it comes to pafs, that fome who make a confpicuous Figure in the World, (thro' their Ignorance of this Noble Principle,) falfly imagine themfelves to be treading in the Paths of Honour, while they are but greedily purfuing their Ambitious Defigns, and Impatiently Gratifying their Lufts of Pride and Covetoufnefs.

Honour indeed, according to the vulgar Notion of it, is nothing more than an empty Name. The Actions of many Men, fpeak their Sentiments of it ; and render it Obvious, that they fuppofe it to confift only in Flattering Titles, and high Pofts and Preferments, be they Acquir'd in the moft Shameful and Difhonourable Ways. But how often do fuch Precipitate themfelves into Open Shame ? and when they fondly imagine they have grafp'd the Airy Phantom, and arriv'd to the utmoft Pitch of Honour, Behold, it Vanifhes into nothing, perifhes even in the ufing, and leaves a lafting Brand of Infamy on their Memory.

Now feeing nothing is more pernicious, than a Principle of Action not rightly apprehended, it may not be improper, Firft, To hint at fome Things, which have the Shadow and Appearance of Honour, but in reality are Infamous and Difhonourable ; and Then, to give fome brief Defcription of this Superior Principle.

With refpect then to Pofts of Honour and Honourary Titles, (and fome Men have no other Idea of Honour than what refults from fuch Empty Names as thefe,) it may be faid in the Words of an Ingenious Writer, " But whatever Wealth " and Dignities Men may arrive at, they ought to confider, " that every one ftands as a Blot in the Annals of his Coun- " try, who arrives at the Temple of Honour, by any other " Way than through that of Vertue". He that advanceth himfelf to Pofts of Honour, by curfed Bribery, or fordid Flattery, or any other bafe and unworthy Arts, lays his Honour in the Duft, and Expofes himfelf to lafting Infamy and Reproach. It is alfo highly Difhonourable for a Man, when any particular Accomplifhment is requifite to Qualify him for Preferment, to climb thereto by Sham Pretenees, and meer Impofture. He that will thus Impofe on the World, it is no Wonder, if he Act by *Secret Commiffions*, and carry on Defigns in the Dark that are ruinous to his Country, and Infamous to himfelf. But the true Reafon why Men are guilty of fuch Actions is, Their Breafts were never once warm'd with one fingle Spark of true Honour.

It is alfo Difhonourable, for men to rife to Places of Honour, by Calumny and Detraction, or other fordid Arts, which their Envy, Ambition, or Avarice prompt them to Improve, the more eafily to undermine and fupplant others, who are perhaps more Righteous and worthy of Honour than themfelves.

But above all, how vile and inglorious is it, for Men horely to purfue Preferment with this Defign and View, that they may Squeefe and Opprefs their Brethren ; that they may Crufh and Trample them in the Duft ? How amazing is it, that Men who pretend to Reafon and Religion, fhould thus Defire to Act the Tyrant and the Brute ! May we not reafonably conclude of Such, that they never yet Entertain'd a Juft Idea of true Honour. The Driving of fuch Men, is commonly like the Driving of the Son of *Nimfhi* ; and to fuch a high Degree of impetuofity, do their Paffions fometimes fwell, that the Man is Difmounted, loofes the Reins, and is Dragg'd whither the fury of the Beaft directs.

Men of Arbitrary Spirits, what wont they comply with ? Through what Rules of Vertue and Humanity will they not

break, that they may attain their Ends ? Too many fuch there are, (fays Mr. *Dummer*, In his Defence of the N. E. Charters, pag. 42.) who are contented to be Saddled themfelves, provided they may Ride others under the chief Rider.

Men of Tyrannical Principles, with what abhorrence are they to be Look'd on, by all who have any Senfe of Honour ? Such, it may be prefum'd, had they Power equal to their Will, would foon, not only Sacrifice Honour, and Confcience, but even all Mankind, to their Voracious Appetites. They are to be Efteem'd, (as Dr *Cotton Mather* calls them) the Bafeft of Men. Such Sons of *Nimrod*, *Nero*, & old *Lewis*, are viler than the Earth they tread on ; it groans under them as an Intolerable Plague, and infupportable Burthen. Tyranny and Honour, cannot Reign together in the fame Breaft.

And (to mention nothing more) it is very Difhonourable, for Men to make rafh and hafty Promifes, relating to any Thing Wherein the Intereft of the Publick is nearly concern'd, and then to fay, they will retain their Integrity forever, or till *Doomfday*, pretending it is for fear of violating their Word and Honour. The Talents, Intereft, or Experience of fuch Men (fays one) make them very often ufeful in all Parties, and at all Times. They Ridicule every Thing as Romantick, that comes in Competition with their prefent Interefts ; and treat thofe Perfons as Vifionaries, who dare ftand up in a corrupt Age, for what has not its Immediate Reward annexed to it.

But let us now change the Scene, and fee what true Honour is. And no doubt, the reverfe of what has been faid is truly Honourable. True HONOUR, (as a Learned Writer defines it) is the Report of Good and Vertuous Actions, iffuing from the Confcience into the Difcovery of the PEOPLE with whom we live, and which (by a Reflection on our felves) gives us the Teftimony of what others believe concerning us, and to the Soul becomes a great Satisfaction. True Honour, (fays another) tho' it be a different Principle from Religion, is that which Produces the fame Effects. The Lines of Action, tho' drawn from different Parts, terminate in the fame Point. Religion Embraces Vertue, as it is enjoin'd by the Laws of GOD ; Honour as it is Graceful and Ornamental to Humane Nature. The Religious Man fears, the Man of Honour fcorns to do an ill Action. A Noble Soul, would rather die, than commit an Action that fhould make his Children Blufh, when he is in his Grave, and be look'd upon as a Reproach to thofe who fhall live a Hundred Years after him.

In a Word, He is the Honourable Man, who is Influenc'd and Acted by a Publick Spirit, and fir'd with a Generous Love to Mankind in the worft of Times ; Who lays afide his private Views, and foregoes his own Intereft, when it comes in competition with the Publick : Who dare adhere to the Caufe of Truth, and Manfully Defend the Liberties of his Country when boldly Invaded, and Labour to retrieve them when they are Loft. Yea, the Man of Honour, (when contracted fordid Spirits defert the Caufe of Vertue and the Publick) will ftand himfelf alone, and (like *Atlas*) bear up the Maffy Weight on his Shoulders : And this he will do, in Spite of Livid Envy, Snakey Malice, and vile Detraction.

This is true Honour indeed : and the Man who thus Glorioufly acquits himfelf, fhall fhine in the Records of Fame, with a peculiar Luftre : His Name fhall be mention'd with Reverence in Future Ages ; and all Pofterity fhall call him Bleffed.

PHILANTHROPOS.

To the Author of the New-England Courant.

SIR,
IT may not be improper, in the firft Place to inform your Readers, that I intend once a Fortnight to prefent them, by the Help of this Paper, with a fhort Epiftle, which I prefume will add fomewhat to their Entertainment.

And fince it is obferved, that the Generality of People, now a days, are unwilling either to commend or difpraife what they read, until they are in fome meafure informed who or what the Author of it is, whether he be *poor* or *rich*, *old* or *young*, a *Schollar* or a *Leather Apron Man*, &c. and give their Opinion of the Performance, according to the Knowledge which they have of the Author's Circumftances, it may not be amifs to begin with a fhort Account of my paft Life and prefent Condition, that the Reader may not be at a Lofs to judge whether or no my Lucubrations are worth his reading.

At the time of my Birth, my Parents were on Ship-board in their Way from *London* to *N. England*. My Entrance into this troublefome World was attended with the Death of my Father, a
Misfortune

Fig. 2.4 George Heap, The East Prospect of the City of Philadelphia, in the Province of Pennsylvania, *1755.*

(fig. 2.4). Presenting himself at Andrew Bradford's (where it turned out he was not needed), he learned that a failed printer from London named Samuel Keimer had just set up the second press in Philadelphia but had yet to print anything. Thus Franklin's arrival in Philadelphia coincided with the advent of a competing printer in the middle colonies; in fact, he was present at the primal scene of rivalry. In Andrew's shop Franklin was surprised to see William Bradford, whom he had just left in New York and who had come down by a more direct route. Andrew thought Keimer might need a hand, and William, who was curious to meet Keimer himself, offered to accompany Franklin to Keimer's shop. William cunningly concealed his identity, a ruse that led to a scene of comic misunderstanding brilliantly dramatized in the *Autobiography:*

> Neighbor, says Bradford [to Keimer], I have brought to see you a young Man of your Business, perhaps you may want such a One. He ask'd me a few Questions, put a Composing Stick in my Hand to see how I work'd, and then said he would employ me soon, tho' he had just then nothing for me to do [fig. 2.5]. And taking old Bradford whom he had never seen before, to be one of the Townspeople that had a Goodwill for him, enter'd into a Conversation on his present Undertaking and Prospects; while Bradford not discovering that he was the other Printer's Father; on Keimer's Saying he expected soon to get the greatest Part of the Business into his own Hands, drew him on by artful Questions and starting little Doubts, to explain all his Views, what Interest he relied on, and in what manner he intended to proceed. I who stood by and heard all, saw immediately that one of them was a crafty old Sophister, and the other a mere Novice. Brad-

Fig. 2.5 (Above) L'Opération de la casse (Composing room), in Denis Diderot et al., Encyclopédie, ou Dictionnaire raisonné des sciences, des arts et des métiers, 1761–89. The compositor on the left is setting type from a "pair of cases," upper and lower.

Fig. 2.6 (Left) Composing stick, 1740–60. This composing stick was used by Franklin.

Fig. 2.7 Ink balls, eighteenth century. With an ink ball in each hand, the pressman picked up ink from the ink block and applied it to the type with a dabbing, rolling, and beating motion before each pull of the press.

ford left me with Keimer, who was greatly surpris'd when I told him who the old Man was. . . These two Printers I found poorly qualified for their Business. Bradford had not been bred to it, and was very illiterate; and Keimer tho' something of a Scholar, was a mere Compositor, knowing nothing of Presswork. He . . . was very ignorant of the World, and had, as I afterwards found, a good deal of the Knave in his Composition.[4]

Fig. 2.8 Attributed to Gustavus Hesselius, Portrait of James Logan, ca. 1728–35.

Thus Franklin first dimly saw how he might make his way as a rival to both men. His next step was to seek a job with Keimer, which he did in a typically straightforward way.

Keimer's Printing-House I found, consisted of an old shatter'd Press and one small worn-out Fount of English [type], which he was then using himself, composing in it an Elegy on Aquila Rose before-mentioned . . . a pretty Poet. Keimer made Verses, too, but very indifferently. He could not be said to write them, for his Manner was to compose them in the Types directly out of his Head; so there being no Copy, but one Pair of Cases [that is, the upper and lower cases of type], and the Elegy likely to require all the Letter, no one could help him. I endeavour'd to put his Press (which he had not yet us'd, and of which he understood nothing) into Order fit to be work'd with; and promising to come and print off his Elegy as soon as he should have got it ready, I return'd to Bradford's. . . . A few Days after Keimer sent for me to print off the Elegy. And now he had got another Pair of Cases, and a Pamphlet to reprint, on which he set me to work. [fig. 2.6]

A copy of this elegy has recently come to light, and it demonstrates how much care Franklin lavished on this, the first thing he printed in Philadelphia. It is a large broadside, about 15½ by 12½ inches with the elegy in English type as set by Keimer in two columns. Franklin added a mourning border headed by a woodcut memento mori, perhaps of his own design, consisting of skulls, cross bones, and an hourglass symmetrically arranged. The presswork is impeccable. This chef-d'oeuvre got him a job as Keimer's press man.[5]

Almost immediately Franklin drew the attention of the governor of Pennsylvania, Sir William Keith, who happened to see a letter of Franklin's, explaining his reasons for leaving Boston. Keith was struck by how well written it was and concluded that Franklin deserved encouragement. Keith called on Franklin while he was at work, ignoring Keimer, who "star'd like a Pig poison'd." In due course Keith offered to advance Franklin the capital needed to set up on his own, and he promised to get Franklin the printing contract for government publications. At the end of 1724 Franklin set out for London to buy printing equipment (fig. 2.7), believing that Keith had entrusted letters of credit to various suppliers to the captain's bag of mail. Upon arrival the bag was opened and the promised letters were nowhere to be found. Franklin was stranded in London. He believed that he had been duped, but characteristically he made the best of it, contriving to meet Andrew Hamilton, legal counsel to the Penn family, the proprietors (hereditary rulers) of Pennsylvania, to whom he gave information damaging to Keith, thus securing for himself a lasting and more powerful patron.[6]

It seems likely that Keith had wished to set up Franklin as the third printer in town in order to have privileged access to the press for his own political purposes. Pennsylvania was in the midst of an economic depression; the surpris-

ingly large loaves Franklin describes in his autobiography as receiving for his
last three coppers testified to the fall in local grain prices. The old merchant
elite, led by the Penn family agent James Logan (fig. 2.8), had taken no action
in response to the crisis, and many of them were ousted from the Pennsylvania
Assembly in the election of 1721. The new, somewhat more populist Assembly

passed a controversial paper money bill in 1722. To confuse matters further, the proprietor William Penn had died in 1718, leaving his widow's title to the province clouded and her authority uncertain. The governor was supposed to represent the interest of the proprietor, but Keith had allied himself with the Assembly. All these changes had passed almost unnoticed in Bradford's newspaper, the *American Weekly Mercury,* but Keith's strategy (as it turned out) was to use another printer to appeal directly to the people, vilifying Logan and flouting Hannah Penn's authority. So why did he dupe Franklin? The most likely explanation is that he changed his mind and decided to employ the more pliant Keimer, figuring either that Philadelphia could not support three printers or that with three printers, neither party could control the press.[7]

With Franklin out of the way in London, Keimer began to print steadily for Keith, and the rivalry between Bradford and Keimer burst into the open with an explosion of print relating to the political crisis. It might be supposed that Bradford would print for the proprietary party and Keimer for Keith, but in fact both printers were printing for both sides. In many of these pamphlets no printer is named, and the two printers used similar type, the same small folio format, and the same page layout so that no one could tell who printed them. When there was just one printer, there was never any doubt; now that there were two, there was never any certainty.

Rivalry between Bradford and Keimer was most deadly just where the printer's role was most traditionally fixed: printing for the Friends. Just before Keimer arrived on the scene, Bradford had persuaded the Philadelphia Friends to underwrite his publication of an edition of five hundred copies of Sewel's *History of the Quakers.* This was to be a massive folio, by far the largest book yet attempted in the colonies. Bradford dawdled and haggled over the price, so when Keimer offered to print the book for substantially less money, the Friends gave the job to him. Meanwhile, Bradford, without telling the Friends, had ordered five hundred copies of a new London edition that had just gone to press, hoping the Friends would prefer to buy the better edition now in stock rather than wait for Keimer to print his. The Friends resented Bradford's tactics, however, and decided to stay with Keimer's cheaper edition, leaving Bradford with five hundred copies to sell and most potential customers already committed to Keimer. In retaliation Bradford refused to let Keimer have paper from his Rittenhouse family mill in Germantown, of which he was part owner; finally, James Logan himself interceded after a long delay. Thus the printing of Keimer's edition of Sewel dragged on for years.[8]

Franklin, meanwhile, having spent a pleasant and educational eighteen months in London working for two different printers, decided to return to Philadelphia as a merchant's clerk. However, his employer soon died, and Franklin reluctantly agreed to return as foreman to Keimer's shop, where he was badly needed to finish off the interminable Sewel job. He quickly saw that despite the appearance of having a flourishing trade, Keimer was deeply in debt and certain to fail. He therefore positioned himself to take Keimer's place, and then plotted to hasten his downfall. He borrowed money from the father of his coworker Hugh Meredith and ordered press and type from London; after these arrived in the middle of 1728 he and Meredith gave notice. At the time he left Keimer, forty sheets of the Sewel (nearly a quarter of the book) remained unprinted; through the influence of his friend Joseph Breintnall, a member of the Junto, a

Fig. 2.11 Colonial currency: 15 shilling note, Pennnsylvania 1757; 20 shilling note, Delaware 1758; and 5 pound note, Pennsylvania 1759, all printed by Franklin and Hall. Franklin developed a way to print leaves by casting them in metal and using them to print in the same manner as printing type.

self-improvement club founded by Franklin, Franklin persuaded the Friends to transfer the job of finishing the printing to his new office. Thus Franklin got his start as an independent printer by stealing from Keimer the job Keimer had stolen from Bradford.

At the same time Franklin laid plans to start a second newspaper, which would easily outsell Bradford's newspaper, "a paltry thing, wretchedly manag'd, no way entertaining; and yet it was profitable to him." But Keimer found out about Franklin's plan and beat him to it, publishing the first issue of the *Pennsylvania Gazette* in the last days of 1728. In a prospectus Keimer ran down Bradford's paper ("a Scandal to the very Name of Printing . . . *Nonsense in Folio*") and promised a better paper, but he did not have the wit to provide one. The *Gazette* did not print much news but rather filled its space by serializing Chambers's *Cyclopaedia,* starting in the first issue with a pedantic philological disquisition on the letter *A.* Franklin retaliated by satirizing Keimer's paper ruthlessly in a series of letters signed "Busy-Body" which he and his friend Breintnall published in Bradford's newspaper; Keimer's circulation dropped almost to nothing, and Franklin bought the paper in the fall of 1729 for a trifle while it was still struggling through the article on "Air" (fig. 2.9). Thus Franklin used one competitor's newspaper to destroy the other's. [9] Around the end of 1729 Keimer sold the rest of his printing business to his apprentice David Harry and moved to Barbados; within a year Harry had given up and followed him.

The departure of Keimer coincided with the end to the exchange of political pamphlets that had been so brisk since 1725. A paper war required not only a disaffected party but also two printers both willing to be drawn in, and Franklin was not. In his first publication as a printer and an author he adopted the even-handed, modest, consensus-seeking posture that was to characterize not only his whole political career but also his press and, through his influence, the presses of many printers over the next generation. Instead of opening his press to controversy, he used it (and his skill as a writer) to propose solutions to controversy. Paper money was still the issue of the day. By now nearly everyone agreed that it was helping the economy, but Logan's party still wanted strict limits on the amount in circulation and the length of time it circulated. Franklin entered the fray with an anonymous pamphlet, *A Modest Enquiry into the Nature and Necessity of a Paper-Currency*, which supported a compromise on those limits, us-

Fig. 2.12 *Title page of Richard Saunders [Benjamin Franklin], *Poor Richard improved . . . , [1757]. This is the last *Poor Richard *written by Franklin; it includes the first appearance of "Father Abraham's Speech," later published as *The Way to Wealth, *into which he wove many of the best aphorisms from the previous twenty-five years.*

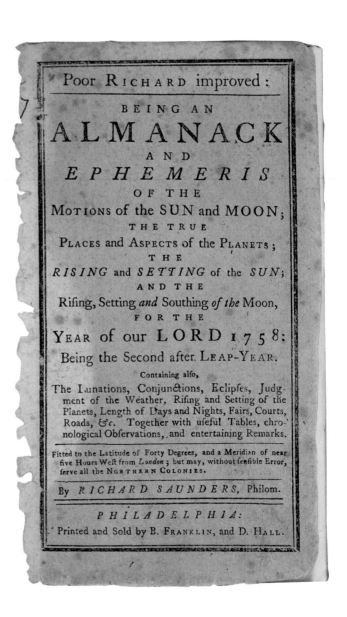

ing arguments borrowed from European economists deftly adapted to the needs of Pennsylvania (fig. 2.10). In the *Autobiography* he wrote, "It was well receiv'd by the common People in general; but the Rich Men dislik'd it; for it increas'd and strengthen'd the Clamour for more Money; and they happening to have no Writers among them that were able to answer it, their Opposition slacken'd, and the Point was carried by a Majority in the House." As a reward his friends in the Assembly got him the lucrative job of printing the money, which had previously been Bradford's (fig. 2.11).[10] Thus Franklin invented a new way of being the second printer, quite different from Keimer's: he consciously used his press to shape the political discussion.

The *Gazette* was the centerpiece of Franklin's printing business and the key to his success. As a prototypical second newspaper, it was more lively, more topical, and better written than Bradford's paper. In one of its first issues (as Franklin later wrote), "some spirited Remarks of my Writing on the Dispute then going on between Governor Burnet and the Massachusetts Assembly, struck the principal People, occasion'd the Paper and the Manager of it to be much talk'd of, and in a few Weeks brought them all to be our Subscribers. . . . This was one of the first good Effects of my having learned a little to scribble. Another was that the leading Men, seeing a Newspaper now in the hands of one who could also handle a Pen, thought it convenient to oblige and encourage me." Franklin's ability as a writer helped him carve out his niche, but it was his firm hand as an editor that kept him secure in it. He was scrupulously evenhanded in his coverage of politics: "In the Conduct of my Newspaper I carefully excluded all Libelling and Personal Abuse . . . Whenever I was solicited to insert anything of that kind, and the Writers pleaded as they generally did, the Liberty of the Press, and that a Newspaper was like a Stage Coach in which any one who would pay had a Right to a Place, my Answer was, that I would print the Piece separately if desired, and the Author might have as many Copies as he pleased to distribute himself, but that I would not take upon me to spread his Detraction."[11]

The distinction Franklin made in this passage is crucial to understanding his open-press policy. An open press was open to all parties: it would not print anything that would make it impossible for an opponent to reply with dignity in the same columns. As an editor Franklin actively shaped his paper's content, negotiating the material in every piece with its writer, reserving the right to refuse access not in order to abridge the liberty of the press but to preserve it from the greater repressive force of the law of libel. However, as this passage shows, when a printer was printing a pamphlet for an author who covered all the costs and took the whole edition away with him, he was merely a trades-

Fig. 2.13 H. S. Grimm and J. Macky, *Caricature of Benjamin Franklin, 1789. Franklin is seen here distilling stories, proverbs, and other material written by others into his own abundant writings.*

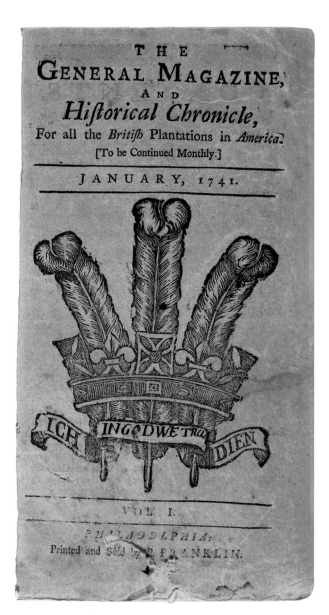

Fig. 2.14 Front page of The General Magazine, and Historical Chronicle, For all the British Plantations in America, *January 1741. Franklin's was the second magazine published in the colonies, preempted by his rival Andrew Bradford's* The American Magazine.

man who manufactured print to the customer's specifications. In those circumstances, the press *was* like a stagecoach. This was the safety valve that made the open-press strategy work. If the printer did not want his name associated with the pamphlet, he could issue it without an imprint. Franklin's open-press policy was imitated by nearly every printer in the middle colonies. Until the end of the colonial period, newspapers were edited by their printers, and none was in the control of a political party or religious group. Keeping an open press made good business sense, too, since a newspaper that was available to all parties was likely to be read by all people; one that embraced a fac-

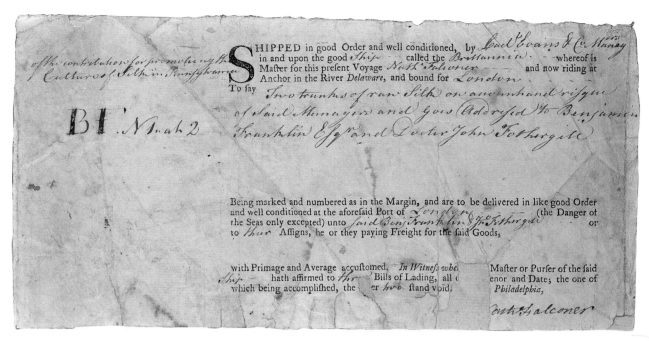

Fig. 2.15 Bill of lading, ca. 1740–48, printed by Franklin.

tion would attract a few subscribers but alienate a great many more. The open press promoted a stable environment for public discussion and for business.

William and Andrew Bradford were the first American printers who performed all the offices and functions later deemed necessary for success as a colonial printer: publisher of newspapers and almanacs, job printer, book printer, postmaster, government printer, wholesale paper merchant, stationer, retail and wholesale bookseller, book publisher. But though the Bradfords did all these things, they did not make all the elements function as a coherent, commercially viable system. Franklin imitated or appropriated all their jobs in competition with the Bradfords, and in every instance, he expanded or improved upon them. It was he who made the system work, producing a reliable product for readers and a reliable source of income and capital for the printer. Most subsequently established colonial printers imitated the Franklin system, as did most printers outside the main seaport towns until well into the nineteenth century.

His newspaper was the mainstay of Franklin's business, as newspapers were for nearly all subsequent printers in colonial America. The *Gazette* produced revenue from subscriptions at ten shillings a year and even more from advertisements at five shillings per insertion. Almanacs were the next most profitable products of his press (fig. 2.12). Like the Bradfords and Keimer, Franklin printed several almanacs of different formats and character by different compilers, but the first almanac written by Franklin was *Poor Richard, 1733*. "I endeavour'd to make it both entertaining and useful, and it accordingly came to be in such Demand that I reap'd considerable Profit from it, vending annually near ten Thousand."[12]

It retailed for five pence, but he sold copies in bulk to storekeepers and peddlers for three and a half pence. It was so popular that it was in demand even in latitudes where its astronomical observations were not correct; and Franklin's accounts show him sending hundreds of copies to booksellers as far north as Boston and as far south as Charleston, South Carolina, at threepence a copy (fig. 2.13).[13] The monthly magazine was another kind of periodical, midway in

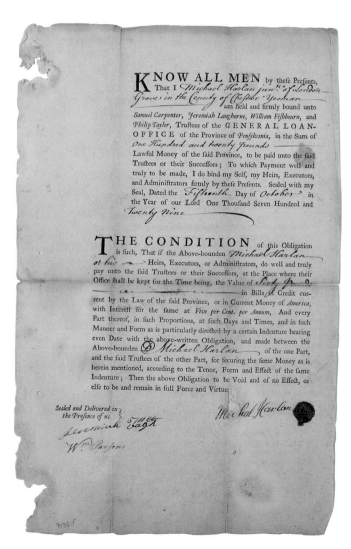

Fig. 2.16 *General Loan Office of Pennsylvania, blank mortgage bond, 1729.*

Fig. 2.17 *Title page of George Webb,* Batchelors-Hall; a Poem, *1731.
This pamphlet is an example of printing by Franklin done at the
author's expense. Webb, a member of Franklin's Junto, announced
the pamphlet in the* Pennsylvania Gazette *on April 1, 1731, with the
notice "There is but a small Number printed, so that few will be left
for Sale after the designed Presents are made by the Author."*

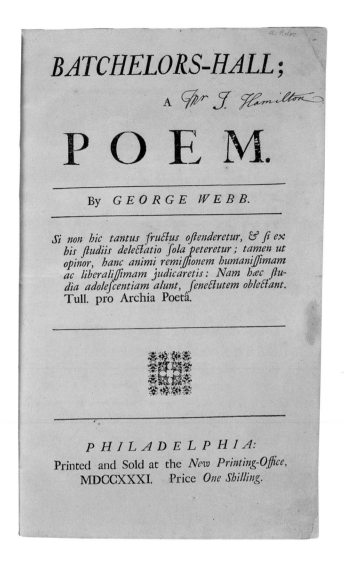

frequency between the weekly newspaper and the annual almanac. The first
successful English monthly was *The Gentleman's Magazine,* begun in 1732. In
1741 Franklin announced that he was going to publish the first American magazine, *The General Magazine, and Historical Chronicle, For all the British Plantations in America* (fig. 2.14); but Bradford rushed out his competing *American
Magazine* three days before Franklin's was published. Once again Franklin was
second. Neither magazine had enough of a market to succeed, however, and both
expired after a few issues.

The category of job printing subsumes many types of printed materials:
blank business forms (fig. 2.15), single-sheet programs, announcements, advertisements, and handbills. The Bradfords made part of their living from job
printing, but Franklin made it a specialty. In 1730 he added a stationer's shop to

his printing business and, with the help of his Junto friend Breintnall, offered "Blanks of all Sorts the correctest that ever appear'd among us" (fig. 2.16).[14]

Another source of income was what Franklin called "book work"—that is, books (or more usually pamphlets) published at the request and expense of civil or religious corporate bodies or individual authors. From 1728 to 1748 (when he retired from active involvement in the printing business) Franklin printed 432 identified books, pamphlets, and broadsides, of which 241 (56 percent) can be shown by his records to have been published (that is, paid for) by others (fig. 2.17). The Bradfords never produced a fraction of his output. This was extremely profitable work: Franklin later wrote that he charged his customers for book work by computing the cost in wages for setting the type and printing the sheets, then multiplied by three, adding in the cost of the paper, if not supplied by the customer, plus a commission for securing the paper.[15]

In his appointments as printer to the Assembly and as postmaster, Bradford seemed immune to competition, but Franklin deviously finagled away both jobs. He secured the job of printer to the Assembly by "elegantly and correctly" reprinting a document that Bradford had printed in a "coarse blundering manner." (Andrew Hamilton used the two versions to persuade the Assembly to give Franklin the job.) We have already seen how Franklin's pamphlet on paper money helped secure him the job of printing paper money. Getting the postmastership away from Bradford was in the long run just as important to him. The postmaster controlled the source of most news as well as the means of distributing newspapers in the country. He was also able to send and receive letters at no charge, thus facilitating the flow of remittances, news, and advertising

Fig. 2.18 Unknown artist, Cartoon of a post rider from the newspaper Boston Post-Boy, *1750–54. This woodcut may have been a caricature of Franklin.*

copy. Bradford was postmaster of the colony when Franklin began his business,
and for years he prohibited post riders from delivering Franklin's *Pennsylvania
Gazette.* To keep his newspaper alive, Franklin was compelled to bribe the riders (fig. 2.18). The postmastership gave Bradford "better Opportunities of obtaining News," wrote Franklin, so "his Paper was thought a better Distributer of
Advertisements than mine, and therefore had many more, which was a profitable
thing to him and a Disadvantage to me." But Bradford was "rich and easy," and
"not very anxious about the Business." In 1737 the postmaster general finally became fed up with Bradford's sloppy accounts and gave the job to Franklin. As
he wrote in his *Autobiography,* "tho' the Salary was small, it facilitated the Correspondence that improv'd my Newspaper, increas'd the Number demanded, as
well as the Advertisements to be inserted, so that it came to afford me a very considerable Income. My old Competitor's Newspaper declin'd proportionably."[16]

Franklin also broke the Bradford family monopoly on printing paper manufactured by the Rittenhouse family. At first Franklin had to use imported paper for everything he printed. In 1733 he was reduced to selling half an edition
of a psalter to Bradford just to get the paper to print it with. He must have then
resolved never again to allow his supply of paper to be controlled by a competitor, since a few months later he began to set up mills of his own, becoming Bradford's rival in the paper business.[17]

When Franklin first came to Philadelphia, "there was not a good Bookseller's Shop in any of the Colonies to the Southward of Boston. In New York and
Philadelphia the Printers were indeed Stationers, they sold only Paper, etc., Almanacs, Ballads, and a few common School Books. Those who lov'd Reading
were oblig'd to send for their Books from England."[18] When Franklin opened
his printing office in 1728, he added such a shop, managed by his wife, Deborah; she sold far more stationery than almanacs and more almanacs than books.
In fact, books were the smallest part of the store business; sidelines such as cloth
and groceries were more remunerative (fig. 2.19). By 1734, however, he was beginning to advertise a few imported books, and by the early 1740s his lists of
books for sale occupied whole columns of the *Gazette.* Nevertheless, the largest
part of his trade as a bookseller lay in retailing and wholesaling the pamphlets
and books he published.

The publisher is the most entrepreneurial of all the members of the book
trade, the person who seeks out authors, pays them, and brings their books into
print. Most of the books and pamphlets Franklin printed were paid for by their
authors, but occasionally he would publish an original work in pamphlet form

Lambert Emerson Dr for paper	3	—
William Monkredy Dr for 3 Quires of paper 2 of 2 Shilins 1 of one and sixpence	3	6
Jacob Lankester Dr for almanacks	3	6
Stephen Potts Dr for Cash	3	
Rober Grose Dr for paper and ink	1	3
26 Recd of Mr Wm Vere in full settled	1..1	—
Jewace Farowat Egg harbour Dr for 1 Doz Almanacks	3	6
Mrs Merredey Dr for almanacks	5	3
26 John Hud Shoemaker Dr for all	1	9
Bernard Reyser Dr Lampblack paid	5	
Thos Meredith 1 doz Alm. some time ago	3	6
Thomas Merredy Dr for almanacks	3	8
Hugh Davey Dr for Bills Lading	3	—
James Mackey Dr for wax	—	10
29 Benja Shoemaker Dr for the Ballance of Kedges Acct	1	7	6
Neighbour Wollaston Dr 1/2 doz Alm	1	9
Johnson Firm Wafers	—	6
Recd of Peter Bard Cash	9	2
Freight	12	—
Which is in full	1..1	2
Mr Reckless Dr		
for 3 Dictionaries	1.15	—
3 Doz Almanacks	10	6
1 Doz E. Man his own Dr	8	—
1/2 Doz Jonath Dickinson	6	—
1/2 Doz Watts Songs	3	—
1/2 Doz Hockey Books	—	
1/2 Doz Pocket Farrier	4	—
1 box of Idelnes and pride	3..6..6	
	4	

Nov 29	Mr Eastburn Bucks County 1 Doz Almanacks	3	6
	Mr Mogridge Dr For 2 Books for the Lead Comp	10	—
	Samuel Boulton Dr for Religues Cortship of Milton paid	6	—
	Stephen Potts Dr for Cash	3	—
	William Morgon Dr for paper	5	—
	Messrs Montgomary Dr for 3 Doz allmanacks	10	6
	Mr Johnson of Allentown 3 Doz of allmanacks	2	2	—
	James Jordon Dr for 1 box of Bound Books	1	4	—
	1 box of Idelnes and pride Books		4	
	1 box of almanacks	3	6
	Nathanel Jonkins Dr for a Book Baptist minister	2	—
	John Crocker Dr for things she of mrs Read	7	—
December 2	Ivan wornor Dr for Lamblack	2	6
	mrr Farrel Dr for a pound Lamblack	15	
	mrs Fetis Limner Dr for a book of silver	2	—
	Jack Brown Dr for almanack	—	5
	mrs Wittsover at Gloster Dr	2	9
	my Maid Gatten Dr Cash settled	1	3
3	Stephen Potts Dr for Cash	3	
	mr David Evans Minister in new Brilintown Ship in Bucks County Dr for a Book and almanack	5	5
	Samuel Scott good Dr for one half box of Plagitterstone ware one half box Pots two box of almanacks one box of Bonds	12 10 7 3	
	Mrs Merredey Dr for a Ferment	1	
	Joseph Lane Dr for Inkanopots Joseph Lane Dr for a tapoo Ink	6	
5	Samuel Colts Dr for almanack	8	6
	Edward Lewis Dr for Cash	5	
	Mr Ford Dr of Long Island Flushing for 6 Doz Almanacks	1.1.	
	Mr Zenger New York Dr For 1 grofs of Almanacks the Post before last, & 200 Almanacks Ps last		

M. T. CICERO's
CATO MAJOR,

OR HIS

DISCOURSE

OF

OLD-AGE:

With Explanatory NOTES.

PHILADELPHIA:

Printed and Sold by B. FRANKLIN,

MDCCXLIV.

at his own expense (and risk). Only once did he publish an original, full-sized book at his own expense, James Logan's translation of Cicero's *Cato Major* (fig. 2.20). He printed it in large type on creamy paper to flatter the Quaker grandee and to show off his own prowess as a printer, but he did not make a penny from it. In that instance he was playing the courtier more than the entrepreneur.[19]

All the other full-sized books Franklin published were reprints of books previously published in Britain, and many had been previously published in America as well by other printers. In book publishing, too, Franklin was second, but so was every other American printer because they were all preceded by the booksellers of London. Most of the books colonial Americans read were imported. American printers could not afford the risk and expense of publishing a book which had not already proven its popularity in Britain and been tested in the American market through importation. But these standard books were simply the ones most frequently imported, and colonial printers had to be cautious about reprinting editions of books easily obtainable by importation in smaller numbers and possibly at lower prices. Only an insatiable demand could justify such a risk.

The Great Awakening created just such a demand, and Franklin's response to it shows how careful he was about reprinting full-sized books. The tour undertaken by the British evangelist George Whitefield between 1739 and 1741 sparked an enthusiastic revival of religion that was perhaps the first great public event in the colonies mediated by—and to some degree created by—print. Pamphlets for and against Whitefield, by and about him, streamed from the presses of both Franklin and Bradford in unprecedented numbers. The newspapers were full of him too. His charismatic preaching was attracting crowds as large as fifteen thousand, and his appeals for funds for his Georgia orphanage extracted huge sums from normally frugal Pennsylvanians. Franklin knew from personal experience that there was money in Whitefield, since he had once gone to hear him preach vowing not to give him a single copper; before Whitefield's oration ended, Franklin had emptied his pockets into the collection plate.

At first Bradford got the jump on Franklin, bringing out pamphlet editions of several of Whitefield's sermons. But Franklin soon befriended Whitefield, lodged him in his house, and received his permission to reprint the London edition of his *Sermons* and *Journals* in volume form. Franklin advertised for subscribers and found more than he had printed copies, enabling him to sell only to those who had paid in advance or came to his shop with cash in hand. Never had there been so many auguries favorable to a really big publication, and Franklin the entrepreneur was the man to do it. Yet his edition of the *Sermons* and *Jour-*

Fig. 2.20 (Opposite) Title page of James Logan, trans., M. T. Cicero's Cato Major, or his Discourse of Old-Age . . . , 1744. Franklin printed this book at his own expense to flatter Logan, whose patronage he sought for many years.

from English warehouses. Nor would American readers trust a Bible not printed by authority. Nonetheless, as C. William Miller showed conclusively from Franklin's accounts, Franklin did print a New Testament. No copy of this Testament is known, but one may yet turn up, for it is likely that Franklin printed it under a false London imprint so that it would escape notice. Thus he competed with the imports by camouflaging his book as one of them. As with *Pamela,* the success of this venture is questionable. It was printed on cheap brown paper to keep the cost down, and a large part of the edition was sent in sheets to New York and Boston, perhaps to allow it better to pass as an import. Even so, Franklin still had fifty-one copies on hand three years later. If Isaiah Thomas is correct in saying that a Bible with a London imprint was printed in Boston in the 1750s, then Franklin's Testament was not unique, but nevertheless it offered no real challenge to the dominance of the British Bible publishers in the colonies. [21]

Franklin was one of the first Americans to see the mainland British colonies as a potential political and cultural unit. Long before he proposed the Albany Plan

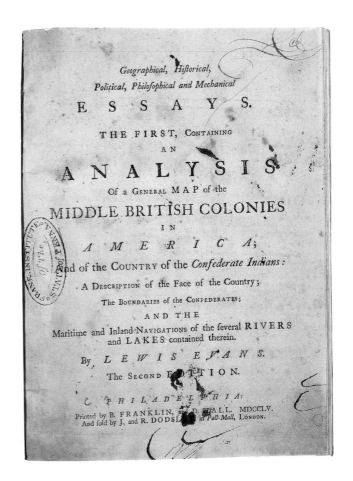

Fig. 2.23 Title page of Lewis Evans, Geographical, Historical, Political, Philosophical and Mechanical Essays: The First, Containing an Analysis Of a General Map of the Middle British Colonies in America . . . , *2d ed., 1755. This pamphlet, printed by Franklin's partner David Hall, accompanied the first authoritative map of the middle colonies, the territory encompassed by Franklin's communications network.*

Fig. 2.24 (Opposite) Benjamin Franklin, Directions to the Deputy Post-Masters, for keeping their Accounts, *1753? When Franklin and William Hunter received their joint appointment as deputy postmasters general of North America in 1753, they set about reforming post-office procedures, especially those relating to how accounts were kept.*

DIRECTIONS to the DEPUTY POST-MASTERS, for keeping their ACCOUNTS.

THE second Book referred to in your Instructions must be in *Folio*, of Post or Demy Paper, about fifteen Inches long, and Eighteen and a Half wide. The Quantity of Paper to be contained in it must be determined by the Number of Letters you receive and dispatch: A Book that will contain three, four, or more Years Transaction, will be best. You are to begin it with an Account of *Letters sent from your Office*, according to the following Specimen, mark'd B. Every Time you dispatch a Mail, you are to turn to this Account, and fill it up from the Post-Master's Bills you send to each Office. After heading this Account (that you may have Room to carry it forward from Time to Time, as the Pages become fill'd) you are to leave a Quantity of blank Paper after it, extending to about the Middle of your Book, where you must enter an Account of *Letters received into your Office*, according to the Form mark'd C.

B. LETTERS sent from the Post Office, at

[Complex tabular account of unpaid, paid, and free letters sent, with columns for Date of the Bills sent; To what Office the Letters were sent; Number of Unpaid Letters (Single, Double, Treeble, Packet); Sums unpaid (Dwt. Grs.); Number of paid Letters; Sums paid; Free Letters; Ship Letters. Entries dated October 4, 10, 12, 18, 25; November 1, 8, 15, 22, 30; December 1, 13, 21, 31, for offices including Boston, Rhode-Island, New-York, Amboy, Brunswick, Trenton, Burlington, Williamsburg, Annapolis, New-Castle.]

C. LETTERS received into the Post-Office, at

[Complex tabular account with columns: Time of Receiving; Names of the Offices, and Ships, from whence they were received; Date of the Bills received; Unpaid Letters; Way Letters received; Undercharged from other Offices; Overcharged; Overcharged transmitted to other Offices; Paid Letters received from other Offices; Forwarded to other Offices, being mis-sent; Ship Letters (Number sent for; Belonging to this Office only). Entries for 1753 October and November and December, with ships Charles, Harriet, John, Amy, Friendship, Happy, Adventure, Sea-Horse, Hester from London, Bristol, N. Carolina, Jamaica, Barbados, etc.]

That you may be at no Loss to fill up each Column of this Account (mark'd C) properly, observe the following Directions. On the Receipt of any Mail, lay all the Post-Masters Bills before you (having first examined whether they are right or no, as directed in the third Instruction.) Enter the Time of receiving in the first Column. From each of the Bills enter the Name of the Office in the second Column: The Date of the Bill in the Third: The Pennyweights and Grains of the Unpaid Letters you receive from such Office in the fourth Column, exactly according to the Foot of the Bill, whether right or wrong cast up, whether under or overcharged, because the 6th and 7th Columns will rectify the Mistake, if any. Enter the Amount of the Way Letters you receive from the Post-Man, belonging to your Stage only, and also the Amount of the Letters you deliver him from your Stage (not being charged to you in any Bill) to be left on the Road, for which he is to pay you the Postage, in the 5th Column. Enter the Under and Overcharges of each Bill in the 6th and 7th Columns, opposite to the Name of the Office where such Under or Overcharges were made. Enter the Amount of Paid Letters you receive from each Office, in the 8th Column, opposite to the Name of such Office. When you receive any Letters in the Mail, mis-sent, and which you have forwarded to other Offices, place the Amount of such Letters, as charged to you in the Bill, in the 9th Column. When you receive Letters from on board any Ship or Vessel, you are to enter the Name of such Vessel in the 2d Column; the Number of Letters you have paid the Captain or others for in the 10th Column; and the Amount of such of them as belong to your Office only, in the 11th Column, marking the Rates on them at the Time of receiving. Hence you may with little Trouble make up your Quarterly Account, as follows.

D. Dr. The POST-OFFICE at ___ in Account with the GENERAL POST-OFFICE of America, **Cr.**

	For one Quarter, ending	Dwt.	Gr.	£.	s.	d.
1	To Postage of Letters which remained in the Office last Quarter,					
2	To Postage of paid Letters sent from this Office this Quarter,	46	8			
3	To Postage of unpaid Letters received from other Offices Ditto,	3616	16			
4	To Postage of Way Letters belonging to this Office Ditto,	65	16			
5	To Postage of Letters undercharg'd from other Offices Ditto,	20				
6	To the Amount of Ship Letters belonging to this Office Ditto,	113				

	Day of ___ 17	Dwt.	Gr.	£.	s.	d.
1	By Postage of dead Letters sent to the General Post-Office this Quarter,					
2	By Postage of Letters remaining in this Office,					
3	By Letters mis-sent, being forwarded to other Offices,	21	16			
4	By Overcharge of Letters from other Offices,	44	16			
5	By 199 Pence, paid for Ship Letters,					
6	By a Quarter's Allowance for Salary, and Incidents, per Ct.					
7	By Ditto, paid the Rider between this Office and ___					
8	Balance carried to the Credit of the General Post-Office,					

On the Debtor Side,

Article 1*st.* Will be the same Sum as the second Article on the Creditor Side of your preceding Quarterly Account.
2*d.* From the Account of *Letters sent from your Office*, take the Amount of the paid Letters for the Quarter.
3*d.* Turn to the Account of *Letters received into your Office*, and from the fourth Column take the Amount of unpaid Letters received from other Offices.
4*th.* From the fifth Column in the said Account, take the Amount of Way Letters.
5*th.* From the sixth Column, take the Amount of Letters which came to you from other Offices, undercharged.
6*th.* From the eleventh Column, take the Amount of Ship Letters.

On the Creditor Side,

Article 1*st.* Will be the Amount of dead Letters, you send with your Quarterly Account to the General Post-Office.
2*d.* Take the Amount of the Letters you keep in your Office, and place the Sum in Pennyweights and Grains opposite to this Article.
3*d.* From the ninth Column of the Account of *Letters received into your Office*, take the Amount of Letters sent by Mistake, and by you forwarded to other Offices.
4*th.* From the seventh Column of the said Account take the Amount of Letters overcharg'd.
5*th.* Fill this up from the tenth Column, with the Sum you have paid for ship Letters during the Quarter.
6*th.* Your Quarter's Salary or Allowance.
7*th.* The Wages you pay the Riders.
8*th.* The Balance due to the General Post-Office.

Sum up the whole Amount of Pennyweights and Grains, on both Sides, and extend it in the current Coin of your Province, in the Columns for that Purpose, at the Rate you receive for Pennyweights and Grains. Then strike a Balance, due from you to the General Post-Office.

Some of the Articles in the above Account will be often unnecessary, as when during the whole Quarter, you have received no mis-sent Letters; have not been under or overcharged; where the Office is not a Sea-port, &c. so that in the printed Account sent to the General Post-Office every Quarter, some of these Articles will remain blank.

It will be proper to copy the Quarterly Account you send to the General Post Office into the latter Part of your Book.

You have now only an Account to raise for the General Post-Office; which, as it will take up but little Room, may be on the last Folio of your Book save one: To the Creditor Side of which Account, you must carry all your Quarterly Balances; and on the Debtor Side, charge all the Money you remit to, or pay by Order of, the Post-Master-General, the Comptroller, or either of them.

In placing the aforementioned Accounts in different Parts of your Book, as directed, you may contrive it, as nearly as possible, that every Part of your Book may be filled at one and the same time.

B. FRANKLIN.

of Union or conceived the American Philosophical Society, he was fashioning a cooperative intercolonial network of printers. He began as early as 1733, when his apprentice Lewis Timothy, having finished his apprenticeship, wanted to set up on his own. The last thing Franklin wanted was another printer in Philadelphia; but the only printer in Charleston had just died, so he sent Timothy there. Franklin provided a press and type, in return for which the partner would remit half his profits. Timothy was primarily a newspaper and job printer, but he also sold Franklin's publications and reprinted pieces from his newspaper. In later years Franklin established similar partnerships in New York, New Haven, Connecticut, Annapolis, Maryland, and Antigua. He also maintained close business ties with the widow and son of his brother James in Newport, Rhode Island, and with bookbinder friends in Boston who were especially useful in distributing his publications. To extend his reach into the German-speaking backcountry of Pennsylvania he bankrolled a German printing office in Philadelphia from 1748 to 1758, at the same time trying repeatedly to establish a printing office in Lancaster.[22]

Imitating Franklin's business plan, the partners worked to win the government printing contract, to edit the best newspaper, and to attract most of the job printing. In addition, they published the occasional book and helped Franklin distribute his publications. When Franklin became postmaster general of the colonies, he had several of these printer partners named postmasters, thus helping their individual businesses as well as the interactions among them. When he retired, he maintained an interest in his Philadelphia office by means of a partnership with his foreman David Hall (fig. 2.23). Thus he transformed a brood of potential rivals into a sophisticated intercolonial communications network, one of the most dynamic in the world, with himself at the center (fig. 2.24).[23]

From the 1740s to the 1760s (when more master printers began to emigrate from Britain) most of the printers in the middle colonies, with the exception of the Bradfords, rose through Franklin's extended network. (In New England, consanguinity—especially in the prolific Green family—replaced partnership as the organizing principle.) The striking uniformity and stability of the print culture of the middle colonies in this period is probably due to this shared experience and culture. In everything from the type they used to their editorial policies, they all imitated Franklin.

The most effective of all Franklin's partners was his successor, David Hall, the only partner bred in the British book trade, who emigrated in 1745 specifically to work for Franklin. Hall was the close friend and favorite journeyman of the London printer William Strahan (fig. 2.25). For many years Frank-

Fig. 2.25 (Opposite) Joshua Reynolds, Portrait of William Strahan, 1783.

lin's acquaintance with Strahan was strictly epistolary, but the two men became
close friends, perhaps because they were both printers. Strahan was the only
printer in London who managed to acquire enough copyrights to become an important publisher. This three-way friendship was the basis of the most successful book-importing enterprise in the colonial period.

Because Hall was so capable, Franklin was able to retire in 1748 to devote
himself to scientific research and politics, activities his business and his position

as a newspaper editor had precluded. His partnership agreement with Hall was like the others, with one difference: Franklin took half the profits of the printing, but whatever money Hall made from bookselling was all his own. The effect of this clause, whether intended or not, was to divert even more of Hall's energy to importing books and away from printing them, until his book business grew to be larger than his printing work.[24] Hall not only made Franklin's career as a scientist and a diplomat possible, he made the business transatlantic just as Franklin himself was becoming a transatlantic personage (fig. 2.26).

Throughout Franklin's subsequent career as scientist, diplomat, and finally founder of the new United States, he continued to refer to himself as a printer. To the end of his life he was in the habit of making copies for friends of a humorous epitaph he said he had written for himself in 1728, at the beginning of his career as a master printer. It read,

The Body of
B. Franklin,
Printer;
Like the Cover of an old Book,
Its Contents torn out,
And stript of its Lettering and Gilding,
Lies here, Food for Worms.
But the Work shall not be wholly lost:
For it will, as he believ'd, appear once more,
In a new & more perfect Edition,
Corrected and amended
By the Author.[25] [A variant appears in figure 2.27.]

Though God would ultimately correct all his errata, the work that was Franklin's life, in its material earthly form, was wrought by the printer himself. In a very real sense, Franklin created himself by means of print. Printing was his way to wealth, the trade by which he acquired a fortune, but it was also the means he used to acquire the power and influence to try to make a better world. In an age when the first requisite for a political career was mastering the art of oratory, Franklin never addressed a large assembly for more than a minute or two. He found his public in the disembodied sphere of print; and even then he seldom wrote in his own voice, preferring to use an array of pseudonyms and elusive personae: Poor Richard, Father Abraham, Silence Dogood. This mode of

Epitaph
on Doctor Franklin
Written by Himself.

The Body
of
Benjamin Franklin, Printer,
(Like the cover of an Old book,
Its contents torn out,
And stript of its lettering & Gilding)
lies food for Worms:

Yet the Work itself shall not be lost
For it will (as he believed) appear once more

In a new

And more beautiful Edition
Corrected and amended
By
The Author.

writing, he said, made people evaluate what he had to say more objectively than if they were hearing it in his own voice. It also provided him with a dizzying variety of masks that kept everyone guessing, then and now, about what he really thought and who he really was. Even in his *Autobiography*, the most self-revelatory work of its time and the basis of much of what we know about him, he created yet another character, his most perfectly realized persona. Of all Franklin's many identities, the one that tells us the most about all the others and the one that he clung to most tenaciously through life was Benjamin Franklin, printer.

Fig. 2.27 (Opposite) Benjamin Franklin, Epitaph, 1728.

Chapter 3

Benjamin Franklin, Civic Improver

BILLY G. SMITH

When he first landed at Philadelphia's Market Street Wharf on October 6, 1723, Benjamin Franklin embarked on one of the most famous walks in American history. "I was in my working Dress," he remembered. "I was dirty from my Journey; my Pockets were stuff'd out with Shirts and Stockings; I knew no Soul, nor where to look for Lodging."[1] Strolling up the hill from the wharf into the city, he began a personal journey that led from rags to riches, from obscurity to fame. In the process, and concomitant with his practical innovations, Franklin invented many elements of the material success story that would come to define the American dream. Too often forgotten, however, is his deep, enduring commitment to his community. From founding the self-improvement society known as the Junto (commonly called the Leather Apron Club) at the age of twenty-one to serving as president of the Pennsylvania Society for Promoting the Abolition of Slavery in the final years of his life, Franklin dedicated himself to improving the city of Philadelphia in particular and the country in general. Franklin excelled in that capacity, as in virtually all others. He was either totally or partially responsible for establishing a university, a hospital, a library, a learned society, a militia, a firefighting company, and a fire insurance company, as well as for successfully advocating lighting, cleaning, paving, and policing of the city streets. Franklin also promoted smallpox inoculation, which saved thousands of lives, and, toward the end of his life, took a prominent

Fig. 3.1 Peter Cooper, The South East Prospect of The City of Philadelphia, *ca. 1718. Cooper embellished the town's appearance, adding, for example, pinnacles to the Quaker meetinghouses and a tower to the Court House.*

stand against slavery, the premier moral issue of his day. Franklin epitomized the best of what it is to be a citizen, either in the eighteenth or in the twenty-first century.

The seventeen-year-old who landed in Philadelphia entered a provincial village considerably different from the "greene country town" envisioned by William Penn four decades earlier. Instead of large airy blocks extending westward, Penn's lots were now divided by drab alleys, the residents crowded north and south along the Delaware River. Peter Cooper's *South East Prospect of the City of Philadelphia* (fig. 3.1), the oldest surviving painting of a North American urban center, distorts a few of the buildings, yet it still conveys what Franklin initially may have seen from his boat. By the time of Franklin's death in 1790, Philadelphia had changed a great deal more, maturing into the new nation's premier social and cultural metropolis, hailed by the architect Benjamin Henry Latrobe as "the Athens of the Western world." By following Franklin on his initial walk around Philadelphia in 1723, we shall be able better to appreciate the myriad ways in which the city subsequently reaped the fruits of Franklin's tremendous energy, intellect, and dedication to enhancing the quality of everyday life.[2]

Hungry, searching for a job, and perpetually curious, Franklin set out to explore the city on foot (fig. 3.2). Had this been a Saturday or Wednesday market day rather than a Sunday, he would have joined the throng of people who crossed the river from New Jersey to Philadelphia, heading for the stalls in the middle of Market Street to sell or shop for food. At the top of the hill rising from

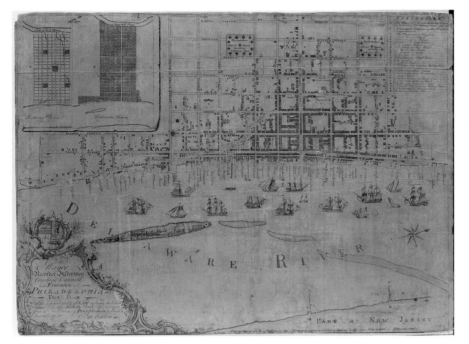

Fig. 3.2 Map of Philadelphia, 1762. Known as the Clarkson-Biddle map, this is the first detailed map of the interior, settled part of the city, locating institutions and identifying streets and alleys. Mary Biddle was the daughter of Franklin's friend and fellow Junto member Nicholas Scull.

the wharf, he passed the outdoor area where women sold their husbands' catch of fish and oysters. Crossing Front Street, Franklin proceeded by the London Coffee House, an impressive edifice where customers conducted all manner of business. Merchants, shopkeepers, and ship captains drank coffee and rum here while making business deals, many of which revolved around maritime trade, the foundation for the city's economy. The urban center was an entrepôt through which European manufactured goods flowed to be sold throughout the Delaware Valley; meanwhile, farmers brought the region's abundant grain and livestock products into the city for shipment abroad. Most residents, directly or indirectly, depended on commerce with people scattered throughout the Atlantic world, from Native Americans in the backcountry to small farmers and storekeepers in the neighboring countryside to planters, manufacturers, and merchants operating from the West Indies to Portugal to Britain. Mariners and merchants earned money managing the trade, carters and stevedores stowed staples on ships, and coopers created barrels to store flour bound for sea. Housing construction likewise formed a vital cornerstone of the economy as carpenters and laborers built structures to accommodate the city's rapid population growth from a handful of people in 1682 to somewhat more than five thousand inhabitants when Franklin arrived. The economy, however, depended largely on European trade and suffered from the boom-and-bust cycles associated with maritime commerce.[3]

Wealthier Philadelphians also congregated at the London Coffee House to barter human property. A "Very likely breeding Negroe Woman, and a Boy about two Years old" numbered among the hundreds of black people forcibly imported into the province in the 1720s, usually from West Africa via the West Indies, and sold as slaves at auctions at the coffee house, as illustrated in the nineteenth-century image created by William Breton (fig. 3.3). When Franklin arrived in the city, slaves accounted for one of every seven Philadelphians, working as domestics, laborers, mariners, and skilled artisans. Reflecting the rising racial tensions in the town, white workers complained about the competition created by "the hiring out of negroes by their masters." Indeed, Franklin occupied a tenuous position in this regard, technically still bound as an apprentice to his brother in Boston but, like so many unfree Americans, claiming his liberty by taking flight. It is thus little wonder that the youthful Franklin was asked "several sly Questions" meant to determine whether he was a "Run-

Fig. 3.3 William L. Breton, London Coffee House, *ca. 1830. In this scene showing the coffeehouse near the city's main wharf, merchants are selling newly imported slaves.*

away." In the coming years, Franklin purchased his own slaves, although he eventually advocated ending racial bondage.[4]

Continuing along Market Street, Franklin unknowingly passed the future meeting place of the Leather Apron Club, from which many civic improvement projects would emanate, as well as the house where he would establish the first subscription library in North America. "I met a Boy with Bread," Franklin remembered, "and, inquiring where he got it, I went immediately to the Baker's he directed me to in Second Street." If similar to John Bryant's nearby bakery at the entrance to Laetitia Court (named after William Penn's daughter, who owned a house there), the shop measured twenty-three feet wide and stretched seventy-two feet deep. Pleasantly surprised at the cheapness of bread, Franklin purchased "three great Puffy Rolls . . . and, having no room in my pockets, walk'd off, with a Roll under each Arm, and eating the other. Thus I went up Market Street" (fig. 3.4).[5] The Quaker open-mindedness regarding religious freedom had encouraged diverse groups of immigrants, and Franklin consequently heard a medley of tongues along the way. Philadelphia residents spoke not only English but also Dutch, German, French, Spanish, Portuguese, and Gaelic, as well as a host of African and Native American languages.

The next few blocks in the center of town illustrate some urban problems that Franklin eventually would attempt to rectify. He paused to read some of the official notices—including announcements of the *assize* (price) of bread and broadsides concerning market regulations—posted on the courthouse in the middle of the street. Recent flyers enjoined city watchmen to detain anyone walking the streets (especially "negroes" and "others who may be found gaming") during the "time of Divine worship," although the watchmen often were too incompetent (and sometimes too drunk) to enforce this restriction or to detain the many people who broke the law.[6]

Criminals who were apprehended frequently suffered public punishment at the courthouse, usually on market days when a great number of people could enjoy the spectacle; as a result, one observer commented wryly, "the price of eggs went up much." In an era of corporal punishment, Richard Evans was one of many who "received 39 Lashes at the publick Whipping-post, having been convicted of Bigamy." At another time, "Griffith Jones, and one Glascow an Indian, stood an hour in the Pillory together, and were afterwards whipt round the Town at the Carts Tail, both for Assaults with Intent to ravish" a woman and a young girl.[7] The year Franklin arrived, a new prison had been constructed at the corner of Market and Third Streets, with debtors in the north wing and convicts occupying the workhouse (fig. 3.5). Three years

Fig. 3.4 David Rent Etter, Franklin with Loaf of Bread, *ca. 1830. The iconic scene from Franklin's Auto-biography, here depicted on the decorative side panel of a fire engine, shows the seventeen-year-old Franklin strolling through Philadelphia's Head House Square with little money in his pocket and a loaf of bread under his arm. In reality, this market did not exist when Franklin first arrived in the city.*

later, disgruntled by the criminal system, Philadelphians rioted, destroying the pillory and stocks in protest.[8] Franklin, of course, helped organize a police force better capable of capturing lawbreakers.

The butchers' shambles, where animals were slaughtered and sold on Sundays, abutted the courthouse, and Franklin wandered along the smelly, fly-

Fig. 3.5 Unknown artist, Stone Prison at Philadelphia, 1728, *ca. 1830. Franklin walked past this newly constructed prison during his initial stroll around the city.*

infested booths and the adjacent covered food stalls that stood in the middle of Market Street. (Figure 3.6 provides an antiseptic interior view, devoid of dirt and people, of the market eighty years later.) Like the Scarecrow in the *Wizard of Oz,* Philadelphians feared fire in a city containing numerous frame structures. Announcements on the courthouse (where Franklin's Fire Insurance Company would later meet) banned smoking tobacco in the wooden market stands or anywhere within the "built part" of town. Fatigue forced Franklin to stop a while at the Friends' meetinghouse on the corner of Second and Market, where he slept through the Quaker worship service. This corner was the only paved section of the city's streets, and one of the few areas where pedestrians did not choke on the dust raised by carts and horses or stagger in the mud and gullies created by heavy rains. Hogs and dogs ran wild, eating trash. Indeed,

Fig. 3.6 William Birch and Thomas Birch, High Street, From the Country Market-place Philadelphia, *1798. In reality, the market was rarely so clean or so empty. On his return to Philadelphia in 1726, Franklin settled in High Street (now Market Street). All his subsequent homes and shops were located along this central thoroughfare.*

the streets sometimes became so foul with garbage and manure that, as one resident noted, they called the town "Filthy-dirty" as a pun on the city's name. Continuing westward, Franklin passed the First Presbyterian Church and the Indian King Tavern, where the Junto eventually would meet. At the corner of Fourth and Market, Franklin's path was halted by a ditch, the residue of Dock Creek, where water sometimes flowed so deep that a drunken man drowned there a few years later. Franklin later took the lead in organizing a fire company and fire insurance association, as well as in paving, cleaning, and lighting the streets.[9]

Turning south onto soggy Fourth Street, he passed the Indian Queen, a prominent public house offering both lodging and alcohol, and a future meeting site of the American Philosophical Society, founded by Franklin. About a hundred licensed taverns—approximately one for every dozen adult males—served the hard-drinking population of the city. Franklin walked a block, then "turn'd and went down Chestnut Street and part of Walnut Street, eating my Roll all the Way, and coming round found my self again at Market Street Wharf, near the Boat I came in." Along his route, Franklin undoubtedly passed people scarred by smallpox, one of the most common and deadly diseases in eighteenth-century Philadelphia, but an ailment that Franklin helped bring under control by campaigning for inoculation. "When I first walk'd about the Streets of Philadelphia," Franklin reported, "I saw most of the Houses in Walnut Street between Second and Front streets with Bills on their Doors, to be let; and many likewise in Chestnut Street, and other Streets; which made me think the Inhabitants of the City were one after another deserting it." The bursting of the South Sea Bubble and the concomitant collapse of the money supply in London had beleaguered the city's economy.[10]

In 1723 Philadelphia was an economically depressed, obscure country town on the edge of the British Empire. It hardly seemed a settlement poised to develop into the premier social, cultural, and political capital of a new nation, boasting such distinguished institutions as the Pennsylvania Hospital, the University of Pennsylvania, and the Library Company. The town possessed some valuable assets—including a good harbor and central geographic location—talented artisans and merchants, and an unusual measure of broadmindedness about religious and ethnic diversity, the latter being especially valuable in attracting immigrants. Yet it had fallen far short of its Quaker founder's ideal of a "greene country town." Except for churches and a few private schools, Philadelphia was devoid of cultural institutions. Its government was nearly nonexistent, unresponsive to the needs of its citizens, and unwilling to levy taxes to pay for urban improvements. In this situation, private rather than public action was essential to effect the necessary reforms. Part of Franklin's genius was his ability to understand how to make incremental changes by enlisting his friends, mostly young artisans on the make, to collaborate with him on public projects.

The initial energy that drove many early civic improvements emanated from the Leather Apron Club, subsequently called the Junto, founded by Franklin in 1727. The original name, taken from the customary attire of artisans, reflected the organization's membership and goals. Among its first dozen members were Franklin's partner and fellow printer Hugh Meredith, the apprentice printer George Webb, the shoemaker William Parsons, the joiner

William Maugridge, the glazier Thomas Godfrey, and the surveyor Nicholas Scull. (Scull later "directed" the engraving of the *East Prospect* of Philadelphia seen in figure 2.4 and drew the map of Pennsylvania in figure 3.7.) Only Robert Grace, a "gentleman" member with family money, belonged to the upper class. Divisions between the wealthy elite and artisans of the middle class had long existed in Britain and America; in a phrase misattributed to William Shakespeare, "the gentry think scorn of leather aprons." Well aware of the differences in the status and value accorded to the opinions of, in his words, the "*poor* or *rich, old* or *young,* a *Schollar* or a *Leather Apron Man,*" Franklin consciously invited men primarily of the latter group to join the club. The Junto was where his public service began.[11]

Of course, Franklin had personal ambitions for the club as well. From his own experience, he realized that his father's limited economic means as a candlemaker had imposed restrictions on his own life. As a youth, Benjamin was unable to continue his formal grammar school education, attend college, become a minister (as his father desired), pursue his love of poetry, follow a career as a ship's officer (rather than the dead-end vocation of a common seaman), or become a cutler's apprentice—largely because of his father's inadequate assets. Indeed, his apprenticeship as a printer to his brother, which Benjamin strongly resisted, occurred in part because it did not cost his father a shilling. Benjamin also noted that "the Straitness of His [father's] Circumstances, keeping him close to his Trade," prevented the elder Franklin from contributing his many talents to "public Affairs." It should be of little wonder, then, that the young Franklin pursued his own economic independence with such passion, not merely to get rich but as a means to escape the financial binds that restricted the lives and options of most artisans. He formed the Leather Apron Club, in part, to help him achieve that objective.[12]

By establishing the club, Franklin followed the long tradition of artisans who created mutual aid societies to assist one another during times of financial distress, to acquire friends with common occupational interests, to celebrate their identity as craftspeople, and to help advance their own careers. Franklin also credited Cotton Mather's *Essays to Do Good* as an inspiration for the club, and he appears to have modeled its rules and queries on the neighborhood benevolent societies that the New England Puritan Mather had proposed to promote religion and morality. Trained by his father to do "what was good [and] just" in the world, yet a deist who could not work through religious institutions to effect social change, Franklin sought different means to improve

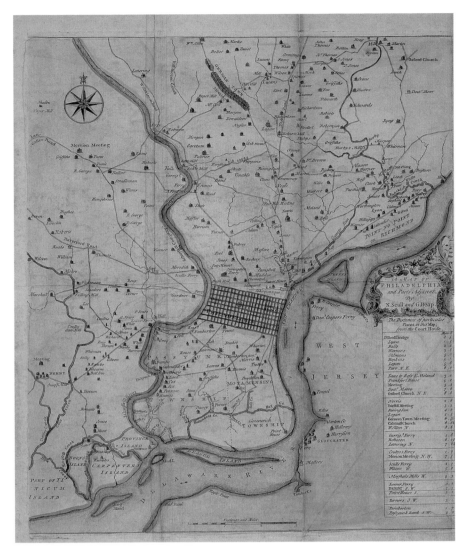

Fig. 3.7 Nicholas Scull and George Heap, A Map of Philadelphia and Parts Adjacent, *1753. Scull was an original member of Franklin's Junto (Leather Apron Club), a group composed primarily of artisans interested in self- and civic improvement. Heap was one of the original subscribers of the Library Company.*

his community. He combined artisan customs with a secularized version of Mather's form of organization, to which Franklin added the vital goals of intellectual self-improvement and civic enhancement.[13]

The club considered specific "Standing Queries" at each meeting, along with such questions as "Does the importation of servants increase or advance the wealth of our country?" Following the dual spirit of the association, members took a keen interest in debating issues that would benefit both themselves and their society, trying to determine where individual self-interest overlapped with the communal good, where self-improvement led to civic improvement. This theme of enlightened self-interest came to dominate Franklin's approach to changing society. "Few in public affairs," Franklin believed, "act from a meer View of the Good of their Country." What inspired citizens instead was when they "primarily consider'd that their own and their Country's Interest was united." Franklin introduced many of his ideas about public improvement at the club meetings, then subsequently published the deliberations, usually using a pseudonym, in his newspaper. The Leather Apron Club became a nursery of early urban reform, as Franklin developed the topics discussed by the members into concrete proposals for creating a subscription library, a tax-supported police force, a volunteer fire company, and an institution of higher learning.[14]

To raise the level of informed debate, Franklin suggested that the members of the club pool their books to form a library. The accumulated volumes filled only one end of the room on Market Street furnished by Robert Grace; after a year, "for want of due Care" of the books, and because members were loath to part with their best volumes, the collection was disassembled. However, Franklin's "first Project of a public Nature" grew out of this experiment. In 1731 he proposed plans for a subscription library; rather than pooling their books, members would pool their financial resources, thereby creating funds

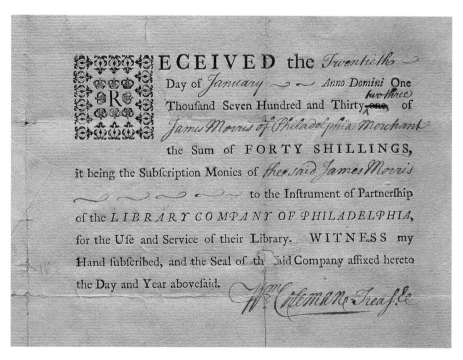

Fig. 3.8 James Morris's subscription receipt for the Library Company, 1732.

to establish a communal library greater than any of them could have built individually. For an initial payment of forty shillings and an annual renewal fee of ten more, subscribers could borrow books from the library (fig. 3.8). This was no small sum for working people, many of whom earned only ten shillings a week. "The Majority of us," Franklin remembered, were "so poor, that I was not able with great Industry to find more than Fifty Persons, mostly young Tradesmen, willing to pay down for this purpose."[15]

After consulting with James Logan, formerly William Penn's secretary and one of the best-read men in the colonies, Franklin spent the hundred pounds raised from fifty subscriptions to order forty books from London. When the volumes arrived in 1732, the Library Company of Philadelphia was located "at the House of Mr. Louis Timothee . . . in the Ally next to the Boar's-Head Tavern" and was open once a week; it remains a flourishing research institution to this day. On behalf of the library's board of directors, nearly all of whom came from the Junto, Secretary Joseph Breintnall petitioned the colony's proprietor Thomas Penn for his support (fig. 3.9). This and other developments, they hoped, would make their city "the future Athens of America." Reflecting the seriousness with which he took his civic responsibility, Franklin wrote a motto for the Library Company that found godly approval for public service: "To pour forth benefits for the common good is divine" (fig. 3.10).[16]

Within a decade the number of subscribers had doubled and the library's holdings increased fourfold. The library's *Catalogue of Books,* printed by Franklin in 1741, included 375 titles, most focusing on history, literature, and science (fig. 3.11). The writings of John Locke, the Enlightenment philosopher, outnumbered those of any other author. "Reading became fashionable," Franklin reported, and he took advantage of the book collection to complete his own education. The Library Company served, in Franklin's words, as the "Mother of all the North American Subscription Libraries," as institutions patterned on this model sprouted throughout the colonies. In Philadelphia, craftspeople and tradesmen started the Union Library Company in 1747, and a decade later the Amicable and Association Libraries opened. By 1769 the Library Company of Philadelphia had absorbed these independent institutions, making it the best library in the colonies. "These Libraries," Franklin proudly proclaimed, "have improv'd the general Conversation of the Americans, [and] made the common Tradesmen and Farmers as intelligent as most Gentlemen from other Countries." While his claim may have been exaggerated, the system of subscription libraries did help shape early America by disseminating Enlightenment ideas among both the common people and the elite.[17]

Fig. 3.9 (Right) Title page of Francis Hopkinson, copied after Joseph Breintnall and Benjamin Franklin, A Book of Minutes, containing An Account of the Proceedings of the Directors of the Library Company of Philadelphia, Beginning November 8th, 1731, taken by the Secretary to the Company, Vol: 1st, 1759. In 1759 Hopkinson became secretary of the Library Company and copied all the fragmentary minutes he could find from the previous years when first Breintnall and later Franklin were secretary.

Fig. 3.10 Philip Syng, Jr., Seal of the Library Company, ca. 1731–33. Syng, a silversmith, engraved the seal. Its motto, composed by Franklin, reads, "Communiter Bona profundere Dêum est," which translates freely as "To pour forth benefits for the common good is divine."

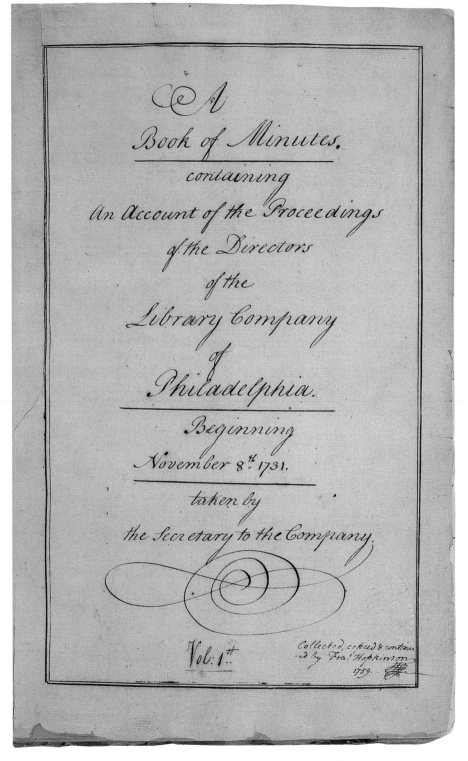

Franklin remained occupied primarily with earning a living by working in his print shop, so it took three more years before he once again turned his attention "a little to public Affairs" when he focused on improving law enforcement. At this time, constables appointed residents to walk their ward in the city, alert for criminal activity. Citizens could pay a fine of six shillings to avoid the duty, and the constables would then search for substitutes, often finding drunks in taverns and paying them a small token and a good deal of rum. As a result, tipsy watchmen performed poorly, if at all. Franklin wrote a paper, initially discussed by the Leather Apron Club in 1735, proposing that taxes be instituted to pay for qualified, full-time watchmen. Figure 3.12 shows a nineteenth-century rattle similar to ones watchmen used to alert residents of danger. Reflecting his class and artisanal perspective, Franklin advocated

Fig. 3.11 (Left) Title page of A Catalogue of Books belonging to the Library Company of Philadelphia, *1741. Although broadsheet catalogues of the Library Company's books may have been issued in 1733 and 1735, no copy of either survives. This small octavo of fifty-six pages is the earliest surviving catalogue of the library's holdings and lists the 375 titles then in the library.*

Fig. 3.12 Rattle, nineteenth century. Watchmen roused the neighborhood to the danger of fire by the use of rattles. Made of wood with a lead weight in the toe reinforced with brass plates, rattles are capable of a loud, distinctive sound.

Fig. 3.13 (Right) Full-sized side-crank hand pumper, 1753.

Fig. 3.14 (Below, top) Fire bucket inscribed "Library Company of Philadelphia," late eighteenth–early nineteenth century. Volunteer firefighters were required to own at least two buckets to help keep the engine pumper filled with water.

Fig. 3.15 Salvage bag inscribed "John Coburn PHIL AD," late eighteenth century. In the eighteenth century, the most useful task that firefighters could accomplish when a house was burning was to save as many of its contents as possible. They carried valuables out in cloth bags like this one that they were required to bring to the fire.

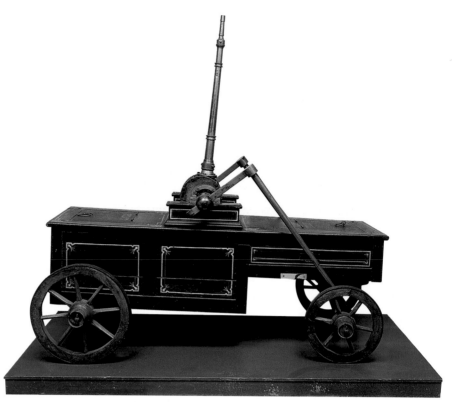

a "more equitable" tax system to carry out the project, proportionate to the value of the citizen's property. It was unjust, he reasoned, that "a poor Widow Housekeeper, all [of] whose Property to be guarded by the Watch did not perhaps exceed the Value of Fifty Pounds," had to bear the same burden as "the wealthiest Merchant who had Thousands of Pounds worth of Goods in his Stores." It took seventeen years, "when the Members of our [Leather Apron] Clubs were grown into more Influence," before the Assembly ordered tax-supported, regular police patrols.[18]

Franklin enjoyed more immediate success in organizing volunteer fire companies, in part because fire posed such a threat to towns with wooden structures. Franklin's newspaper routinely carried notices about fires in Philadelphia; one of the most serious occurred in April 1730, when a blaze burned all the stores on the wharf, then jumped Front Street and consumed three of the finest houses in the city. Franklin calculated the total damage at five thousand pounds—an enormous sum of money—and editorialized that "if the People had been provided with good [fire] Engines and other suitable Instruments, the Fire might easily have been prevented spreading" (figs. 3.13–3.15). Several years later, Franklin once again wrote a paper for discussion by the

Junto, subsequently published in his newspaper under the name "Pennsylvanus," in which he praised the "brave men" and "good Citizens, or Neighbours, capable and worthy of civil Society who fought fires."[19]

In February 1735 Franklin published an anonymous letter in the *Gazette* proposing a solution to the problem of fire. Declaring, like Poor Richard, that an "Ounce of Prevention is worth a Pound of Cure," he provided instructions on how to avoid home fires, then asserted, perhaps based on personal experience, that "when your Stairs [are] in Flames, you may be forced, (as I once was) to leap out of your Windows, and hazard your Necks to avoid being over-roasted." Because Philadelphians lacked "Order and Method" in fighting these catastrophes, Franklin suggested that they follow the example of Boston by establishing "a Club or Society of active Men belonging to each Fire Engine; whose Business is to attend all Fires with it whenever they happen." While Franklin typically emphasized volunteer associations as a means to civic improvement, he also recognized that compensation was essential; he thus advocated that firefighters be paid through an abatement of their taxes.[20]

As in all of his proposals, Franklin detailed his recommendations about the best method of fighting fires: "Firewards [wardens], who are distinguish'd by a Red Staff of five Feet long, headed with a Brass Flame of 6 Inches" (fig. 3.16) would command the companies. These men would "direct the opening and stripping of Roofs by the Ax-Men, the pulling down burning Timbers by the Hookmen, and the playing of the Engines" (figs. 3.17–3.18). Figure 3.19, showing firefighters in action, illustrates the type of organization Franklin believed would result in more effective firefighting. Following up on his proposal, Franklin organized twenty men into the Union Fire Company in 1736, and he specified its rules in the company's original articles (fig. 3.20). Franklin kept the minute book for this fledgling organization, and his strong, clear writing inventories their early meetings (fig. 3.21). Like the Leather Apron Club and the Library Company, Franklin's fire company spawned numerous similar organizations. As a result, by the time of the American Revolution, when

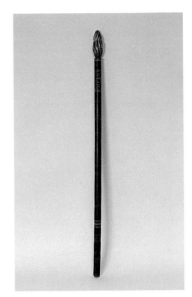

Fig. 3.16 (Top) Fire warden's staff, nineteenth century. Franklin recommended that "a Red Staff of five Feet long, headed with a Brass Flame of 6 Inches" should be carried by fire wardens as a means to identify their authority in the chaos of firefighting.

Fig. 3.17 Fire ax, ca. 1865.

Fig. 3.18 Fire hook, nineteenth century. Hooks on long poles were used to open ceilings and pull down plaster to allow access to flames or smoldering materials above the ceiling.

most of Philadelphia's male property owners belonged to a company, Franklin doubted "whether there is a City in the World better provided with the Means of putting a Stop to beginning Conflagrations."[21]

To further safeguard the citizens of Philadelphia, Franklin and his fire company colleagues conceived the idea of an insurance fund for company members. From this initial plan eventually resulted the nation's first successful property insurance company, the Philadelphia Contributionship for the Insurance of Houses from Loss by Fire, today America's oldest fire insurance company, founded in 1752. Franklin held the first seat on the Contributionship Board and printed the company's first policies (fig. 3.22).

In 1736, the same year that he founded the Union Fire Company, Franklin suffered a deep personal tragedy. His four-year-old son Francis, like many children in early America, contracted smallpox and died. A cruel irony is that during this period, when the efficacy of smallpox variolation (an early, effective form of inoculation) was fiercely debated, Franklin strongly supported the practice. In the early 1730s, his newspaper had carried stories praising the success of variolation in Boston as well as a detailed description of how to perform the procedure. Franklin had intended to inoculate his son as soon as he recovered from the "Flux" (dysentery), but by then it was too late. When rumors circulated that Francis had died from variolation, Franklin was disturbed that "some People are, by that Report . . . deter'd from having that Operation perform'd on their Children." So he set the record straight in the *Ga-*

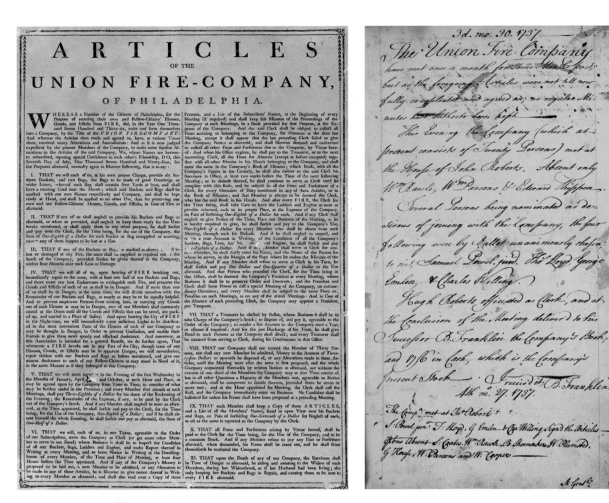

Fig. 3.20 Articles of the Union Fire-Company, of Philadelphia, 1794. *The original articles were recorded in manuscript form in 1736.*

Fig. 3.21 Page of the minute book of the Union Fire Company, 1736–85. *These minutes, written by Franklin, begin, "The Union Fire Company have met once a month for some Months past, but as the foregoing Articles were not till now fully completed and agreed on, no regular Minutes have hitherto been kept. This Evening the Company (which at present consists of Twenty Persons) met at the House of John Roberts." It is followed by a list of names.*

zette: "I do hereby sincerely declare, that he was not inoculated, but receiv'd the Distemper in the common Way of Infection."[22]

Smallpox was the most dangerous disease in early America. It was endemic in urban centers, afflicting most children, some adults, and a considerable number of recent immigrants. Besides mourning his son's death, Franklin, typically, took action. Not only did he continue to praise inoculation in his newspaper but, several decades later, he also persuaded William Heberden,

Fig. 3.22 John Stow, Philadelphia Contributionship fire mark, 1752–53. At the first meeting of the Contributionship's Board of Directors in 1752, the silversmith Philip Syng, Jr., was asked to devise a seal for the company, "being four Hands united." This is the earliest issued fire mark, featuring the company's seal, which would be affixed to houses to show that they were insured.

a noted London physician, to explain the ease with which anyone could perform the procedure. Variolation cost a good deal of money when performed by a physician, putting it beyond the financial reach of many working people. Heberden's *Plain Instructions for Inoculation in the Small-Pox* appeared in 1759. Franklin sent fifteen hundred copies of the pamphlet from Britain to Philadelphia, instructing his business partner David Hall to give them away free as a guide for poorer residents. The endorsement of inoculation by Franklin and others helped save thousands of lives, and the virulence of smallpox gradually declined in the city during the eighteenth century.[23]

Working with his friend John Bartram, a Quaker botanist who helped establish the foundation for American environmentalism, Franklin proposed a plan for a type of Junto on a larger, more sophisticated scale. In 1743 Franklin published *A Proposal for Promoting Useful Knowledge among the British Plantations in America,* which outlined an organization for the exchange of information and ideas. The group would "be formed of Virtuosi or ingenious men residing in the several colonies, to be called *The American Philosophical Society*" (fig. 3.23). The society's goal was to encourage learned men to correspond and converse about matters that would benefit their own lives, their communities, and "Mankind in general." Franklin's familiar emphasis on practical knowledge was broadened to include complex scientific information as well. Topics suitable for consideration thus might range from "new-discovered Plants" to "new-discovered Fossils" to "New Discoveries in chemistry" to "New Mechanical Inventions for saving Labour."[24]

Because of its strategic geographic location at the center of the colonies where postal and maritime routes converged (and since Franklin lived there), Franklin decided that Philadelphia should host the new society. He volunteered to serve as secretary, and the early membership list included associates of the Leather Apron Club such as the glazier and mathematician Thomas Godfrey and the shoemaker William Parsons (who also had served as librarian of the Library Company). Other notable members were Thomas Hopkinson (a director of the Library Company), the Philadelphia physician Thomas Bond, the future Pennsylvania governor Robert Hunter Morris, and the prominent New York politicians Cadwallader Colden and James Delancey. The society met sporadically beginning in 1744, but Franklin was disappointed in its elite members, complaining about the lack of commitment on the part of "very idle Gentlemen" who "will take no pains." Moreover, in this plan Franklin not

Fig. 3.23 Membership certificate for the American Philosophical Society, signed by Benjamin Franklin, 1786. The oldest scientific society in the United States, the American Philosophical Society was founded in Philadelphia in 1743 by Franklin and John Bartram, and revived in 1768; Franklin was elected president in 1769.

only was ahead of his time (as usual) but also premature and too ambitious in his efforts. In the 1740s communications remained so rudimentary and localism so strong that they prevented scholars in other colonies from being drawn into an effective collaborative network centered in Philadelphia. Meetings thus discontinued in 1746.[25]

During the 1760s, when Franklin was in London but conditions were more suitable for establishing such a society, Philadelphia intellectuals revived his proposal on a smaller scale. Shortly after the American Society for Promoting and Propagating Useful Knowledge was founded in 1766, Franklin's original plan was reinvigorated. The organizations merged three years later to produce the American Philosophical Society, held at Philadelphia, for Promoting Useful Knowledge. By the 1790s, the organization had spread nationally and developed into the principal learned society in the new republic. This, the first learned institution in America, enlisting members ranging from Thomas Jefferson to Albert Einstein, continues to shape the intellectual and cultural life of the country today.

Benjamin Franklin was one of the few founding fathers (along with Thomas Paine) who had to earn a living by laboring with his hands. Unlike Thomas Jefferson, George Washington, John Hancock, or Robert Morris, Franklin would have starved if he had not worked during the early years of his life. While writing his autobiography, Franklin recounted in impressive detail the precise cost of room and board and the exact wages he had earned decades earlier—a habit of exactitude in fiscal details common to working-class people who, as Franklin put it, "rubb'd on from hand to mouth." That experience shaped his philanthropic endeavors, as evident by his establishment of the Leather Apron Club and its various institutional progeny and by his emphasis on enlightened self-interest. It also helped create his youthful artisan radicalism, when he sought to empower ordinary laboring folk (for example, when he circulated do-it-yourself instructions for smallpox inoculation). In addition, he advocated progressive taxation to pay for improving the urban environment. In a sweeping departure from the past, Franklin likewise proposed that common militia soldiers elect their officers. Like many artisans, Franklin also subscribed to the labor theory of value, a philosophy that challenged the emerging free market ideas of the era. "Trade," he contended, "being nothing else but the exchange of Labour for Labour, the Value of Things is . . . most justly measured by Labour." He shared other radical perspectives with work-

Fig. 3.24 (Opposite) Robert Feke, Portrait of Benjamin Franklin, ca. 1738–46. This is the earliest known portrait of Franklin.

Fig. 3.25 Title page of Benjamin Franklin, Proposals Relating to the Education of Youth in Pensilvania, 1749. *Franklin wrote and printed* Proposals *to promote the establishment of a college. His efforts led to the founding of the Philadelphia Academy (now the University of Pennsylvania) in 1751. Franklin was the first to promote higher education in Philadelphia.*

Fig. 3.26 (Opposite) First page of "Account of School Money . . ." (tuition book) belonging to the Philadelphia Academy, 1751–57. This account book lists the students enrolled and the people responsible for paying their tuitions.

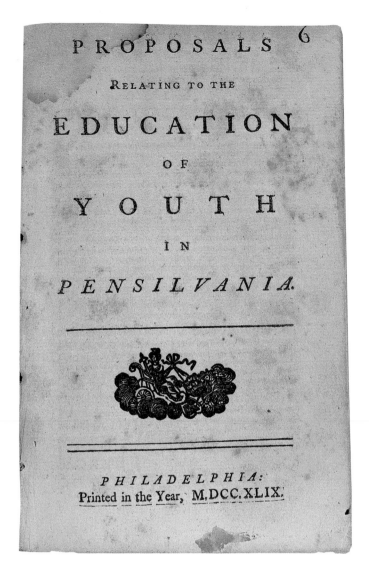

ing people in his view of wealth itself. As he confided to a friend, "What we have above what we can use, is not properly *ours*, tho' we possess it."[26]

Franklin's actions, especially in his early life, mirrored his beliefs. Revealingly, when he had acquired sufficient wealth to live on by the youthful age of forty-two, he retired, rather than pursue even greater riches, in order to dedicate his life to public service. "I would rather have it said," he wrote his mother at the time, "'*He lived usefully,*' than, '*He died rich.*'" His view of wealth obviously was much more complex than a simplistic recounting of his rags-to-riches story or the popularity of his most reprinted tract, *The Way to Wealth,* would suggest. Franklin rejected "the general Foible of Mankind, in the Pursuit of Wealth to no end." Instead, he thought of work and the quest for pros-

Anno 1751.

Acco.t of School-Money from the 7. January 1750/1. to the 6. January 1752. inclusive.

Remaining due 6 Janua.y 1752

When entered	Expences Stationy &c.al Mr. Masters.	Quarters paid Ditto	Scholars Names	By whom entered, or sent to School.	Quarters	Months	Days	£	s	d
			A							
1750/1								£	s	d
January. 7.	1.	3	John Allen	William Allen Esq.r	1	—			1	
	1.	3	Andrew Allen	Ditto	1	—			1	
	1.	3	James Allen	Ditto	1	—			1	
June. 5.	1.	1	Ralph Ashton	Susanna Ashton	1	1	1		1	7
			B							
1750/1										
January. 7.	1.	3	John Boudenot to pay	Elias Boudenot	1	—			1	
	1.	2	Jn.o Burroughs to 7 July	Cap.t Arthur Burrough	1	—			1	
	1.	3	Elias Boudenot	Elias Boudenot	1	—			1	
9.	1.	2	Edward Biddle	William Biddle	1.	2.	28	1.	19.	6
	1.	2	Thomas Bond	D.r Thomas Bond	1.	2.	28	1.	19.	6
February 5.	1.	2	Arthur Burroughs	Cap.t Arthur Burroughs	1	2	—	1.	13.	4
March 11.	1.	1	Henry Bambridge	James Bambridge	2.		26	2.	5.	8
23.	1.	2	Joseph Boude	Thomas Boude	1		12	1.	2.	9
April. 15	1	2	Samuel Bard	Peter Bard	0.	2.	22	0..	18.	3
20.	1	1	Rob.t Bridges to 20 8ber	Cornelia Bridges	1.	0.	0	1.		
Novem. 5.	1.	0	Davis Bevan	Awbry Bevan	0.	2.	0		13.	4
26	1	0	Thomas Bradford	William Bradford	0.	1.	11		9.	2
			C							
1750/1										
Janua.y 12.	1	3	William Clifton	John Clifton	0.	2.	25		18.	9
March 11	1	2	Lindsay Coates	John Coates	1.	0.	26	1.	5.	8
April 15	0	0	Samuel Chew	D.r Thomas Bond	2.	2.	22	2.	18.	2
	0	0	John Chew	Ditto	2.	2.	22	2.	18.	2
May 17.	1	1	Henry Chadd		1.	1.	20	1.	11.	—
June. 3	1	1	John Cadwalader	D.r Tho.s Cadwalader	1.	1.	3	1.	7.	5
—	1	1	Lambert Cadwalader	Ditto	1.	1.	3	1.	7.	5
Sepr. 3	1	0	John Child	Cap.t James Child	1.	1.	3	1.	7.	5
Octob.r 9	1	0	William Coates	John Coates	0.	2.	28		19.	6
—	1	0	John Caryll	Reese Meredith	0.	2.	28		19.	6
14.	1	0	Philemon Loyd Chew	D.r Adam Thomson	0.	2.	23		18.	6
Novem. 6	1	0	Langton Carlisle		0.	2.	0		13.	4
11	1	0	Gerardus Clarkson	Rev.d Gilbert Tennant	0.	1.	26		12.	4

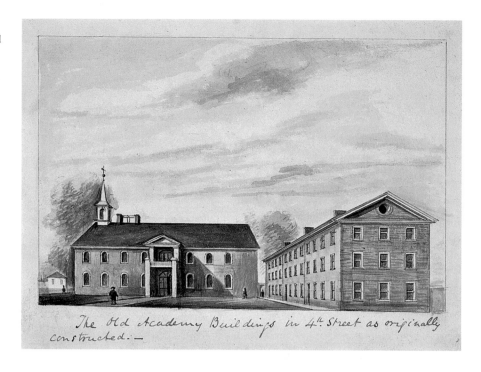

perity as a means to an end, whether the goal was the "decent competency" and
independence sought by most artisans or a foundation on which people could
create their own happiness and contribute to the common good. In his "Hints
for those who would be Rich," Poor Richard advised, "The use of Money is
all the Advantage there is in having Money." Robert Feke, a self-taught artist,
captured Franklin on canvas at this juncture in his life (fig. 3.24). As one art
historian observed, the comparatively "plain and unpretentious manner" in
which Franklin is represented (when compared to the style of contemporary
portraits) reflected the values and sensibilities of both artist and subject. [27]

Franklin underwent a renewed dedication to public service when he retired from his printing business. Whether pursuing practical inventions—like
the lightning rod and the Franklin stove—serving as a politician, or establishing philanthropic institutions, Franklin continued to enhance the quality of
people's daily lives. By realizing his own financial success, Franklin had escaped the monetary and time constraints that so often limited the participa-
tion of artisans (including his father) in civic affairs. He was now free to pursue
projects designed for the public good, and he did so with a passion that super-
seded his commitment to his business, to his scientific pursuits, and even to

his family, from whom he was absent for years while he worked as a politician and diplomat.

Immediately after his retirement, Franklin pursued the twin goals of establishing a college and a hospital. Building on an idea that he had discussed with the Leather Apron Club six years earlier, in 1749 Franklin published a pamphlet called *Proposals Relating to the Education of Youth in Pensilvania* that defined a public academy unique in early America (fig. 3.25). An educational radical, Franklin challenged the dominant classical elite approach that emphasized instruction for the glory of God and learning for its own sake. Rather than serving the privileged (as did the four existing colonial colleges: William and Mary, Princeton, Yale, and Harvard), Franklin's academy would provide training in practical matters and prepare young men for future careers.

Fig. 3.28 William Marchant after Gilbert Stuart, Provost William Smith, *1871. Smith and Franklin struggled for years about the direction of the educational institution (which became the University of Pennsylvania) founded by Franklin.*

"As to their Studies," he wrote, "it would be well if they could be taught every Thing which is useful, and every Thing which is ornamental: But Art is long, and their Time is short." Enlightenment ideas, his own self-education and experiences, and his egalitarian commitment to the needs of Philadelphia's diverse classes and religious groups all shaped Franklin's perspective. In addition, in typical Franklin fashion, he felt that higher education should enrich the community by cultivating in its students "an *Inclination* join'd with an *Ability* to serve Mankind, one's Country, Friends and Family."[28]

Franklin solicited several thousand pounds in donations, and the Philadelphia Academy opened in 1751 as the equivalent of a high school, divided into a Latin and an English component (figs. 3.26 and 3.27). Franklin was elected president of the academy board, but he soon lost control of its direction. The Anglican priest William Smith (fig. 3.28), who became professor and provost of the academy, persuaded the wealthy, religiously committed trustees to redefine Franklin's priorities, moving the institution closer to a classical view in training the sons of affluent Anglican merchants rather than the children of artisans or people of other religious denominations. In 1755 Smith established the College of Philadelphia, geared for more advanced students. Franklin and Smith grew to be bitter enemies, and the academy became a political football during the revolutionary era when the trustees proved to be Tory sympathizers. The Pennsylvania Assembly consequently took control of the institution, changed its administrators, and renamed it the University of Pennsylvania in 1791. Even though his democratic designs were thwarted, Franklin continued as a trustee throughout his life and hailed the college as one of his greatest accomplishments.[29] Near the end of his life, Franklin was a patron of yet another

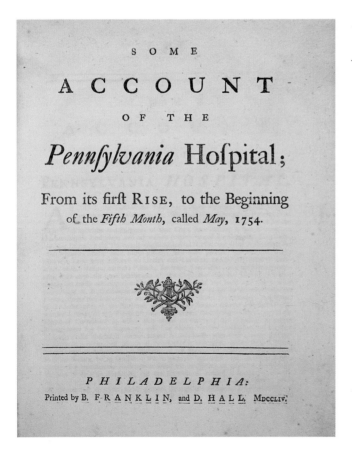

Fig. 3.30 Title page of Benjamin Franklin, Some Account of the Pennsylvania Hospital . . . , 1754. Franklin wrote this history of the founding of the hospital to gain financial support for the fledgling institution.

A South-East Prospect of the Pensylvania Hospital, with the Elevation of the intended Ft.

This Building, by the Bounty of the Government, And of many private Persons, Was Piously founded, for the Relief of the Sick and Miserable

TAKE CARE OF HIM
MT WILL REPAY
THEE

Built A.Dom. 1755. From No. 1 to 2

Fig. 3.31 Henry Steeper and John Dawkins, A South-East Prospect of the Pensylvania Hospital with the Elevation of the intended Plan, *1755. The institution is still located near the corner of Eighth and Pine Streets.*

college, which was named after him when in 1787 he gave the first large donation of two hundred pounds (fig. 3.29). Franklin College later merged with another school and became Franklin and Marshall College in 1853.

Within a few weeks of the academy's opening, Franklin began to set the groundwork for a hospital. Doctor Thomas Bond, a fellow member of the American Philosophical Society and trustee of the academy, campaigned for a hospital "for the reception and cure of poor persons," especially those "whose poverty is made more miserable by the additional weight of a grievous disease." Bond appealed to his friend Franklin, the great organizer of such endeavors. Franklin realized that like so many of his schemes, this large project required government aid in addition to private donations. When he petitioned the Assembly, however, backcountry delegates resisted because they perceived little benefit to funding an exclusively urban institution. Franklin's ingenious response was to propose a matching grant: the Assembly would provide two thousand pounds if citizens contributed an equal sum. Franklin used the Assembly's commitment to leverage private donations: "We urg'd the conditional Promise of the Law as an additional Motive to give, since every Man's Donation would be doubled." As a result, the "Subscriptions accordingly soon exceeded the requisite sum."[30]

Reflecting its clientele by its name, the Pennsylvania Hospital for the Sick Poor—the first public hospital in the colonies—began treating patients in 1752 (fig. 3.30). "A convenient and handsome Building was soon erected," Franklin wrote years later, and "the Institution has by constant Experience been found useful." (Figure 3.31 is an engraving of the hospital made soon after it was built.) The original building was constructed well out of town, near the corner of Pine and Eighth Streets, to shield more respectable residents from the perceived threat posed by impoverished patients. Once again, though, Franklin had been the principal moving force in creating an institution that catered primarily to people of the poorer classes.[31]

By the time of the Constitutional Convention in 1787, Benjamin Franklin was so infirm from kidney stones and other ailments that he could hardly walk. While being carried by four men in a sedan chair from his home to the convention, he may have compared the major urban center he observed through his window to the small country town he had strolled through on his arrival

Fig. 3.32 Rendering of the Franklin block of Market Street, ca. 1949. This watercolor is said to have been painted by a descendant of Franklin's English friend Polly Stevenson.

Fig. 3.33 William Birch and Thomas Birch, Back of the State House, Philadelphia, *1799. The new brick building of the American Philosophical Society can be seen through the trees at the rear right.*

in 1723, readily recognizing that vast changes had occurred, even if some similarities remained. The number of residents had expanded eightfold, to about forty-one thousand, owing primarily to a large influx of immigrants, which produced an even more diverse racial, religious, and ethnic population than Franklin had known in his youth. The city had grown considerably more prosperous, even though the basic economic structure had not changed fundamentally; much of the economy still rested on trade. Visible from the sedan were enormous new mansions, like that of William Bingham on Third Street, and elegant buildings on Second Street such as the City Tavern, the meeting place of wealthy merchants. Yet not too far away stood two of the largest, most congested structures in America: the Walnut Street Jail and the almshouse. What might have troubled Franklin the self-made man, then, was that material inequality had intensified, class lines had hardened, and poverty and crimi-

nality had increased. Emerging residential segregation was yet another sign of the greater social and economic gulf. Reflecting his status, Franklin himself lived in a grand house on Market Street (between Third and Fourth Streets), the central area of the city where the elite congregated (fig. 3.32); meanwhile, poorer citizens frequently settled on the city's fringes and in the dark alleys cutting between the major thoroughfares.[32]

Philadelphia had become the social, cultural, and political capital of America, in no small part because of Franklin's influence. Many of the institutions for which he was responsible were not far from his home. The College of Philadelphia, for which Franklin remained a trustee until the end of his life, stood a few blocks north of his house at Fourth and Arch Streets. One block east of his home, on Chestnut Street, was the newly opened Philadelphia Dispensary, an outpatient clinic for the poor. It recalled the still-flourishing Pennsylvania Hospital that Franklin had founded, and the fact that he had always advocated free inoculation for smallpox, something the dispensary provided. As a result, deaths from the disease had declined significantly in the city. Across from his home on Chestnut Street was Carpenter's Hall, which temporarily contained the book collection of the Library Company Franklin had created. The Harmony Fire Company, one of the many offshoots of the Union Fire Company Franklin had established, stood a block south of Franklin's home.

Traveling to the Constitutional Convention at the Pennsylvania State House (later renamed Independence Hall), the sedan-chair carriers turned west on Market Street in front of Franklin's house, then carried him over the sewer being constructed along Fourth Street. Turning onto Fifth Street, they may have stumbled on the gravel road, one of the few unpaved avenues in the downtown area. Franklin, of course, had helped organize paving and cleaning the city streets. The hall of the American Philosophical Society was under construction near Chestnut and Fifth Streets and would be finished in 1789, a year before Franklin's death (fig. 3.33). The short journey to the State House and the immediate area around his own home may have warmed Franklin with the knowledge that so much of his civic vision had turned into grand accomplishments.[33]

Chapter 4

Benjamin Franklin at Home

PAGE TALBOTT

No residence closely associated with Benjamin Franklin has survived on American or French soil. Franklin's family home on Milk Street in Boston, the several houses that he rented in Philadelphia, and the mansion house he built there in 1764 (on Market Street between Third and Fourth Streets) have long since been torn down. Likewise the elegant *hôtel* in Passy, near Paris, where Franklin lived for nine years, is no longer standing. Only the Georgian house owned by the widow Margaret Stevenson at 7 (now 36) Craven Street in London, where Franklin lived between 1757 and 1775, remains to represent Franklin's domestic environment, and this site contains none of his possessions (fig. 4.1).[1]

No Mount Vernon, Monticello, or Montpelier exists where trained interpreters and curators can devote their skills to a multisensory, multidimensional examination of this extraordinary man. Franklin's personal belongings were long ago scattered among his descendants and others, beginning with a sale of his household effects within months of his death. In the intervening two centuries, some of these artifacts have been deposited in public institutions, among them the American Philosophical Society, the Franklin Institute, and the Library Company of Philadelphia, but few are on permanent display. A. C. Carlton, the former director of the Franklin Institute, noted in 1954, "The widespread dispersion of Franklin relics . . . prevents anyone from seeing

Fig. 4.1 When he was in London, Franklin lodged at 7 (now 36) Craven Street.

many of them without a great deal of travel." The Franklin Tercentenary project has brought to light and reunited many of these important artifacts for exhibition, study, inspection, and appreciation.[2]

The principal sources for this chapter are these artifacts, Franklin's letters to his family and friends and their letters to him, and key documents such as household accounts, newspaper notices, and the 1790 inventory of Franklin's estate. While Benjamin Franklin wrote extensively about his worldly goods, relatively few of his letters identify specific possessions. But his correspondence, together with the other primary documents, does convey his taste and buying habits. Although occupied with matters of business, civic vision, useful knowledge, and affairs of state, he was never too busy to direct his wife and daughter regarding fashion, interior decoration, and household purchases; and he took pleasure in purchasing European goods for their enjoyment back home.

Franklin's concentration on domestic details may seem remarkable, but Franklin paid extraordinary attention to all aspects of his life and wrote voluminously on a wide variety of subjects, from the exotic to the mundane. When he was absent from Philadelphia, as he was for nearly thirty years altogether, he sought to maintain both control of and connection to his home and household. As he wrote regretfully to his wife in August 1765, "I wish you would give me a particular Account of every Room, who and what is in it, 'twould make me seem a little at home."[3]

Few have written about the domestic life of Franklin. The most notable exception is Claude-Anne Lopez, who published three important books focusing on his personal life that described various aspects of it, including his family, his residences, and his possessions.[4] But even Lopez's account leaves out a great deal of what we can glean about Franklin's family and residences from the material possessions pictured here.

In his *Autobiography,* Franklin wrote that he first laid eyes on his future wife, Deborah Read, the day he arrived in Philadelphia—October 6, 1723. Franklin courted Deborah briefly before heading to London for two years, where he seemingly forgot "by degrees" his attachments to her (one of the "great Errata" of his life). In the meantime Deborah wed a successful potter and apparent bigamist named John Rogers, who exhausted his wife's dowry before she parted company with him, refusing to "cohabit or bear his name." Rogers fled the country, and Deborah, finding herself neither married nor free to marry another, was receptive when Franklin returned from England, ready to settle down and eager to renew his relationship with her. Stymied by Debo-

Fig. 4.2 Mather Brown, Portrait of William Franklin, ca. 1790. Descended in the family of Sally's oldest son, Benjamin Franklin Bache.

Fig. 4.3 Attributed to Samuel Johnson, Portrait of Francis Folger Franklin, ca. 1736. Descended first in the family of Sally's third daughter, Deborah Bache Duane, then in the family of Benjamin Franklin Bache, through purchase.

rah's uncertain marital status, they joined in a common-law marriage in 1730, beginning a forty-four-year liaison.[5]

As the mother of Franklin's two children—Francis (Franky) Folger and Sarah (Sally)—and stepmother to Franklin's illegitimate son, William, Deborah was the constant in her household as her husband pursued his multifaceted interests. Yet motherhood proved trying for Deborah. Benjamin Franklin's first son, William, whose mother has never been identified, was a source of considerable resentment for Deborah, who was required to rear another woman's child from infancy.[6] Young William received the finest education available in Philadelphia, traveled extensively at home and abroad with his father, and benefited from his father's reputation and power. An ardent admirer of the British crown, William Franklin eventually became governor of New Jersey and took the side of the loyalists during the Revolutionary War, much to the dismay of his father (fig. 4.2).

The Franklins' beloved Franky died tragically and ironically of smallpox in 1736 at the age of four. A portrait of Franky, painted posthumously by an unknown artist, remained a constant reminder of their loss and was obviously considered a family treasure (fig. 4.3).[7] Seven years after Franky's death, Deborah gave birth to Sally. As Franklin became increasingly preoccupied with business, politics, and his other affairs, Sally received relatively little of her father's personal attention. Yet with gentle and loving concern, Franklin offered guidance from afar, and gifts of cloth and clothing, accessories, and books were plentiful. From London in 1758, for example, Franklin sent his daughter "a newest fashion'd white Hat and Cloak, and sundry little things which I hope will get safe to hand . . . a pair of Buckles, made of French Paste Stones, which

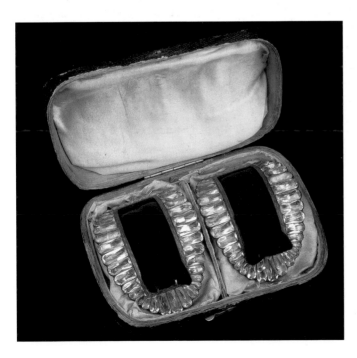

Fig. 4.4 Shoe buckles given by Benjamin Franklin to his daughter Sally, ca. 1758. Descended in the family of Deborah Bache Duane.

are next in Lustre to Diamonds, they cost 3 Guineas, and are said to be cheap
at that Price" (fig. 4.4). She, in turn, wrote him often, hoping to receive his approval, to stay in his thoughts, and to requisition items that could only be purchased in London.[8]

On one occasion, however, Franklin expressed his strong disapproval of
her intentions—when he learned that she planned to marry Richard Bache.
Franklin questioned Bache's ability to support a wife, given his lack of a trade.
Despite her father's displeasure, Sally and Richard married on October 29,
1767, and moved into the house recently built by her mother. They lived there

for twenty-five years and reared their seven surviving children (one daughter died in infancy), enjoying the generosity of her parents. Sally served as her father's housekeeper after her mother died, and later was hostess and caregiver for her father when he returned home from France (fig. 4.5). Sally's children were prolific, and all living Franklin descendents come from her family.[9]

Philadelphia, 1723–57

From 1730 to 1748, Deborah Franklin worked steadfastly by Franklin's side as they nourished their printing, stationery, and post-office business. Deborah's regular entries in their shop book are testimony both to her daily involvement with sales and inventory—initially ranging from slates to sealing wax to spectacles, later including chocolate, codfish and cheese—and to her propensity toward phonetic spelling (see fig. 2.19). Franklin acknowledged his wife's diligence when he wrote, "We have an English Proverb that says, He that would thrive Must ask his Wife; it was lucky for me that I had one as much dispos'd to Industry and Frugality as myself. She assisted me cheerfully in my Business, folding and stitching Pamphlets, tending Shop, purchasing old Linen Rags for the Paper-makers."[10]

Deborah and Franklin "throve together and . . . mutually endeavor'd to make each other happy." By 1732 they were free of debt and on their way to amassing a fortune that eventually allowed Franklin to retire from active busi-

Fig. 4.6 Famille Rose bowl, ca. 1760–70. Descended in the family of Sally's second son, William Bache, until the early nineteenth century.

Fig. 4.7 (Top) Elias Cachart, Spoon, 1771–72. Descended in the family of Deborah Bache Duane.

Fig. 4.8 Philip Syng, Jr., Baptismal bowl for Sally Franklin, engraved "D. EVANS to S. FRANKLIN," ca. 1743. This bowl is believed to have been given as a baptismal gift to Sally Franklin by Dr. David Evans, Presbyterian minister to the Welsh congregation in Tredyffrin, Pennsylvania, and an author published by Franklin. Descended in the family of Benjamin Franklin Bache.

Fig. 4.9 Elias Boudinot, Tankard, 1733–52. Descended in the family of Polly Stevenson Hewson, the daughter of Franklin's landlady at 7 Craven Street.

ness in 1748 at the age of forty-two. To a great extent this financial success was due to the couple's frugality, a trademark attribute of which they both boasted. Yet one of the first references to the Franklins' household goods, recounted in the *Autobiography,* suggests that both Deborah and Benjamin were well aware of the symbolic power of material possessions:

We kept no idle Servants, our Table was plain and simple, our Furniture of the cheapest. For instance my Breakfast was a long time Bread and Milk, (no Tea,) and I ate it out of a twopenny earthen Porringer with a Pewter Spoon. But mark how Luxury will enter Families, and make a Progress, in Spite of Principle. Being Call'd one Morning to Breakfast, I found it in a China Bowl with a Spoon of Silver. They had been bought for me without my Knowledge by my Wife, and had cost her the enormous Sum of three and twenty Shillings, for which she had no other Excuse or Apology to make, but that she thought *her* Husband deserv'd a Silver Spoon and China Bowl as well as any of his Neighbors. This was the first Appearance of Plate and China in our House, which afterwards in a Course of Years as our Wealth increas'd, augmented gradually to several Hundred Pounds in Value.

A well-used (and extensively repaired) Chinese bowl made as early as 1740 and an equally worn English silver spoon bearing Franklin's coat of arms remain from these highly symbolic purchases made by Deborah (figs. 4.6 and 4.7). The spoon, one of a dozen by Elias Cachart of London, bears London hallmarks for 1771–72 and is said to have been made according to Franklin's order to replicate the famous porridge spoon.[11]

This "first Appearance" of luxury items in the Franklins' house, probably in the 1730s, was succeeded by the acquisition of an extensive array of fine household goods, ranging from silver and china to handsome furniture and elegant fabrics (fig. 4.8). By the mid-1740s their furnishings represented the most fashionable available, including several pieces of silver embellished with a coat of arms that Franklin baldly "borrowed" from an unrelated family in Yorkshire, England, named Franklin or Franklyn.[12]

Writing as "Philomath" in the *Pennsylvania Gazette* on October 20, 1737, Franklin proclaimed, "The first Thing requisite in an Almanack-Writer, is, That he should be descended of a great Family, and bear a Coat of Arms, this gives Lustre and Authority to what a Man writes, and makes the common People to believe, that Certainly this is a great man." Franklin's father, Josiah, weighed in on the subject of coats of arms in a letter to his son dated May 26, 1739, saying that his brother Benjamin had "made inquiry of one skilled in heraldry, who told him there is two coats of armour, one belonging to the Franklins of the north, and one to the Franklins of the west. However our circumstances have been such as that it hath hardly been worth while to concern ourselves much about these things, any farther than to tickle the fancy a little."[13]

Bearing out Philomath's proclamation and despite his illegitimate claim to its use, Benjamin Franklin's assumed arms consist of a variety of heraldic emblems, including a pair of lions' heads, two doves, and a dolphin, as well as an idiosyncratic crest of a so-called lucy's (or pike's) head between two olive branches. The full coat of arms can be seen on an elegant silver tankard made by Elias Boudinot, Franklin's neighbor until 1753 and father of the future president of the Continental Congress. Perhaps one of the earliest uses of the arms, the tankard also bears the inscribed initials F/B*D, for Deborah and Benjamin Franklin (fig. 4.9). The distinctive crest motif was also used on Franklin's silver serving pieces. A Franklin descendant owns a marrow spoon embellished with the pike's head from his adopted crest (fig. 4.10). Franklin's fine, unmarked mid-eighteenth-century English fish slice is also engraved with the signature fish (figs. 4.11 and 4.12).

The finest rendering of the crest is found on the beautifully printed passports Franklin produced at his press at Passy (see fig. 7.11). The passports are the first official documents printed by Franklin on his French press, and they served to authenticate the travel of American citizens before the U.S. government printed such documents. "Nos Armes," as they were called in the text of the passport, were now being used to make the document look official in the eyes of the French, as Franklin had previously used his wax seal, also bearing his arms, to validate correspondence.

Although Franklin had early used his coat of arms as a vehicle for acceptance by the aristocracy, by the time he was minister plenipotentiary to France he was no longer trying to impress with his noble ancestry. But he was trying to impress on the French that the United States was a credible nation, and his coat of arms was a necessary tool. Writing to his daughter, Sally, Franklin declared that honoring one's descendants purely on the grounds of heredity "is not only groundless and absurd but often hurtful to posterity." Furthermore, he claimed that inherited aristocracy or nobility was "in direct opposition to the solemnly declared sense of their country."[14]

Unlike the silver bearing Franklin's crest, his furniture and ceramics are

Fig. 4.10 Detail of Benjamin Franklin's marrow spoon, showing the fish from the coat of arms, ca. 1770. Descended in the family of William Bache.

Fig. 4.11 (Right) Detail of fig. 4.12, bearing the pike's head from Franklin's adopted family coat of arms.

Fig. 4.12 Fish slice, ca. 1760–70. Descended in the family of Benjamin Franklin Bache.

difficult to authenticate. Over the years a vast number of household furnishings have been said to have been owned by Deborah and Benjamin Franklin. In some instances the history of ownership is extremely tenuous, consisting merely of wishful thinking and family tradition. In other instances, however, claims of provenance are accompanied by information that satisfies the researcher.[15]

Among the earliest examples of well-documented furniture purchased by Deborah and Benjamin Franklin are a dressing table and a set of three chairs in the Queen Anne style popular in the 1740s and 1750s. The chairs may be the ones listed as "three best crookt foot" chairs in the 1748 ledger entry of Philadelphia cabinetmaker Solomon Fussell, who provided goods and services to Franklin for at least nine years (fig. 4.13).[16] These handsome walnut chairs are similar in form and style to a somewhat plainer armchair, also purported to have been owned by Franklin (fig. 4.14). Likewise, Franklin's maple dressing table was made in the fashion of the 1740s, perhaps by Fussell's former apprentice William Savery (fig. 4.15). Also attributed to Savery and owned by Frank-

Fig. 4.15 Attributed to William Savery, Dressing table, ca. 1745–55. Probably descended in the family of either Benjamin Franklin Bache or Deborah Bache Duane. Purchased by William S. Vaux at the Great Central Fair in aid of the U.S. Sanitary Commission, Philadelphia, 1864.

Fig. 4.13 (Top) Attributed to Solomon Fussell, Side chair, ca. 1748. Descended in the family of Benjamin Franklin Bache.

Fig. 4.14 Armchair, ca. 1750–70. George H. Chickering of Boston is said to have purchased this chair at the French Fair in Boston ("The Fair in Aid of the Destitute People of France" during the Franco-Prussian War) in April 1871.

Fig. 4.16 (Left) Attributed to William Savery, probably after a design by Benjamin Franklin, Four-sided music stand, ca. 1770. Descended in the family of William Bache until the early nineteenth century.

Fig. 4.17 Tilt-top table and firescreen, ca. 1740–70. Franklin may have designed this ingenious table. Descended in the family of William Bache.

lin was a revolving four-sided music stand, perhaps designed by Franklin himself (fig. 4.16). The stand, which includes a storage area for sheet music and candle slides, reflects Franklin's lifelong interest in and love of music: he wrote songs, learned to play several instruments, even invented an instrument, his beloved glass armonica (see fig. 7.20). A related ingenious piece, also thought to have been designed by Franklin and with nearly identical legs, is a combination small tilt-top table and firescreen (fig. 4.17).

Both Fussell and Savery had civic and political, as well as business, connections to Franklin beyond their roles as chair and cabinetmakers, a not uncommon aspect of Franklin's web of associations. Given Franklin's widespread involvement with nearly every aspect of city life, he made a point of encouraging and patronizing local craftsmen as well as drawing them into his other activities. For example, the cabinetmaker Fussell is known to have turned parts for Franklin's scientific apparatus, and Franklin appointed William Savery ward assessor in 1754.

Along with other scientific-minded Philadelphians such as Ebenezer Kinnersley and Provost William Smith of the Philadelphia Academy (now the University of Pennsylvania), Franklin encouraged local clockmakers to develop their craft. Among these was Edward Duffield, who was active in Philadelphia in the 1740s and 1750s and from whom Franklin purchased as many as three tall clocks. The earliest of these—in the Queen Anne style—descended in the family of Benjamin Franklin Bache, Franklin's beloved grandson, who died prematurely in 1798 (fig. 4.18). Like Fussell, Savery, and Boudinot, Duffield had a personal relationship with Franklin; he was an executor of Franklin's will and the two shared common interests, including membership in the American Philosophical Society, by which Duffield was commissioned to make a specialized timepiece for the observance of the transit of Venus in 1769.[17]

When Franklin was no longer involved in the daily operations of the print shop, Deborah continued to manage their financial and business matters, and from 1757 until her death in 1774 she was left alone, for all but two years, to carry on her husband's interests at home while he lived in England. As Franklin wrote in a letter to Deborah, "I leave home, and undertake this long Voyage more cheerfully, as I can rely on your Prudence in the Management of my Affairs, and Education of my dear Child."[18]

London, 1757–75

Shortly after he arrived in London in July 1757, Franklin wrote to his wife, "As you desire to know several Particulars about me, I now let you know that I lodge in Craven Street near Charing Cross, Westminster; We have four Rooms furnished, and every thing about us pretty genteel, but Living here is in every respect very expensive."[19] In London he resided in the home of Margaret (Mrs. Addinell) Stevenson, a widow, and her daughter Mary, called Polly (fig. 4.19). For sixteen years, these lodgings were the base for his many experiments, writings, and political negotiations, including those with William Pitt, the Elder, 1st Earl of Chatham, on the eve of the American Revolution. Mrs. Stevenson and Polly became his London family, and Franklin served as head of the household (fig. 4.20).

Soon after Franklin arrived in London, he eagerly began to acquire household furnishings of every type, most of which he sent home to his family. After all, his selection of household goods far exceeded what was available in Philadelphia, and he obviously enjoyed shopping for the most up-to-date items. In one letter to Deborah he describes in extraordinary detail his most recent purchases:

4 Silver Salt Ladles, newest, but ugliest, Fashion; a little Instrument to Core Apples; another to make little Turnips out of great ones; Six coarse diaper Breakfast Cloths; they are to spread on the Tea Table,

Fig. 4.18 Edward Duffield, Tall case clock, ca. 1750. Descended in the family of Benjamin Franklin Bache.

Fig. 4.19 Unknown artist, Portrait of Polly Stevenson as a young woman, ca. 1765. Descended in the family of Polly Stevenson Hewson.

for no body breakfasts here on the naked Table, but on the Cloth set a large Tea Board with the Cups; . . . In the great Case, besides the little Box, is contain'd some Carpeting for a best Room Floor. There is enough for one large or two small ones; it is to be sow'd together, the Edges being first fell'd down, and Care taken to make the Figures meet exactly: there is Bordering for the same. This was my Fancy. . . . There is also 56 Yards of Cotton printed curiously from Copper Plates, a new Invention, to make Bed and Window Curtains; and 7 Yards Chair Bottoms printed in the same Way, very neat; these were my Fancy; but Mrs. Stevenson tells me I did wrong not to buy both of the same Colour. . . . There is also a Snuffers, Snuff Stand and Extinguisher, of Steel, which I send for the Beauty of the Work; the Extinguisher is for Sperma Ceti Candles only, and is of a new Contrivance to preserve the Snuff upon the Candle. . . . No. 2 contains cut Table Glass of several Sorts.

Silver, kitchen utensils, fabrics printed with the newest technology, and the latest in candle snuffers . . . nothing was too insignificant to warrant a comment, or a purchase![20]

Franklin seems to have had particular affection for ceramics, which he purchased in vast quantities and variation. "In the large Case is another small Box, containing some English China; viz. Melons and Leaves for a Desert of Fruit and Cream, or the like; a Bowl remarkable for the Neatness of the Figures, made at Bow, near this City; some Coffee Cups of the same; a Worcester Bowl, ordinary. To show the Difference of Workmanship there is something from all the China Works in England; and one old true China Bason mended, of an odd Colour. . . . Look at the Figures on the China Bowl and Coffee Cups, with your Spectacles on; they will bear Examining."[21]

Fig. 4.20 Benjamin Franklin's handwritten calling card from when he lived in England, ca. 1757–75.

Although Franklin identifies the bowls and cups with the neat figures as Bow, he may have been referring to the porcelain from Worcester that later descended in William Bache's family (fig. 4.21). A bowl and cups are part of a set with transfer-printed bucolic designs etched and engraved by Robert Hancock, who had been an employee at Bow but moved to Worcester by 1757. Given Franklin's interest in innovative techniques, we should not be surprised that he bought wares decorated by the best-known English engraver, whose innovative work is found on mid-eighteenth-century English porcelains and enamels. When Franklin returned to England the second time, he purchased more Worcester coffee cups and saucers, this time hand-decorated in London with gilded, naturalistic, leafy floral sprays and sprigs (fig. 4.22).[22]

Franklin's affection for Deborah is demonstrated through yet another purchase, "a large fine Jugg for Beer, to stand in the Cooler." He writes his wife that "I fell in Love with it at first Sight; for I thought it look'd like a fat

Fig. 4.22 Twelve-piece tea service,
ca. 1765–75. Descended in the family
of Benjamin Franklin Bache.

jolly Dame, clean and tidy, with a neat blue and white Calico Gown on, good natur'd and lovely, and put me in mind of—Somebody. It has the Coffee Cups in its Belly, pack'd in best Chrystal Salt, of a peculiar nice Flavour, for the Table, not to be powder'd."[23]

As further testimony to his fondness for Deborah, Franklin commissioned the British painter Benjamin Wilson in 1757 to copy Deborah's "small Picture," recently sent from Philadelphia (fig. 4.23). Deborah's portrait hung in his London apartments, while Wilson's companion portrait of Franklin, completed in 1759, was sent back to Philadelphia (fig. 4.24). Both Wilson portraits were hanging in the Franklins' Philadelphia house in 1778, when Franklin's portrait was taken as a prize of war by Major John André during the British occupation of the city, leaving Deborah's portrait, as Franklin wrote, "a sort of a widow."[24]

Not all Franklin's British purchases were shipped home, however. "I am about buying a compleat Set of Table China, 2 Cases of silver handled Knives and Forks, and 2 pair Silver Candlesticks; but these shall keep to use here till my Return, as I am obliged sometimes to entertain polite Company," he wrote. Among his "polite Company" was the king of Denmark, whom Franklin proudly entertained at Craven Street, sending a sketch of the seating arrangement home for his family to see (fig. 4.25).[25]

Philadelphia, 1762–64

In November 1762, Franklin left London for a two-year hiatus in Philadelphia. During this time, he and Deborah had the opportunity to plan and start building their first house, only a few steps from where they had first laid eyes on each other. At last they would have room to display their assembled furnishings and their "elegant appurtenances shipped from London." The house was set in the center of a courtyard well off Market Street, on a group of contiguous properties, some inherited by Deborah and others purchased by Benjamin. Measuring thirty-four feet square, the spacious house, built by the prominent Philadelphia carpenter Robert Smith, was still under construction when Franklin returned to England in December 1764.[26]

Franklin next saw his handsome three-story brick house eleven years later, but he was nonetheless deeply involved in its embellishment and furnishing, and he regretted that he could not oversee the project. As he wrote in February 1765, "I almost Wish I had left Directions not to paint the House till my Return. But I suppose tis done before this time." Of course, if he had done so, the house would have remained unpainted for more than a decade![27]

As with his letters regarding purchases made in London, Franklin's letters to Deborah about the new house, and her responses to his, offer extraordinary detail about all aspects of its construction, embellishment, and furnishing. These letters, together with Gunning Bedford's insurance survey at the Philadelphia Contributionship dated August 5, 1766, help us visualize this elegant mansion. Furthermore, they demonstrate that Franklin's taste, to a large degree, dictated the interior decoration. Lacking floor plans, Franklin requested details so that he might order the necessary fittings for the house, such as curtains, furniture, and carpets (fig. 4.26). In one letter, for example, he requested of Deborah, "Let me have the Breadth of the Pier, that I may get a handsome Glass for the Parlour. I want also the Dimensions of the Sash Panes in the Buffets of the little North Room: and the Number of them. Also the Dimensions of the Windows for which you would have me bring Curtains, unless you chuse to have the Curtains made there." Once he received the necessary measurements, he was able to proceed with his orders for fabric. For a second-floor chamber he stipulated, "The blue Mohair Stuff is for the Curtains of the Blue Chamber. The Fashion is to make one Curtain only for each Window. Hooks are sent to fix the Rails by at Top, so that they may be taken down on Occasion."[28]

All the while, Franklin seems to have anticipated his imminent return to Philadelphia to oversee some of these activities. "Have you mov'd every thing,

and put all Papers and Books in my Room, and do you keep it lock't?" he wrote. "Is the Passage out to the Top of the House fixed with Iron Rails from Chimney to Chimney? As to oiling the Floors, it may be omitted till I return: which will not be till next Spring." Deborah gave him the particulars he requested. Her colorful, phonetic letter from early October 1765 illustrates both her attention to detail and her desire to please her absent husband. First she described Franklin's room: "Now for the room we Cale yours thair is in it your Deske the armonekey maid like a Deske a large Cheste with all the writeings that was in your room down stairs the boxes of glases for musick and for the Elicktresatecy and all your close and the pickters as I donte drive nailes leste it shold not be write." Deborah was loath to hang the "pickters" without his approval of their placement, for, as she said later in this letter, "O my Child there is graite odes [odds] between a mans being at home and a broad as every bodeey is a fraid thay shall doe wrong so every thing is lefte undun."[29]

Knowing that Franklin would be specifically interested in the Music Room (or Blue Room) on the third floor, she was particular in her description. The room "has the Armoneyca and the Harpseycord in it the Gilte Sconse a Carde tabel a seet of tee Chaney [china] I bought sens you wente from home the worked Chairs and Screen a verey hansom mohoganey Stand for the tee kittel to stand on and the orney mental Chaney but the room is not as yit finished for I think the paper has loste much of the blume by paisteing of it up thair-fore I thought beste to leve it tell you Cume home[. T]he Curtins [for

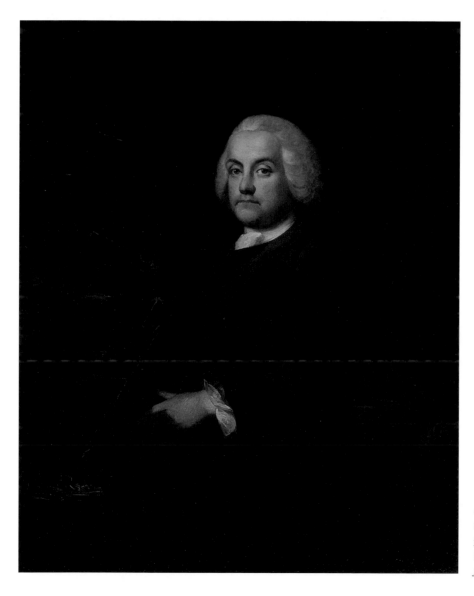

Fig. 4.24 Benjamin Wilson, Portrait of Benjamin Franklin, ca. 1760. This portrait was owned by the earls of Albermarle, Quidenham Hall, Norfolk, for a century and a half.

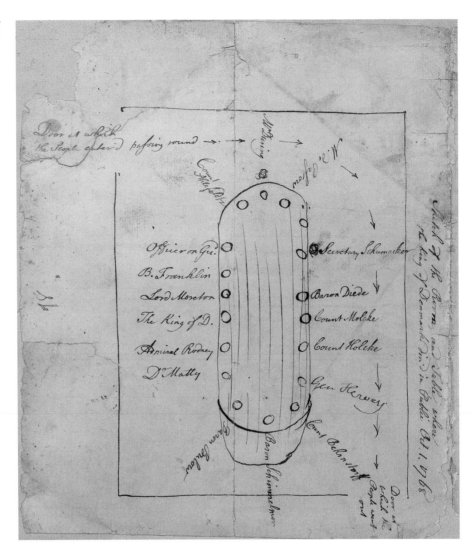

which he had earlier sent home the blue mohair] is not maid nor did I pres for them as we had a verey graite number of fleys as it is observed thay air verey fond of new painte."[30]

Getting this extraordinary room just right preoccupied both husband and wife for some time. Finally, nearly two years later, Franklin wrote, "I suppose the blue Room is too blue, the Wood being of the same Colour with the Paper, and so looks too dark. I would have you finish it as soon as you can, thus. Paint the Wainscot a dead white; Paper the Walls blue, and tack the gilt Border round just above the Surbase and under the Cornish. If the Paper is not equal Coloured when pasted on, let it be brush'd over again with the same Colour:

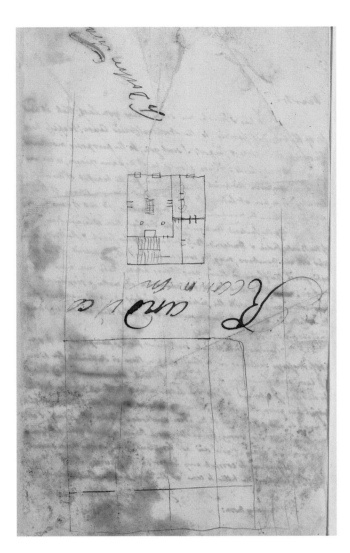

Fig. 4.26 Floor plan of the first floor of the Franklin house in Philadelphia, ca. 1765. The entry to the house is at the top of the picture.
One of two plans found among Franklin's papers, each on the back
of another document, which have been established beyond doubt
as rough plans of the first and second floors of Franklin's house as
completed and occupied in 1765. They may have been sketched by
Franklin.

and let the Papier machée musical Figures be tack'd to the middle of the Ciel-
ing; when this is done, I think it will look very well. "³¹

Franklin's British purchases for the new house were primarily smaller
items that could easily be shipped: fabric, china, silver, cloth, and so on. Although Deborah mentions "the beed which you sente from Ingland," which she
placed in the northwest chamber, used for guests, and Franklin writes about
"a Mohogany Press . . . I brought from England," which he recommended stor-
ing in the garret, their house primarily contained furniture from their earlier
life—such as the "old black wolnot chairs" in Deborah's chamber—and, later,
items that Deborah herself purchased from local Philadelphia cabinetmakers.
Describing her dining room set, she wrote, "In the rom down stairs is the sid

bord that you be spoke which is verey hansum and plain with two tabels maid to sute it and a Doz of Chairs allso[.] I sold to mr. Foxcrofte the tabeles we had as they did not sute the room by aney meens[. T]he potterns of the Chairs air a plain Horshair and look as well as a Paddozway [paduasoy] everey bodey admiers them." In this letter, then, we begin to see the decision-making role that Deborah was assuming in her effort to create a home she could call her own. She was happy to leave certain details to her husband ("as to Curtins I leve it to you to due as you like your self or if as we tolked be fore you went"). On the other hand, she expressly requested a "turkey Carpet," a luxury that Franklin was only able to provide for her following the repeal of the Stamp Act many months later. [32]

Several examples of furniture that probably belonged to Franklin and were made in Philadelphia between 1765 and 1775—the years he was abroad— are known today. These include a marble-top mixing table (a table for mixing drinks), a dining or side chair, and a high chest (figs. 4.27–4.29). All are in the

Fig. 4.27 Marble-top mixing table, ca. 1750–60. Used for mixing drinks, among other functions, this table descended in the family of William Bache.

Fig. 4.28 Side chair, ca. 1765.
Descended in the family of
William Bache.

elegant Chippendale style and feature claw-and-ball feet and carved cabriole
legs. Both the table and chair descended in the family of Franklin's grandson
William Bache. Perhaps the mixing table is the one that Deborah purchased
in 1766 at the sale she expedited on behalf of the estate of her deceased sister-
in-law, who died a mere six weeks after her husband, Peter, Benjamin Franklin's last surviving brother. A bill to Deborah reads, "To Goods bought at Mrs.
Mary Franklin's Vendue," and includes "a Marble Table" at £1.2.0. The high
chest was owned by descendants of Benjamin Franklin Bache and may be the
"large Cheste" that Deborah describes as being in Franklin's chamber, filled
with "all the writeings that was in your room down stairs."[33]

The gifts kept coming. Throughout his years in London, Franklin regularly mailed packages home filled with presents such as "a fine Piece of Pom-
pador Sattin . . . a Silk Negligee . . . a Gimcrack Corkscrew. " Some purchases
were made at the request of Sally or Deborah, while others were on Franklin's
own initiative. Sally, for example, wrote, "We have no plates or Dishes fit to
set before your Friends, and the Queens ware is thought very eligent here particularly the spriged. I just mention this as it would be much cheaper for you
to bring them than to get them here and you have them much handsomer." In

March 1769, Franklin was excited at describing a surprise purchase for Sally, "1/2 a Dozen Caudle Cups and Saucers of my Choice . . . they cost 3 Guineas, are in my Opinion great Beauties." These two-handled cups were an appropriate gift for his daughter, who was expecting her first child, because they were used for drinking "caudle," a warm spiced gruel often recommended for pregnant women.[34]

Among the English-made furnishings that Franklin purchased in London are several items that have descended in his family and are now in both public and private collections. These British purchases include a flat-top desk, several pieces of silver, and a variety of ceramics. The largest of these English furnishings is the so-called writing table, often now called a partner's desk. Franklin purchased the desk in 1772 from John Mayhew, a prominent London cabinetmaker and furniture designer, and used it in his lodgings in Craven Street and later in his library in his Philadelphia home at Franklin Court. The large, flat surface of the desk provided Franklin with a place to examine his large folios and to store his copy press, which was valued together with the desk in Franklin's inventory at £15 (fig. 4.30).[35]

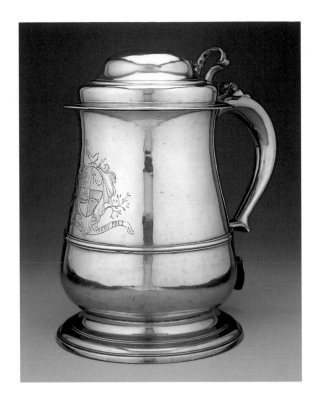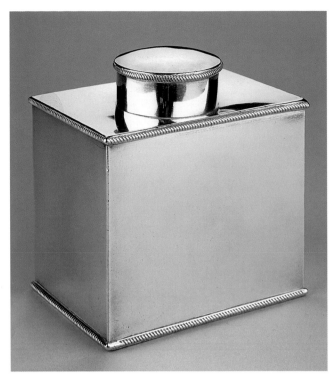

Fig. 4.31 (Left) Robert Gurney and Thomas Cook, Tankard, ca. 1750. Owned by Richard Bache, Jr., purchased by William Duane, then returned to the family of Richard Bache, Jr., by descent.

Fig. 4.32 Tea caddy, 1771. Descended in the family of Deborah Bache Duane.

Silver bought by Franklin in London includes a tankard, a tea caddy, and an inkstand (figs. 4.31–4.32). Now showing signs of heavy use, the tankard was purchased secondhand by Franklin from the silver left on the death of Alexander Macdonell, the 5th earl of Antrim, in 1755. The family faced serious financial losses during the following years and had to divest itself of many of its assets. With his letter of July 4, 1771, Franklin sent Deborah "two plated Canisters and a Sugar ditto, which I hope will be agreeable to you. I bought them lately from Sheffield."[36] Like most of Franklin's furnishings, the tankard and canisters were left to Sally and descended in her family. The inkstand, on the other hand, was a gift from Franklin to Polly Stevenson, his landlady's daughter, and remained in her family into the twentieth century. Made by London silversmiths Edward Aldridge, Sr., and John Stamper in 1758, the delicate inkstand consists of a gallery with four compartments, a silver-mounted glass inkwell, and a sander.

When a bitter Franklin returned to Philadelphia on November 9, 1775, fresh from his humiliation in the chambers of the British Privy Council, he arrived at a city preparing for war. The "sundry crates, containing his books, papers and household furniture, which were in his use when he lived in London, and which were imported for his own use and not for sale," were added to the rest of his furnishings that would be left in place should the family need to flee. As Franklin wrote to his son-in-law, "We have just receiv'd Advice of the burning of Falmouth Casco Bay; and are assur'd that Orders are come over to burn, ravage and destroy all the Sea Coast; such is the Government of the best of Princes! If the People of Philadelphia, to be more at their Ease in defending the City should think fit to remove their Families, and some of their Goods, do you after taking Care of Sally and the Children, remember to secure my Account Books and Writings which are in the Glass Desk and two Trunks in my Library. I hope too that the Library may be sav'd; but we must run all Risques, that being to bulky to be remov'd." His fears proved valid, for the house was occupied by the British in 1778. By that time, however, Franklin had been sent to France to represent American interests at the court of Louis XVI.[37]

Paris, 1776–85

Arriving in Paris on December 3, 1776, accompanied by his two grandsons, seven-year-old Benjamin Bache and sixteen-year-old William Temple Franklin, Benjamin Franklin soon found accommodations in "a fine House" in Passy, "situated in a neat Village, on high Ground, half a Mile from Paris, with a large Garden to walk in" (fig. 4.33). His residence from March 1777 to July 1785, the house was on the elegant estate of Jacques Donatien Le Ray de Chaumont, a financier who helped provide supplies for the American army. Called the Hôtel de Valentinois after a former owner, the estate was purchased in 1776 by "Monsieur de Chaumont," as he preferred to be called. Initially at no charge, Chaumont hosted Franklin and his entourage in a garden pavilion in the "basse cour"; after he became minister plenipotentiary Franklin moved to the main house, where he and his staff occupied the right wing. Throughout Franklin's stay, Chaumont's major-domo, M. Montaigne, oversaw the kitchen to the American guests' liking.[38]

Few furnishings remain from Franklin's time in Paris. Probably he purchased relatively little in the way of furniture, for no doubt Chaumont's house was furnished. What he needed he primarily rented from a *tapissier* from whom he leased furniture in three-month increments. An exception is a set of secondhand chairs, which he apparently purchased. These descended in the family of Polly Stevenson, who might have bought them at a sale of Franklin's personal effects.[39]

In August 1778, Louis Carrogis de Carmontelle drew a small ink, crayon, and watercolor portrait of Franklin, showing him seated in a rococo-style armchair (fig. 4.34). This amateur artist was a member of the household of the duc d'Orléans, where he served as professor of mathematics, librarian, dramatist, and stage designer. A letter suggests the day on which Franklin agreed to have his portrait painted. Following up on a previous invitation from Franklin, Madame Herbaut de Marcenay invited herself and others to dine at Franklin's house on August 30, 1778. Among the suggested guests was Carmontelle, who had already completed a portrait of Madame Marcenay and probably suggested doing Franklin's over dinner.[40]

Although Franklin's relaxed countenance in this portrait is in itself attractive and engaging, this view is all the more interesting because of the rococo chair on which Franklin sits next to the Constitution of Pennsylvania, a symbol of liberty with rich meaning for his French admirers. Many of Carmontelle's subjects—he made approximately five hundred portraits of eminent persons of his day, mostly in profile—were painted in a chair of this type, but Franklin owned a set of chairs that resembled the one in his picture (fig. 4.35).

Fig. 4.35 One of at least three English armchairs in the French style owned by Franklin, ca. 1765. Descended in the family of Polly Stevenson Hewson.

Made around 1765, the chairs were probably acquired by Franklin in London, where they were perhaps made by a French cabinetmaker or possibly by an Englishman working in the French style. Franklin may have brought the chairs to Paris, where they would have been appropriate for his apartment, although somewhat old-fashioned by French standards.[41]

As did his diplomatic colleagues Thomas Jefferson and John Adams, Franklin purchased a set of so-called Chantilly sprig pattern tea wares from the factory of Dihl and Guérhard shortly before he returned to Philadelphia. Franklin's hard-paste porcelain service is, in fact, an assemblage of patterns, all with the hallmark blue sprig but bearing a variety of embellishments: flowered

borders, gilt edges, and so forth. Established under the patronage of the five-year-old duc d'Angoulême, son of the comte d'Artois (brother of Louis XVI and the future Charles X of France), this factory (located on rue de Bondy) enjoyed "a leading position and considerable prosperity," most notably in reference to its wares decorated with blue, yellow, and green enameled cornflowers. Perhaps Franklin had met Antoine Guérhard, a Parisian burgher with ties to Germany, when in 1782 he presented a paper to the Académie des Sciences on the mining of cobalt in Saxony and Silesia for use in porcelain manufacture. A gift for his daughter Sally, the set (probably consisting of a teapot, matching cups and saucers, milk jug, and sugar bowl) descended in the family of Franklin's grandson William Bache and is now scattered among a number of public and private collections (fig. 4.36). Franklin also purchased a large earthenware dinner service in 1780 from expatriate British potters working in France who were selling their version of "Queens Ware."[42]

Another example of French porcelain acquired by Franklin in Paris is a small sprig-decorated porcelain spirit barrel, given to him by the comte d'Artois. The stand, resembling a Roman temple on wheels, reportedly was made by Franklin. Probably an early product of the porcelain factory at Faubourg Saint-Denis, a facility under the protection of the count, the spirit barrel

Fig. 4.37 Probably from the Faubourg Saint-Denis porcelain factory, Spirit barrel, ca. 1780. The so-called punch keg was a gift to Franklin from the comte D'Artois. It was given in 1875 to the National Museum (established during the Centennial as a shrine to the American Revolution) by "a descendant of the owner."

Fig. 4.38 François Joubert and François-Nicholas Rousseau, Spirit Lamp, ca. 1775–81. Descended in the family of Richard Bache, Jr.

is missing its spigot yet it still evokes Franklin's luxurious Parisian way of life (fig. 4.37).[43]

A final memento of Franklin's years in France is a silver spirit lamp and holder made around 1775 by two separate craftsmen: François Joubert made the round vessel, and François-Nicholas Rousseau created the legged stand (fig. 4.38). The spirit lamp is an accessory for the table, designed to keep a serving dish or plate of food warm. It consists of two separable elements: a covered container for liquid spirits with a hole for a projecting wick, which could be lighted to provide a low flame; and a stand or frame to hold the container of liquid. That Franklin understood the merits of such a contraption is evident in his description of the difficulties of eating at sea. "A spirit-lamp, with a blaze-pan, may enable you to cook some little things for yourself; such as a hash, a soup, &c."[44] Although some have suggested that he used this lamp to conduct experiments in his chambers at Passy, more likely it was a convenient way to warm up his late evening snack.

Philadelphia, 1785–90

Upon returning to Philadelphia after his latest (and final) service overseas, Franklin determined that his three-and-a-half-story house could not accommodate the many possessions he had accumulated abroad, nor was it large enough for his growing family, which now consisted of Sally and Richard Bache and their seven children. Describing his familial state of affairs to his sister "Jenny" (Jane Mecom) in Boston, he noted, "I have ordered an Addition to the House I live in, it being too small for our growing Family. There are a good many hands employ'd, and I hope to see it cover'd in before Winter. I propose to have in it a long Room for my Library and Instruments, with two good Bedchambers and two Garrets. The Library is to be even with the Floor of my old best Chamber: & the Story under it will for the present be employ'd only to hold Wood, but may be made into Rooms hereafter. This Addition is on the Side next the River.—I hardly know how to justify building a Library at an Age that will so soon oblige me to quit it; but we are apt to forget that we are grown old, and Building is an Amusement."[45]

Franklin had been denied the opportunity to witness the building of the original house; now with this addition at last he was able to supervise every detail in person, and when he died five years later these latest rooms were

Fig. 4.39 (Left) Armchair, ca. 1770. A gift from Catherine Wistar Bache (wife of William) to Dr. David Hosack, who gave the chair to the Literary and Philosophical Society of New York in January 1822.

Fig. 4.40 Library chair with folding steps, 1760–80. This ingenious chair may have been designed by Franklin.

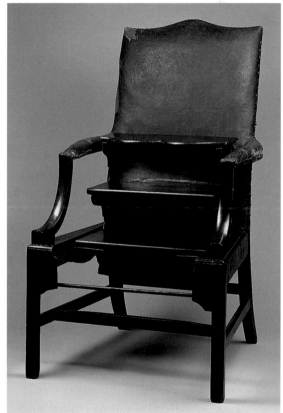

full of his favorite possessions: his vast library of books, his scientific instruments, his beloved glass armonica, and numerous comfortable chairs in the alcoves and near the desk. Since 1822 a mahogany armchair, probably purchased in Philadelphia, has been designated by Columbia University "The Library Chair of Dr. Benjamin Franklin" (fig. 4.39). Because of its relative size and mass, this chair would have been a suitable companion to Franklin's writing table as well as to his own considerable bulk.[46]

Infirm and often in pain, Franklin continued to conjure up conveniences that would assist daily living, including "an Instrument for taking down Books from high Shelves" and a library chair with a concealed ladder beneath the hinged seat. The latter may have worked for him on his stronger days, when he

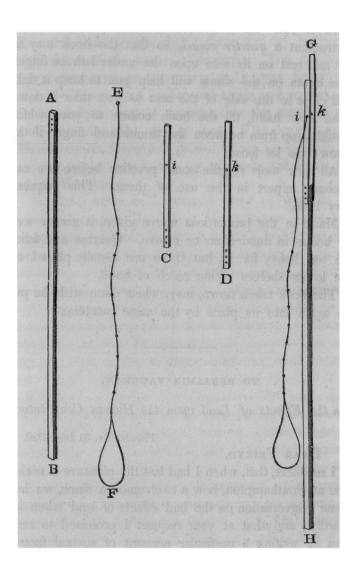

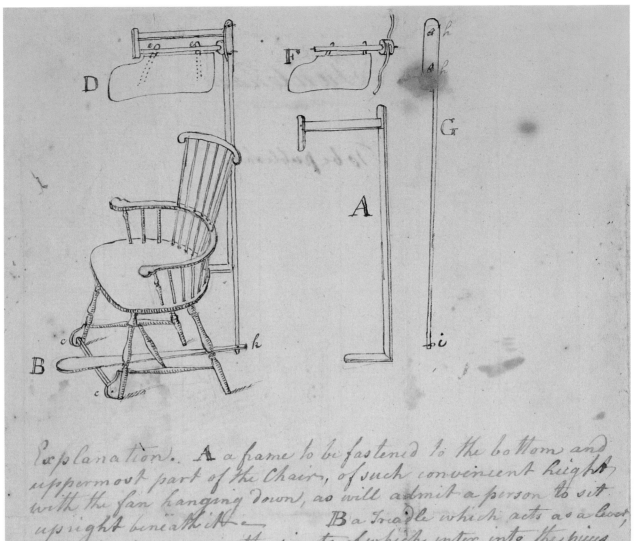

Explanation. A a frame to be fastened to the bottom and uppermost part of the Chair, of such convenient height, with the fan hanging down, as will admit a person to set upright beneath it.⸺ B a Treadle which acts as a lever, working by an axis, the pivots of which enter into the pieces c, c, fastened to the front legs of the Chair. D the fan, made of paste-board; to which are fastened two spring catches that go into mortices in the mooving axis at e, e. This axis has a pulley, to which are fastened two pieces of leather, to moove it in reverse directions, as may be better understood by the figure F, each piece of leather after being once turned round the pulley are fastened into the piece G at the holes h, h, and needs no other fastning to the frame above; at the bottom the end i, is hinged to the treadle B at the extremity k.

had the strength to move the chair as needed (fig. 4.40). But imagine Franklin's new library, with "Windows at each End, and lin'd with Books to the Ceiling, and one can well understand his need for such a contraption" as the long-arm pole (fig. 4.41). As he explained, "Old men find it inconvenient to mount a ladder or steps for that purpose, their heads being sometimes subject to giddinesses, and their activity, with the steadiness of their joints, being abated by age; besides the trouble of removing the steps every time a book is wanted from a different part of their library. For a remedy, I have lately made the following simple machine, which I call the Long Arm."[47]

In his final years, Franklin regularly received visitors at Franklin Court. While some met him outdoors, where he held court under "a very large Mulberry" tree, others had the privilege of visiting the new library, including the naturalist Manasseh Cutler, who wrote a detailed description of "the largest, and by far the best, private library in America." Cutler was astounded by the array of curiosities, including "a rolling press, for taking the copies of letters or any other writing. . . . It is an invention of his own, and extremely useful in many situations in life. He also showed us . . . his great armed chair, with rocker and a large fan placed over it, with which he fans himself, keeps off flies, etc., while he sits reading, with only a small motion of his foot"(fig. 4.42).[48]

A technophile his entire life, Franklin had long been interested in devices that simplified or enhanced living. He is credited, for example, with the introduction into America of the sabotière-style bathtub (one shaped like a lady's shoe), popular in France and mentioned in his famous commentary on the chess game Madame Brillon played entirely from her bath. And upon his return to Philadelphia he installed a special round "tepid bath" with spigots for hot and cold water and a newly designed heating unit. These were located in Franklin's "Bath room" along with fifteen pounds' worth of furniture.[49]

During the time he was presiding over the Constitutional Convention in 1787, George Washington described seeing "a Machine at Doctr. Franklins (called a mangle) for pressing, in place of Ironing, clothes from the wash. Which Machine from the facility with which it dispatches business is well calculated for Table cloths & such Articles as have not pleats & irregular foldings and would be very useful in all large families." Such devices had been patented in England by 1774; the mangle Washington saw was probably one that Franklin had brought home with him. And to assist himself as he grew weaker, Franklin installed a pulley device whereby he could unlock his bedroom door without getting out of bed. Furthermore, the doors of the chambers were "lined or edged with green baize, to prevent noise when shutting."[50]

When his addition was complete, Franklin wrote his sister Jane Mecom in Boston, describing the house and suggesting future alterations. "I forgot to mention, that there is no Staircase in the new Part of my Dwelling as it would have incommoded my Library Room. But knowing the Convenience of two Staircases in a large House, I shall recommend that one be made when I am gone & the Books taken away, which shall go up from the Cellar to the Garret; and that the Long Rooms be divided by Partitions each into two, whereby the Addition may serve to accommodate on occasion a distinct Family."[51] His optimistic foresight did not alter the fate of the house, however.

Shortly after Franklin's death, his daughter and her family moved out of Philadelphia. The Franklin Court mansion was subsequently rented out and then served successively as "a boarding house, the home of a female academy, a coffee house and hotel." Finally, in 1812, the house was razed to make room for a street and several much smaller houses. By this time the building was long since emptied of Franklin's furniture, some having gone to his daughter and grandchildren, others sold at public auction.[52]

For those few short years in Philadelphia, Franklin clearly cherished his home and furnishings as a symbol of how far he had come since his youth, when he lived in a two-room dwelling with his family of fourteen. In a postscript to his sister, Franklin reflected, "When I look at these Buildings, my dear Sister, and compare them with that in which our good Parents educated us, the Difference strikes me with Wonder; and fills me with humble Thankfulness to that divine Being who has graciously conducted my Steps, and prospered me in this strange Land to a degree that I could not rationally have expected, and can by no means conceive my self to have merited. I beg the Continuance of his Favour but submit to his Will[,] should a Reverse be determin'd."[53]

Chapter 5
Benjamin Franklin's Science
E. PHILIP KRIDER

Benjamin Franklin had extraordinary curiosity and a lifelong interest in "natural philosophy," or science, because it gave him pleasure to understand the laws of nature and because he thought that advances in science could lead to practical benefits for humankind. He created and disseminated new knowledge all his life, and he encouraged others to do the same. Franklin's many scientific contributions were in areas as diverse as health and medicine, geology, weather, oceanography, and electricity, and he invented or promoted practical devices ranging from the flexible catheter to bifocals to the lightning rod. Eventually, Franklin's reputation as a natural philosopher helped him in the diplomatic arena as well.

Benjamin Franklin was very interested in health, and he wrote often on that topic. In *Poor Richard's Almanack* for 1742 he advised those who would like to "enjoy a long Life, a healthy Body, and a vigorous Mind": "Eat and drink such an exact Quantity as the Constitution of thy Body allows of, in reference to the Services of the Mind," and " Eat for Necessity, not Pleasure, for Lust knows not where Necessity ends," and in the *Almanack* for 1747 he noted, "We are not so sensible of the greatest Health as of the least Sickness." Franklin also wrote about the importance of regular exercise, and he was particularly fond of swimming. He swam all his life; when he was young, he devised hand-held paddles and special sandals to help propel his body through the water. Once he even used a kite to pull himself across a pond. On his first trip to London, Franklin taught swimming and almost became a full-time swimming instructor; later, he wrote instructions to help others learn how to swim (fig. 5.1).[1]

Franklin wrote a pamphlet on *The Art of Procuring Pleasant Dreams* and works on the causes and cures of common colds, vaccinations against smallpox, and treatment for the gout. He even came up with a novel way of bathing —sitting naked in cold air while reading or writing letters. In 1752, to help treat his brother's kidney stones, Franklin designed a flexible catheter, an instrument that was the first of its kind in America. He was also among the first to document the symptoms and dangers of lead poisoning.[2]

As Franklin grew older, his eyesight worsened, and eventually he needed glasses. In 1785 he described why and how he invented bifocal lenses (fig. 5.2): "I imagine it will be found pretty generally true, that the same Convexity of Glass, through which a Man sees clearest and best at the Distance proper for Reading, is not the best for greater Distances. I therefore had formerly two Pair of Spectacles, which I shifted occasionally, as in travelling I sometimes read, and often wanted to regard the Prospects. Finding this Change troublesome, and not always sufficiently ready, I had the Glasses cut, and half of each kind associated in the same Circle, thus, [Illustration Inserted] By this means, as I wear my Spectacles constantly, I have only to move my Eyes up or down, as

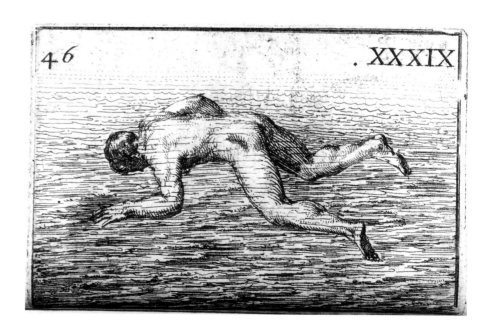

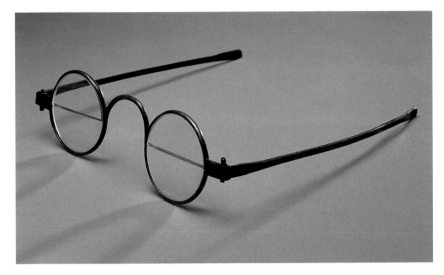

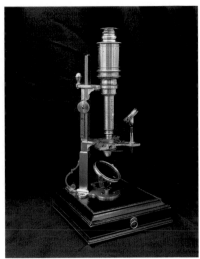

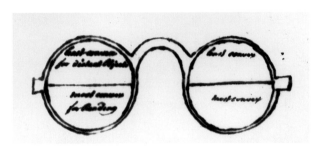

I want to see distinctly far or near, the proper glasses being always ready" (fig. 5.3).[3]

Franklin was insatiably curious about the world around him on all spatial scales. In 1751 he published a description of how a microscope "opened to us . . . a World utterly unknown to the Ancients," and how common materials looked under high magnification (fig. 5.4). His descriptions illustrate the compact, entertaining style of Franklin's writing:

> Flies are found by the Microscope to be produced from Eggs laid by the Mothers, from whence they are hatched in the Form of Maggots, or small Worms, which are afterwards transformed into Aurelias, and these into perfect Flies. . . . They have a great Number of Eyes fixed to their Heads, so that they see on all Sides around them, without turning their Heads or Eyes. . . . [T]he Stings of Moths and Bees appear to be Instruments finished to the highest Perfection; their Points, and saw-like Teeth, being perfectly polished and sharp. . . . By the help of the Microscope, the innumerable and inconceivably minute Animal-

Fig. 5.5 James Trenchard after William Bartram, Franklinia alatamaha, *ca. 1786. The discovery of this plant was published in Bartram's Travels Through North & South Carolina, Georgia, East & West Florida, 1791. Discovered along the Altamaha River (the correct spelling) in Georgia in 1765, saved from extinction, and named in honor of Franklin, this tree was among the most famous of John and William Bartram's botanical discoveries.*

cules in various Fluids are discovered. . . . In the Melt of a single Codfish ten Times more living Creatures are contained, than the Inhabitants of Europe, Asia, Africa, and America."[4]

Benjamin Franklin liked plants and understood the fundamental importance of agriculture for the economy of North America. He was a good friend of John Bartram, a naturalist and explorer who was a prominent early American botanist. Franklin communicated many of Bartram's discoveries to England, and Bartram and his son William named a new tree that they found in Georgia in Franklin's honor, the *Franklinia alatamaha* (fig. 5.5).[5] Bartram gathered many new and unusual plants, and when he could he grew specimens in his botanical garden and nursery in Philadelphia. He also sold plants from North America to collectors in England, such as Peter Collinson, a Fellow of the Royal Society of London who would later play an important role in communicating Franklin's experiments and observations on electricity to the Royal Society and elsewhere (fig. 5.6). John Bartram's fossils fascinated Franklin, and Franklin supported Bartram's expedition to remote areas of New York and Pennsylvania to find new specimens (fig. 5.7).

In 1760 Franklin used logic and known scientific principles to speculate about the origin of fossils on geologic timescales in ways that anticipated the

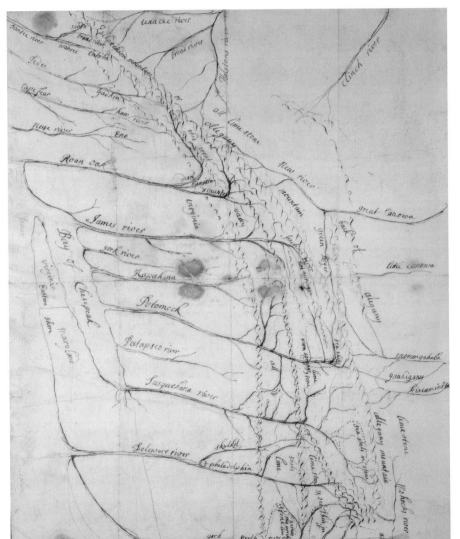

Fig. 5.6 (Above) J. S. Miller, Portrait print of Peter Collinson, 1770. Collinson, a prominent London merchant, was the Library Company's agent in London from 1732 on. He helped Franklin set up the American Philosophical Society's library and furnished him with tracts on electricity and electrical equipment. Collinson communicated Franklin's letters on electricity to the Royal Society, and later published them for the benefit of the learned world.

Fig. 5.7 John Bartram, Map of the Allegheny Ridge, ca. 1745–47. Bartram presented this map, along with several fossils, to Franklin, who inscribed it "Mr. Bartram's Map very curious."

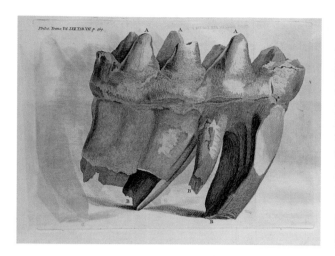

Fig. 5.8 (Left) Illustration of a mastodon tooth fossil from Philosophical Transactions of the Royal Society, *vol. 57, pt. 1, 1768. Mastodon bone fossils were collected in Big Bone Lick, Kentucky, near the Ohio River, by George Groghan, an Indian agent and land speculator. In 1767 he sent fossils to Franklin and the earl of Shelburne.*

Fig. 5.9 Mastodon tooth fossil. Found at Franklin Court close to the ruins of Franklin's mansion, this tooth matches the description of a "large pronged" tooth sent to Franklin by George Groghan.

work of Charles Lyell, the founder of modern geology, in the nineteenth century: "It is evident from the quantities of sea shells, and the bones and teeth of fishes found in high lands, that the sea has formerly covered them. Then, either the sea has been higher than it now is, and has fallen away from those high lands; or they have been lower than they are, and were lifted up out of the water to their present height, by some internal mighty force, such as we still feel some remains of, when whole continents are moved by earth-quakes." After mastodon bones and teeth (figs. 5.8–5.9) were found in Ohio, Franklin commented, "It is remarkable, that elephants now inhabit naturally only hot countries where there is no winter, and yet these remains are found in a winter country; and it is no uncommon thing to find elephants' tusks in Siberia, in great quantities, when their rivers overflow, and wash away the earth, though Siberia is still more a wintery country than that on the Ohio; which looks as if the earth had anciently been in another position, and the climates differently placed from what they are at present."[6]

Weather and climate were important factors in colonial America because unexpected storms or outbreaks of freezing temperatures could be disastrous for people and agriculture. Franklin wrote long-term predictions of weather and climate and reproduced numerous weather proverbs in *Poor Richard* and his newspaper, the *Pennsylvania Gazette*. In about 1751 he wrote *Physical and Meteorological Observations, Conjectures, and Suppositions*, in which he used scientific reasoning to explain one of the most important factors in controlling large-scale wind patterns—the rotation of the earth: "The earth turning on its axis in about twenty-four hours, the equatorial parts must move about fifteen miles in each minute. In Northern and Southern latitudes this motion is gradually less to the Poles, and there nothing."[7] Now, if a parcel of air starts at the equator and moves northward, following the curved surface of the earth, the distance between that parcel and the vertical north-south axis of the earth's rotation will become smaller, and because of this the speed of the air to the east must increase in order to conserve angular momentum. This effect is like that achieved by twirling ice skaters who bring their hands in toward their bodies to speed up and push their hands out to slow down. Similarly, if an air parcel moves from north to south along a line of longitude, the distance from the axis will increase, and the parcel will accelerate to the west. Today these accelerations are known as the "Coriolis effect." Franklin knew that air will tend to rise above a warm surface and sink above a cool one, so he could speculate about the form of large-scale circulations of air between the equator and the poles and the causes of the easterly trade winds. Today we know that the earth's general circulation is more complicated than Franklin's model, but his basic suppositions were correct.

On a day when Franklin wanted to observe an eclipse of the moon in Philadelphia, an intense storm arrived with damaging winds from the northeast, and the clouds blocked his view for two or three days. Later, he received a newspaper account from Boston (about four hundred miles northeast of Philadelphia) that described the eclipse in detail, and a letter from his brother in Boston verified that the eclipse had been visible there *before* the storm arrived in Philadelphia. Franklin checked newspaper reports and found that the storm actually began in the southern colonies and was stronger there, then moved to the northeast even though the winds near the ground were going in the opposite direction. Franklin explained this remarkable finding with the following hypothesis: "Thus to produce our North-East storms, I suppose some great heat and rarefaction of the air in or about the Gulph of Mexico; the air thence rising has its place supplied by the next more northern, cooler, and therefore denser and heavier, air; that, being in motion, is followed by the next more northern air, &c. &c. in a successive current, to which current our coast and inland ridge of mountains give the direction of North-East, as they lie N.E. and S.W." Franklin's hypothesis anticipated thermal theories of cyclone formation developed in the nineteenth century.[8]

Franklin was fascinated by accounts of whirlwinds, waterspouts, and tornadoes, and he once followed a dust devil for miles on horseback to learn more about its characteristics. He summarized his thoughts on the causes of whirlwinds in 1753, using as an illustration the suggestion that if a tract of land were receiving more heat from the sun than its surroundings, the air near it would become less dense and "the Consequence of this should be, as I imagine that the heated lighter Air being press'd on all Sides must ascend, and the heavier descend; and as this Rising cannot be in all Parts or the whole Area of the Tract at once, for that would leave too extensive a Vacuum, the Rising will begin precisely in that Column that happens to be the lightest or most rarified; and the warm Air will flow horizontally from all Points to this Column, where the several Currents meeting and joining to rise, a Whirl is naturally formed, in the same Manner as a Whirl is formed in the Tub of Water by the descending fluid flowing from all Sides of the Tub to the Hole in the Center." Franklin's explanation of this phenomenon is still valid today, and in the nineteenth century Herman von Helmholtz was able to describe this behavior in mathematical terms.[9]

In 1768, while Franklin was deputy postmaster general for North America, his correspondents in England asked him why ships carrying the mail took longer to go from England to North America than the other way. In response, he noted one important factor: the Atlantic Ocean has a regular, large-scale circulation that brings warm water north from southern latitudes along the east coast of North America, then east to the British Isles, and eventually south along the west coast of Europe. The speed of this "Gulph Stream" is

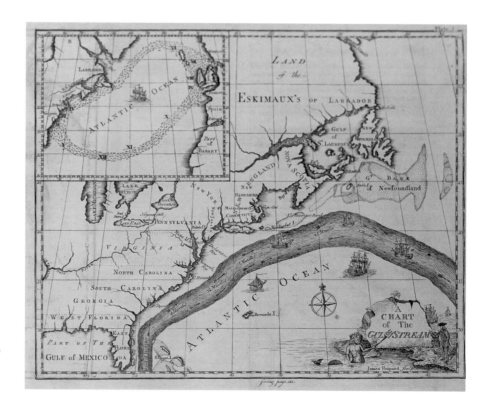

Fig. 5.10 James Poupard after Georges-Louis Le Rouge, A Chart of The Gulf Stream, from Benjamin Franklin, "Maritime Observations," in Transactions of the American Philosophical Society 2, 1786.

Fig. 5.11 Charles Willson Peale, Portrait of David Rittenhouse, 1772. An astronomer and maker of clocks and mathematical instruments, Rittenhouse became, with Franklin, a central figure in the intellectual life of mid-eighteenth-century Philadelphia.

sixty to seventy miles per day, and even though the Gulf Stream had been discovered by Spanish explorers, it was not well known in England. Franklin, however, knew that American whaling captains used the Gulf Stream to optimize their catches and minimize their travel time to and from port; therefore he asked his cousin Timothy Folger, a Nantucket sea captain, to make a map showing the dimensions, course, and strength of the Gulf Stream, and in 1769, he published this together with instructions on how to avoid the opposing current when sailing from Europe to America. The water temperature is higher in the Gulf Stream than in the surrounding ocean, and when he crossed the Atlantic from England to America in 1775, and to and from France in 1776 and in 1785, Franklin systematically measured the ocean temperature and made weather observations, which he published in 1786 (fig. 5.10).[10]

While Franklin was en route from England to Philadelphia in 1762, his ship stopped in Madeira, where he refilled one of his sea lamps with oil. The bottom third of the glass had water with oil floating on top of it, and Franklin noticed that the interface between the water and the oil "was in great commotion, rising and falling in irregular waves, which continued during the whole evening." In 1783 he summarized a long-standing interest in what happens when oil is poured over water and described his attempts to still wind-blown waves with oil: "and there the Oil tho' not more that a Tea Spoonful produced an instant Calm, over a Space several yards square, which spread amazingly, and extended itself gradually till it reached the Lee Side, making all that Quarter of the Pond, perhaps half an Acre, as smooth as a Looking Glass." Franklin performed this experiment to amuse his friends, but he also wanted to know why there was a "sudden, wide and forcible Spreading of a Drop of Oil on the Face of the Water" and "to understand whence it arises." In these experiments Franklin came surprisingly close to determining the size of the oil molecules, even though the molecular theory of matter had not yet been formulated. It was not until the late nineteenth century that Lord Rayleigh and

Fig. 5.12 Astronomical transit telescope, ca. 1769. David Rittenhouse built this instrument to use during his observation of the transit of Venus in 1769.

Fig. 5.13 Unknown artist, Joseph Priestley, L.L.D. F.R.S. *(portrait print), 1782. A pioneer in electrical science and chemistry, Priestley was Franklin's protégé and close friend in London; their correspondence continued until Franklin's death.*

Agnes Pockels pioneered the field of surface physics, using experiments similar to Franklin's.[11]

In 1766 Franklin traveled to Germany with his friend Sir John Pringle, a future president of the Royal Society of London. While they were in Holland, they noticed that their canal boat was moving slower than usual, and the boatman told them that the horses had to pull harder because the water level was low, even though the boat was not yet touching the bottom of the canal. Franklin realized that there must be a reason for the extra drag, and he traced it to the fact that as the boat moved forward through the water, the water displaced by the boat must also move back through the narrow space between the boat and the walls of the canal. England was then in the process of building a large

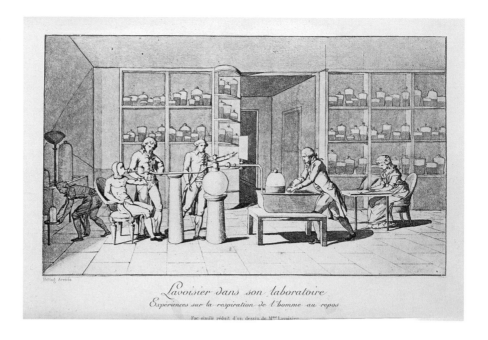

Fig. 5.14 V. Vitold Rola Piekarski, Lavoisier dans son laboratoire, *1888. Antoine Lavoisier is considered the founder of modern chemistry. The experiment being shown involves human respiration.*

number of canals, so Franklin conducted experiments with a model boat in a trough of water using different depths and measuring the time it took the boat to cross a known distance with a constant force. The results of this experiment showed that there was significantly less drag in deeper water, and he published the findings in the 1769 edition of his *Experiments and Observations.*[12]

In June 1783, while Franklin was in Paris leading the peace negotiations that ended the American Revolution, a large volcano erupted in Iceland and produced a catastrophic amount of air pollution over Iceland and much of northern Europe. The pollution took the form of a blue haze or dry fog that persisted for several months. Franklin published a description of this "constant Fog" and its effects on the weather, and then suggested two possible causes, meteorites and (correctly) volcanoes. The year 1783 came to be known as "the year without a summer" in Europe. The effects of the volcanic fog killed 24 percent of the people in Iceland and 75 percent of the livestock, and created economic hardships throughout the region. Today volcanic eruptions and meteorites are widely recognized as having important effects on weather and climate.[13]

Franklin also studied astronomy, and among the phenomena that were of particular interest in the eighteenth century were the transits of Mercury and Venus across the disk of the sun. The British astronomer Edmond Halley had shown that if the precise times that the front and rear edges of Venus enter and exit the disk of the sun (two times at ingress and two at egress) are measured at widely separated (and known) locations, these times can be used to determine the angle that would be subtended by Earth if it were viewed from the center of the sun. This angle or "solar parallax" can in turn be used to compute the distance from the Earth to the sun, or the astronomical unit, a fundamental parameter in astronomy. Before the transit of Mercury in 1753, Franklin was among the first to distribute information to observers in the American colonies, and before the transits of Venus in 1761 and 1769, Franklin assisted James

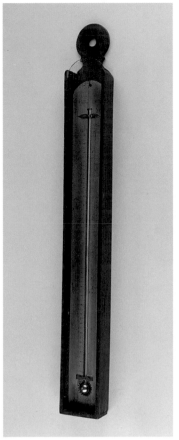

Fig. 5.15 (Above) Edward Nairne, Thermometer, ca. 1760. Franklin bought this and other scientific instruments from Nairne, a leading London instrument maker.

Fig. 5.16 George Adams, Double-acting pneumatic air pump, ca. 1740–70. The air pump was commonly used in scientific experiments to remove air from a container to show the effects of air pressure or to pump air into a container to show the effects of pressure higher than normal. Franklin's pump was made by George Adams, the Mathematical Instrument Maker to His Royal Highness the Prince of Wales, later King George III.

Bowdoin, John Winthrop, and others in acquiring apparatus to observe and measure transits. In 1761, Winthrop, a distinguished professor at Harvard, led an expedition to Saint Johns, Newfoundland, to observe the transit of Venus, and in 1769, David Rittenhouse, a talented instrument maker and surveyor, made careful observations in Philadelphia (fig. 5.11). Rittenhouse's measurements were the best, and for this work he constructed his own transit telescope (fig. 5.12), equal-altitude instrument, and precise clock.[14]

While he was in London, Franklin actively participated in meetings of the Royal Society, and when he was in Paris he attended meetings of the Académie des Sciences. At such meetings and elsewhere, Franklin met many of the leading Enlightenment scholars. Franklin could recognize outstanding ability in others, and he assisted or encouraged many of these scholars in their work. In England he helped the young Joseph Priestley write *The History and Present State of Electricity* (1767); Priestley then went on to discover oxygen and several other important gases, and developed techniques for manufacturing carbonated water (fig. 5.13). Franklin corresponded with Jan Ingenhousz, physician to the court of Austria, who extended some of Priestley's work and independently discovered photosynthesis, the process whereby living plants convert carbon dioxide into oxygen in the presence of sunlight. While he was in Paris, Franklin befriended many scholars, including Antoine Lavoisier and his wife, Marie-Anne. Antoine Lavoisier later showed that mass is conserved in chemical reactions, and today he is viewed as the father of modern chemistry (fig. 5.14).

Benjamin Franklin was interested in scientific instruments such as the thermometer and the air pump, which he regularly purchased from British makers, and he enjoyed making scientific measurements (figs. 5.15 and 5.16). He was also talented at making things, so it should not be surprising that he became a well-known inventor. When Franklin was just starting out in business as a printer in Philadelphia, he published *A Modest Enquiry into the Nature and Necessity of a Paper-Currency* anonymously; shortly thereafter he was asked to print paper money for the government of New Jersey. In order to do this job, he "contriv'd a Copper-Plate Press for it, the first that had been seen in the Country." Later he developed techniques for printing paper currency using impressions of tree leaves to minimize forgeries.[15]

In 1744 Franklin published *An Account Of the New Invented Pennsylvanian Fire-Places*, which detailed how to construct a wood-burning stove that would provide more heat with less fuel (fig. 5.17). The design was clever but was not

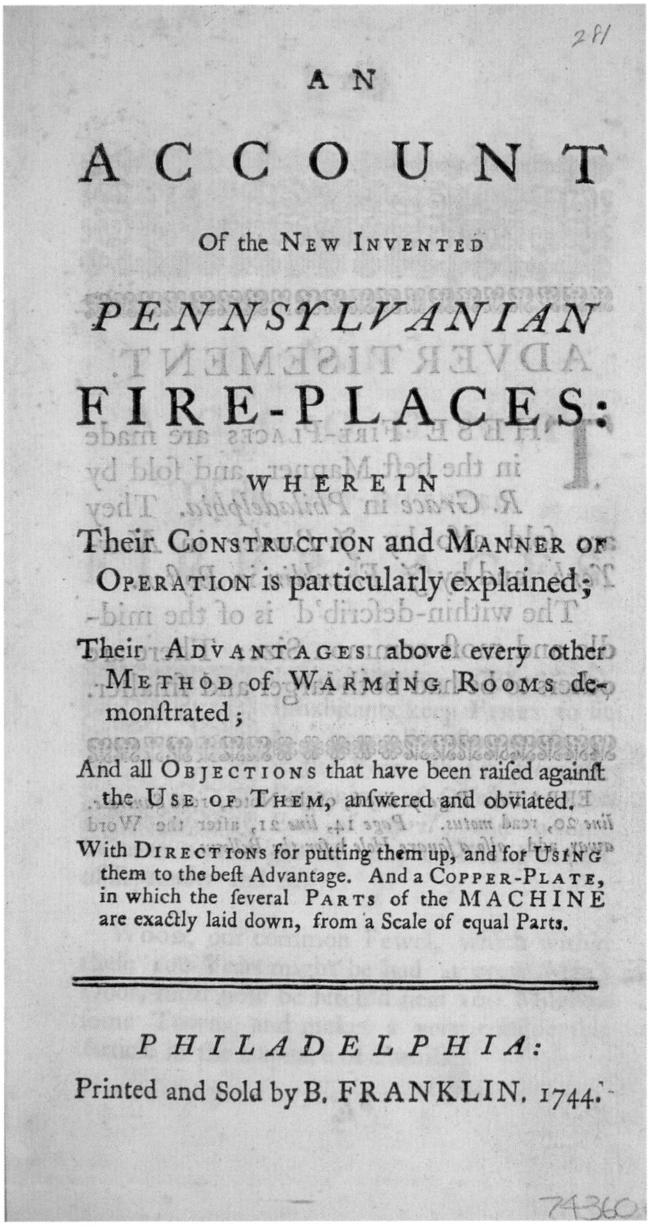
AN

ACCOUNT

Of the NEW INVENTED

PENNSYLVANIAN

FIRE-PLACES:

WHEREIN

Their CONSTRUCTION and MANNER OF OPERATION is particularly explained;

Their ADVANTAGES above every other METHOD of WARMING ROOMS demonſtrated;

And all OBJECTIONS that have been raiſed againſt the USE OF THEM, anſwered and obviated.

With DIRECTIONS for putting them up, and for USING them to the beſt Advantage. And a COPPER-PLATE, in which the ſeveral PARTS of the MACHINE are exactly laid down, from a Scale of equal Parts.

PHILADELPHIA:

Printed and Sold by B. FRANKLIN, 1744.

Fig. 5.17 Front page of Benjamin Franklin, An Account Of the New Invented Pennsylvanian Fire-Places . . . , *1744. Franklin printed this tract to explain and promote his efficient "Franklin Stove."*

widely adopted, apparently because of deficiencies in venting the smoke. Later Franklin gave considerable thought to heating technology, and he performed experiments which demonstrated that metals (such as lead) conduct heat better than insulators (like dry wood). He also showed that dark colors absorb the heat in sunlight more readily than light colors. In a letter to Ingenhousz in 1785, Franklin asked, "What is it then which makes a *Smoky Chimney,* that is,

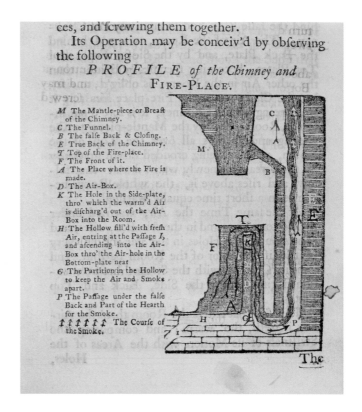

ces, and screwing them together.

Its Operation may be conceiv'd by observing the following

PROFILE of the Chimney and FIRE-PLACE.

M The Mantle-piece or Breast of the Chimney.
C The Funnel.
B The false Back & Closing.
E True Back of the Chimney.
T Top of the Fire-place.
F The Front of it.
A The Place where the Fire is made.
D The Air-Box.
K The Hole in the Side-plate, thro' which the warm'd Air is discharg'd out of the Air-Box into the Room.
H The Hollow fill'd with fresh Air, entring at the Passage *I*, and ascending into the Air-Box thro' the Air-hole in the Bottom-plate near
G The Partition in the Hollow to keep the Air and Smoke apart.
P The Passage under the false Back and Part of the Hearth for the Smoke.
↑↑↑↑↑↑ The Course of the Smoke.

The

a Chimney which instead of conveying up all the Smoke, discharges a part of it into the room, offending the eyes and damaging the furniture?" He then described nine possible causes of this problem and the ways to fix each of them. Although Rittenhouse and others improved Franklin's stove design, today most free-standing metal fireplaces are termed Franklin stoves (fig. 5.18).[16]

Franklin was appointed postmaster of Philadelphia in 1737 and deputy postmaster general for North America in 1753. Because the British colonies were growing rapidly, it was important that the postmaster understand postal operations and arrange the post offices and routes in ways that minimized the cost. To aid in this effort, Franklin devised a three-wheel odometer to measure the length of post roads (fig. 5.19). Using a similar idea, he also designed a three-wheel clock that was later manufactured by James Ferguson in London but credited to Franklin. This clock had minute and second hands, but the hour hand went completely around once every four hours rather than every twelve (fig. 5. 20), on the assumption that most people could estimate the time to within four hours from their daily activities or the position of the sun.[17]

In 1736 Franklin was appointed clerk of the Pennsylvania Assembly. As clerk he could not take part in the debates, "which were often so unentertain-

Fig. 5.19 (Left) Odometer, ca. 1763. To help him measure the length of postal roads and make them more efficient, Franklin may have designed this odometer; he fitted it to the wheel of his carriage to measure the distance during his inspection of post offices in 1763; the total miles clocked on the odometer amounted to 1,600.

Fig. 5.20 J. Lodge, Diagrams of a three-wheel clock from James Ferguson, Select Mechanical Exercises: Showing How to Construct Different Clocks, Orreries, and Sun-Dials, on Plain and Easy Principles, 2d ed., 1778. Designed by Franklin and manufactured by Ferguson in London, this twenty-four-hour, three-wheel clock was much simpler than other clock designs.

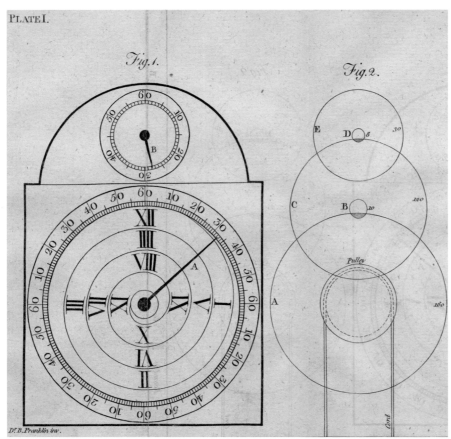

Fig. 5.21 Benjamin Franklin, Magic square, ca. 1765. Franklin claimed this sixteen-by-sixteen square was the "most magically magical of any magic square ever made by any magician."

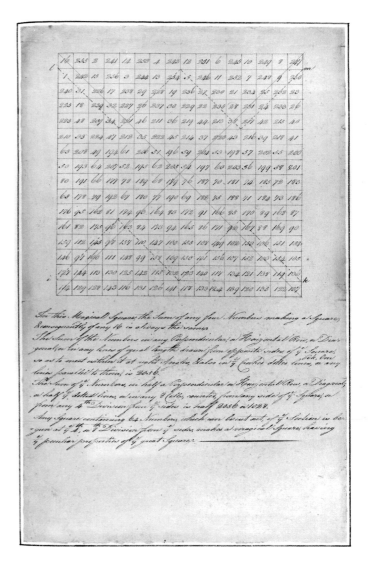

ing, that I was induc'd to amuse myself with making magic Squares, or Circles, or any thing to avoid Weariness." Figure 5.21 is an example of one such square that contains consecutive numbers, no two of which are the same; it is constructed so that the sums of all the numbers in each row, column, and diagonal are 2,056. Franklin also noted another special property of this sixteen by sixteen square, namely, any four by four square hole "being cut in a piece of paper of such a size as to take in and shew through it, just 16 of the little squares, when laid on the greater square, the sum of the 16 numbers so appearing through the hole, wherever it was placed on the greater square, should likewise make 2056." Franklin allowed "this square of 16 to be the most magically magical of any magic square ever made by any magician." The magic circles in figure 5.22 contain numbers from 12 to 75, and the sum of all the numbers within each circle and along each radial is 360. When his friend James Logan, the mayor of Philadelphia, asked Franklin whether making magic squares had any practical use, he replied that the amusement might not be

Fig. 5.22 *Benjamin Franklin*, A Magic Circle of Circles, *ca. 1765.*

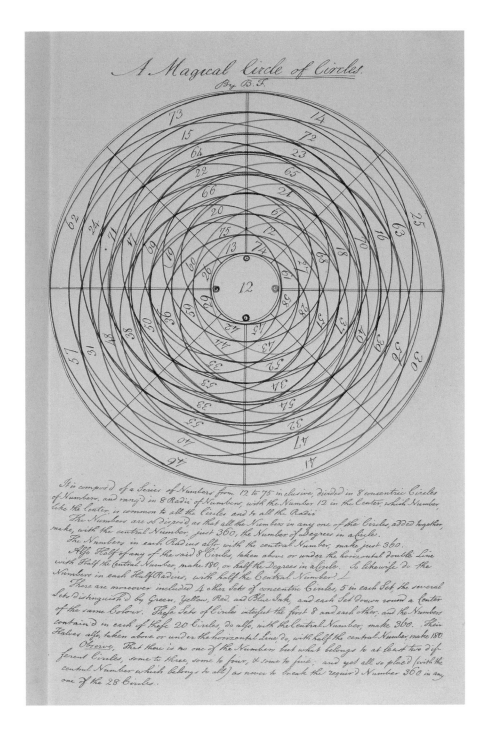

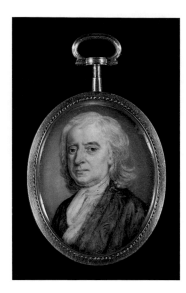

Fig. 5.23 After John Vanderbank, Miniature portrait of Isaac Newton, after 1725. When Newton died, Franklin (as Poor Richard) called him the "prince of astronomers and philosophers."

altogether useless "if it produces by practice an habitual readiness and exactness in mathematical disquisitions, which readiness may, on many occasions, be of real use."[18]

The Philadelphia experiments and observations on electricity are good examples of how adopting a systematic, scientific method, such as the one Isaac Newton described in the *Opticks,* can lead to significant discoveries (fig. 5.23). This work also illustrates how fundamental, curiosity-driven research can lead to significant practical benefits. Franklin's method started with a question, which he would investigate through careful experimentation. Next, he would formulate hypotheses and conjectures about the way nature behaves, and he would test these by making predictions and further experiments. If necessary, he would revise a hypothesis to reflect the results of the experiments, and the process would continue until what started as a conjecture became a principle or law that could be communicated to and tested by others. As we have seen, Franklin had excellent powers of observation and experimental skills, and he could communicate his observations in a concise, entertaining style. The Philadelphia experiments on electricity led to the application of tall, grounded rods for lightning protection, and they also represent the beginning of modern physics.[19]

Franklin and his colleagues, principally Ebenezer Kinnersley, Thomas Hopkinson (fig. 5.24), and Philip Syng, Jr., began experimenting with static electricity in 1746 after they saw some electrical demonstrations and parlor tricks that were then popular in Europe. They received apparatus from Peter Collinson, and instructions on how to use it came from an article published in *The Gentleman's Magazine.*[20]

The first Philadelphia experiments were described in five letters that Franklin sent to Collinson between 1747 and 1750 and that Collinson communicated to the Royal Society. In April 1751 Collinson published these letters in a small (eighty-six-page) pamphlet entitled *Experiments and Observations on Electricity, made at Philadelphia in America, by Mr. Benjamin Franklin, and Communicated in several letters to Mr. P. Collinson, of London, F.R.S.* (fig. 5.25). Supplements were added in 1753 and 1754, and the work was soon translated into French, German, and Italian.

In his first letter Franklin described "the wonderful Effect of Points, both in *drawing* off and *throwing* off the Electrical Fire." He showed that the effects of point discharges are seen quickly over large distances, that sharp points work better than blunt points, that metal points work better than dry wood, and that the pointed object should be touching something (or grounded) in or-

Fig. 5.24 Robert Feke, *Portrait of Thomas Hopkinson*, 1746. *A collaborator in electrical experiments with Franklin, Hopkinson devised a series of experiments to show the "Power of Points"—the ability of pointed objects to both "draw off" and "throw off" electricity. Franklin's interest in these phenomena led to the development of the lightning rod.*

Fig. 5.25 Title page of Benjamin Franklin, Experiments and Observations on Electricity . . . , *1751. In 1751 the British merchant and naturalist Peter Collinson brought several of Franklin's letters about his electrical experiments before the Royal Society and arranged for them to be published by Edward Cave.*

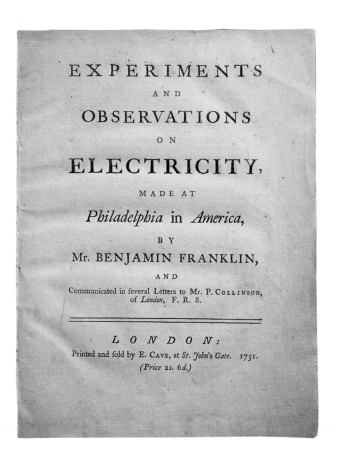

der to obtain the maximum draw effect (fig. 5.26). Next, Franklin introduced the idea that rubbing glass with leather does not actually create electricity (fig. 5.27); rather, at the instant of friction, the glass simply takes some "Electrical Fire" out of the leather and leaves a deficiency behind. Whatever amount is added to the glass, an equal amount is lost by the leather. The terms *plus* and *minus* were used to describe these electrical states; the glass was assumed to be electrified *positively* and the rubbing material *negatively*. Franklin's ideas that there are two states of electricity, positive and negative, and that charge is never created or destroyed but merely transferred from one place to another were profound, and today this principle is known in physics as the "conservation of electric charge."[21]

In his second letter, Franklin started with the concept of equal positive and negative charges, then posited that glass is a perfect insulator. These assumptions enabled him to explain the electrical behavior of a Leyden jar, the first electrical capacitor, and predict its behavior in further experiments (fig. 5.28). "So wonderfully are these two States of Electricity, the plus and minus combined and balanced in this miraculous Bottle!"[22]

In his third letter, Franklin began to use terms like *charging* and *discharging* in describing the action of a Leyden jar, and he noted the importance of grounding when charging and discharging the jar. He also showed that the electricity in such a device is stored entirely in the glass and not on the conductors inside and outside the jar (fig. 5.29). He described how several Leyden jars could be charged in series with the same effort as charging one by hooking them together, and he constructed an *"Electrical Battery"* using panes of window glass sandwiched between thin lead plates; he then discharged them together so that they provided the "Force of all the Plates of Glass at once thro' the Body of any Animal forming the Circle with them."[23]

In his fourth letter, Franklin began to apply his knowledge of electricity

Fig. 5.26 (Left) Electrical apparatus, ca. 1742–47. Franklin used this apparatus to generate static electricity for his experiments; his grandson Benjamin Franklin Bache gave it to the Library Company of Philadelphia in 1792. The electricity was drawn off the glass sphere by metallic points.

Fig. 5.27 Glass tube for generating static electricity, ca. 1747. Peter Collinson sent this tube to Franklin.

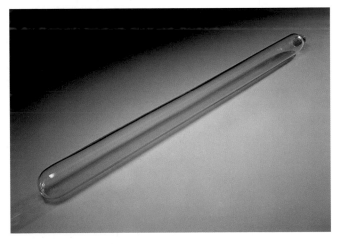

Fig. 5.28 (Left) Bells attached to a Leyden jar capacitor, late eighteenth century. The bells ring whenever the Leyden jar capacitor is charged with electricity.

Fig. 5.29 "Electrical Battery" of Leyden jars, ca. 1760–69. Franklin connected numerous jars together to increase the amount of electricity in his experiments.

to lightning by introducing the concept of the *sparking* or *striking distance*. If two gun barrels that are electrified "will strike at two Inches Distance, and make a loud Snap; to what great a Distance may 10,000 Acres of Electrified Cloud strike and give its Fire, and how loud must be that Crack!" Based on his previous observations of the "Power of Points," Franklin then speculated that if an electrified cloud passes over a region, it might draw electricity from, and discharge electricity to, high hills and trees, lofty towers, spires, masts of ships, chimneys, and the like. This supposition led to practical advice for remaining safe from lightning that is still valid today: it is dangerous to take shelter under an isolated tree during a thunderstorm; it is better to crouch in an open field because there the chances of a nearby strike will be lower and one's clothing will tend to be wet, which will help keep the current outside the body. Franklin's analogy was "a wet Rat cannot be kill'd by the exploding Electrical Bottle, when a dry Rat may."[24]

In his fifth letter, Franklin attempted to explain the power of points in fundamental terms. He noted that discharges between smooth or blunt conductors occur with a "stroke and crack," whereas sharp points discharge silently and produce large effects at greater distances. He then described what he termed a "Law of Electricity, That Points as they are more or less acute, both draw on and throw off the Electrical Fluid with more or less Power, and at greater or less Distances, and in larger or smaller Quantities in the same Time." Given his interest in lightning and the effects of pointed conductors, it was a short step to the lightning rod: "I say, if these Things are so, may not the Knowledge of this Power of Points be of Use to Mankind; in preserving Houses, Churches, Ships, etc. from the Stroke of Lightning; by Directing us to fix on the highest Parts of those Edifices upright Rods of Iron, made sharp as a Needle and gilt to prevent Rusting, and from the Foot of those Rods a Wire down the outside of the Building into the Ground; or down round one of the Shrouds of a Ship and down her Side, till it reach'd the Water? Would not these pointed Rods probably draw the Electrical Fire silently out of a Cloud before it came nigh enough to strike, and thereby secure us from that most sudden and terrible Mischief!"[25]

Clearly, Franklin's initial supposition was that the effects of silent discharges from one or more sharp points might reduce or eliminate the electricity in the cloud and thereby reduce or eliminate the chances of being struck by lightning and the damage it might produce. From his earlier experiments, Franklin knew that silent discharges from points work best when the conductors are grounded, and he also knew that lightning tends to strike tall objects. Therefore, even if the silent discharges did not neutralize the cloud, the tall rod would create a likely place for the lightning to strike, and if it did, then the grounded conductor would provide a safe path for the current to go into ground. In the next paragraph, Franklin proposed an experiment to determine whether thunderclouds contain any electrical "Fire": "On the Top of some high Tower or Steeple, place a Kind of Sentry Box big enough to contain a Man and an electrical Stand. From the Middle of the Stand let an Iron Rod rise, and pass bending out of the Door, and then upright 20 or 30 feet, pointed very sharp at the End. If the Electrical Stand be kept clean and dry, a Man standing on it when such Clouds are passing low, might be electrified, and afford Sparks, the Rod drawing Fire to him from the Cloud" (fig. 5.30).[26] It should be noted that the purpose of the sentry box (and later the kite) experiment was to determine whether thunderclouds are electrified; for this, the rod (or the conducting kite string) must be carefully insulated from ground. To protect against lightning, the rod must be connected to ground.

From 1749 to 1753, the Reverend Ebenezer Kinnersley, a leading electrical experimenter and a friend of Franklin's, traveled the East Coast giving lectures

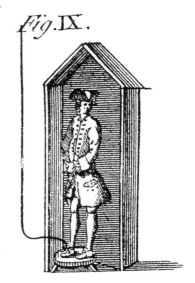

Fig. 5.30 Thomas Jefferys after Lewis Evans's original sketch, Illustration of a sentry box from Benjamin Franklin, Experiments and Observations on Electricity . . . , *1751. Sketch shows an insulated iron rod twenty to thirty feet long mounted on the side of a sentry box. The stool at the base of the rod is insulated from ground, and the sentry box protects the insulator from rain.*

Fig. 5.31 Model of a "thunder house,"
late eighteenth century. Eighteenth-
century "electricians" used model
houses to demonstrate that grounded
conductors would protect structures
from lightning damage.

and demonstrations on electricity. He told people that lightning is an electrical discharge, and he showed them how grounded rods would protect model "thunder houses" from sparks that simulated lightning (fig. 5.31). These lectures were widely advertised, and the associated broadsides represent the first public disclosures that grounded rods will protect buildings from lightning damage (fig. 5.32).[27]

Unbeknownst to Franklin or Collinson at the time, on May 10, 1752, a retired French dragoon acting on instructions from Thomas-François Dalibard, who had translated Franklin's *Experiments and Observations* into French, succeeded in drawing sparks from a tall rod that had been carefully insulated from ground at the village of Marly-la-Ville, just north of Paris (fig. 5.33). These sparks demonstrated, for the first time, that thunderclouds contain electricity and that lightning is an electrical discharge. These findings were sensational

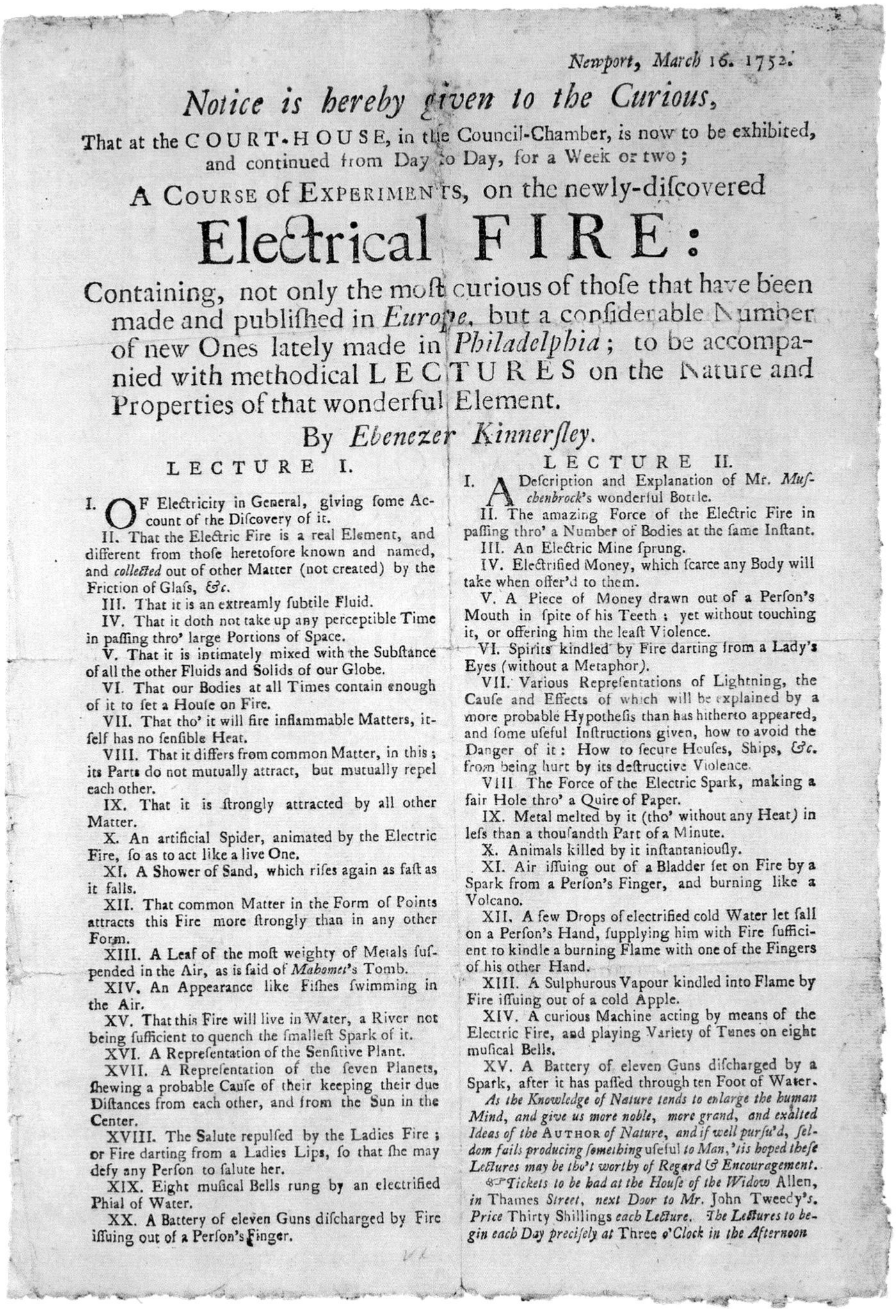

Newport, March 16. 1752.

Notice is hereby given to the Curious,

That at the COURT-HOUSE, in the Council-Chamber, is now to be exhibited, and continued from Day to Day, for a Week or two;

A COURSE of EXPERIMENTS, on the newly-diſcovered

Electrical FIRE:

Containing, not only the moſt curious of thoſe that have been made and publiſhed in *Europe*, but a conſiderable Number of new Ones lately made in *Philadelphia*; to be accompanied with methodical LECTURES on the Nature and Properties of that wonderful Element.

By *Ebenezer Kinnerſley.*

LECTURE I.

I. OF Electricity in General, giving ſome Account of the Diſcovery of it.

II. That the Electric Fire is a real Element, and different from thoſe heretofore known and named, and *collected* out of other Matter (not created) by the Friction of Glaſs, *&c.*

III. That it is an extreamly ſubtile Fluid.

IV. That it doth not take up any perceptible Time in paſſing thro' large Portions of Space.

V. That it is intimately mixed with the Subſtance of all the other Fluids and Solids of our Globe.

VI. That our Bodies at all Times contain enough of it to ſet a Houſe on Fire.

VII. That tho' it will fire inflammable Matters, itſelf has no ſenſible Heat.

VIII. That it differs from common Matter, in this; its Parts do not mutually attract, but mutually repel each other.

IX. That it is ſtrongly attracted by all other Matter.

X. An artificial Spider, animated by the Electric Fire, ſo as to act like a live One.

XI. A Shower of Sand, which riſes again as faſt as it falls.

XII. That common Matter in the Form of Points attracts this Fire more ſtrongly than in any other Form.

XIII. A Leaf of the moſt weighty of Metals ſuſpended in the Air, as is ſaid of *Mahomet's* Tomb.

XIV. An Appearance like Fiſhes ſwimming in the Air.

XV. That this Fire will live in Water, a River not being ſufficient to quench the ſmalleſt Spark of it.

XVI. A Repreſentation of the Senſitive Plant.

XVII. A Repreſentation of the ſeven Planets, ſhewing a probable Cauſe of their keeping their due Diſtances from each other, and from the Sun in the Center.

XVIII. The Salute repulſed by the Ladies Fire; or Fire darting from a Ladies Lips, ſo that ſhe may defy any Perſon to ſalute her.

XIX. Eight muſical Bells rung by an electrified Phial of Water.

XX. A Battery of eleven Guns diſcharged by Fire iſſuing out of a Perſon's Finger.

LECTURE II.

I. A Deſcription and Explanation of Mr. *Muſchenbrock's* wonderful Bottle.

II. The amazing Force of the Electric Fire in paſſing thro' a Number of Bodies at the ſame Inſtant.

III. An Electric Mine ſprung.

IV. Electrified Money, which ſcarce any Body will take when offer'd to them.

V. A Piece of Money drawn out of a Perſon's Mouth in ſpite of his Teeth; yet without touching it, or offering him the leaſt Violence.

VI. Spirits kindled by Fire darting from a Lady's Eyes (without a Metaphor).

VII. Various Repreſentations of Lightning, the Cauſe and Effects of which will be explained by a more probable Hypotheſis than has hitherto appeared, and ſome uſeful Inſtructions given, how to avoid the Danger of it: How to ſecure Houſes, Ships, *&c.* from being hurt by its deſtructive Violence.

VIII The Force of the Electric Spark, making a fair Hole thro' a Quire of Paper.

IX. Metal melted by it (tho' without any Heat) in leſs than a thouſandth Part of a Minute.

X. Animals killed by it inſtantaniouſly.

XI. Air iſſuing out of a Bladder ſet on Fire by a Spark from a Perſon's Finger, and burning like a Volcano.

XII. A few Drops of electrified cold Water let fall on a Perſon's Hand, ſupplying him with Fire ſufficient to kindle a burning Flame with one of the Fingers of his other Hand.

XIII. A Sulphurous Vapour kindled into Flame by Fire iſſuing out of a cold Apple.

XIV. A curious Machine acting by means of the Electric Fire, and playing Variety of Tunes on eight muſical Bells.

XV. A Battery of eleven Guns diſcharged by a Spark, after it has paſſed through ten Foot of Water.

As the Knowledge of Nature tends to enlarge the human Mind, and give us more noble, more grand, and exalted Ideas of the AUTHOR *of Nature, and if well purſu'd, ſeldom fails producing ſomething* uſeful *to Man, 'tis hoped theſe Lectures may be tho't worthy of Regard & Encouragement.*

☞ *Tickets to be had at the Houſe of the Widow* Allen, *in* Thames *Street, next Door to Mr.* John Tweedy's. *Price* Thirty Shillings *each Lecture. The Lectures to begin each Day preciſely at* Three *o'Clock in the Afternoon*

Fig. 5.32 Broadside advertising Ebenezer Kinnersley's lecture tour, March 16, 1752. Kinnersley toured the colonies in 1751–52, giving lectures and demonstrations on electricity. Broadsides advertising these lectures constitute the first public disclosures that grounded rods protect structures from lightning damage.

and were verified within days by a collaborator in Paris and soon by many others throughout Europe. When Dalibard reported his results to the Académie des Sciences, he acknowledged that in performing the sentry box experiment he had followed the path that Franklin had traced for him: "En suivant la route qu'il nous a tracée, j'ai obtenu une satisfaction complette."[28] Later, the king of France, Louis XV, would send Franklin, Collinson, and the Royal Society of

Fig. 5.35 Edward Fisher after Mason
Chamberlin, Benjamin Franklin of
Philadelphia, L.L.D., F.R.S., 1763. In
one of his favorite likenesses, which he
distributed to friends and relatives,
Franklin is shown next to the bells that
he used to study thunderstorm electricity. A grounded rod of his improved
design is shown in the background on
the right.

In the late fall of 1752, Franklin published the following instructions for
installing a lightning rod in *Poor Richard's Almanack*:

How to secure Houses, etc. from Lightning

 It has pleased God in his Goodness to Mankind, at length to
discover to them the Means of securing their Habitations and other
Buildings from Mischief by Thunder and Lightning. The Method is
this: Provide a small Iron Rod (it may be made of the Rod-iron used

A View of the State-House in Philadelphia.

Fig. 5.36 Unknown artist, A View of the State House in Philadelphia (now Independence Hall) from The Gentleman's Magazine, September 1752. The lightning rod on the tower of the State House was probably the first "Franklin" rod ever attached to a building for lightning protection. Constructed in accordance with Franklin's recommendations, the State House lightning rod protected the building for 208 years, with only one recorded instance of lightning damage.

by the Nailers) but of such a Length, that one End being three or four Feet in the moist Ground, the other may be six or eight Feet above the highest Part of the Building. To the upper End of the Rod fasten about a Foot of Brass Wire, the Size of a common Knitting-needle, sharpened to a fine Point; the Rod may be secured to the House by a few small Staples. If the House or Barn be long, there may be a Rod and Point at each End, and a middling Wire along the Ridge from one to the other. A House thus furnished will not be damaged by Lightning, it being attracted by the Points, and passing thro the Metal into the Ground without hurting any Thing. Vessels also, having a sharp pointed Rod fix'd on the Top of their Masts, with a Wire from the Foot of the Rod reaching down, round one of the Shrouds, to the Water, will not be hurt by Lightning.

Since lightning was a significant threat in Philadelphia, protective rods were soon installed on the spires of the Philadelphia Academy and the Pennsylvania State House (fig. 5.36).[32]

In 1753 Dr. John Lining repeated Franklin's kite experiment in Charleston, South Carolina, but when he tried to install a tall rod on his house, the

local populace objected. They thought the rod was presumptuous—that it would interfere with the will of God or that it might attract lightning and be dangerous. In April of that year, Franklin commented on religious presumption in a discussion of the abbé Nollet (fig. 5.37), the leading electrical experimenter in France and a strong opponent of protective rods: "He speaks as if he thought it Presumption in Man to propose guarding himself against the *Thunders of Heaven!* Surely the Thunder of Heaven is no more supernatural than the Rain, Hail, or Sunshine of Heaven, against the Inconvenience of which we guard by Roofs and Shades without Scruple. But I can now ease the Gentleman of this Apprehension; for by some late Experiments I find, that it is not Lightning from the Clouds that strikes the Earth, but Lightning from the

Earth that Strikes the Clouds."[33] In the next few years, Franklin's experiments and observations on electricity were repeated in Italy by Giambattista Beccaria, who discovered several new phenomena in atmospheric electricity and became a strong advocate for using grounded rods to protect against lightning.

Franklin continued to gather information about lightning and lightning damage, and in March 1761, Ebenezer Kinnersley sent Franklin a detailed description of a lightning flash that struck the house of William West in Philadelphia. The West house had been equipped with a protective rod similar to the one described in *Poor Richard's Almanack*, and at the time of the strike an observer reported that "the Lightning diffused over the Pavement, which was then very wet with Rain, to the Distance of two or three Yards from the Foot of the Conductor." Further investigation showed that the top of the brass needle had been melted, as happened to the rod in figure 5.38, but otherwise there was no damage to the house. Kinnersley concluded: "Surely it will now be thought expedient to provide Conductors for the Lightning as for the Rain."[34]

Before receiving Kinnersley's letter, Franklin had received reports of two similar strikes to houses that had been equipped with protective rods in South Carolina. In one case, the lightning had melted the points and a length of the brass grounding conductor, and in the other three brass points mounted on top of an iron rod, each about seven inches long, had evaporated, and the links and joints of the iron grounding conductor, which was about half an inch in diameter composed of several sections with links hooked together, were unhooked by the discharge. Almost all the staples that held this conductor to the outside of the house had also been loosened or removed. "Considerable cavities" had been made in the earth near the ground rod (sunk about three feet into the earth), and the lightning also created several furrows in the ground "some yards in length."[35]

Franklin was pleased by these reports because even though the conductor "when too small, may be destroyed in executing its office," the rods had indeed saved the houses from substantial damage. In his reply to Kinnersley, Franklin transcribed the reports from South Carolina and then recommended larger, more substantial conductors and a deeper, more extensive grounding system to reduce the surface arcing and to keep explosions in the soil away from the foundation of the house.[36]

Franklin published Kinnersley's letter and his reply in the 1769 edition of *Experiments and Observations* together with some "Remarks" on the improved design of protective rods. He began with an acknowledgement that "like other new instruments, this appears to have been at first in some respects

Fig. 5.38 Top portion of a lightning rod, ca. 1756, from the Wister house on High Street (now Market Street) Philadelphia. Like William West, John Wister was an early proponent of mounting lightning rods. The tip was probably melted by a lightning strike and weakened; it was subsequently bent by wind. This is believed to be one of the earliest rods erected by Franklin.

imperfect; and we find that we are, in this as in others, to expect improvement from experience chiefly." He then repeated his recommendations that pointed air terminals be mounted five or six feet above the highest part of the building, that "a rod in one continued piece is preferable to one composed of links or parts hooked together," and that the grounding conductors should go deep into the soil and be kept away from the foundation of the building.[37]

In the 1780s, Franklin noted that Rittenhouse had examined the lightning rods that were installed in the city of Philadelphia with his telescope to see whether they had been struck by lightning and, if so, whether they had worked properly. Rittenhouse found "that the Points of a Number of them have also been melted; and we have no Instance of any considerable Damage done to any House that was furnished with a compleat Conductor; and very few of Damage to any other Houses in the City since Conductors became common."[38]

Today most authorities agree that the main functions of lightning rods and the associated grounding conductors are to define and control the point(s) where lightning will attach to the structure and to provide one or more safe paths for the current to go into the ground. In his reply to Kinnersley, Franklin noted, "Indeed, in the construction of an instrument so new, and of which we could have so little experience, it is rather lucky that we should at first be so near the truth as we seem to be, and commit so few errors." Lucky indeed— today virtually every lightning protection code in the world recommends Franklin rods for ordinary structures, and the basic elements of their design and installation are, in essence, the same as Franklin's improved design.[39]

When Franklin went to France in 1776, seeking military and financial aid for the newly declared United States of America in the war against Great Britain, he was already world famous as a scientist, particularly for his work on lightning. He had been congratulated by Louis XV in 1752 for his electrical experiments, and when Franklin visited France in 1769, he dined with the king and queen at Versailles in the "grand couvert" ceremony. In 1772 Franklin was made a Foreign Associate of the Académie des Sciences, one of only eight foreigners who were given that distinction, and by then his work in electricity had called attention to his other writings in science, politics, economics, and moral philosophy.

In 1776, then, the intellectuals of France viewed Franklin as one of their own, and the ordinary people idolized him and received him warmly everywhere he went. John Adams, who served with Franklin in France (and hated him), later described Franklin's reputation at that time:

Nothing, perhaps, that ever occurred upon this earth was so well calculated to give any man an extensive and universal celebrity as the
discovery of the efficacy of iron points and the invention of lightning
rods. The idea was one of the most sublime that ever entered a human
imagination, that a mortal should disarm the clouds of heaven, and almost 'snatch from his hand the sceptre and the rod!'

His reputation was more universal than that of Leibnitz or Newton, Frederick [the Great] or Voltaire, and his character more beloved
and esteemed than any or all of them. His name was familiar to government and people, to kings, courtiers, nobility, clergy, and philosophers, as well as plebeians, to such a degree that there was scarcely
a peasant or a citizen, a valet de chambre, coachman or footman, a
lady's chambermaid or a scullion in a kitchen, who was not familiar with it, and who did not consider him as a friend to human kind.
When they spoke of him, they seemed to think he was to restore the
golden age.[40]

That extraordinary reputation gave Franklin entrance into the cream of
French society, and he used this access, as well as his considerable ability to
communicate, to achieve his political goals. His earlier service in the Pennsylvania Assembly and as a colonial agent in London had given Franklin experience in diplomacy: he knew the British ministers and members of Parliament,
and he also understood the French and their protocols and customs. Franklin understood that the French resented the harsh terms of the 1763 Treaty of
Paris and wanted to minimize Britain's influence in North America. To merchants, he frequently pointed out the advantages of future commerce with an
independent United States of America. To the French military leaders he presented himself as a colonial insurgent and an ally against Britain, their traditional foe. Although Louis XVI was initially wary of Franklin's presence
because the king wanted to remain on good terms with Britain, Franklin's
scientific reputation and diplomatic ability won him over; by 1777 even Ma-
rie Antoinette was referring to Franklin as "l'Ambassadeur Electrique." Anne-
Robert-Jacques Turgot, the distinguished French economist and finance minister, may have best summed up the link between Franklin the scientist and
Franklin the diplomat with his prophetic epigram of 1775, "Eripuit coelo fulmen, sceptrumque tyrannis" (He snatched the lightning from the skies and the
scepter from the tyrants).[41]

Chapter 6

Benjamin Franklin, Pragmatic Visionary: Politician, Diplomat, Statesman

ROBERT MIDDLEKAUFF

Linking the words *pragmatic* and *visionary* may seem strange and undoubtedly is, but in the case of Benjamin Franklin such a linkage suggests just how extraordinary his public life was. He was always a practical man who recognized the force of circumstances and the realities of life. Yet he had dreams too, in particular a powerful idea that one should always use what was apparent in the world to bring into existence something that was not. At times that something turned out to be of extraordinary importance.

In particular, he wanted to serve humankind, to make the lives of others around him better, and he looked to politics, defined broadly, for the means. He tried many techniques for improving human life, beginning with his own and working outward. After he gained experience and perspective on the world, he became convinced that the British Empire held immense promise for delivering good—by which he meant liberty—to people on both sides of the Atlantic. This conviction gave way finally in the crisis of the American Revolution, when he came to realize that it was rather the American republic that offered a model for free men everywhere.

Politician

Franklin was a natural in politics. He did not have a grand and imposing personality, he had something more useful: an understanding of men. And in his own way he had a quiet charisma. People of all sorts looked to him for leadership and felt comfortable asking him for it.

As a small boy he organized other small boys. He tells us in his autobiography that he was "commonly allow'd to govern" in the affairs of the boys with whom he played. Thus, at an early age he developed rudimentary skill as a leader. Franklin learned other skills as a boy that would be helpful in public life. One was how to persuade others of his point while retaining their friendship. When he was a youth he was fond of argument; he was even of a disputatious turn, to the point of making enemies out of those who might have been his friends. Realizing this, he gave up disputation in favor of maneuvering his friends into uncomfortable positions by assuming the role of "humble Enquirer." He would trick his opponent by asking those innocent questions that have a trap at their end—"loaded questions," in modern parlance. This style of argumentation was a perversion of the Socratic Method, which he had admired, and he soon gave it up. Instead he found a new way of talking with others: he used terms of "modest Diffidence" and stopped showing off, discovering in the process that modesty combined with a desire to learn could win him friends and open up the doors of learning.[1]

The political man who wished to do good followed naturally from the boy. His talents were on display in the organization he called the Junto, a group of young tradesmen and artisans determined to advance society as they advanced themselves. Franklin, by now a skilled printer in Philadelphia, won appointment as Pennsylvania's public printer. From a political standpoint, it proved to be a valuable post in several ways. As printer he became visible to the public as a person of some substance. His charitable work prospered, and in 1731 he led the way in the creation of the Library Company of Philadelphia, the first circulating library in the United States. Not long afterward he founded the American Philosophical Society. His appointment as clerk to the Pennsylvania Assembly almost inevitably occurred in this period of good works, as did his subsequent election in 1751 to the Assembly as a representative from Philadelphia. He now took his place in a powerful legislative body and in a sense began to operate as a conventional politician.

But Benjamin Franklin was not simply a conventional politician, though he mastered the usual legislative arts quickly and though he would soon demonstrate by his actions an almost intuitive understanding of the work of government. Certainly he did his share of the work as a legislator, sitting in meetings, drafting messages, and conferring with his colleagues about legislative bills, appropriations, revenue, and how to deal with the governor.

The governor, along with the Assembly, under the Charter of Privileges of 1701—the constitution that had been issued by William Penn, founder of the colony—provided the colony's leadership. The governor answered only to the proprietor, a member of the Penn family, which controlled the colony by royal grant; the Assembly, popularly elected under a liberal franchise, represented the people. By the time Franklin took his seat in the legislature, it had attained great power but not as much as it wanted and not enough to serve fully the interests of the electorate. Thomas Penn, who had succeeded to the proprietorship on the death of his father, William, thought the Assembly was too aggressive and smelled plots against himself in much that it did, or proposed to do.

Among the things the Assembly proposed, long before Franklin joined, was taxing the proprietor's lands in the colony. These lands were no small item—Penn was the largest landowner in the colony, and he refused to pay taxes on any of his holdings. To forestall any inclination in his governors to yield to the importunities of the legislature, he handed each in turn written instructions defining the limits of his power. Requiring every governor to post a bond, which would be forfeited if he transgressed those limits, stiffened spines.

The obstinacy of the proprietor and his governors distressed Franklin even more than the pacifism of the Quakers who dominated the legislature. The 1750s were dangerous years, with the Indians to the west threatening colonial settlements and the French urging them on (figs. 6.1 and 6.2). Franklin admired many things about the Quakers, but he felt that their refusal to organize a militia was carrying principle too far. Confronted by a proprietor who was blind to the danger to provincial safety and a Quaker party apparently unwilling to see the merit in self-defense, Franklin acted. In 1747 he published a tract called *Plain Truth* that urged Pennsylvanians to form an association for their own defense.[2] Franklin did not ordinarily speak in public meetings, but he put aside his usual reticence and addressed gatherings of tradesmen and mechanics, gentlemen and merchants, urging them to organize a military force. In addition to this extraordinary action he seems to have resorted to more conventional means favored by politicians—he quietly sought out the Philadelphia Corporation, the governing body of the city, and the Pennsylvania Council, an advisory group to the governor. These agencies, along with other men of substance, vocally endorsed organized private action for defense.

Franklin acted to make the association work by raising money from local merchants for cannons and other weapons as well as recruiting a militia: a thousand men signed up (fig. 6.3). In an astute political move, he refused to

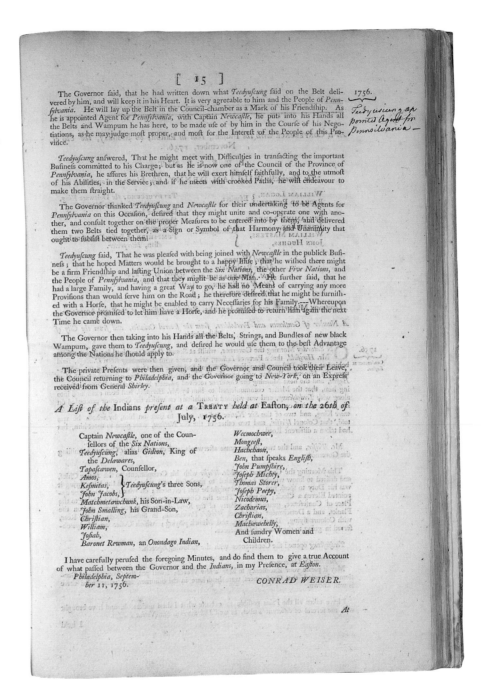

claim a position of command, choosing to serve instead as a common soldier. However, nothing he did—neither his abnegation nor his organizing spirit—pleased Thomas Penn, who greeted the news of private defense efforts with dismay. The "people of America," he wrote, "are too often ready to act in defiance of the Government they live in, without associating themselves for the purpose." He feared a "Military Common Wealth" and sensed treason in what was transpiring in his colony. As for Franklin, Penn called him "a dangerous Man" and wrote the colony secretary, Richard Peters, that he would be "very glad" if Franklin "inhabited any other Country" but Pennsylvania. Where Penn's suspicion and fear would have led him had the war continued is not clear, but it ended, and with peace his uneasy spirit seemed to find rest.[3]

Both the peace and Penn's peace of mind proved temporary: in 1754 war broke out in America and two years later in Europe, as Britain once more engaged with its old enemy France. Just before this new war began—known as the French and Indian War in America and the Seven Years' War in Europe—Franklin attempted with others, including Thomas Hutchinson, then a member of the Massachusetts Council, to prepare the colonies for conflict. At a conference held in Albany he offered a plan of union that would pull the colonial governments together in an imperial parliament, an organization he thought would enable them to fight the French and the Indians more effectively. It was a daring idea, implying a loss of autonomy, and it frightened American legislatures, all of whom either ignored or rejected it (fig. 6.4). Nor did the government in Britain accept the plan. Western Pennsylvania tasted the bitter fruits of this failure ten years later when the Paxton Boys, a group of rioters from the village of Paxton, slaughtered several groups of Indians living in Lancaster and adjacent counties (fig. 6.5). The murders began in December 1763; by early February the killers were threatening to march on Philadelphia, where some of the fleeing Indians had been sheltered. In panic, Governor John Penn, nephew

Fig. 6.2 Daniel Smith and Robert Sharp, Milk jug, 1765. Franklin's friend and physician in London Dr. John Fothergill gave him this jug, perhaps in 1775, engraved, "Keep Bright the Chain," a motto adopted by Franklin from treaties with Indians, referring to the chain of friendship. Here Fothergill refers to their mutual efforts to prevent the American Revolution.

Fig. 6.3 Association for Defense, Second Philadelphia lottery ticket, 1748. Franklin printed the tickets for this lottery, whose proceeds helped defray the cost of strengthening the defenses for the city of Philadelphia. The most tangible benefit of this second lottery was the construction of the Association Battery at Wicaco on the Delaware River, just south of Philadelphia.

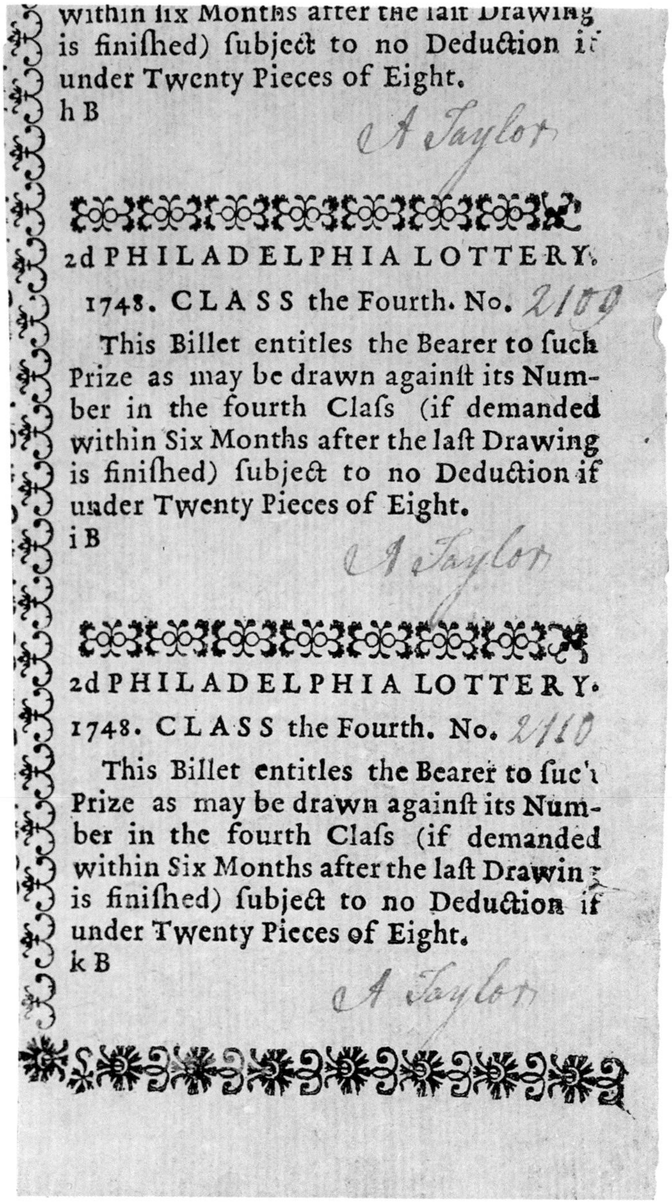
within ſix Months after the laſt Drawing is finiſhed) ſubject to no Deduction if under Twenty Pieces of Eight.
h B
A Taylor

2d PHILADELPHIA LOTTERY.
1748. CLASS the Fourth. No. 2109
This Billet entitles the Bearer to ſuch Prize as may be drawn againſt its Number in the fourth Claſs (if demanded within Six Months after the laſt Drawing is finiſhed) ſubject to no Deduction if under Twenty Pieces of Eight.
i B
A Taylor

2d PHILADELPHIA LOTTERY.
1748. CLASS the Fourth. No. 2110
This Billet entitles the Bearer to ſuch Prize as may be drawn againſt its Number in the fourth Claſs (if demanded within Six Months after the laſt Drawing is finiſhed) ſubject to no Deduction if under Twenty Pieces of Eight.
k B
A Taylor

of Thomas, fled to Franklin's house in the middle of the night. Franklin had just issued a denunciation of the frontier rioters, *A Narrative of the late Massacres* (fig. 6.6). He not only opened his doors to the governor, he joined a delegation to persuade the rioters, intercepted at Germantown, to return home. Just before this he had signed up as a foot soldier in a temporary militia to defend the city. With quiet restored he laughed about the whole affair, remarking that "within four and twenty hours" he had been "a common soldier, a Counsellor, a kind of Dictator, an Ambassador to the Country Mob, and on their Returning home *Nobody*, again."[4]

This "nobody" soon discovered that not even war could alter the proprietor's authoritarian policies. By 1764 Franklin had had enough and proposed that the crown replace the proprietor with a royal governor. There was almost no evidence that the people of Pennsylvania wished for such a change, and soon there was a great deal of evidence that they did not. But before the popular will could be ascertained, Franklin persuaded the legislature to pass a petition requesting that the crown replace the proprietorship with a royal government. Even after he discovered that public opinion was against the move, he fought for election to the Assembly on the proposed change. He subsequently lost his seat; fortunately for him the Quaker party (his party) retained control. Apparently undiscouraged, he carried the petition to Britain that fall.

But Franklin had miscalculated. He had read the people incorrectly, and he had allowed himself to be carried away by his sense of outrage at Thomas Penn. It was a rare mistake—his spirit, in a fury, had overpowered his head. Though he never admitted it, he probably recognized later the irony of appealing for a royal government on the eve of a massive revolution to expel the king and all his works from America.

The issues dividing the province and the proprietor had not disappeared in the Indian crisis and now took on renewed urgency. But Franklin's politi-

Fig. 6.4 "Join, or Die" cartoon from the Pennsylvania Gazette, *May 9, 1754. Franklin published (and possibly drew) this cartoon urging the colonies to join together against the French. At the Albany conference, Franklin proposed a joint military partnership for the united British colonies.*

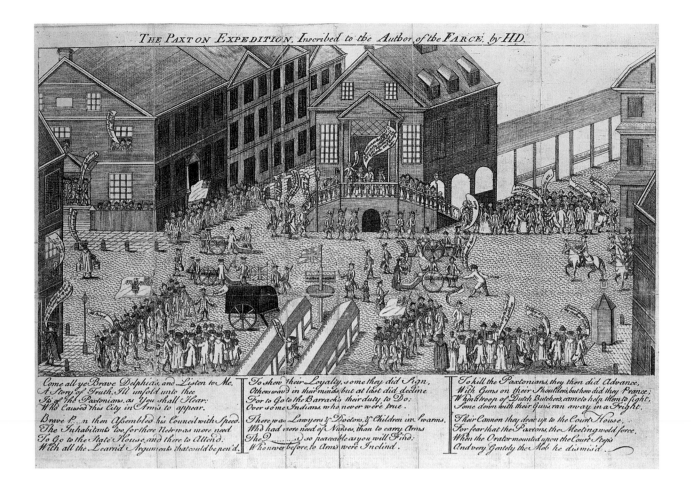

THE PAXTON EXPEDITION. *Inscribed to the Author of the* FARCE. *by* HD.

Come all ye Brave Delphia's, and Listen to Me. | To shew their Loyalty, some they did Sign, | To kill the Paxtonians, they then did Advance,
A Story of Truth, Ill unfold unto thee | Others wavd in their minds, but at last did decline | With Guns on their Shoulders, but how did they Prance;
Its of the Paxtonians, as You shall Hear, | For to Go to the Barrack's their duty to Do: | Whon troop of Dutch Butchers, came to help them to fight,
Who caused this City in Arms to appear. | Over some Indians, who never were true. | Some down with their Guns ran away in a Fright.

Brave P—n then Assembled his Council with Speed. | There was Lawyers & Doctors, & Children in Swarms, | Their Cannon they drew up to the Court House,
The Inhabitants too, for there Neir was more need | Who had more need of Nurses, than to carry Arms | For fear that the Paxtons, the Meeting wold force,
To Go to the State House, and there to Attend: | The Q——s so peaceable as you will Find: | When the Orator mounted upon the Court Steps
With all the Learnd Arguments that could be pen'd. | Who never before, to Arms were Inclind. | And very Gentely the Mob he dismisd.

Fig. 6.5 Attributed to Henry Dawkins,
The Paxton Expedition, *1764. One in
a series of political cartoons concerning the Paxton Boys.*

cal principles remained consistent and faithful to the interests of Pennsylvania
and the ideals of its founder—personal liberty, tolerance of religious dissent,
and representative government as the agency best designed to serve the people's wishes. These convictions, fair-minded and balanced as they were, failed
to reckon with those of the British governing classes, who found it impossible
to give equal treatment to colonists. Indeed, they found the idea unthinkable,
holding instead that colonies and their peoples were by definition subordinate
to their imperial masters in the home country.

In the years he was in London, between 1764 and 1775, Franklin discovered that his skills in politics were inadequate—he could not even get a hearing in English governing circles when he presented the petition asking for
royal government for his colony. Penn ignored his complaints, as did the English officials, who instinctively shared the proprietor's sense of superiority.
There was, of course, no public discussion in Britain of the request for royal

administration—the king's government did not work in such a manner. In August 1768 the colonial secretary Lord Hillsborough informed Franklin that the crown did not favor the petition. The struggle for royal government was over, and Franklin, so skillful in local politics before this crisis, had to accept the fact that he had failed both as a provincial and an imperial politician.

If holding the British Empire together in 1775, after a decade of revolutionary crisis, were considered a test of his mettle as a politician, he also failed to meet that challenge. But no single man, no matter how gifted, could have prevented the Revolution. Franklin did his best; indeed, he tried to persuade both sides to avoid bloodshed even after he apparently lost hope that it could be done. As the agent representing Pennsylvania, New Jersey, Georgia, and, at a crucial moment, Massachusetts, he acted responsibly and honestly throughout the revolutionary upheaval. He wanted the colonies to remain in the em-

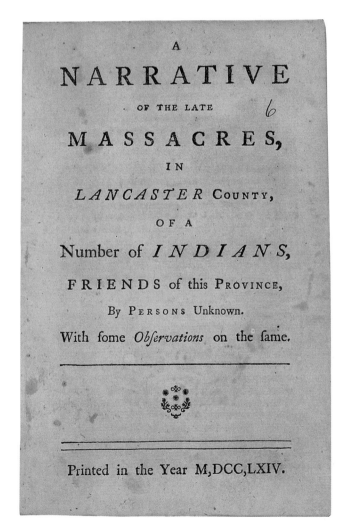

Fig. 6.6 Front page of Benjamin Franklin, A Narrative of the late Massacres, in Lancaster County, of a Number of Indians . . . , *1764.*

Fig. 6.7 (Opposite) Mason Chamberlin, Portrait of Benjamin Franklin, 1762. Chamberlin was a leading portraitist and founding member of the Royal Academy in London. He portrayed Franklin as the world first knew him: the man who tamed lightning (see fig. 5.35). Knowledge of Franklin's electrical experiments had preceded him to England, and his fame as a scientist provided an introduction to individuals and groups essential to the success of his mission. This work was commissioned by a friend, and the depiction met with Franklin's approval.

pire; he admired Britain, asking in 1763, "Why should that pretty Island, which compared to America is but like a stepping Stone in a Brook, scarce enough of it above Water to keep one's Shoes dry; why, I say, should that little Island, enjoy in almost every Neighbourhood, more sensible, virtuous and elegant Minds, than we can collect in ranging 100 Leagues of our vast Forests."[5] It was a judgment he repented of in the next ten years.

Franklin used all the techniques of a politician-agent in these years. He was also able to rely on his fame as the man who had pulled lightning from the clouds. The learned men of Europe had by this time come to terms with the fact that one of the world's most important natural philosophers (as scientists were called) lived in America. But though his distinction in scientific research probably helped open British doors to Franklin, his own efforts counted for more (fig. 6.7). To be sure, in representing his colonies, he did the same things other agents did. He passed on information from the colonies to the secretary of state for the southern department, which included colonial affairs. The Board of Trade, an advisory body to the Privy Council, also drew his attention. Lord Shelburne, the secretary for the southern department in 1766–67, became a friend, only one of a number of officials Franklin cultivated over lunches and dinner. Shelburne looked to Franklin for ideas about reducing imperial expenses in America; he and Henry Seymour Conway, then leader of the House of Commons, must have been surprised when Franklin used the opportunity not just to advise on cutting costs but to argue for lifting the ban on paper money as well.

Information flowed both ways across the Atlantic, and Franklin took pains to report what the British ministry was doing whenever colonial interests were at stake. Part of Franklin's political strength came from his wide acquaintance in Britain and America; people in and out of government found him a comfortable man who was always interested in others. They talked to him easily, sensing his curiosity in a broad array of subjects. There was nothing false in Franklin's willingness to listen, and much that he heard was relayed to his American masters.

This openness did not imply that he made no judgments of his own. His strong will and his devotion to American liberties might not find expression in every encounter with British officials who were given to looking down their noses at colonials. But when the issue was important to colonial rights, Franklin made clear how colonials saw things. In 1771, for example, he ran up against Lord Hillsborough. Hillsborough had practiced sneering at colonials ever since his appointment in 1768. When he looked at Franklin, he saw someone

Fig. 6.8 Paper embossed with tax stamp, 1765. All newspapers and public and legal documents in the American colonies were required to be printed on paper sent from England bearing an embossed seal, or "stamp." The stamp certified the payment of the tax, the cost of which was passed on to the purchaser, adding to the expense—and difficulty—of carrying on daily life. The Stamp Act symbolized for Americans the heavy hand of Britain on their commerce, and their reaction was predictable. This sheet was pulled from a bonfire in which New Yorkers burned quantities of the stamped paper. Sent to Philadelphia and displayed in the coffeehouse, it served as a constant reminder of the offense. (The official stamp is the embossed mark, to the right of the inked mark).

Fig. 6.9 (Opposite) Front page of The Pennsylvania Journal; and Weekly Advertiser, *October 31, 1765. The day before the Stamp Act took effect, William and Thomas Bradford, publishers of the* Pennsylvania Journal; and Weekly Advertiser, *printed the edition with a skull and crossbones on the masthead and a vow to discontinue publishing until the tax was repealed. William took up the cause of independence, becoming a leader of Philadelphia's Sons of Liberty. He ultimately left his son, Thomas, in charge of the paper, joined the Continental Army, served in the New Jersey campaign, and was severely wounded at the Battle of Princeton.*

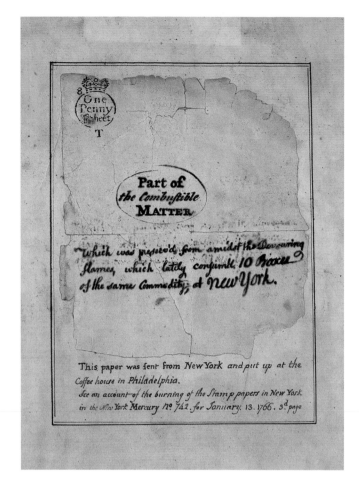

who had to be put in his place. The way to do that was to deny official status to Franklin when he presented his credentials as an agent of the Massachusetts lower house. Hillsborough dismissed the notion that the house alone could appoint an agent, arguing that the only legitimate means to such a standing was through a legislative act—in other words, the house might approve a bill for Franklin's appointment, but the governor had to sign the bill into an act. Both men knew there was no chance of Thomas Hutchinson, the governor, giving his consent. Franklin argued his case to no avail and went away furious, commenting to a friend on Hillsborough's "wrongheadedness" and his "insolent" style.[6] It was a representative episode in Franklin's gradual estrangement from Britain, symptomatic of much in the imperial atmosphere and revealing the limits of Franklin's patience.

That patience had been much in evidence earlier, during the crisis over the Stamp Act of 1765 in which Parliament levied a tax on the colonies (fig.

Thurſday, *October* 31, 1765. THE NUMB. 1195.

PENNSYLVANIA JOURNAL; AND WEEKLY ADVERTISER.

EXPIRING: In Hopes of a Reſurrection to LIFE again.

I AM ſorry to be obliged to acquaint my Readers, that as The STAMP-ACT, is fear'd to be obligatory upon us after the *Firſt of November* enſuing, (the *fatal To-morrow*) the Publiſher of this Paper unable to bear the Burthen, has thought it expedient TO STOP a while, in order to deliberate, whether any Methods can be found to elude the Chains forged for us, and eſcape the inſupportable Slavery; which it is hoped, from the juſt Repreſentations now made againſt that Act, may be effected. Mean while, I muſt earneſtly Requeſt every Individual of my Subſcribers, many of whom have been long behind Hand, that they would immediately Diſcharge their reſpective Arrears, that I may be able, not only to ſupport myſelf during the Interval, but be better prepared to proceed again with this Paper, whenever an opening for that Purpoſe appears, which I hope will be ſoon.

WILLIAM BRADFORD.

Remember, O my friends! the Laws, the Rights,
The generous plan of power deliver'd down,
From age to age, by your renown'd fore-fathers;
O let it never periſh in your hands!
But piouſly tranſmit it to your children.
Do thou, great Liberty, inſpire our ſouls,
And make our lives in thy poſſeſſion happy;
Or our deaths glorious in thy defence.
ADDISON'S Cato.

LIBERTY is one of the greateſt Bleſſings, which human beings can poſſibly enjoy: When we are deprived of this earthly happineſs, we are fettered with the Chains of inimical ſervitude. Nations, who are born for the mutual ſupport of each other, ſhould preſerve a ſteady attachment to the welfare and happineſs of that nation with whom they are united, that their mutual alliance of friendſhip might be ſincere and permanent. When this union is ſeparated by the illegal encroachments on that Liberty, which is the Soul of Commerce, and the Support of Life, it degenerates into implacable Enmity, which in time grows inveterate, and finally recoils upon thoſe who have been the means of its unhappy diſſolution. The *Liberty of the Preſs* has very juſtly been eſteemed one of the main Pillars of the Liberty of the People. While this is maintained, the firſt Steps to Oppreſſion are detected, and the Attention of the People ſeaſonably awakened. When this is ſuppreſſed, the Suſpicion of the People, and their Ruin may admit of ſo ſudden a tranſition, as renders the Succeſs of the firſt impracticable, and the Miſeries attending the latter unavoidable. So dangerous is this to lawleſs Power, that the fartheſt approaches to it are reſolutely oppoſed, or rigorouſly puniſhed. So eſſential is this to Freedom, Property, and Happineſs, that the moſt plauſible Attempts to curtail it even in the ſmalleſt Degree, have always been moſt ſtrenuouſly oppoſed by the virtuous, free, and unbiaſſed Patriot. It is the Priviledge of Britons to ſpeak Truth with impunity, and even to fear no Danger from ſpeculative Error whether in Religion or Politicks. The want of attending to this has produced needleſs Enquiries, and unjuſtifiable Cenſures of what is true in Fact or no more than falſe in Speculation.---But how unhappily is it to be debarr'd from this laſt Relief in a dangerous and ſickly State! How melancholly to pine and die while no kind Phyſician is allowed to explore the Cauſe, or preſcribe the Cure of our manifold Diſorders? The love of Eaſe, and abſence of Pain in ſome Diſtempers, is a fatal Symptom of the deſperate Circumſtances of the Patient. And in all political Diſorders the more contented we are under them, ſo much the worſe are they, and ſo much the worſe are we for them. It is a very happy Circumſtance attending public Virtue and public Spirit, that the more it is vilified, the more illuſtrious it always appears. No Falſhood formed againſt it can proſper, for it at once detects and confutes the darkeſt and moſt inveterate Calumny. But although public Virtue cannot be affected by the Indulgence of the moſt unlimited Freedom of ſpeaking or writing, yet Oppreſſion and Tyranny as it derives all its Influence from its Secrecy, may be extremely benefited by the Reverſe. For this reaſon, in Countries ſubjected to the inſatiable Demands of Power and Avarice, the firſt Attempts to inſpire People with a juſt Senſe of their Condition, are commonly nipt in the Bud. It is of the laſt Importance to the Views of deſigning Men to ſhut up the moſt ſucceſsful and univerſal Channel of Information from the People, when they are forming ſuch Schemes as need only to be known in order to be Oppoſed. Beſides the Deprivation of our whole Liberty may be juſtified on the ſame Principles as the Deprivation of any individual Part, ſuch as the Liberty of the Preſs undoubtedly is.

How amiable is the Enjoyment of Liberty! But how deteſtable are the Bonds of Servitude! 'Tis therefore ſincerly to be hoped, that the old *New-England* Spirit ſo exemplarily free in former Times, will never condeſcend in Submiſſion to new and unwarrantable Reſtrictions.

A Day, an Hour of virtuous Liberty,
Is worth a whole Eternity in Bondage.

May we all as loyal Subjects, and free born Britons exert our utmoſt to preſerve the Rights and Liberties of our Country, in a Manner that ſhall add Honour to our Endeavours; that future Poſterity may reap the Benefit, and bleſs the Hands which were the Inſtruments of procuring it.---

That Glory then, the brighteſt Crown of Praiſe,
Which every Lover of his Country's Wealth,
And every Patron of Mankind deſerves;
Will gracefully adorn ſuch Patriot's Deeds,
And leave behind an Honour that will laſt
With Praiſe immortal to the End of Time.

Thurſday laſt arrived here the ſhip Philadelphia Packet, Capt. Budden, from London, by whom we have the following advices.

R O M E, *July* 24.

THE harveſt in this country hath not proved ſo good as we hoped. This event hath engaged the congregation eſtabliſhed for inſpecting into the ſupplies of proviſions for this capital, to ſeek all poſſible means to prevent a freſh ſcarcity.

St. James's, Auguſt 17. The king has been pleaſed to appoint the moſt honourable the Marquis of Rockingham to be lord lieutenant of the weſt-ridings of the county of York, and of the city of York, and county of the ſame city: and alſo Cuſtos Rotulorum of the north and weſt-ridings in the ſaid county of York and of the city of York, and county of the ſame city; and Ainſty, otherwiſe Aynſtry, of York.

The king has been pleaſed to appoint the right hon. William Earl of Dartmouth, Soam Jenyns, Edward Elliot, John York, George Rice, John Roberts, Jeremiah Dyſon, and William Fitzherbett, Eſqrs; to be commiſſioners of trade, and for inſpecting and improving his majeſty's plantations in America, and elſewhere.

The king has been pleaſed to grant unto the right hon. Richard Viſcount How, the office of treaſurer of his Majeſty's navy.

St. James's, Auguſt 27. By the laſt letters from Col. Deſmaretz, his majeſty's commiſſary at Dunkirk, we are aſſured, that orders were given by the French miniſtry, for immediately ſetting about the demolition of the Jettees, which are the ſupport of the harbour of Dunkirk.

Warſaw, Auguſt 1. The tribunal of Great Poland, held at Poſnania, has granted permiſſion to the Lutherans at Lobſcutz to open their church, which has been ſhut near twenty years, to provide a miniſter, and to perform divine ſervice in public.

Corunna, July 17. The detachment of one hundred men drafted for Louiſiana, are on the march for Ferrol, where they are to embark on board the Unicorn frigate with a governor, two capuchin friars, a commiſſionary at war, and ſome civil officers.

Cadiz, July 23. Letters brought by the laſt poſt from Gibralter ſay, the report before ſpread, that the Algerines have killed their Dey, and declared war againſt all the European powers except England and France, proves not true.

L O N D O N.

Auguſt 17. On Thurſday at the king's arms tavern in Cornhill, an elegant entertainment was given by the committee of North-American merchants to Richard Glover, and Charles Garth, Eſqrs; when thoſe gentlemen received the thanks of that body, for their endeavours to prevent the ſoldiery from being billeted upon the private houſes of their fellow-ſubjects in America.

Part of a letter from an officer in the Eaſt-India ſervice, dated from the Arietur camp, January 8, 1765.

"In my laſt I acquainted you that we did at laſt reduce Madure. The army has ſince conquered the Arietur country for the Nabob, of 100,000l. revenue a year. We are now under orders to attack another chief, or polyagor contiguous to this country; both chiefs have mutually maintained an independency of the Nabob till now; meerly on account of the impenetrable woods they are poſſeſſed of. You certainly have heard before of the memorable battle Major Munro gained at Bengal over Suja Dowla, one of the moſt formidable powers of India: The conſequence of this battle gives the company the command of trade in the greateſt part of the Mogul's dominions; and, without exaggeration, the Eaſt-India company at preſent may be brought in comparriſon with Alexander the Great, whoſe command, from the river Indus to the river Ganges, was not ſo much reſpected as their's."

It is ſaid the new m-----y, taking into conſideration the preſent deplorable ſituation of the Canadians, have determined to take up all the Canada bills at par, with intereſt to the preſent time; and afterwards to demand, in the moſt ſpirited terms, *immediate* and *full* payment of France, under pain of all the conſequences that can reſult from a refuſal.

The new lords of trade and plantations will hold a board on Monday next, for the firſt time, at the Cockpit Whitehall.

We hear the rent rolls of the ſeveral proprietary eſtates in America, obtained by former grants under the crown are ordered to be made out, as alſo an eſtimate of the annual produce of their land tax, in order to introduce a more equitable form of levying his majeſty's revenues in that part of the world.

They write from Gibralter, that Engliſh officers and ſeamen are engaging both there and at Minorca by foreign agents, to ſerve on board his Sardinian majeſty's ſhips of war in the Mediterranean.

Auguſt 20. The right honourable the Earl Cornwallis, lieutenant colonel to the 12 regiment of foot, is appointed one of his majeſty's aids de camp, with the rank of colonel of foot in the army.

We are informed, that a gentleman lately very popular in this country, is ſoon to reſide at Louſanne, in Switzerland, where he intends publiſhing his friend Mr. Churchill's poems, with explanatory notes; and we are likewiſe informed, that he has an intention of publiſhing, at the ſame place, a hiſtory of England wrote by himſelf.

By a veſſel arrived at Guernſey from Belleiſle there is advice, that the French are errecting ſeveral batteries at Sandy Bay, on the ſouth eaſt of the iſland, and in the great road where the deſcent was made in the late war by the ſeamen and troops under Admiral Keppel and General Hodgſon.

Aug. 21 We hear lord Viſcount Spencer is ſhortly to be created an earl.

All thoughts of any farther changes are ſaid to be entirely laid aſide.

It is reported, that a perſon of high rank, on being lately offered a great employment, refuſed it, ſaying, "that he could not poſſibly accept of it, conſiſtently with the love he bore to the Britiſh nation, which would ever be the object of his care and attention."

Monday ſome diſpatches ſaid to be of importance, were received here from Holland, but the ſubject has not yet tranſpired.

Private letters from Paris mention, that the true reaſon

An Emblem of the Effects of the STAMP.

O! the fatal STAMP.

Adieu, Adieu to the LIBERTY of the *PRESS*.

[1]

The EXAMINATION of Doctor
BENJAMIN FRANKLIN, *before an*
AUGUST ASSEMBLY, *relating to the Repeal of*
the STAMP-ACT, &c.

Q. WHAT is your name, and place of abode?
A. Franklin, of Philadelphia.
Q. Do the Americans pay any considerable taxes among themselves?
A. Certainly many, and very heavy taxes.
Q. What are the present taxes in Pennsylvania, laid by the laws of the Colony?
A. There are taxes on all estates real and personal, a poll tax, a tax on all offices, professions, trades and businesses, according to their profits; an excise on all wine, rum, and other spirits; and a duty of Ten Pounds per head on all Negroes imported, with some other duties.
Q. For what purposes are those taxes laid?
A. For the support of the civil and military establishments of the country, and to discharge the heavy debt contracted in the last war.
Q. How long are those taxes to continue?
A. Those for discharging the debt are to continue till 1772, and longer, if the debt should not be then all discharged. The others must always continue.
Q. Was it not expected that the debt would have been sooner discharged?
A. It was, when the peace was made with France and Spain----But a fresh war breaking out with the Indians, a fresh load of debt was incurred, and the taxes, of course, continued longer by a new law.
Q. Are not all the people very able to pay those taxes?
A. No. The frontier counties, all along the continent, having been frequently ravaged by the enemy, and greatly impoverished, are able to pay very little tax. And therefore, in consideration of their distresses, our late tax laws do expressly favour those counties, excusing the sufferers; and I suppose the same is done in other governments.
Q. Are not you concerned in the management of the Post-Office in America?
A. Yes. I am Deputy Post-Master General of North-America.
Q. Don't you think the distribution of stamps, by post, to all the inhabitants, very practicable, if there was no opposition?
A. The posts only go along the sea coasts; they do not, except in a few instances, go back into the country; and if they did, sending for stamps by post would occasion an expence of postage, amounting, in many cases, to much more than that of the stamps themselves.
Q. Are you acquainted with Newfoundland?
A. I never was there.
Q. Do you know whether there are any post roads on that island?
A. I have heard that there are no roads at all; but that the communication between one settlement and another is by sea only.
Q. Can you disperse the stamps by post in Canada?
A. There

A

6.8). Before the passage of the act Franklin had met with George Grenville, the king's first minister, and along with other agents he offered to see about raising money in the form of requisitions, the standard method by which the colonies taxed themselves for the crown. All they needed was some idea of the sum the Grenville ministry wanted. They were never told, and the Stamp Act yielded a near revolution in America but no revenue, for it was nullified by colonial action, then repealed by Parliament. (fig. 6.9).

When the act passed, Franklin, out of touch with American opinion, had obtained the appointment of John Hughes, a Philadelphia supporter, as stamp distributor for Pennsylvania. Unfavorable popular reaction in the colony compelled Hughes to renounce his office even before the statute went into effect. Franklin soon learned of the overwhelming opposition to the act; he also

Fig. 6.11 Attributed to Benjamin Wilson, The Repeal, Or the Funeral of Miss Ame-Stamp, 1766. In the most famous satire on the Stamp Act, a funeral procession carries the remains of bills and other unpopular taxes. Among the participants is the Stamp Act's principal proponent, Treasury Secretary George Grenville, who carries a child's coffin marked "Miss Ame Stamp 1766." Franklin sent a copy of this cartoon home to his wife; it was redrawn and altered to include American references, and published in America.

realized—somewhat tardily—that it violated the constitutional principle that taxes could be imposed upon British subjects only by their representatives. And no American sat in Parliament, nor was Parliament likely to invite colonials to do so. "No taxation without representation" expressed a constitutional truth that now took on special meaning for Americans and for Franklin.

Testifying before the House of Commons on behalf of the forces opposed to the act, Franklin gave a brilliant performance. Some of the questions he was asked had been rehearsed in an agreement with the Rockingham ministry, which took over from Grenville's largely to repeal the Stamp Act; others had not, coming as they did from members who opposed repeal (fig. 6.10). In the course of his answers to questions from both sides Franklin argued on constitutional terms that the act violated the privileges and liberties of Americans and was unconstitutional. But the principal thrust of his answers was to reinforce the fear planted by others that if Parliament persisted in its policy of taxing a people not represented in its ranks, it would inevitably stimulate the economic independence of the colonies. To the question "What used to be the

Fig. 6.12 Mather Brown, Portrait of Alexander Wedderburn, 1st earl of Rosslyn, 1791. Wedderburn attacked Franklin before the Privy Council over Franklin's role in the affair of the Hutchinson-Oliver letters.

pride of the Americans?" Franklin answered, "To indulge in the fashions and manufacturers of Great Britain." And to the question that followed—"What is now their pride?"—he crisply stated, "To wear their old cloaths over again, till they can make new ones."[7]

Franklin was dazzling—the politician as prophet of imperial rupture unless Parliament heeded the good advice he and scores of British merchants were offering it (fig. 6.11). These merchants probably produced even more powerful impressions on Parliament, but Franklin's words clarified the full implications for the empire of the Stamp Act in ways neither the merchants nor any other Britisher could do. This episode also marked him as a man of political substance, someone whom British officials might turn to in crisis.

Some turned to him again in 1773 when the crisis reached feverish proportions at the time of the Boston Tea Party, the Coercive Acts, and the meeting of the Continental Congress. Others turned on him. The cause producing the reaction of this second group was an affair involving letters that mysteriously came into his hands written by Thomas Hutchinson and Andrew Oliver, the governor and deputy governor of Massachusetts. Written several years earlier, the letters seemed to provide evidence that the changes in British policy that Americans found so repellent had first been proposed by the two Massachusetts officials. Franklin interpreted the letters in this fashion and sent them off to the Speaker of the Massachusetts legislature, Thomas Cushing, with instructions to handle them with care and not to allow them to become public. Cushing, however, could not resist publishing them, to an immense uproar in America.

In Britain there was a feeling of outrage and betrayal, especially in the ministry, which took its revenge on Franklin in January 1774 when he presented the petition from Massachusetts calling for the dismissal of Hutchinson and Oliver. The hearing on the petition occurred in the Cockpit, a large meeting room of the Privy Council, with the solicitor general, Alexander Wedderburn, making a relentless attack on Franklin—"a thief," Wedderburn said (in Latin), who "has forfeited all the respect of societies and of men" (fig. 6.12).[8] The listeners to Wedderburn's rant included Lord North, now the king's first minister; Edmund Burke; members of the Privy Council; and other men of influence in Britain.

The petition was rejected, and Franklin, who had stood silent while the blows rained down upon him, left the room largely without hope for the future of relations between Britain and America (fig. 6.13). When petitions expressing grievances become "so odious to government that even the mere pipe which conveys them becomes obnoxious," he wrote to Cushing, "I am at a loss to know how peace and union is to be maintained or restored between different parts of the empire."[9] Still, he remained in England for a little more than a year, leaving for good in March 1775.

In these last months his friends John Fothergill and David Barclay attempted to open new avenues between him and the British government. (fig. 6.14) Their attempts brought him face to face with Caroline Howe, her brother Admiral Lord Richard Howe, and the elder William Pitt, now Lord Chatham. Caroline Howe proved to be a charming conduit between Richard Howe

Fig. 6.13 Robert Whitechurch after Christian Schussele, Franklin Before the Lords in Council, 1774, 1859. This mid-nineteenth-century engraving depicts Franklin before the lords of the Privy Council in the Cockpit, a building erected on the site of Henry VIII's actual cockfighting pit. Here Franklin was publicly berated for his involvement in the Hutchinson-Oliver affair.

Fig. 6.14 François Dumont, Snuffbox with portrait of Benjamin Franklin, 1779. Like Barclay and Fothergill, Jonathan Shipley, bishop of St. Asaph, was a staunch supporter of American liberties and a proponent of Franklin's efforts to avoid a revolution. This snuffbox was a gift from Franklin to Shipley's daughter, Georgiana, and the portrait on its cover was one of Franklin's favorites. He later borrowed it so that it could be copied by other artists.

and Franklin. Lord Howe, who seems not to have had the full support of the ministry—perhaps no support at all—sought to enlist Franklin as an advocate for reconciliation on terms that could not have found acceptance in America because they did not include provisions for colonial self-government. Franklin gently turned him aside with the reminder that he, Franklin, had no official standing.

Lord Chatham, by this time an extinct volcano in British politics, could not use his reputation, immense though it was, to force a compromise acceptable to the government. It is unlikely that what he seemed to have in mind—acknowledgment of old colonial rights within a framework of unrestrained parliamentary sovereignty—would have appealed to Americans in any case. Franklin admired Chatham, but he could not have supported the terms Chatham wished the government to accept. Chatham got nowhere, and Franklin left England convinced that no accommodation could be found.

Even while he had struggled with Thomas Penn in the 1760s, Franklin had found himself advocating the interests of all the American colonies. The reason he could play such a role lay in the general American belief that British policies were unconstitutional, even oppressive. When he came back to America early in 1775, Franklin discovered just how far American resistance to British measures had gone, and he then took his place in a Continental Congress organizing for war. At that moment Franklin's understanding of his public life was transformed: action pursued in the political realm though principled had been in a sense provincial—he was acting only on behalf of Pennsylvania and Massachusetts and occasionally some of the other colonies. In the Congress he felt himself to be part of a great cause, the liberty of a nation—and soon afterward, he sought not only its liberty but its independence.

His service in Congress was of short duration. Yet it was full, demanding service for he was made a member of a variety of committees, including a secret committee charged with finding weapons, munitions, and other supplies for the Continental Army and a committee of correspondence that wrote to Europeans in an attempt to establish relations that would produce aid and support. He also offered a plan, "Articles of Confederation," for governing the new nation. This plan, though rejected by Congress, anticipated the principle of federalism later embodied in the Federal Constitution of 1787. He sat with Thomas Jefferson (fig. 6.15) and John Adams on the special committee to draft a declaration of independence (fig. 6.16). The resulting document was almost entirely Jefferson's composition, but Franklin offered several editorial suggestions that were accepted (fig. 6.17). As if this work in congressional deliberations were not enough, Congress sent Franklin to Canada on a mission to add a fourteenth state to the new union. He found traveling in the northern wilderness taxing, and he failed in his mission; indeed, he did not even try his considerable powers of persuasion on the Canadians once he had fought his way through to Montreal, for the British army had revived and was pushing the American force there into full retreat. Back in Philadelphia, Franklin was dispatched to New York to meet his old friend Lord Richard Howe, now commander of British naval forces in North America, who claimed to have an offer the Americans could not resist. The offer was the same old thing, and it came much too late for a nation that had declared its independence three months earlier.

Fig. 6.15 Jean-Antoine Houdon, Portrait bust of Thomas Jefferson, 1787. This bust may have been given to its owner, the astronomer and clockmaker David Rittenhouse, by Jefferson himself.

Fig. 6.16 Begun by Robert Edge Pine and finished by Edward Savage, Congress Voting Independence, ca. 1784–1801. Pine's painting is considered one of the most realistic renditions of this historic event. Several key political figures can be identified in the painting, including the members of the committee to draft the Declaration: Jefferson is the tall man depositing the Declaration of Independence on the table. Benjamin Franklin sits to his right. Fellow committee members John Adams, Roger Sherman, and Robert R. Livingston stand behind Jefferson. John Hancock is behind the table in the center.

Diplomat

Among Franklin's tasks during these months was to write the instructions for Silas Deane of Connecticut, who was dispatched by Congress as a commissioner to Paris to enlist support for the new nation. In October 1776, Congress sent Franklin himself to join the two commissioners, Deane and Arthur Lee of Virginia, with the charge to seek aid and commercial arrangements with France (fig. 6.18). Franklin arrived in Paris in December ready, as always, to give his best. The politician now turned to diplomacy.

The France he entered in 1776 was still a great power, but not as great as it had been before the Seven Years' War, which had depleted the country's treasury; the French fleet had not yet recovered from the pounding the British navy had given it. The war had also affected the European state system, which France had dominated for much of the century. After the French defeat in 1763, the old alignments fell apart. Instead of three great powers, France,

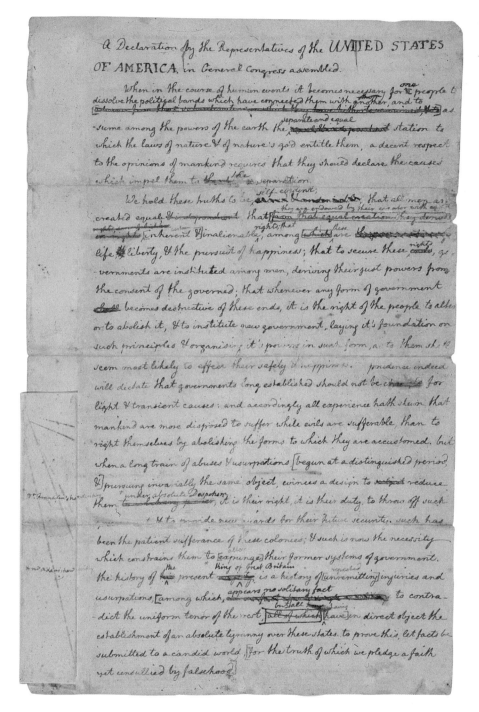

Fig. 6.17 "Original Rough draught" of the Declaration of Independence, June 1776, including the changes made later by John Adams, Benjamin Franklin, other members of the committee, and Congress. This draft of the Declaration includes a passage, later deleted, advocating the elimination of the slave trade. Jefferson sent the draft to Franklin for suggestions; his most memorable and enduring edit was substituting the word self-evident *for Jefferson's* sacred & undeniable.

Britain, and Austria, there were now five, including Russia, under Catherine the Great, and Prussia under Frederick II. In this new arrangement, Britain was isolated. British policy had been to ally itself with any European state that had the ability to counter French power. With France apparently in decline, or at least weakened, Britain's old allies, Prussia and Austria, no longer needed its

friendship. Russia might have become an ally, but only if Britain agreed to pay a subsidy.

These shifts in power did not embolden the French to plunge into the American war of independence. Under the monarchy of Louis XVI (fig. 6.19), France sought to reduce British strength wherever it existed. This desire was intensified by an old-fashioned motive: a yearning to settle old scores with the country's ancient enemy. But realism induced caution, for the changes on the continent required France to be wary of the rising powers led by Catherine and Frederick II.

Franklin probably came to his mission in Paris largely ignorant of the nature of the new alignments on the continent. But he certainly knew of the old animosities: he had shared British feelings toward France. In the new diplomatic environment, however, he thought that France and other European states might be induced to come to the aid of the Americans. But throughout his service in France, he had to deal with Silas Deane and Arthur Lee, who did not always advance the work of the commission. Deane was recalled in September 1777 and left early the next year. Then Congress abolished the three-member commission in September 1778 and appointed Franklin sole commissioner, yet Lee lingered in France until June 1780. Meanwhile, John Adams (fig. 6.20) had arrived in April 1778 as Deane's replacement, but he had to return home after Congress made Franklin sole diplomatic representative. Congress sent other men to Europe seeking aid, Francis Dana to Russia and Ralph Izard to Tuscany.

Dana was never a problem for Franklin—the others were. Deane, who had enjoyed some success in getting money and supplies for the United States, had aroused Lee's suspicions of his handling of public funds. Soon Lee began to include Franklin in his suspicions and harassed him with complaints about almost everything having to do with commission business. Ralph Izard never made it to Tuscany, but he did not seem to mind because he found abusing Franklin so satisfying. John Adams was a special case—he was a man of great ability and extraordinary patriotism—but he too came to dislike Franklin, whom he considered to be lazy, immoral, and subservient to the French, and did not bother to conceal his feelings. Among his names for Franklin, the "old Conjurer" was a favorite.[10]

Franklin met all that came his way with patience, and when he occasionally gave expression to deeper feelings, he buried them in letters to his tormentors that he never sent. The diplomacy required to maintain civil relations with the group around him taxed him more than that required to get along with the French. Beneath the foolish behavior of his colleagues, Franklin recognized a serious misconception concerning the strategy best suited to those representing America. Deane, Lee, and Adams all favored an assertive, even aggressive, style in approaching European powers for help. Their methods, Franklin believed, would turn away European governments, not bring them to the American side.

Congress had instructed the commissioners to secure a treaty of amity and commerce, instructions that implied that they should find a way to gain French recognition of the new United States—recognition that would lead to war between Britain and France. Until a treaty could be brought into being, the commissioners were to find as much aid as possible—money to fuel the war and to buy arms, gunpowder, and supplies of all kinds—for the army of the new country needed everything (fig. 6.21). Although Franklin was the best known of the three commissioners—indeed, a man famous throughout Europe—he

Fig. 6.18 (Opposite, top) Etienne Palliere, Allegory of the Franco-American Alliance, ca. 1778. Depicting Franklin, sporting a fur cap and glasses, arriving in France, this print is a reflection of his immediate fame. Although this allegorical print places Louis XVI at the wharf on Franklin's arrival, his image is there only to represent the monarchical state of France, not to suggest the king's actual presence.

Fig. 6.19 Louis Sicardy, Miniature portrait of Louis XVI, 1784. Louis XVI presented this miniature portrait to Franklin upon his retirement as minister plenipotentiary to France. The portrait was originally surrounded by three circles of 408 diamonds, but Sarah Franklin Bache, who inherited the miniature, sold many of the diamonds to finance her first trip to England.

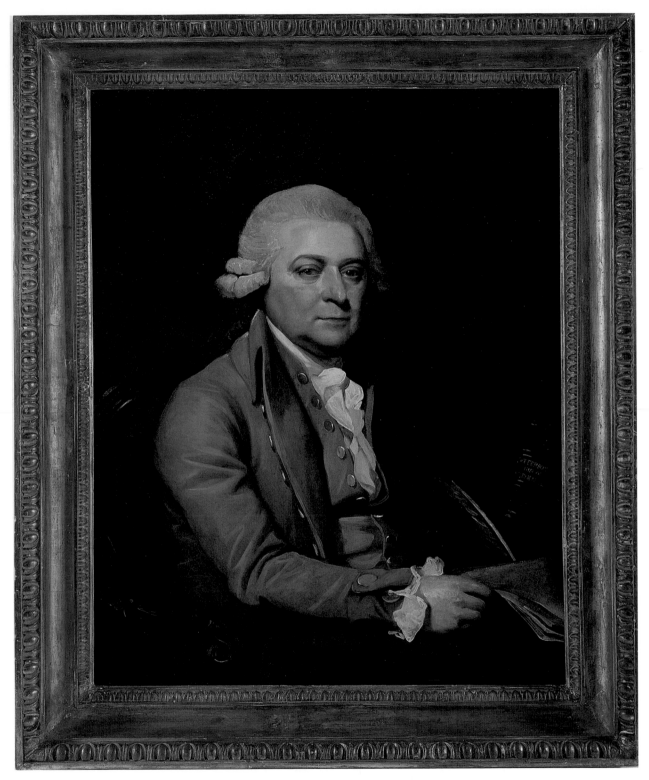

Fig. 6.20 *Mather Brown, Portrait of John Adams, 1788. Adams was sent to join Franklin as commis-sioner to Paris; he later served with Franklin as peace commissioner.*

was not quite first among equals, and he could not claim any formal authority over the others. Throughout the first year he seems to have acted in concert with them, though as the months passed Lee grew querulous and more difficult in every way.

Franklin's particular task, as he seems to have understood it, was to hold the commission together whatever its inner tensions. And so, as the commission went to work he concealed the uneasiness he felt at the way the commissioners chose to deal with the French. At first he seems to have agreed with their tactics, in part perhaps because they reflected the desires of the Congress. The original instructions adopted by Congress in September and October 1776 declared, "It is highly probable that France means not to let the United States sink in the present Contest," but because France might overestimate American ability to support the war "on our own Strength and resources, longer than in fact we can do, it will be proper for you to press for the immediate and explicit declaration of France in our Favour, upon a suggestion that a reunion with Great Britain may be the consequence of a Delay."[11] The idea of pressing France appealed to Lee and Deane, both men disposed to action without much thought. Restraint probably comes to revolutionaries only late in their revolutions; this one found Lee and Deane, both naturally impatient, wanting to get on with their assignment and unable to see why France might hesitate to commit itself. Franklin joined in the early meetings with the comte de Vergennes, the French foreign minister (fig. 6.22), and like Lee and Deane urged the French to act according to American prescriptions. He and his fellow commissioners soon learned that the French would not rush to war.

The French had been trying to repair their navy. They knew that going

Fig. 6.21 Hubert Robert, The Departure of Lafayette for America in 1777, *ca. 1800. The first aid to the American cause came not from the government but from an individual Frenchman. The young marquis de Lafayette, an ardent supporter, chartered a vessel,* La Victoire, *which sailed from Bordeaux in March 1777 laden with arms and military supplies he purchased with his own funds.*

Fig. 6.22 After Antoine-François Callet, Portrait of Charles Gravier, comte
de Vergennes, ca. 1781. Franklin negotiated the alliance between France and
the United States with the foreign minister, Vergennes.

to war with Britain before the colonies gave evidence that they were not going
to give up—thereby leaving France on a very shaky limb—would be rash and
destructive. In October 1777 the Battle of Saratoga, and the British general
Burgoyne's humiliation there, provided the evidence France needed. Early
the next year, France entered into treaties of commerce and alliance with the
United States and by June was at war with Britain (fig. 6.23).

Long before these treaties Franklin had recovered his natural caution and
attempted to rein in his colleagues. In March 1777 he put his understanding
of how the commission should conduct itself in a letter to Arthur Lee: "I have
never yet changed the Opinion I gave in Congress, that a Virgin State should
preserve the Virgin character, and not go about suitering for Alliances, but

wait with Decent Dignity for the applications of others. I was over-ruld; per-haps for the best."[12] Lee did not heed his colleague and took himself to Spain, where he failed to gain recognition for the United States but did extract a loan of 187,500 livres and promises of military supplies. Emboldened, Lee next tried the Germans in Berlin and brought back nothing. Of all the Americans who practiced the aggressive style, called by historians "militia-diplomacy,"[13] only Adams was able to bring in great rewards by it. And Adams succeeded in the Netherlands late in the war, well after France became an ally.

While waiting for the French to come openly to America's aid, Frank-lin strove to tap the French treasury for loans and gifts, money that could be used to buy arms, clothing, shoes, and other supplies needed by the Ameri-can army. Vergennes approved a loan of two million livres early in 1777, an act that partly relieved the disappointment of the American commissioners when he spurned their requests for a treaty. There were to be other subventions from the French in the years following. These loans and French military and naval help played vital roles in the final outcome of the war (fig. 6.24).

A second great battle, fought at Yorktown in October 1781, forced the Brit-ish to negotiate for peace. Not that they yielded easily: there was fierce oppo-sition at home to the idea of giving up the American colonies and settling with them and France. For a time the king resisted the idea. But his chief minister, Rockingham, who had replaced North early in 1782, was in favor of peace, as was Shelburne, his colonial secretary. Shelburne took the first steps toward ne-gotiations by sending Richard Oswald, a Scottish merchant, to talk with Frank-lin about an exchange of prisoners. It was a cautious opening, but gladly ac-cepted by Franklin, who now served on the revised commission to make peace. As the senior commissioner he in effect acted as chief of the group, which soon shrank to two members besides himself: John Adams, so involved with negotia-tions for a commercial treaty with the Dutch that he refused to return to Paris until late October, and John Jay, who did not appear until late June.

Negotiations proceeded far more slowly than Franklin desired. He had to act under the requirements Congress had imposed on the commission to keep the French informed of every step in the process, to seek their advice and approval, and to conclude no agreement without their concurrence. Af-ter he rejoined the commission in Paris, Jay expressed anger at this tying of the commission's hands, and Franklin, who had kept Vergennes informed of Shelburne's approaches, agreed to ignore the injunction. He and Jay did not agree on every tactic; Jay wanted the British to recognize the United States as a sovereign nation at the beginning of negotiations, a point Franklin did not

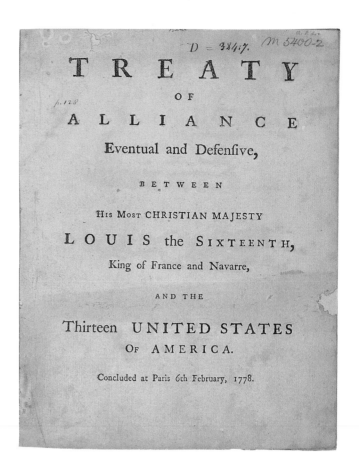

Fig. 6.23 Front page of Treaty of Alliance Eventual and Defensive, between His Most Christian Majesty Louis the Sixteenth, King of France and Navarre, and the Thirteen United States Of America *(Treaty of Amity), 1778. The alliance, negotiated by Franklin and the other commissioners, provided military and financial assistance that was a decisive factor in the American victory. There are multiple copies of the treaty in the United States and France.*

insist upon. The question of recognition was further complicated by a second British envoy, Thomas Grenville, sent out by Charles James Fox, secretary of state for foreign affairs, with the cabinet's authorization to negotiate with Vergennes. Fox had his own game, a plan by which Britain would make peace with the Americans, who would then break their alliance with France. Free of the American war, Britain, in Fox's scheme, would then make a pact with Prussia and Russia to carry the war to France and its ally Spain, which had come into the war in 1779.

Franklin saw the danger to the United States in British recognition on such terms and wanted no part of an arrangement that would betray France. Fox's scheme never made it through the cabinet and was abandoned when Shelburne became first lord of the treasury following Rockingham's death. Franklin probably did not expect that Shelburne's accession to power would smooth the path to peace. If he did, he was disappointed. The British continued to drag their feet.

Shelburne retained hopes that independence might be avoided. When the British admiral George Rodney defeated the comte de Grasse and the French navy off the Iles de Saintes in the West Indies, in April 1782, his hopes were quickened. In August a commission was provided for Oswald, but it met with Jay's objection because of its ambiguity regarding American independence. Not until late September did Shelburne provide Oswald with a new commission that recognized the United States as an independent nation.

The terms of a preliminary draft treaty of peace took form by early November in discussions largely between Jay and Oswald. Those terms included an explicit recognition of the independence of the United States, established the boundaries of the new country (the critical boundaries were the Mississippi River in the West and the thirty-first parallel in the South; see figure 6.25), acknowledged fishing rights off Newfoundland, and included a vague commitment by the Americans to compensate Loyalists for their loss of property. The treaty constituted a major diplomatic triumph, so impressive that Vergennes did not seriously protest being shut out of the negotiations. These preliminary provisions were made permanent the next year. The extraordinary success of the commission owed something to Jay's persistence, little to Adams' dithering, and much to Franklin's insight and patience (fig. 6.26).

Franklin did not completely avoid mistakes in his treaty negotiations. Early in the discussions with Oswald he suggested that Britain might voluntarily cede Canada to the United States. Because giving up Canada in response to an American demand might be "humiliating," Franklin gently pointed out that a voluntary renunciation of ownership might serve British interests better. The Americans, he said, would react with pleasure and accept the condition that vacant Canadian lands be sold "to indemnify the Royalists for the Confiscation of their Estates." Franklin's was a generous mind, but he soon realized his proposal implied that the Americans had an obligation to compensate Loyalists, a proposition that should not have been conceded though it might provide a subject for bargaining.[14]

This was a rare lapse. Throughout the negotiations he almost always displayed restraint and caution. He also proved to be extraordinarily patient with Shelburne, initially showing a willingness to wait for that worthy to instruct Oswald to acknowledge American independence as a precondition to settlement. When Shelburne delayed and left Oswald dangling, Franklin stopped the discussions, insisting that until independence was recognized, "Propositions and Discussions seem on Consideration, to be untimely."[15] A little more than two weeks later Shelburne came through with a commission to Oswald

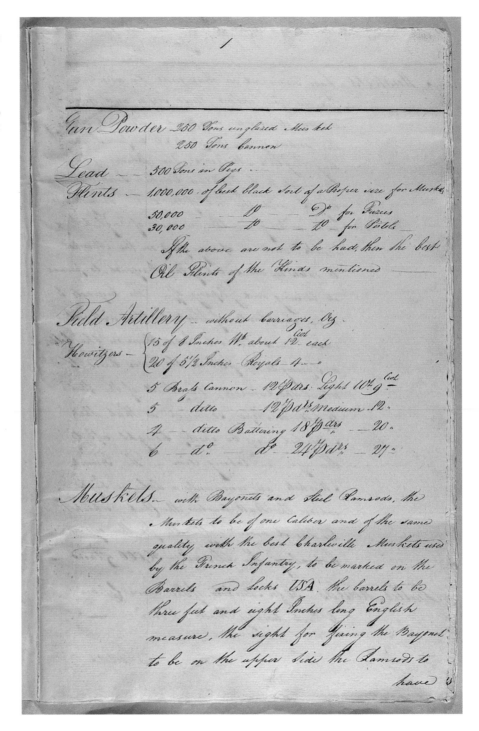

Fig. 6.24 First page of Congressional order for supplies, July 1779. Congress sent this list of needed military equipment to Franklin in France. Franklin had to place the order and then persuade the French to foot the bill. Many of these acquisitions were subsequently captured at sea by the British and sold at auction in London.

that satisfied Franklin and Jay. Franklin had demonstrated that patience combined with a sense of timing would carry the day.

His confidence in his own style was well-founded—he knew what he was doing; he kept himself informed of parliamentary politics; and he read his British opposites shrewdly. Before Fox lost out to Shelburne in the government, Franklin offered the following judgment of his agent, Grenville, and of Oswald. Grenville, he said, was "clever" and "seems to feel Reason as readily as Mr. Oswald. Tho not so ready to own it!" Oswald, "plain and sincere" and "old," seemed to have "no Desire but that of being Useful in doing Good." Grenville, in contrast, was young and ambitious to acquire "Reputation" through the negotiations, and in Franklin's assessment seemed "to think the whole Negotiation committed to him," thus stretching the terms of his commission beyond their meaning. Ever tactful, Franklin proved he could work with both men.[16]

Fig. 6.25 John Wallis, The United States of America laid down From the best Authorities, Agreeable to the Peace of 1783, *1783. This important map shows the new boundaries of the United States determined by the Treaty of 1783, and is the first map to portray the American flag with thirteen stars and stripes as evidence of American sovereignty.*

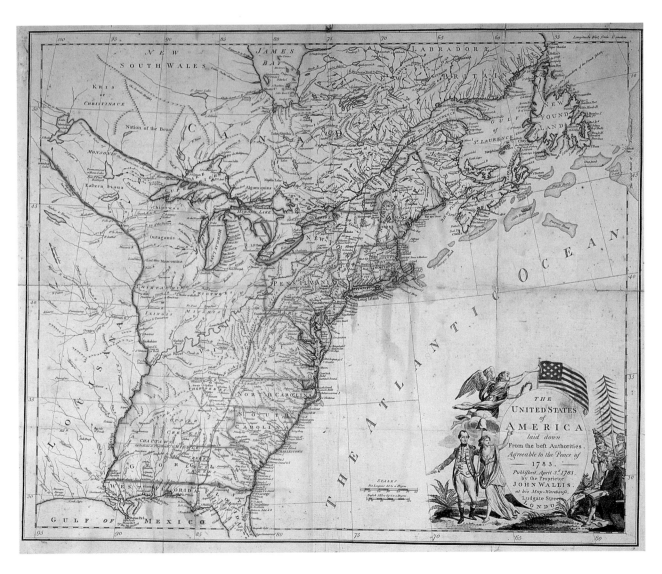

Fig. 6.26 Benjamin West, American Commissioners of the Preliminary Peace Negotiations with Great Britain, 1783–84. The group portrait commemorating the preliminary peace treaty between Great Britain and America was originally intended to include the British commissioner Richard Oswald and his secretary Caleb Whitfoord, in addition to the Americans (from left to right): John Jay, John Adams, Benjamin Franklin, Henry Laurens, and Franklin's grandson William Temple Franklin. But Oswald refused to pose, and the painting was never finished.

Fig. 6.27 Attributed to Jacques-Louis David, Portrait of Benjamin Franklin, n.d. This seldom seen drawing, signed "David," is thought to have been drawn in France by one of the country's leading artists.

He exercised the same sort of tact in dealing with his colleagues on the commission. Adams, returning from the Netherlands, had to force himself even to call on Franklin; Jay was easier and liked the old man (fig. 6.27). By the time the discussions had led to an admirable treaty (fig. 6.28), even Adams had mastered his revulsion for Franklin and admitted that his tactics had led to a treaty that served America's interests far more than praise could acknowledge (fig. 6.29).

Statesman

Franklin attended the Constitutional Convention of 1787 as a delegate from Pennsylvania. That was his formal designation; in reality, as everyone knew, he represented all the people of the new nation. He had by this time more than established his reputation as a statesman: a man wise in the ways of the world, with immense talent and achievements in the service of mankind. Indeed, he possessed more than a reputation—he had fame as well, and the trust of nations worldwide. In America a convention to draft a constitution for the new republic was inconceivable without him.

The Constitution disappointed him in several respects: it created a bicameral legislature, when Franklin saw no need for a senate; it also gave the

Fig. 6.29 Anton Van Ysendyck, Proclamation of the Treaty of Paris, ca. 1827. This historical painting evokes the spirit of celebration accompanying the signing of the long-awaited Treaty of Paris at the Tuileries, November 25, 1783.

president power to veto legislation. Franklin preferred a plural executive without such a power. He had also by this time become a firm opponent of slavery—the Constitution left the slaves in bondage (fig. 6.30). Yet Franklin supported ratification of the Constitution. It provided for a republican form of government and a large measure of personal liberty. His own vision, had it been honored, would have brought even more democracy to the new republic. But statesmanship demanded that he give his support to the frame of government devised by the convention. The Constitution, after all, was made by men he admired, and it supplied a government that might nourish the liberties of its citizens. His service in political life and diplomacy had always reflected his feeling that others must be trusted until their weakness became apparent. Statesmanship called for restraint as much as imagination. This was the judgment of a man who had hopes for mankind but recognized the realities of politics in America. He remained a pragmatic visionary to the end of his life (fig. 6.31).

Fig. 6.30 (Left) U.S. Constitution, 1787. Franklin's copy of the Constitution bears his notes in the margins. This is the first printing of the Constitution as adopted by the Constitutional Convention.

Fig. 6.31 Fugio penny, 1787. This coin was made according to a design suggested by Franklin, to show the chain of union between the thirteen colonies. The obverse reads, "We are one United States," and the reverse shows a sundial with the legend "Fugio [I fly] 1787 Mind your business."

Chapter 7

The Printer at Passy

ELLEN R. COHN

Franklin's diplomatic mission to France from 1777 to 1785 was hardly, as John Adams sneered, "a Scene of continual discipation" (fig. 7.1). Franklin won treaties of alliance and commerce, he secured loan after improbable loan from the French government to finance the American Revolution, and he single-handedly negotiated the framework for the peace treaty with Great Britain. These are among his most spectacular successes as minister to the French court. But as anyone knows who has leafed through the sixteen volumes of his edited papers that have so far been published from this French period (covering the first six years),[1] the amount of day-to-day business was staggering, and Franklin tackled it with resignation if not always good humor. The problems of securing supplies for the American army far exceeded anything he had imagined, and he grumbled about having to deal with the complaints, excuses, and demands and defaults of agents and manufacturers throughout France and the Netherlands. He was deeply angered to learn, through the scores of letters he received from captured American sailors who were languishing in British jails, about the inhumane conditions they were subjected to, and he fought a long, frustrating battle with the British authorities to arrange for their exchange. In the meantime, he saw to it that these men were given assistance on site, and he helped hundreds of escapees get back to French ports and ship out again on privateers. Dealing with the French court, dealing with the demands of

VIR

Congress, dealing with merchants, agents, ships' outfitters, sea captains, Americans in need, Europeans begging for help—Franklin struggled with a tremendous workload, especially after 1779, when he was appointed sole minister plenipotentiary.

Franklin repeatedly pleaded with Congress to send him a secretary and appoint consuls in the major port cities who could relieve him of having to rule on affairs that he had neither the expertise nor the interest to sort out, long-distance, from Paris. The consuls never came, and until the war's end he remained saddled with such unwelcome tasks as evaluating the validity of prize ships captured by American privateers and brought into Nantes or Lorient or Bordeaux. Each case generated its own paperwork. As for secretarial help, he managed primarily with his grandson William Temple Franklin, who was just sixteen years old when he accompanied Franklin across the Atlantic (fig. 7.2), and a French medical student named Jean L'Air de Lamotte, the nephew of an old friend. The two helped Franklin with correspondence, financial accounts (never his strong suit), and keeping copybooks.

Still, if Franklin was so taxed with business, his legendary social life tends to obscure that fact in the minds of many. Masses of visitors streamed through his door. Some, as John Adams observed, were "Phylosophers, Accademicians and Economists" seeking a few hours of stimulating conversation; others were "humble friends in the Litterary way," who helped him translate his writings into French (Adams preferred to study French grammar in the evenings by candlelight); still others were "Women and children" come solely for the honor of being able to tell their friends they had seen "the great Franklin" (fig. 7.3).[2] Lively dinners at the homes of intelligent and influential men and women, late-night chess games, intimate tea parties, musical soirées, the exchanging of clever songs and playful letters: Franklin's wit and gift for friendship continue to cast his French mission in a glow of flirtation and bonhomie (fig. 7.4).

How else did he relax, besides with this delightful company? Historians of printing, charmed by the playful letters and essays now known as bagatelles that he printed as keepsakes for his circle of intimates, decided that Franklin must have set up a press at his residence in Passy "for his amusement." It was "a relief from the vexations of his daily life," they asserted, a nostalgic reversion to his early occupation designed "principally for his own entertainment and pastime."[3] These statements were based on very little evidence. Franklin left no written descriptions of the press at Passy and rarely mentioned it in his letters. His *Autobiography,* which provides such rich detail about his Philadel-

Fig. 7.2 John Trumbull, Miniature portrait of William Temple Franklin, 1790. Franklin had helped to rear and educate his grandson "Temple," who served as his secretary in Paris. Temple later collected and published his grandfather's voluminous writings.

Fig. 7.3 Anne-Rosalie Boquet Filleul, Portrait of Benjamin Franklin, 1778 or 1779. Filleul and her husband, Louis, were acquaintances of Franklin in Paris. The portrait was specifically made as the model for an engraving by Louis Jacques Cathelin and published by Filleul's father, Blaise Boquet. Exhibited at the French Salon of 1779, the engraving was praised for its likeness.

phia printing office, stops far short of his stay in France. None of the historians of printing quoted above, or the many others who followed their lead, actually knew when Franklin established the press, what its purpose was, or even where he obtained his type. This latter question is of more than antiquarian interest. Type—whose tiny, delicate shapes had to be carved and chiseled by hand onto steel rods before being cast—varied considerably from foundry to foundry, and the public recognized typefaces by the name of the master typefounder who had "cut" the letters. A printer of Franklin's discernment and prominence would not have made his choice lightly.

All these authors had at their disposal the study by Luther S. Livingston, *Franklin and His Press at Passy* (1914), which presented enough examples of

Fig. 7.4 "Depense journaliere du Vin pendant le mois de 7bre. 1782" (Chart of daily wine consumption for the month of September 1782). This is the only such record of daily alcohol consumption that has survived. It shows the Passy household consuming only one bottle of red wine per day except on Sundays, when Franklin customarily hosted dinners. The well-stocked cellar included beers, cider, spirits, and two varieties of champagne.

Franklin's printing to contradict this view. But even Livingston invites us in his preface to "imagine the old philosopher, past seventy, with glasses on his nose and a printer's stick in his hand, *playing at the art* that he had begun to practice as a boy of twelve in his brother's printing shop in Boston more than sixty years before" (emphasis mine).[4] The picture of a kindly old printer seems to be nearly irresistible.

Where does it come from? The image may be traced to Franklin's own grandson, Temple, who unwittingly influenced two centuries of historical interpretation with one careless sentence. When Temple published his inheritance—in the form of a three-volume edition of Franklin's writings—his only mention of the press at Passy was the following: "Notwithstanding Dr. Franklin's various and important occupations, he occasionally amused himself in composing and printing, by means of a small set of types and a press he had in his house, several of his light essays, *bagatelles,* or *jeux d'esprit,* written chiefly for the amusement of his intimate friends."[5]

Small set of types? It weighed nearly eight thousand pounds. Light essays? Not exclusively. Temple deliberately ignored the thousands of other sheets issued from the press: passports, bonds, promissory note forms, payment authorization forms, loan certificates, reprints of congressional broadsides, prize ship condemnation forms, even two small books. Franklin did not buy a printing press in order to escape from work; he established a press to help him do it. By printing official forms he saved himself and his two assistants countless hours of laborious copying by hand.

In addition to its practical purpose, the press had a symbolic function as well. Congress was counting on Franklin to represent the newly declared United States in a way that would inspire confidence, gain allies, and loosen coffers. His mission was to persuade the European world of the fledgling nation's viability and promise. He expertly played on his own personal stature in order to further this goal; the various portraits of himself, reproduced throughout Europe in hundreds of engravings, attest to his savvy when it came to orchestrating a media campaign. Likewise with his printing press. Printed documents, as befit any established government, enhanced America's prestige. Everywhere these forms were carried—from coastal villages to the court at Versailles—they presented an authoritative image of the new nation. Some resembled the routine government printing that Franklin had done earlier in his career. Others, however, were typographically distinctive in a way that symbolized innovation and vigor: they displayed three unusual typefaces commissioned by Franklin that were unique to his press.

Where did Franklin obtain his type? Historians of printing have speculated about who must have sold it to him, but in fact, most of it was not purchased at all. It was made for him in a foundry that he installed on the grounds of his residence at Passy, the Hôtel de Valentinois (fig. 7.5). Franklin established this typefoundry for a reason he never advertised: he hoped to furnish fresh type to American printers, who were cut off from their British suppliers and had no foundries of their own. As he feared, the risks of trans-Atlantic transportation during wartime proved insurmountable, and he was forced to abandon the plan. But his foundry continued to cast type until it produced a full range, sufficient to stock any printing office. This was the type that Franklin and his younger grandson, Benjamin Franklin Bache, brought back to America in 1785 and that Bache, who had been trained in France as a printer and typefounder, used in his printing office on Market Street in Philadelphia. Identifying the origins of Franklin's type is the first step toward a full appreciation of what Franklin printed in France.[6]

The Typefoundry

Franklin was on the lookout for typefounding equipment as soon as he arrived on French soil. In June 1777 his friend Jean-Baptiste Le Roy wrote that "a gentleman of my acquaintance . . . has heard [that] you intend to buy what we call in French *une fonderie de Caractères*." This gentleman "knows a person who has one to Sell very compleat and which you will have at a very mod-

erate Price." Nothing came of this offer, but a year later Franklin was approached again on the same topic, this time by an enterprising well-wisher who counseled him to take advantage of an extremely rare opportunity: the chance to acquire a local typefoundry. Foundries usually remained in families, the writer explained; this particular one was highly regarded and well-equipped. It would be unwise to ship the equipment across the sea during wartime, however. The French government would undoubtedly object to its being exported and if the equipment were lost or captured, it could not be replaced. If Franklin were to buy the foundry, he should hire workmen to keep it producing for French presses until the end of the conflict. The writer, Lefebvre de Longeville, also sent a memoire stressing America's need for foundries if the new nation were to become self-sufficient. Franklin did make inquiries of the typefounder's widow, but it seems that Lefebvre de Longeville had mistaken her desire to sell.[7]

Franklin hardly needed to be reminded of America's desperate need for type. Newspapers were becoming faint and marred by broken letters. "I thank you for the Boston newspapers," he wrote a friend in 1779, "tho' I see nothing so clearly in them as that your Printers do indeed want new Letters. They perfectly blind me in endeavouring to read them. If you should ever have any Secrets that you wish to be well kept, get them printed in those Papers." Although several New England printers inquired into the feasibility of ordering type from France, only two printers, James Watson and Nathan Strong from Connecticut, actually sent money for the purpose. This was in the summer of 1778. Their request, addressed to Franklin and his then–fellow commissioner Silas Deane, was endorsed by Governor Jonathan Trumbull. They also asked whether a typefounder could be persuaded to emigrate with all his equipment; if so, Watson would take him into partnership.[8]

Franklin deposited the printers' considerable sum with his banker and set about filling their order. As a first step he ordered a font of 10 point type (called in French *petit romain,* equivalent to the English "long primer") from the most highly regarded foundry in Paris. This was the firm established by the famous Pierre-Simon Fournier le jeune, author of the *Manuel typographique* (1764-66). After Fournier's widow died in 1775, the foundry descended to their eldest son, Simon-Pierre Fournier le jeune, who was about twenty-eight years old when Franklin met him. The younger Fournier completed the order by early February 1779: two boxes of petit romain, roman, italic, and spaces, weighing 274 pounds and costing 470 livres, approximately one-third of the total amount sent by Watson and Strong. Fournier never got the commission for the remainder of the type. He even had to wait several weeks before Franklin would allow him to deliver this font and collect his payment.[9] For one thing, in early February, Franklin was stricken with a painful attack of gout. Then, on February 12, he received a dispatch from Congress that transformed his mission: Congress had appointed him sole minister plenipotentiary to the French court.

Franklin's appointment was both a relief and a vindication. He was finally released from the exasperating obligations of having to work as a member of a three-man team that was plagued by bickering and intrigue. One of the original members, Silas Deane, had already been recalled by Congress and replaced by John Adams, whose disapproval of Franklin's style made group decisions difficult. Far more irritating, however, was Arthur Lee, whose jealousies and paranoia taxed Franklin's resolve to present a united front to the French ministry. In the same packet that brought him the congressional letter of appointment, Franklin had also received private letters from Philadelphia warning

Fig. 7.6 (Above) Type matrices, ca. 1740, probably made by Claude Mozet. Purchased by Franklin and used to cast type at Passy. Franklin gave them to his grandson Benjamin Franklin Bache in 1785 when setting up a printing office for Bache in Philadelphia.

Fig. 7.7 Type ladle, ca. 1785.

him that Lee and Ralph Izard (an ally of Lee's who was also in Paris) were accusing him of disloyalty and urging Congress to remove him. Congress, rather than recalling Franklin, recalled Adams and Lee. [10]

Elated by the news of his appointment, cognizant of the responsibilities that now lay on his shoulders alone, and finally free to make his own decisions, Franklin determined to set up a press and establish a typefoundry that would supply the needs of American printers as well as his own. Within two weeks he received a visit from a man who left his name and address: "Hémery, typefounder, rue St. Jacques at the home of Mr. Canon the shoemaker across the street from Mr. Dépré."[11]

Hémery, to judge by the scanty biographical information available, had had almost fifty years' experience as a master typefounder when he answered Franklin's inquiry. He had spent thirty of them as foundry director for the Fourniers before buying a foundry of his own in 1760. The previous owner, Claude Mozet, had moved the foundry from Paris to Nantes. Hémery brought it back to the capital and set up on the rue du Haut-Moulin.[12]

Franklin persuaded Hémery to move his foundry to the Hôtel de Valentinois. By the beginning of April he was on Franklin's payroll, buying metal and supplies, and firing up the furnace. Over the next two years he operated the foundry almost continuously, employing between two and five workers and producing a complete set of type ranging from double canon (56 point) to nonpareil (6 point). Franklin used only a fraction of this type for his own purposes at Passy. Nearly all of it, however, along with the characteristic ornaments Franklin used, can be seen in Claude Mozet's 1754 type specimen book, which Hémery inherited.

Fig. 7.8 Pierre-Simon Fournier le jeune, "Fourneau à fondre les Lettres" (Typefoundry), in his Manuel typographique, *[1764].*

None of this type has survived. One set of matrices—an alphabet of capital letters—does survive, however, and it is shown in figure 7.6. Matrices are the forms from which type is cast. In order to make a matrix, a master typefounder must first sculpt and chisel the shape of a given letter—paying particular attention to its height, width, and depth—onto the end of a steel rod known as a punch. (This exacting process is called punchcutting.) The punch is then hammered, or "struck," into a brass tile known as a matrix. The matrix, being of a softer metal, accepts the deep impression. The typefounder places this matrix at the bottom of a letter mold—an immensely complicated and precisely regulated assemblage of some fifty iron parts enclosed in a wooden shell. He (or more likely an assistant) then pours molten typemetal into the mold by means of a tiny ladle (fig. 7.7). The resulting slugs of lead are then subjected to many stages of trimming and polishing. (Fournier's depiction of a typefoundry with its furnace and benches is shown in figure 7.8. The letter mold, resembling a large wooden yo-yo with a long, looped metal spring, is shown on the edge of a shelf on the right, above the furnace.)

The activities of the Passy foundry can be glimpsed through the entries in Franklin's personal "Cash Book." Never known for meticulous record keeping, Franklin did take care to record these particular expenses, including materials and wages. For the first six months, he knew only the names of the master founder and his assistant, Beauville. The lower-paid workers were listed by generic type: "Girl," "Boy" or "Gar" (spelled variously and presumably short for *garçon*, "boy"), and "Beauville's brother." On November 13, their identities emerge: Rocque, Madelon, and Geard. After a few weeks Franklin reverted to generic nouns, this time in French: "femme," "garcon," and "son frere." But by mid-December he settled into a consistent pattern of referring to the workers by name (fig. 7.9). This may well signal the period when Franklin began spending more time in the foundry. We know from the two inventories that survive—faded and confusing jumbles of phonetically spelled French from Hémery with partial translations by Franklin—that Franklin did cast some "large Letters."[13]

On March 6, 1780, almost a year after the foundry began operation, Franklin recorded in his Cash Book that a font of *petit texte* (8 point) had been completed for the Connecticut printers Watson and Strong: 327 ½ pounds of type, 15 pounds of rules, 10 pounds of interlines, and 2 ½ pounds of signs and planets, packed in three boxes. The total came to 870 livres, which exhausted the balance of Watson and Strong's account. Franklin sent these boxes to Nantes,

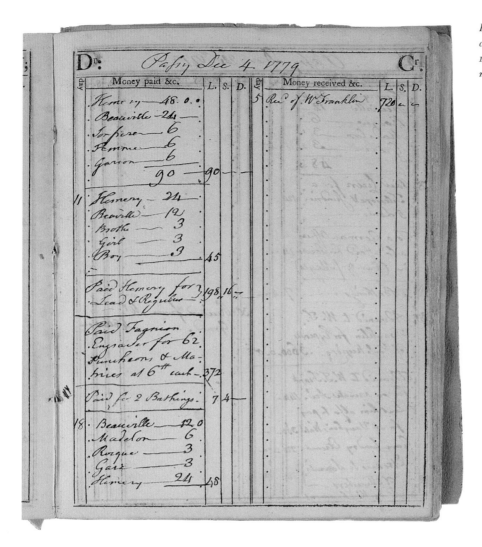

where they were to be loaded onto the *Marquis de Lafayette*—a 1,200-ton transport ship that was preparing to carry to America a long-awaited and desperately needed shipment of supplies for the American army. Plagued by countless mishaps and delays, this shipment was nearly two years in the planning. In the spring of 1780, however, all conditions seemed favorable.

Hémery's three boxes of type were placed next to the two boxes of Fournier's type that for a full year had been waiting for a safe conveyance to America. The *Marquis de Lafayette* set sail under protection of a convoy at the end of March. Halfway into the voyage the ship was separated from the convoy by a storm and captured by the British. The entire cargo (except for the type, which vanished) was sold at public auction in London. It was a disaster for the

Americans, who had to start all over again assembling the critically needed military supplies.[14] Franklin gave up the idea of trying to send type to America during wartime.

He did, however, purchase the entire foundry from Hémery on May 6, 1780. Franklin now owned a complete, coordinated set of punches, matrices, and molds, as well as all the other tools and equipment necessary to cast as much type as he could possibly need, in as much variety as he could reasonably want. The foundry, along with all the Passy type, would eventually be packed into crates by Benjamin Franklin Bache and shipped to Philadelphia. Claude Mozet could never have foreseen that his equipment would be used to produce one of the earliest American type specimens.

The most distinctive of Mozet's types, in his own opinion, were the *italiques rondes* (a rounded, softer italic) that he featured in his 1754 specimen book. Franklin made frequent use of these italics, and favored them almost exclusively in the bagatelles. Livingston described them as "the most easily recognizable of all the Passy types, especially the ornamental capitals."[15] Those ornamental capitals, however, were not part of that font, and did not come from Mozet. To date, their origin is still a matter of speculation. Franklin called them "Fancy Capitals," and they appear on Hémery's inventories as "italique de fantasie." They were made in only one size—cicero, or 12 point— and they appear to have been unique to Franklin.

Franklin commissioned three unique typefaces in all. The second, also cicero, has only recently been noticed and identified.[16] It is a style of letter that had never before been manufactured. Known today as "sloped roman," it is somewhere between a roman-style letter and an italic: roman-shaped letters that slant to the right. Designed for the Académie des Sciences by Jacques Jaugeon in the 1690s as part of the *romain du roi*, a scientifically designed set of typefaces for the royal printing office, the sloped roman letterform was ultimately rejected as being not sufficiently distinctive. The drawings lay unrealized until someone cut this type for Franklin. He reserved it for one very special use: loan certificates that he issued to the French government on behalf of the United States.

Of the three type fonts that Franklin commissioned, the two just mentioned have left no traces in his correspondence. By contrast, the third—a spectacular, large-script type that was cut by Simon-Pierre Fournier le jeune after a design that was undoubtedly suggested by Franklin—has left a documentary trail that shows the collaboration between artisan and client. Fournier sent Franklin a proof of the capital N, P, and ampersand, on the bottom of which he scribbled, "I flatter myself you will find them beautiful." Franklin agreed that they were "well formed," and he conferred several times with Lucien, the metalsmith who was constructing the molds. Fournier finished the font in early 1781 and christened it "Le Franklin."[17]

The Press

Franklin seems to have acquired his first printing press in the spring of 1779, just as Hémery and his crew were beginning their work. A year earlier he had bought a small quantity of type from Jean-François Fournier *fils,* a cousin of Simon-Pierre.[18] This was the type he used for his first imprints. The press was inaugurated for an occasion that held particular significance for Franklin: he printed invitations to an Independence Day celebration, his first as sole minister plenipotentiary (fig. 7.10).

Franklin and John Adams had hosted a similar dinner in Passy the previous year on the Fourth of July, to which they invited the Americans living in

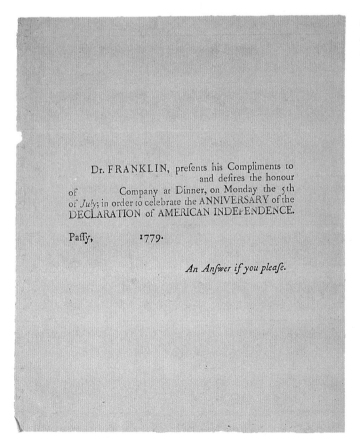

Fig. 7.10 Invitation to a celebration of the anniversary of the Declaration of American Independence, July 5, 1779, printed by Benjamin Franklin.

and around Paris along with selected French friends and dignitaries. Franklin's animosity toward certain of those Americans, especially Ralph Izard, had reached such a pitch that he refused to have any part in inviting them; Adams was forced to issue invitations in his name alone. A year later, exuberant in his post, Franklin needed no prodding. He set his own name in capital letters and delivered printed invitations to the very Americans who had been lobbying Congress for his recall: Ralph Izard and Arthur Lee.

The celebration was a grand banquet attended by about forty people. It was held on July 5, as the fourth fell on a Sunday. Franklin's financial accounts record the magnificence of this occasion: he rented quantities of tableware, including seventeen decorative porcelain figurines; the goblets were filled from more than a hundred bottles of wine; and the platters overflowed with a mouth-watering assortment of poultry, meats, vegetables, and fruits, representing the full summer bounty of the French countryside. The guests dined under a full-length portrait of George Washington holding the Declaration of Independence and the Franco-American Treaties of Alliance and Commerce and trampling the British conciliatory bills. The portrait, painted by Louis Trinquesse, had been brought to France by Lafayette. Toasts were delivered in English and French; poems were recited and distributed; guests received a French translation of Franklin's *Way to Wealth* (*La science du Bonhomme Richard*); a band played military music; and the whole was followed by a ball.[19]

By August, at least, Franklin was using his press for diplomatic purposes: printing French-language passports for American citizens. Any foreign national leaving France was required to carry a passport issued by that country's ambassador.[20] In the early years of the Revolution, passports for Americans were handwritten and signed by all three American commissioners. The wording was adapted from standard passport language and, as custom dictated, the documents required a seal. Lacking a national emblem, the commissioners decided to seal the documents with Franklin's personal seal, his adopted coat of arms.

There is no way of knowing how many passports Franklin issued once he started printing them, as he kept no records. William Temple Franklin started a list of passports granted during 1782, but he gave up after nine months and even the list of those months is incomplete.[21] (Three of the passports issued during that nine-month period have survived, of which Temple noted only one.) Extrapolating from that list and the various references to passports in Franklin's papers, it seems clear that he must have issued at least five hundred. Every captured sailor who had escaped from a British jail and made his

Nous Benjamin Franklin,
Ecuyer, Miniſtre Plénipotentiaire des
Etats-Unis de l'Amérique, près Sa
Majeſté Très-Chrétienne,

PRIONS *tous ceux qui ſont à prier, de*
vouloir bien laiſſer ſûrement & librement paſ-
ſer

ſans   donner ni permettre qu'il   ſoit
donné aucun empêchement, mais au contraire
de   accorder toutes ſortes d'aide et d'aſ-
ſiſtance, comme nous ferions en pareil Cas,
pour tous ceux qui nous ſeroient recommandés.

EN FOI DE QUOI *nous*
avons délivré le préſent Paſſe-port, valable
pour   ſigné de notre main,
contre-ſigné par l'un de nos Secretaires, & au
bas duquel eſt l'empreinte de nos Armes.

DONNÉ *à Paſsy, en notre Hôtel, le*
mil ſept cent quatre-vingt

Par ordre du Miniſtre Plénipotentiaire.

way to Paris, for example, required a passport to return to the coast and ship out again. (If Franklin doubted the man's identity or loyalty, he would make him sign an oath of allegiance.) In addition to these prisoners of war and the diplomats and merchants serving the American cause, a surprising number of Americans of both sexes, with or without servants and children, were crossing

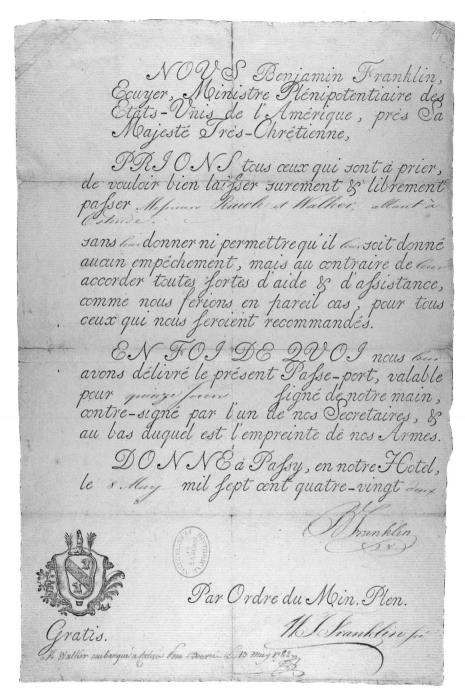

Fig. 7.12 Passport for William Rawle and Benjamin[?] Walker, May 8, 1782, printed by Benjamin Franklin. Franklin printed this with the script type cut for him by Simon-Pierre Fournier le jeune.

national boundaries for private business, study, or pleasure. Every one of them had to procure a passport from Franklin. It is no wonder that he was eager to mechanize the process.

Because they were such ephemeral documents, typically valid for only one month, few of these printed passports have survived. Only thirteen dated examples have been located, ranging from August 1779 to May 1785; one came to light only two weeks before this essay was submitted for publication. Together they indicate that Franklin reset his passport forms at least seven times. Each time he tinkered with small things: he improved spelling, added or changed accent marks, altered hyphenization of certain words (varying between *passe-port* and *passeport,* for example), played with spacing and the heights of initial letters, and varied the style of his italics. In the second printing, he set lines ("rules") along the top and both sides of the text. In the third printing he removed the rules but added an engraved version of his coat of arms to replace the seal he had previously impressed in red wax (fig. 7.11). (He had commissioned a woodblock engraved with his arms from a Mr. Miller exclusively for use on the passports.)[22] The change required him to substitute the word *empreinte* (imprint) in the passport text for *cachet* (seal). The most dramatic alteration in the passports, however, came in the spring of 1782, when he began setting them in the large-script type Fournier had cut for him and that he used only for these forms.

Two versions of the large-script passports have been located. They differ only in the type font used below Franklin's signature. The one shown in figure 7.12 is the only known example of the first version, in which Franklin used the large script throughout. (Notice that he was forced to abbreviate his own title as "Min. Plen." for lack of space. In the second version he reverted to the small italic he had formerly employed, allowing him to spell out his title in full.) The typography of both versions, however, is striking. In the body of the text, the tops and bottoms of the letters touch one another and in some cases intersect— something that is natural in handwriting but impossible with lead type, at least when printed in the conventional manner.

Franklin's trick was to print these forms in two passes, first printing the odd-numbered lines, then the even-numbered ones. In this way, the letters on any given line could invade the space above and below. In figure 7.12, for example, the *j* of *Benjamin* loops halfway through the capital *P* below it. On the two lines directly below that, the graceful foot of the capital *A* rests on the crown of the capital *C* of *Chrêtienne.* Because Franklin could not align the paper in exactly the same position for each of the passes, all these imprints differ slightly, just as every handwritten document is unique. Franklin took the newly developed notion of script type and enhanced its potential to imitate actual script.

The leading text element in the passports, and also the largest, was Franklin's name. The format of these documents was designed to convey to French governors and port officials the ambassador's stature as the representative of

Fig. 7.13 George Peter Alexander
Healy, Franklin Urging the Claims of
the American Colonies Before Louis
XVI, ca. 1847.

his country to the court of Louis XVI (fig. 7.13). Typographically, they did not need to be distinctive. Franklin's using a printed coat of arms was an elegant touch; otherwise, except when he used the large-script type (which he discontinued in 1784), the passports were simply functional: authoritative, dignified, and to some degree routine.

The loan certificates that Franklin printed for the French court, however, were anything but routine. Nearly everything about them was deluxe. Previous to these forms, the American commissioners had acknowledged receipt of the huge sums they received from the French government with handwritten promises of repayment. Franklin envisioned a certificate for the royal treasury whose elegance and ingenuity would represent the new nation with dignity. He would print the certificates on vellum-like wove paper, made according to a technique as yet unknown in France; he would have that paper marbled in an extraordinary way; and he would use distinctive typefaces that he alone possessed.

Franklin's chance opportunity to order this paper came just as he was setting up his press. In June 1779, shortly before he printed his Independence Day invitations, he received an unexpected visit from a British stationer who represented James Whatman, one of Britain's finest papermakers. Whatman had been making wove paper since the 1750s; Franklin knew it well, and his French friends marveled over its uncommonly smooth surface. (French paper makers began manufacturing wove paper within a year of Franklin's importing this stock.) The paper order took nearly a year to complete because Franklin specified that two of the reams—the paper he used for these certificates—

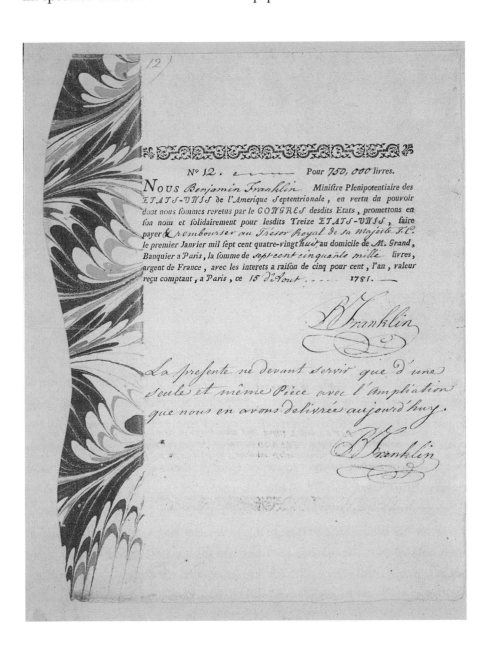

Fig. 7.14 French loan certificate, no. 12, August 15, 1781, printed by Benjamin Franklin. Franklin used two typefaces in this form that were unique to his press: "sloped roman" and what he called "fancy italic" capitals. The end of the first line, "Ministre plenipotentiaire des," is set in sloped roman. The beginning of the second line, "ETATS-UNIS," is set in fancy italic capitals.

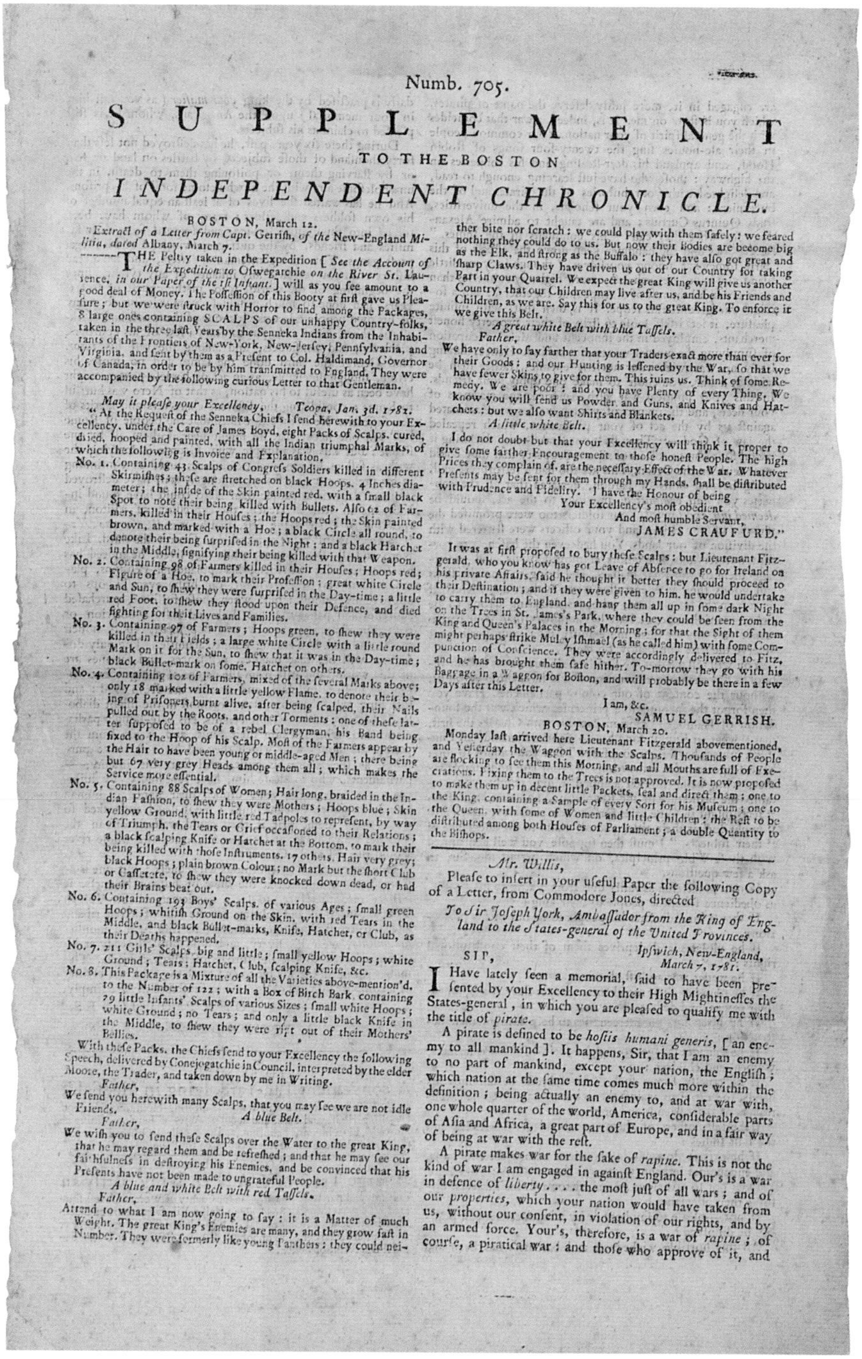

Numb. 705.

SUPPLEMENT

TO THE BOSTON

INDEPENDENT CHRONICLE.

BOSTON, March 12.

Extract of a Letter from Capt. Gerriſh, *of the* New-England *Militia, dated* Albany, March 7.

------THE Peltry taken in the Expedition [*See the Account of the Expedition to* Oſwegatchie *on the River St.* Laurence, *in our Paper of the 1ſt Inſtant.*] will as you ſee amount to a good deal of Money. The Poſſeſſion of this Booty at firſt gave us Pleaſure; but we were ſtruck with Horror to find among the Packages, 8 large ones containing SCALPS of our unhappy Country-folks, taken in the three laſt Years by the Senneka Indians from the Inhabitants of the Frontiers of New-York, New-Jerſey, Pennſylvania, and Virginia, and ſent by them as a Preſent to Col. Haldimand, Governor of Canada, in order to be by him tranſmitted to England. They were accompanied by the following curious Letter to that Gentleman.

May it pleaſe your Excellency, *Teoga, Jan. 3d, 1782.*

"At the Requeſt of the Senneka Chiefs I ſend herewith to your Excellency, under the Care of James Boyd, eight Packs of Scalps, cured, dried, hooped and painted, with all the Indian triumphal Marks, of which the following is Invoice and Explanation.

No. 1. Containing 43 Scalps of Congreſs Soldiers killed in different Skirmiſhes; theſe are ſtretched on black Hoops, 4 Inches diameter; the inſide of the Skin painted red, with a ſmall black Spot to note their being killed with Bullets. Alſo 62 of Farmers, killed in their Houſes; the Hoops red; the Skin painted brown, and marked with a Hoe; a black Circle all round, to denote their being ſurpriſed in the Night; and a black Hatchet in the Middle, ſignifying their being killed with that Weapon.

No. 2. Containing 98 of Farmers killed in their Houſes; Hoops red; Figure of a Hoe, to mark their Profeſſion; great white Circle and Sun, to ſhew they were ſurpriſed in the Day-time; a little red Foot, to ſhew they ſtood upon their Defence, and died fighting for their Lives and Families.

No. 3. Containing 97 of Farmers; Hoops green, to ſhew they were killed in their Fields; a large white Circle with a little round Mark on it for the Sun, to ſhew that it was in the Day-time; black Bullet-mark on ſome, Hatchet on others.

No. 4. Containing 102 of Farmers, mixed of the ſeveral Marks above; only 18 marked with a little yellow Flame, to denote their being of Priſoners burnt alive, after being ſcalped, their Nails pulled out by the Roots, and other Torments: one of theſe latter ſuppoſed to be of a rebel Clergyman, his Band being fixed to the Hoop of his Scalp. Moſt of the Farmers appear by the Hair to have been young or middle-aged Men; there being but 67 very grey Heads among them all; which makes the Service more eſſential.

No. 5. Containing 88 Scalps of Women; Hair long, braided in the Indian Faſhion, to ſhew they were Mothers; Hoops blue; Skin yellow Ground, with little red Tadpoles to repreſent, by way of Triumph, the Tears or Grief occaſioned to their Relations; a black ſcalping Knife or Hatchet at the Bottom, to mark their being killed with thoſe Inſtruments. 17 others, Hair very grey; black Hoops; plain brown Colour; no Mark but the ſhort Club or Caſſetete, to ſhew they were knocked down dead, or had their Brains beat out.

No. 6. Containing 193 Boys' Scalps, of various Ages; ſmall green Hoops; whitiſh Ground on the Skin, with red Tears in the Middle, and black Bullet-marks, Knife, Hatchet, or Club, as their Deaths happened.

No. 7. 211 Girls' Scalps, big and little; ſmall yellow Hoops; white Ground; Tears; Hatchet, Club, ſcalping Knife, &c.

No. 8. This Package is a Mixture of all the Varieties above-mention'd, to the Number of 122; with a Box of Birch Bark, containing 29 little Infants' Scalps of various Sizes; ſmall white Hoops; white Ground; no Tears; and only a little black Knife in the Middle, to ſhew they were ript out of their Mothers' Bellies.

With theſe Packs, the Chiefs ſend to your Excellency the following Speech, delivered by Conejogatchie in Council, interpreted by the elder Moore, the Trader, and taken down by me in Writing.

Father,

We ſend you herewith many Scalps, that you may ſee we are not idle Friends.

A blue Belt.

Father,

We wiſh you to ſend theſe Scalps over the Water to the great King, that he may regard them and be refreſhed; and that he may ſee our faithfulneſs in deſtroying his Enemies, and be convinced that his Preſents have not been made to ungrateful People.

A blue and white Belt with red Taſſels.

Father,

Attend to what I am now going to ſay: it is a Matter of much Weight. The great King's Enemies are many, and they grow faſt in Number. They were formerly like young Panthers: they could neither bite nor ſcratch: we could play with them ſafely: we feared nothing they could do to us. But now their Bodies are become big as the Elk, and ſtrong as the Buffalo: they have alſo got great and ſharp Claws. They have driven us out of our Country for taking Part in your Quarrel. We expect the great King will give us another Country, that our Children may live after us, and be his Friends and Children, as we are. Say this for us to the great King. To enforce it we give this Belt.

A great white Belt with blue Taſſels.

Father,

We have only to ſay farther that your Traders exact more than ever for their Goods: and our Hunting is leſſened by the War, ſo that we have fewer Skins to give for them. This ruins us. Think of ſome Remedy. We are poor: and you have Plenty of every Thing. We know you will ſend us Powder and Guns, and Knives and Hatchets: but we alſo want Shirts and Blankets.

A little white Belt.

I do not doubt but that your Excellency will think it proper to give ſome farther Encouragement to thoſe honeſt People. The high Prices they complain of, are the neceſſary Effect of the War. Whatever Preſents may be ſent for them through my Hands, ſhall be diſtributed with Prudence and Fidelity. I have the Honour of being

Your Excellency's moſt obedient

And moſt humble Servant,

JAMES CRAUFURD."

It was at firſt propoſed to bury theſe Scalps: but Lieutenant Fitzgerald, who you know has got Leave of Abſence to go for Ireland on his private Affairs, ſaid he thought it better they ſhould proceed to their Deſtination; and if they were given to him, he would undertake to carry them to England, and hang them all up in ſome dark Night on the Trees in St. James's Park, where they could be ſeen from the King and Queen's Palaces in the Morning; for that the Sight of them might perhaps ſtrike Muley Iſhmael (as he called him) with ſome Compunction of Conſcience. They were accordingly delivered to Fitz, and he has brought them ſafe hither. To-morrow they go with his Baggage in a Waggon for Boſton, and will probably be there in a few Days after this Letter.

I am, &c.

SAMUEL GERRISH.

BOSTON, March 20.

Monday laſt arrived here Lieutenant Fitzgerald abovementioned, and Yeſterday the Waggon with the Scalps. Thouſands of People are flocking to ſee them this Morning, and all Mouths are full of Execrations. Fixing them to the Trees is not approved. It is now propoſed to make them up in decent little Packets, ſeal and direct them; one to the King, containing a Sample of every Sort for his Muſeum; one to the Queen, with ſome of Women and little Children: the Reſt to be diſtributed among both Houſes of Parliament; a double Quantity to the Biſhops.

Mr. Willis,

Pleaſe to inſert in your uſeful Paper the following Copy of a Letter, from Commodore Jones, directed

To Sir Joſeph York, Ambaſſador from the King of England to the States-general of the United Provinces.

SIR, *Ipſwich, New-England, March 7, 1781.*

I Have lately ſeen a memorial, ſaid to have been preſented by your Excellency to their High Mightineſſes the States-general, in which you are pleaſed to qualify me with the title of *pirate.*

A pirate is defined to be *hoſtis humani generis,* [an enemy to all mankind]. It happens, Sir, that I am an enemy to no part of mankind, except your nation, the Engliſh; which nation at the ſame time comes much more within the definition; being actually an enemy to, and at war with, one whole quarter of the world, America, conſiderable parts of Aſia and Africa, a great part of Europe, and in a fair way of being at war with the reſt.

A pirate makes war for the ſake of *rapine.* This is not the kind of war I am engaged in againſt England. Our's is a war in defence of *liberty* . . . . the moſt juſt of all wars; and of our *properties,* which your nation would have taken from us, without our conſent, in violation of our rights, and by an armed force. Your's, therefore, is a war of *rapine*; of courſe, a piratical war: and thoſe who approve of it, and

Fig. 7.16 Benjamin Franklin, Supplement to the Boston Independent Chronicle, *March 1782. One of Franklin's most elaborate hoaxes, the* Supplement *gave Franklin a chance to publicize British atrocities against Americans.*

Peace" would never last. In order to achieve a true reconciliation and a durable peace, Great Britain would have to offer reparations to the Americans who had suffered at the hands of British soldiers and their Indian allies.[25]

Immediately after Oswald left Paris for London, Franklin used his press to produce one of his most elaborate hoaxes: a one-sheet "supplement" to a Boston newspaper containing two blistering satires and a few fictitious advertisements. The articles gave vent to Franklin's fury against George III, addressing atrocities committed on both land and sea. The centerpiece of the first article, written in the guise of a report by an American militia captain, was a gruesome inventory of civilian scalps taken by the Seneca Indians and proudly presented to the British authorities. The second piece was a letter ostensibly written by John Paul Jones defending himself against the accusation of piracy. In this letter, once again, there appears a catalogue of cruelties, detailing dozens of examples of "horrible wickedness and barbarity" practiced by the king against the Americans, "whom he is still pleased to claim as his subjects." Our war, claimed Jones, "is a war in defence of *liberty* . . . the most just of all wars"; whereas the British war is one of "*rapine; of course, a piratical war.*" The piece intensifies in virulence, asserting that "voluntary malice, mischief, and murder are from Hell," predicting that George III will "stand foremost in the list of diabolical, bloody, and execrable tyrants," and blaming the parliaments "who . . . by different votes year after year, dipped their hands in human blood."[26]

Franklin's double-sided "Supplement to the Boston Independent Chronicle," supposedly from March 1782, was a near-perfect imitation of the actual newspaper—from the number that headed the sheet (no. 705 of Boston's *Independent Chronicle and Universal Advertiser* was actually issued in March) to the representative advertisements from the Massachusetts towns of Medfield, Newburyport, Oxford, and Salem (fig. 7.16). If the British press were to reprint the articles, as he hoped they would, he might be able to influence public opinion at this critical juncture. Franklin sent copies of the "Supplement" to the Netherlands, Spain, and England. It has recently been discovered that, while neither of the articles was published immediately, both were reprinted in England before the year was out. The first to be reprinted, the John Paul Jones letter, appeared in a London newspaper on September 27, just as serious negotiations over the language of a peace treaty were about to begin. Franklin's hoax did not influence those negotiations, but it was certainly discussed in private circles. One reader, at least, guessed its true author.[27]

Did Franklin actually print all these documents? He may well have set the type, inked the forms, wet the paper, and pulled the bar for many of the sheets. There is evidence, however, that he employed other printers during the six years the press was in operation, and he must certainly have hired a printer fluent in French to assist him in 1782 when he issued his most ambitious publications: two small books of political theory.

The authors of these books could not have been more different. One was

Fig. 7.17 Title page of Pierre-André Gargaz, Conciliateur . . .
ou Projet de paix perpétuelle . . . , *1782. Gargaz's proposal for
creating a state of perpetual peace in Europe was one of two
books printed by Franklin at Passy.*

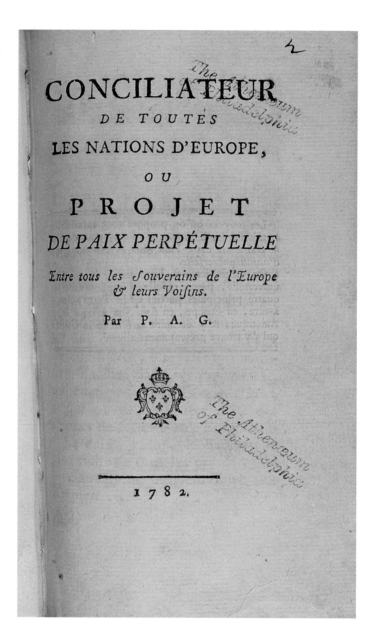

an unknown, the other an old friend (by this time deceased); one was an indi-
gent from Provence, the other a Parisian *grand bourgeois;* one was a convicted
felon, the other a celebrated physician, philosopher, and linguist. Pierre-André
Gargaz and Dr. Jacques Barbeu-Dubourg had only one thing in common: neither man had been able to publish his political treatise in France under the an-
cien régime. Gargaz wrote a proposal suggesting how Europe could achieve
a state of perpetual peace, but was shunned by the aristocracy because of his
humble origins. Franklin welcomed him at Passy and printed a small num-

ber of copies for private distribution (fig. 7.17). Dubourg's *Petit code de la raison humaine*—a deist, vigorously pro-American, and occasionally antiroyalist tract that was dedicated to Franklin—had been banned by the French censors. There is no record of how many copies of the *Petit code* Franklin printed or whether he distributed them outside the circle of friends who had known and loved Dubourg. He could never have imagined that it would see widespread distribution seven years later when the streets of Paris were erupting in revolution and he was safely back in Philadelphia. In 1789, with the presses newly liberated, an anonymous French printer published the work exactly as Franklin had issued it. Comparing it to Rousseau's *Social Contract,* he rushed to bring it before the public because, as he said in the preface, "the time of its triumph had come."[28]

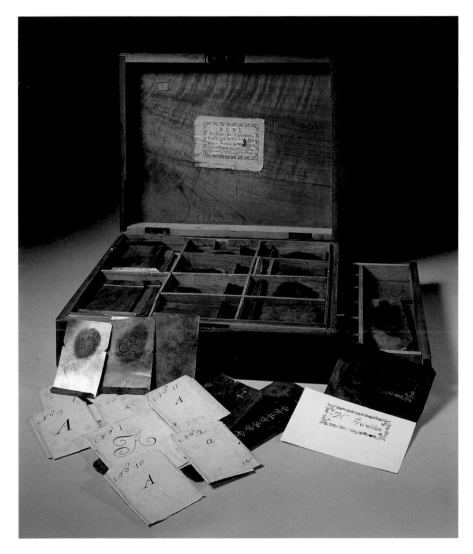

Fig. 7.18 Set of brass stencils in a walnut box, including stencil for "Mr. Franklin," 1781, made by Bery. The set was given to the American Philosophical Society by Franklin's grandson Benjamin Franklin Bache.

Fig. 7.19 Anne Louise Boivin
d'Hardancourt Brillon de Jouy,
"Marche des insurgents," 1778. Madame Brillon was one of Franklin's
closest friends in France; a gifted
composer, she freqently performed
music for him.

Franklin's reputation and expertise as a printer gained him an entrée
into the French typographical community during an unusually innovative
period in its history. In this world, as in so many others, he was involved in
a lively exchange of ideas. He conferred with tradesmen and tradeswomen,
both great and lowly, on matters ranging from press design to papermaking
techniques to ink recipes. In 1781 he purchased a set of exquisite stencils cut
by a M. Bery (fig. 7.18). Franklin ordered several alphabets, both plain and
decorated, and a variety of borders. He also ordered a monogram for himself
(the "BF" that is embossed on the covers of *The Papers of Benjamin Franklin*)

and a calling card for a "Mr. Franklin"—probably Temple, as Franklin himself was always known as "Doctor."

The Bagatelles

The exchanging of calling cards—and visits—was an essential part of the social life that sustained Franklin during the eight and a half years he lived in France. The women and men who formed his coterie of intimates were witty, talented, engaging, and devoted. They doted on him, and he adored them. Franklin loved music, and they indulged his passion—performing for him, playing instruments with him, and composing songs and melodies in his honor. Madame Brillon, a gifted harpsichordist and composer, played and sang for him, often accompanied by her two daughters; Franklin called them his "opera" (fig. 7.19). He, in turn, entertained them by playing Scottish tunes on his glass ar-

Fig. 7.20 Charles James, Glass armonica, ca. 1761–62, owned by Benjamin Franklin. An adaptation of musical water glasses, the glass armonica was Franklin's favorite invention. Its sound was described as "ethereal," and Mozart, among others, composed music for it.

Fig. 7.21 William Temple Franklin, "Three Positions of the Elbow," from M.Lemontey, ed., Mémoires de l'abbé Morellet . . . , 1821. Temple drew this sketch to illustrate a letter Franklin wrote to the abbé Morellet around 1779, in which Franklin maintained that the existence of God could be confirmed by the judicious placement of the elbow. Had the elbow been placed closer to the hand, as in figure 3, or to the shoulder, as in figure 4, we could never succeed in getting a wine glass to our mouth. Thankfully, our elbow is perfectly placed so as to allow us to drink with ease, as in figure 5. "Let us adore therefore," Franklin concluded, "this benevolent wisdom; adore and drink."

monica, the instrument he had invented (fig. 7.20). With the abbé Morellet Franklin sang drinking songs, including pieces each had composed; those that survive are brimming with puns and clever punchlines (fig. 7.21). Franklin also loved to play chess, and his late-night games were curtailed only by the supply of candles (fig. 7.22). His landlord, Le Ray de Chaumont, claimed that Franklin occasionally cheated and had an annoying habit of drumming his fingers on the table when a partner took too long to make a move. At the home of Madame Helvétius (fig. 7.23), whom Franklin (and many others) would have liked to marry, he was surrounded by a stimulating group of scientists and men of letters who called themselves—in a playful reference to the village she lived in—"l'Académie d'Auteuil."[29]

Franklin delighted these friends with witty *jeux d'esprit* composed for their entertainment. He used these pieces—many of which were flirtatious—as French-language exercises, eliciting editing suggestions from many quarters and subjecting them to many drafts (fig. 7.24). Franklin printed one or two of these pieces as broadsides, on single sheets. (Only "The Handsome and the Deformed Leg" survives, but evidence suggests that he also printed "The Morals of Chess" in this way.) Roughly a dozen others he decided to print in pamphlet format, in a small collection he entitled, simply, *Bagatelles*. Franklin did not print these pieces when he wrote them. All evidence suggests that he printed them in early 1784, long after the war was over and as he was beginning to contemplate his return to America. Printing these bagatelles, in other words, was not the reason for Franklin's setting up his press at Passy.

Only two bound copies of the collected bagatelles have survived, and they differ slightly in contents. This is because they were not printed as a book. Each of the pieces is an individual pamphlet with its own pagination; Franklin must have given selections to his friends, who had them bound at a later date. Both of the extant collections, however, begin with the "Dialogue Between the Gout and Mr. Franklin" (fig. 7.25), because the title page to the whole collection was attached to that piece. In addition to the light-hearted compositions, both collections include two essays that Franklin intended for the general public, also printed in 1784 in the same format. These were the dual-language "Information to Those Who Would Remove to America" (fig. 7.26) and "Remarks

Fig. 7.22 Chess set, ca. 1750–80. Franklin owned these chess pieces.

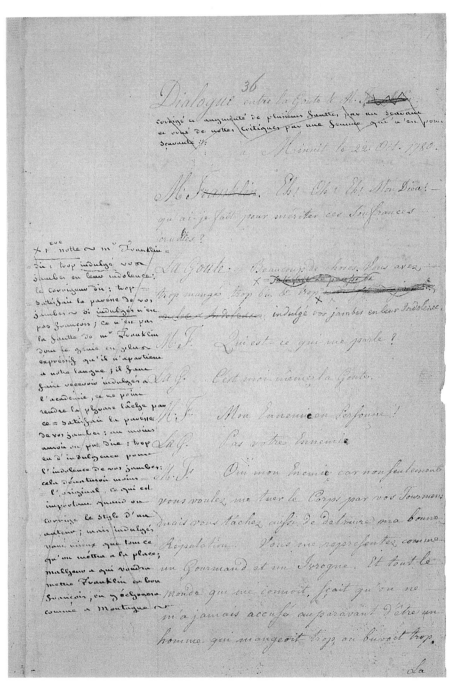

Fig. 7.24 First page of the corrected draft of Benjamin Franklin, "Dialogue entre la Goutte & M. F." (Dialogue between the gout and Mr. Franklin), 1780. Franklin drafted his bagatelles in English and solicited help in translating them into French. This draft of a French translation is a fair copy written by Franklin's French secretary, Jean L'Air de Lamotte. The notes in the margin and below the title are by Madame Brillon.

Upon the Savages of North America." Franklin gave these pamphlets to Europeans who sought his assistance in emigrating, many of whom expected to receive grants of land and other privileges on the basis of their aristocratic birth. In America, he warned in the former, "People do not enquire concerning a Stranger, *What IS he?* but *What can he DO?*"[30]

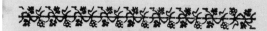

DIALOGUE

ENTRE

LA GOUTTE ET M. F.

à Minuit le 22 Octobre 1780.

M. F.

EH! oh! eh! Mon Dieu! qu'ai-je fait pour mériter ces souffrances cruelles?

LA GOUTTE.

Beaucoup de chofes. Vous avez trop mangé, trop bu, & trop indulgé vos jambes en leur indolence.

M. F.

Qui eft-ce qui me parle?

LA GOUTTE.

C'eft moi-même, la goutte.

M. F.

Mon ennemie en perfonne!

LA GOUTTE.

Pas votre ennemie.

A ij

The New Nation

In the spring of 1783, after the armistice had been declared and as European nations were beginning to explore options for commercial treaties with the United States, Franklin arranged for the publication of a book he had been planning for many years: French translations of the thirteen state constitutions. The book also included the country's other fundamental documents: the Declaration of Independence; the Franco-American treaties of alliance and of amity and commerce (February 1778); and the treaties of amity and commerce with Holland (October 1782) and Sweden (April 1783). The translations were made by the duc de La Rochefoucauld, and Franklin chose as a printer the talented Philippe-Denis Pierres, who was soon afterward named First Printer in Ordinary to Louis XVI. This publication, unlike Franklin's private imprints,

Fig. 7.26 Title page of Benjamin Franklin, Information to those who would remove to america, *1784. Franklin distributed this pamphlet to the many Europeans who wanted to emigrate to the United States once peace had been declared.*

INFORMATION

TO THOSE
WHO WOULD REMOVE
TO AMERICA.

MANY Perſons in Europe having directly or by Letters, expreſs'd to the Writer of this, who is well acquainted with North-America, their Deſire of tranſporting and eſtablishing themſelves in that Country; but who appear to him to have formed thro' Ignorance, miſtaken Ideas & Expectations of what is to be obtained there; he thinks it may be uſeful, and prevent inconvenient, expenſive & fruit-leſs Removals and Voyages of improper Perſons, if he gives ſome clearer & truer Notions of that Part of the World than appear to have hitherto pre-vailed.

He finds it is imagined by Numbers that the In-habitants of North-America are rich, capable of rewarding, and diſpos'd to reward all ſorts of Ingenuity; that they are at the ſame time ignorant of all the Sciences; & conſequently that ſtrangers poſſeſſing Talents in the Belles-Letters, fine Arts, &c. muſt be highly eſteemed, and ſo well paid as to become eaſily rich themſelves; that there are alſo abundance of profitable Offices to be diſpoſed of,

A

required the permission of the French book authorities. As Pierres completed the sections, he was obliged to submit them to the censor.

One hundred volumes of *Constitutions des treize états-unis de l'Amérique* were printed on *papier d'Annonay,* the wove paper now being manufactured in France by the Annonay mills. Franklin had a number of these sumptuously

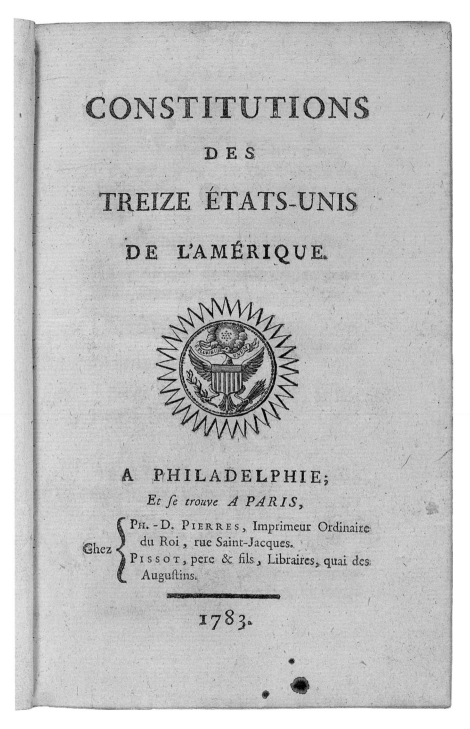

CONSTITUTIONS

DES

TREIZE ÉTATS-UNIS

DE L'AMÉRIQUE.

A PHILADELPHIE;

Et ſe trouve A PARIS,

Chez {
PH. -D. PIERRES, Imprimeur Ordinaire du Roi, rue Saint-Jacques.
PISSOT, pere & fils, Libraires, quai des Auguſtins.

1783.

bound for presentation to the king and queen of France, as well as to all foreign sovereigns and their ministers to the French court. For this edition an engraved block was made of the Great Seal of the United States, and Pierres printed it in the center of the title page (fig. 7.27). This is the first printed appearance of the

Fig. 7.28 Franklin's sketch of the Great Seal of the United States, drawn on the verso of page 17 of his draft of a letter to David Julien Le Roy, begun at Passy in February 1784 and finished at sea in August 1785. That letter—an illustrated compendium of scientific information and observations about seafaring and the ocean—was published by the American Philosophical Society under the short title "Maritime Observations."

Great Seal, which Congress had approved in June 1782. Pierres used it again when he printed for the American commissioners "The Definitive Treaty Between Great Britain and the United States of America, Signed at Paris, the 3d day of September 1783."

In the summer of 1785, at the age of seventy-nine, Franklin reluctantly took his leave of the country he had called "the civilest Nation upon earth."[31] He brought with him the two grandsons who had accompanied him on the previous crossing during a cold November nearly nine years earlier. Franklin's journey back to Philadelphia was his final ocean voyage. It was tinged with as much regret at leaving France as excitement at the prospect of seeing his family and the country he had devoted so much of his energy to helping found. He took advantage of the long weeks at sea to write three scientific papers that for years he had been awaiting the leisure to compose. One of them, known as "Maritime Observations," was a remarkable compendium of inventions, observations, and theories relating to ships and the ocean.

Pausing in the composition of that piece, and forgetting for a moment all thoughts of sail designs, sea anchors, pulleys, and ocean currents, Franklin turned over a sheet and dipped his pen in the inkwell. There, in the middle of an otherwise blank folio page, he drew a circle. Inside he sketched a bald eagle, wings outstretched, grasping a clutch of arrows with one talon and an olive branch with the other. Above the eagle he wrote *e pluribus unum,* underlined by thirteen little crosses (fig. 7.28). In this tiny emblem, drawn in the middle of the Atlantic, lay the essence of everything he had struggled to achieve.

Chapter 8

At the End, an Abolitionist?

EMMA J. LAPSANSKY-WERNER

Observers have spent more than two and a half centuries reappraising Benjamin Franklin. As successive teams of scholars have spent some five decades illuminating his publications and correspondence, the possibilities for exploring the nuances of this complex man have increased exponentially. He has been variously revealed as savvy statesman, wily entrepreneur, innovative scientist, dedicated community builder, internationally beloved ladies' man, convinced religionist (was he Quaker, Episcopalian, deist, all three, or none?), public-spirited philanthropist, and romantic-rationalist philosopher—a long-lived man of labile intellect and prodigious, restless energies. The grist for the reappraisal mill is bountiful, for Franklin invested many gallons of ink in reappraising himself. Many of the issues that concerned Franklin resonate in our own time: how to foster high-minded citizenship, how to harness technology for the public good, how to improve community life. Yet because Franklin was a master of intellectual legerdemain, because he never ceased pursuing new ideas, because he grappled with some of the thorniest issues of his day— and because interpreters in the intervening years have appropriated his image for myriad purposes—some aspects of his thinking remain murky.[1]

As scholars continue the attempt to "penetrate beneath the many images and representations of Franklin . . . and recover the historic Franklin," Franklin's views on race and slavery are paramount among the topics that defy easy analysis. Some of his papers—we do not know how many or which ones—have been lost. During much of his time abroad he wrote little about race, though what he did write suggests that it was very much on his mind. Historians point to his leadership late in life of the Pennsylvania Society for Promoting the Abolition of Slavery and the Relief of Free Negroes Unlawfully Held in Bondage (PAS) as the measure of how his ideas had developed by the time of his death.[2] But what are we to make of this argument since we cannot see the whole picture of his developing thought on the subject, and much of what we *can* see is enigmatic and contradictory? It is tempting to describe Franklin as transforming himself at midlife from a narrow-minded racial bigot to a republican social-justice advocate, but how much of this "transformation" is the construction of later social reformers who appropriated Franklin's image to bolster their own cause? Simplistic analysis—that Franklin transformed himself from a young racist to an old humanitarian—does justice neither to Franklin's insatiable, pragmatic, and life-long inquisitiveness nor to the intransigence of the hydra-headed phenomenon of race in America.

The evidence for reappraisal and recovery is cloudy, for though it may be too strong to describe Franklin as a chameleon, he certainly seems to have both shrouded his true beliefs and changed his mind frequently. After all, Franklin, a religious skeptic, sometimes allowed himself to be mistaken for a Quaker, and Franklin the sophisticated urbanite was often willing to style himself a "woodsman" by donning a coonskin cap.

Late in his life, as he attempted to lay out for his children and his country the wisdom he had gained in his lifetime, Franklin recalled an early experience that exemplified some of the attributes that would make him one of America's most enduring—and enigmatic—heroes. He described how he had become a vegetarian at age sixteen. Learning about the practice through reading a work by the Anabaptist mystic Thomas Tryon, Franklin had changed his diet and found that though some people "chid" him for his "singularity," the experiment had brought the advantage not only of allowing him to feel healthy and moral, but also left him more money to buy books.[3] This anecdote, exemplifying Franklin's penchant for commingling religion and science, also highlights his capacity to continually learn and grow through observation and experimentation, his ability to allow new insights to change his behavior, his penchant for disregarding or challenging his detractors once he became wedded to an idea, and his appreciation for serendipitous offshoots from principled behavior (the extra money to buy books). His abolitionist posture, which he came to in the final decades of his life, reflects these same qualities.

MUSICIENS d'un CALINDA

Franklin's perceptions of race and labor issues surely took shape during his childhood, when Boston's black population mushroomed from a few hundred in the first decade to as many as two thousand by 1720. In the eighteenth-century Atlantic world, with its continuous exchange of wine, cheese, wood, grains, fabric, people, and ideas, Africans were to be found everywhere from Spain to New England, the Caribbean to northern Europe. In fact, Franklin's father allowed slave auctions to be held outside his chandlery. And contemporary genre painters like John Singleton Copley, John Greenwood, and Pierre Eugène Du Simitière routinely included black workers in their depictions of maritime life, reminding us that the life the teenage Franklin admired was filled with black sailors (fig. 8.1). In Boston, Franklin must also have encountered the

The Selling
OF
JOSEPH
A Memorial.

FORASMUCH *as Liberty is in real value next unto* Life: *None ought to part with it themselves, or deprive others of it, but upon most mature Consideration.*

The Numerousness of Slaves at this day in the Province, and the Uneasiness of them under their Slavery, hath put many upon thinking whether the Foundation of it be firmly and well laid; so as to sustain the Vast Weight that is built upon it. It is most certain that all Men, as they are the Sons of *Adam*, are Coheirs; and have equal Right unto Liberty, and all other outward Comforts of Life. GOD *hath given the Earth* [*with all its Commodities*] *unto the Sons of* Adam, *Psal* 115. 16. *And hath made of One Blood, all Nations of Men, for to dwell on all the face of the Earth; and hath determined the Times before appointed, and the bounds of their habitation: That they should seek the Lord.* Forasmuch then as we are the Offspring of GOD &c. Act 17.26,27,29. Now although the Title given by the last ADAM, doth infinitely better Mens Estates, respecting GOD and themselves; and grants them a most beneficial and inviolable Lease under the Broad Seal of Heaven, who were before only Tenants at Will: Yet through the Indulgence of GOD to our First Parents after the Fall, the outward Estate of all and every of their Children, remains the same, as to one another. So that Originally, and Naturally, there is no such thing as Slavery. *Joseph* was rightfully no more a Slave to his Brethren, than they had no more Authority to *Sell* him, than they had to *Slay* him. And if they had nothing to do to *Sell* him; the *Ishmaelites* bargaining with them, and paying down Twenty pieces of Silver, could not make a Title. Neither could *Potiphar* have any better Interest in him than the *Ishmaelites* had, Gen. 37. 20, 27, 28. For he that shall in this case plead *Alteration of Property*, seems to have forfeited a great part of his own claim to Humanity. There is no proportion between Twenty Pieces of Silver, and LIBERTY. The Commodity it self is the Claimer. If *Arabian* Gold be imported in any quantities, most are afraid to meddle with it, though they might have it at easy rates; lest it it should have been wrongfully taken from the Owners, it should kindle a fire to the Consumption of their whole Estate. 'Tis pity there should be more Caution used in buying a Horse, or a little lifeless dust; than there is in purchasing Men and Women: Whenas they are the Offspring of GOD, and their Liberty is,
——— *Auro pretiosior Omni.*

And seeing GOD hath said, *He that Stealeth a Man and Selleth him, or if he be found in his hand, he shall surely be put to Death.* Exod. 21. 16. This Law being of Everlasting Equity, wherein Man Stealing is ranked amongst the most atrocious of Capital Crimes: What louder Cry can there be made of that Celebrated Warning,

Caveat Emptor !

And

tension surrounding slavery, for his home city was home to early antislavery spokesmen like Samuel Sewall, a close friend of the Franklins (fig. 8.2).[4]

As an adult in Philadelphia, Franklin found the black presence equally inescapable. In his *Pennsylvania Gazette,* he frequently printed advertisements for slave sales or for runaways (fig. 8.3), and these ads underscore the diversity of tasks for slaves, from agriculture to crafts, whaling, music making, domestic work, and even some work with relatively high responsibility (fig. 8.4). "Old Alice," a Barbadian slave who apparently had been in Pennsylvania long enough to have personally known William Penn, was entrusted with the task of collecting tolls at Dunk's Ferry near Philadelphia (fig. 8.5). In Boston, in Philadelphia, and later in London and Paris, the economic and social issues raised by these ubiquitous dark-skinned people were never far from Franklin's door and must have been in his consciousness. But Franklin had a practical incentive for taking slavery in stride: advertisements for slave sales or fugitives were among the publishing staples that made him a wealthy man.[5]

Franklin depended upon slaves. The broad array of economic opportunities in colonial America, coupled with British immigration restrictions, made white servants hard to come by and hard to keep. (Franklin himself was a "runaway," having escaped from his apprentice commitment to his brother.) But since personal servants were both a practical necessity and a mark of status for the urban upper classes, who entertained frequently and lavishly, Franklin and many other up-and-coming Philadelphians owned, sold, and brokered slaves. Typical of the American urban gentleman, Franklin employed servants and kept slaves from the 1730s until his death. His slave Peter accompanied him on his travels, and when Franklin's son William traveled with his father, William's black servant King came too. Like many masters, Franklin seems to have been somewhat resigned to the experience of having his slaves run away. Writing home from London in June 1760, he noted simply: "King, that you enquire after, is not with us. He ran away from our house, near two Years ago, while we were absent in the Country; But was soon found in Suffolk, where he had been taken in the Service of a Lady that was very fond of the Merit of making him a Christian, and contributing to his Education and Improvement. As he was of little Use, and often in Mischief, Billy [Franklin's son] consented to her keeping him while we stay in England. So the Lady sent him to school, has him taught to read and write, to play on the Violin and French Horn, with some other Accomplishments more useful in a Servant."[6]

In the same letter home, Franklin wrote that he was able to "rub on pretty comfortably" with his slave Peter by turning a blind eye and a deaf ear to some of Peter's behavior. Quoted out of context, these two passages would seem to indicate the midlife Franklin's acceptance of slavery, and some historians have interpreted them as evidence that he had not yet fully developed his antislavery ideas. But in the context of the entire letter, a reader might draw a different conclusion: that in 1760 London, Franklin was already unhappy with the slave system but his objections lay in what it implied for *white* society's development. In

Fig. 8.3 Page of the Pennsylvania Gazette, *with an advertisement in the left column for the sale of a slave, May 2, 1745, printed by Benjamin Franklin.*

Fig. 8.4 (Opposite) Attributed to John Lewis Krimmel, Worldly Folk Questioning Chimney Sweeps and Their Master Before Christ Church, Philadelphia, *1811–ca. 1813. The African American chimney sweeps pictured in this watercolor held one of many jobs performed by black laborers.*

the paragraph from which these quotes were taken, Franklin expressed his displeasure at the problem black servants present to white society: Peter, he noted, "behaves as well as I can expect, in a country where there are many occasions of spoiling servants. . . . He has as few faults as most of them, and I see with only one Eye, and hear with only one ear; so we rub on pretty comfortably."[7]

Franklin's pragmatic concern for how slavery could negatively affect white society is arguably the kernel of the seemingly humanitarian concern that

underpinned his support for abolition in the last decade of his life. Many of Franklin's abolitionist acquaintances, while deeply disturbed by the plight of the slave, often couched that concern in terms of slavery's effect on the souls of white Americans. Much of our fragmentary evidence of Franklin's views on race indicates that for Franklin, even at the end, slavery may have been as much a metaphor for white society's ills as a humanitarian issue.

Although by 1730 Franklin had published antislavery writings by others, his own first surviving musings, which date from 1751, are more about race than slavery. By that time he had gained intimate knowledge of the black workers who relieved their masters of the drudgery of hauling luggage and freight, preparing meals, procuring wood, sweeping chimneys, caring for children, or struggling to find and hold white apprentices. Slavery, as Franklin saw it in his world, was a necessary economic system, intimately connected with the issue of labor shortages and the need to maximize capitalist production. But he seemed deeply troubled about the effect of slavery on the industriousness of white Americans. He wrote: "The Whites who have Slaves, not labouring [themselves] are enfeebled"; their "Children become proud, disgusted with Labour, . . . educated in idleness . . . unfit to get a Living by Industry."[8] A few years later, in 1757, Franklin wrote a will directing that his slaves be freed upon his death—a decision that historians have often interpreted as proof of his developing abolitionist sensibilities. But was this directive the result of abolitionist sentiment or a wish that his own children be pressed into getting a living by industry? We cannot know.

Franklin the scientist, like his compatriots across the Western world, thought a lot about race. He understood that it was bound up in fundamental and emotionally charged questions of culture, capacity, and one group's estimation of the potential of "Others." In his 1751 essay, "Observations concerning the Increase of Mankind . . . ," Franklin appended twenty-four anthropological "observations," the last of which laid out his thinking about race and society:

> The Number of purely white People in the World is proportionably very small. All Africa is black or tawny. Asia chiefly tawny. America (exclusive of the new Comers) wholly so. And in Europe, the Spaniards, Italians, French, Russians and Swedes, are generally of what we call a swarthy Complexion; as are the Germans also, the Saxons only excepted, who with the English, make the principal Body of White people on the face of the earth. I could wish their Numbers were increased. And while we are, as I may call it, *Scouring* our Planet, by clearing America of Woods, and so making this Side of our Globe reflect a brighter Light to the eyes of Inhabitants in Mars or Venus, why should we in the Sight of Superior Beings, darken its People? why increase the Sons of Africa, by Planting them in America, where we have so fair an Opportunity, by excluding all Blacks and Tawneys, of increasing the lovely White and Red?[9]

Aware that he was on emotionally charged ground, he added a final sentence of humble self-awareness: "But perhaps I am partial to the Complexion of my Country, for such Kind of Partiality is natural to Mankind." Knowing that controversy infused all discussions of race, however, he was not surprised when

Cadwallader Colden, a New York politician who shared Franklin's scientific interests, wrote him in response to the pamphlet: "I am exceedingly pleased with your observations on the increase of mankind. I think with our friend Bartram that the last Paragraph is the only one liable to exception and I wish it had been rather somewhere in the middle than at the end of that discourse because the reader should be the most fully satisfied when you take leave of him."[10] Franklin's readers, of course, would never be fully satisfied with a final paragraph that challenged them to contemplate issues of race.

Franklin's "Observations" ostensibly concerned politics, written in response to his worry over French settlers on the frontier, but race and slavery were everywhere intertwined with religion, philosophy, science, politics, economics, and social reform—the topics that engaged Franklin's mind throughout his life. One of Franklin's favorite authors was the Puritan clergyman Cotton Mather, in whose religious treatises was embedded the belief that American society risked the wrath of God unless slaves were taught religion and made full members of society. Thomas Tryon, whose writings brought Franklin to vegetarianism, advised boycotting meat because eating flesh, like slavery, implied violence. "Refrain at all times from such Foods as cannot be procured without violence and oppression," wrote Tryon, "for know that all the inferior Creatures when hurt do cry and send forth the complaints to their Maker." And Tryon cautioned that "the inferior creatures groan under your cruelties."[11]

Because slavery could not be sustained without violence or the threat of it, the proscription against violence was an important aspect of many antislavery arguments, including those of two Quaker abolitionists whose works Franklin printed while he was still a young man. Franklin was only twenty-three years old in 1729 when he printed Ralph Sandiford's *A Brief Examination of the Practice of the Times* (fig. 8.6). This pamphlet—the first of several antislavery tracts produced in Franklin's shop—was followed the next year by Sandiford's expanded, and more insistent, *The Mystery of Iniquity : In a Brief Examination of the Practice of the Times . . . Unto which is added in the Postscript, the Injury this Trading in Slaves Doth the Commonwealth, Humbly offer'd to all of a Publick Spirit*. Eight years later Franklin printed a similarly strongly worded work by the Quaker abolitionist Benjamin Lay. Lay's indictment, *All Slave-Keepers That keep the Innocent in Bondage . . .* , insisted that slavery and slaveholders invited the wrath of God upon society (fig. 8.7). The following year, Lay, a deformed and wizened man who was passionate about his commitment to ending slavery, stirred up a local scandal by appearing at a Quaker gathering with a container of red berry juice concealed inside a book that looked like a Bible, then dramatizing his conviction that slavery caused bloodletting by piercing the book and splattering the red liquid across the crowd.[12] Franklin had ample evidence that readers were likely to be uneasy if challenged to contemplate the morality of race issues.

No evidence remains of Franklin's thoughts as he published these two works, but Lay's treatise and performance helped launch a struggle within the Religious Society of Friends that dragged on for several acrimonious decades before Philadelphia Quakers finally banned slavery among their membership in the 1770s. Perhaps Lay's passion also planted a seed of change in Franklin as well. Franklin, who had many Quakers among his friends and patrons, could not have been insensible to their struggles. But if Lay's abolitionist seeds were planted in Franklin, their germination was slow and silent. Throughout the 1750s, Franklin—typical of white Americans of his time—still had mostly negative things to say about both slavery and black people. He believed that slavery was financially risky (that is, the initial investment and continuing maintenance might exceed the value of the slave's production) and that because a slave could be expected to be "sullen, malicious, revengeful" and "*by Nature* a thief,"[13] the master's physical and emotional well-being was constantly at risk.

In addition, Franklin shared his compatriots' limited perspective about many varieties of Others, and like many social analysts before and since, he was inconsistent and contradictory about whether "inferior" peoples' negative traits were the result of race, nationality, gender, or experience, and whether or how those traits might be changed. He characterized all Native Americans as drunken "savages that delight in war and take pride in murder," who should be pursued with "large, strong and fierce dogs." He described German immigrants as "Boors" who would "swarm into our Settlements" and make Pennsylvania a "colony of *Aliens.*" Yet he sometimes described Native Americans as justified in their anger at European injustice, and he concedes than under the right circumstances, foreigners might develop sufficient industry and frugality to surpass native white Americans. Similar suspicions about "low" women, Catholics, and Jews marked the narrowness of Franklin's social ideas as he entered his fifth decade. Worried that unsavory settlers would overtake the frontier he wrote in 1754, "Many of our debtors, and loose English people, and German servants, and slaves, will probably desert to [the French]; and increase their numbers and strength, to the lessening and weakening of ours."[14]

By the end of the 1750s Franklin had apparently come in contact with the ardent abolitionist Anthony Benezet. Benezet, a Quaker (whose brother in 1771 married a cousin of Franklin's wife), had experimented with exposing

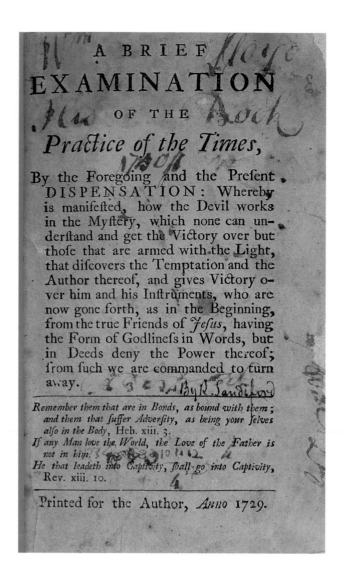

A BRIEF EXAMINATION

OF THE

Practice of the Times,

By the Foregoing and the Present DISPENSATION: Whereby is manifefted, how the Devil works in the Myftery, which none can underftand and get the Victory over but thofe that are armed with the Light, that difcovers the Temptation and the Author thereof, and gives Victory over him and his Inftruments, who are now gone forth, as in the Beginning, from the true Friends of *Jefus*, having the Form of Godlinefs in Words, but in Deeds deny the Power thereof; from fuch we are commanded to turn away.

Remember them that are in Bonds, as bound with them; and them that fuffer Adverfity, as being your felves alfo in the Body, Heb. xiii. 3.

If any Man love the World, the Love of the Father is not in him.

He that leadeth into Captivity, fhall go into Captivity, Rev. xiii. 10.

Printed for the Author, *Anno* 1729.

ALL SLAVE-KEEPERS

That keep the Innocent in Bondage,

APOSTATES

Pretending to lay Claim to the Pure & Holy ChriftianReligion; of whatCongregation fo ever; but efpecially in theirMinifters, by whofe example the filthy Leprofy and Apoftacy is fpread far and near; it is a notorious Sin, which many of the true Friends of Chrift, and his pure Truth, called *Quakers*, has been for many Years, and ftill are concern'd to write and bear Teftimony againft; as a Practice fo grofs & hurtful to Religion, and deftructive to Government, beyond what Words can fet forth, or can be declared of by Men or Angels, and yet lived in by Minifters and Magiftrates in *America.*

The Leaders of the People caufe them to Err.

Written for a General Service, by him that truly and fincerely defires the prefent and eternal Welfare and Happinefs of all Mankind, all the World over, of all Colours, and Nations, as his own Soul;

BENJAMIN LAY.

PHILADELPHIA:

Printed for the AUTHOR. 1737.

Fig. 8.6 (Left) Title page of Ralph Sandiford, A Brief Examination of the Practice of the Times . . . , *1729. Franklin printed this and a number of other antislavery tracts.*

Fig. 8.7 Title page of Benjamin Lay, All Slave-Keepers That keep the Innocent in Bondage . . . , *1737.*

black children to an education similar to that offered white students and concluded that black and white children's intellectual capacities were equal. Benezet's opinions were shared by fellow Delaware Valley Quaker John Woolman, whose 1754 pamphlet *On the Keeping of Negroes* could hardly have escaped Franklin's notice. The Associates of Doctor Bray, whose work Franklin came to know during a stay in London in the 1760s, reached the same conclusion. This group, carrying on the legacy of the Reverend Thomas Bray, had established a number of schools in America aimed at using education to ameliorate the situation of black children.[15]

Franklin, ever the experimental scientist, seemed fascinated that schooling appeared to have a positive effect on both the intellect and the temperament of the Bray Associates' charges. After visiting a Bray Associates school,

Franklin reported having a "higher Opinion of the natural Capacities of the black Race, than I had ever before entertained." So he involved himself with helping the Associates raise funds to open more schools for black and Native American children, and he backed the group's Philadelphia school for black children. Such schools, he theorized, might "imbue the Minds of their young Slaves with good Principles." But at least one modern observer suggests that Franklin's support for black schools was little more than a half-hearted response to pressure from his wife and some of her antislavery friends. Franklin himself wrote in 1758 that slaveowners should be approached to pay the tuition for black students, suggesting that he considered the school as much an economic enterprise as a philanthropic endeavor.[16]

Further indication that Franklin's interest in black education was as much scientific curiosity as philanthropy can be found in some of his other writing from the 1750s, as he contemplated the response of dark-skinned people to climate: "May there not be in negroes a quicker evaporation of the perspirable matter from their skins and lungs, which, by cooling them more, enables them to bear the sun's heat better than whites do?" Continuing with musings about whether it was better to have "negroes rather than whites, to work in the West-India fields," he concluded that he was "persuaded, from several instances . . . that they do not bear cold weather so well as the whites." How much of Franklin's suggestion that black schools be established in other American cities was a function of his desire to experiment with diverse populations and environments?[17]

The following decade provides no more clarity about Franklin's progress toward humanitarian abolitionism. Exposure to the Bray Associates' project probably led Franklin—who had now turned sixty years old—to begin to see black people in a different light, to uncouple slavery from race, and to think of Others as developing behaviors specific to their circumstances. After visiting the Bray school in Philadelphia, Franklin praised the black students' "Apprehension" and "Memory," and by 1769 he was attributing what he perceived as slaves' tendency to steal to their situation of enslavement, rather than their "nature." In fact, as Franklin's view of innate racial characteristics became more nuanced, he began to expand the idea that environment and experience were more important than race in shaping a person's potential. In 1764, after white Americans on the Pennsylvania frontier massacred a peaceful community of Indians, Franklin had defended the Indians, denouncing their attackers as Christian "White Savages." But that same year, in a letter to the lawyer Richard Jackson, an old friend, he expressed his wish that American society would remain populated by white people: "If money *must* be raised from us to support 4 Batallions . . . [a] moderate Duty on Foreign Mellasses maybe collected; . . . [and] the Duty on Negroes I could wish large enough to obstruct their Importation, as they every where prevent the Increase of Whites."[18]

Scholars differ in their identification of the pivotal moment in what one historian has labeled Franklin's transition "from caution to confrontation," but they agree that his first frontal attack on slavery came in the 1770s as a by-product of his frustration over Britain's economic policies. In 1772, when he wrote on the Sommersett Case and the slave trade, his first clearly antislavery statement, he was reacting to a British court case that freed a single fugitive slave. In this essay he challenged British citizens to think about both slavery and the continuation of the slave trade, and he called attention to the brutality of slavery and the absurdity of freeing only one out of hundreds of thousands of black chattel in the British sugar islands. "Can the petty pleasure [of sweetening our tea] . . . compensate for so much misery produced among our fellow creatures?" he asked.[19]

But in this essay Franklin remained defensive about the moral questions raised by the institution. He sidestepped the issue of American slavery by pointing out that only a small minority of white Americans owned slaves and asserted that it was in the owners' economic interest to treat their workers well. He admitted that slavery was troubling, but he disparaged British abolitionists as hypocritical, pointing out that American slavery was as much the fault of the British as of the Americans because British slave dealers "tempted" Americans to purchase more slaves. He further deflected the argument away from his slaveowning compatriots (and himself), by reminding British citizens that the lot of black slaves was no worse than that of the white British soldiers and sailors: both were helpless in the face of the whims and violence of an all-powerful taskmaster. But the issues he raised in his Somerset Case essay were clearly aimed more at disparaging British policies than at denouncing slaveholders. Thereafter, Franklin's writings often combined his anger at Britain with his distress over slavery, blaming British policies both for the presence of slavery in America and for the inability of American employers to attract white laborers from Europe; it is impossible to tell what in them is humanitarian sentiment and what political strategy.[20]

Through the 1750s John Woolman had carried on an outspoken advocacy for both Native Americans and slaves, buttressing his position with the argument that white Americans invited prejudice against black people by dressing them in the "meanest" clothing and consigning them to menial labor. Franklin was just publishing his essay on the Somersett Case and the slave trade when Woolman arrived in London for what would be his last antislavery fundraising tour. And Franklin was still in that city the following year when the Boston slave Phillis Wheatley arrived, her poetry having earned her celebrity status (fig. 8.8). But there is little to suggest that he had developed any empathy for black people themselves. He met with Woolman, but he evidenced his continuing ambivalence about African Americans when he agreed to meet with Wheatley but then expressed relief that the meeting did not take place.[21]

There is no indication that at this time he had moved beyond the perspective apparent when he wrote home to his wife more than a decade earlier expressing sympathy upon the death of one of her black houseboys: "I am sorry for the Death of your black boy [probably Othello], as *you* seem to have had a regard for him. *You must have suffer'd a good deal in the Fatigue of Nursing him* in such a Distemper" (emphasis mine). Franklin's sympathy seems to be only for his wife's suffering, not the suffering of the black child (nor indeed that of child's parents). In 1769 he expressed his concern for "poor Negroe Slaves who are past their Labour, sick or lame" only in terms of their being a "burthen" to the colonies. Referring to Virginia governor Dunmore's recruitment of slaves to the British military during the Revolution, he worried that the British had encouraged Americans to have slaves and were now encouraging those

Fig. 8.8 Unknown artist, Phillis Wheatley, Negro Servant . . . *(portrait print), from Phillis Wheatley,* Poems on Various Subjects, Religious and Moral, *1773. Born around 1753, Wheatley was sold into slavery in Boston in 1761, but within two years she had mastered English, become well-versed in the Bible, and begun studying Latin. Her poetry dealt primarily with religious and moral themes; her first published piece was an elegy to the evangelical preacher George Whitefield. This portrait appeared as the frontispiece to a collection of her poetry published during her lifetime.*

slaves to "murder their Masters Families." And as late as 1782, when he described how his abolitionist friends spoke of slavery as having stained Caribbean sugar with the blood of slaves, he quickly moved on to his concern for the blood of *white* people who had fought for and defended the islands.[22]

Indeed, many of the questions about Franklin stem as much from what he *didn't* write as from what he wrote. What can we infer, for example, from the fact that the slave, King, who ran away in London, had been gone for *two years* before Franklin bothered to mention it to his wife back home? Was King's loss inconsequential, or was Franklin voiceless from pent-up fury? We cannot know. From Franklin's writings while in England, we would never know that Granville Sharp and other British reformers were galvanizing a passionate British abolitionist movement. And through all the years he was abroad, intellectual circles were abuzz with the new racial theories of the Swedish botanist Carolus Linnaeus and the French naturalist Georges-Louis Leclerc de Buffon who were among the many thinkers who tried to comprehend and describe race: What could be discerned about black bodies, minds, and souls, and what might be expected from "hybridization" of the races?[23] It is hard to imagine that a man of Franklin's scientific interests and sexual energies would not have joined in the speculations about sex and race. We know that Franklin corresponded with Linnaeus, and forwarded some of that correspondence to Cadwallader Colden. Yet the Franklin papers that survive from the 1760s and 1770s are largely silent on these issues. His *Autobiography,* which might have filled in some of the blanks, ends with the year 1757.

So when, how, and to what end did Franklin clearly define himself as an abolitionist? Some observers attribute the shift to the early 1770s and his emerging recognition of the incongruity between slavery and the American colonists' bid for freedom. Certainly Franklin saw rising sympathy at home for the slaves' plight, and he praised Benezet's work. During the 1770s, when the Philadelphia Yearly Meeting of Quakers finally banned slaveownership among its members, Franklin also deepened his friendship with the confirmed Philadelphia abolitionist Dr. Benjamin Rush. Perhaps, after all, Franklin's heart was softened by the anguished poetry of Wheatley, who likened the colonists' struggle for freedom to that of her own race. Describing slaves as "snatched from Afric's fancyed happy seat," Wheatley hoped that others would not experience the "tyrannic sway" of bondage. But for more than fifteen years after he published his essay on the Sommersett Case, Franklin was silent on the subject of slavery, apparently too focused on matters of international diplomacy to think much about slavery or race. Only one significant event—when he gave sanctuary to Montague, an abused fugitive slave in France in 1781—offers any indication that he was attentive to the issue of slavery. [24] And there is no evidence that he ever did such a thing again.

Meanwhile, as he negotiated his country's political fate abroad, his home city of Philadelphia became home to an increasingly identity-conscious black community numbering nearly two thousand by 1785. Led by religious visionaries like the former slave Richard Allen (fig. 8.9), a race-focused black community emerged; by 1787 it would crystallize into the Free African Society, which began to define an agenda of liberation. Allen entered adulthood during the revolutionary years and had since his youth been preaching to black worshipers at Philadelphia's Saint George's Church. By the time Franklin returned to America in 1785, Allen, who made his living as a shoemaker and chimneysweep, had a widespread reputation as an industrious, trustworthy, and persuasive leader. Over the succeeding decade, Allen, his friend Absalom Jones (fig. 8.10), and other black leaders would help Philadelphia's African Americans establish strong churches, burial societies, schools, businesses, and other institutions, earning themselves an international reputation that inspired abolitionists across the Atlantic world to memorialize them in popular art and to hold them up as models of the possibilities of black freedom.[25] Returning from abroad, Franklin surely had to see his Philadelphia with new eyes, but we have no record of how he felt about what he saw.

Thus Franklin's modern interpreters have no information about what finally brought Franklin to take a strong abolitionist stand. Did his early reading of Tryon and printing of antislavery tracts put the young Franklin on the road to abolitionism? Did relationships with Benezet, Rush, or the Associates of Doctor Bray help move him along on that road? If so, why is there so little early evidence of Franklin's connection to Benezet, and why is there so little evidence of genuine closeness between the two? Was exposure to literate and thoughtful black people like Phillis Wheatley or Richard Allen the impetus? If so, why was Franklin intent upon keeping his distance from Wheatley? We have no evidence that he ever spoke with Allen, though Allen's home and church were only a few blocks from Franklin's Market Street dwelling. Was abolition no more the natural and logical outcome of Franklin's desire to remove black people from white society? Most of his abolitionist peers, after all, favored educating and Christianizing African Americans before resettling them either in the American West or outside the country.[26] If these behaviors mark him as a "humanitarian" abolitionist, they do so in only the most minimal way.

Fig. 8.9 Unknown artist, Rev. Richard Allen *(portrait print), 1813. From the 1760s until his death in 1831, Allen was a well-respected black religious leader and abolitionist in Philadelphia.*

Fig. 8.10 (Opposite, top) Pitcher with silhouette of Absalom Jones, ca. 1808. Jones was born into slavery in 1746 and learned to read from the New Testament. In 1787 he was elected overseer for the Free African Society; he and Richard Allen were the first two black Americans to receive formal ordination in any denomination.

Fig. 8.11 Title page of "The Constitution and Minutes of the Pennsylvania Society for promoting the Abolition of Slavery . . . ," April 23, 1787.

Fig. 8.12 (Opposite, bottom) Josiah Wedgwood, Am I Not a Man and a Brother? *(anti-slavery medallion), ca. 1787. Wedgwood produced these medallions to raise money for the abolitionists' cause. In 1788 some of the medallions were sent to Franklin in Philadelphia. Franklin thought that they could be as effective as pamphlets in drawing attention to the issue of slavery. This image became so popular that it was replicated in many formats, including buttons, sashes, and decorations on cups and pitchers.*

Upon his return from Europe in 1785, Franklin allowed himself to be drawn into the reorganization of the PAS, and he assumed the society's presidency in 1787. But if the young Franklin's ideas about race and slavery are murky, it is equally difficult to tease out the meaning of his antislavery activities in the last years of his life. When Franklin adopted his abolitionist posture, he appeared to do so with the zeal of the convert. He endorsed the 1787 PAS constitution (fig. 8.11), which proclaimed that God had made "of one flesh, all the children of men," and he accepted the gift created by the British scientist and potter Josiah Wedgwood to publicize and raise money for the cause: a medallion featuring a kneeling slave pleading, "Am I not a man and a brother?" (fig. 8.12), of which hundreds of copies were struck and sold in be-

The Constitution
and
Minutes

of the Pennsylvania Society for promoting the
Abolition of Slavery and the relief of free Negroes
unlawfully held in Bondage; enlarged at Philadelphia
April 23ᵈ 1787

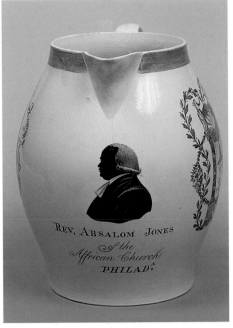

REV. ABSALOM JONES
of the
African Church
PHILADᵃ

AM I NOT A MAN AND A BROTHER

half of the enslaved. Wedgwood, whose intellectual curiosity was nearly the equal of Franklin's, also used the moral authority and economic resources of his thriving ceramics business to lobby for social reform.[27]

Though most analysts conclude that Franklin's pressing health concerns during these years would have dictated that he be more a titular head than an active participant, Franklin—now an octagenarian—seemed to embrace abolitionism with the same "singularity" with which he had adopted vegetarianism more than six decades earlier. Now he appeared to concentrate on the effect of slavery on the *slave*, asserting that the system was an "atrocious debasement of human nature" that stunts "intellectual faculties, and . . . social affections." He promoted abolition and a national program "to instruct, to advise, to qualify" former slaves in preparation for "their future situation in life." Yet in the spring of 1787, as he sat through the Constitutional Convention's bitter debate that ended by reducing a slave to three-fifths of a person, Franklin, the abolitionist convert, was silent. Some historians speculate that this was a strategic move, designed to avoid controversies that might prevent the Constitution from being passed. But we cannot know his motives, and it is possible that the "future situation" Franklin envisioned was one designed to rid white Americans of the burden of black people.[28]

At the same time, perhaps Franklin's prejudices against both Native Americans and slaves had lessened. In 1787, reiterating his developing theory that circumstance might be more important than race, he wrote: "During the Course of a long Life in which I have made Observations on public Affairs, it has appear'd to me that almost every War between the Indians and Whites has been occasion'd by some Injustice of the latter towards the former." And in 1789 he had this to say about slaves: "The unhappy man, who has long been treated as a brute animal, too frequently sinks beneath the common standard of the human species. The galling chains, that bind his body, do also fetter his intellectual faculties, and impair the social affections of the heart" (fig. 8.13).[29]

In the late 1780s, as PAS president, Franklin lived—and endorsed the PAS humanitarian platform—in the Philadelphia where Richard Allen was at work. Other talented African Americans also must have come into the periphery of his vision. Among these was Benjamin Banneker, a former slave living in Maryland who late in the 1780s was befriended by a Quaker named George Ellicott of Bucks County near Philadelphia. Ellicott, discovering that Banneker had spent years studying the stars, wasted no time in broadcasting his interest in the black man's talent. He lent Banneker a telescope, and the two began a long scientific relationship. Franklin surely knew of Ellicott's work, but we have no record of his opinion of Banneker. Two years after Franklin's death, Banneker began publishing an almanac for Pennsylvania, Maryland, Delaware, and Virginia, in which the accuracy of weather forecasts and astronomical predictions rivaled those published decades earlier by Franklin himself. Perhaps Franklin would have taken a scientific interest in Banneker's 1793 almanac, which was republished the next year by Philadelphia's William Young, who used this and an appended biography of Banneker to buttress an antislavery argument (fig. 8.14).[30]

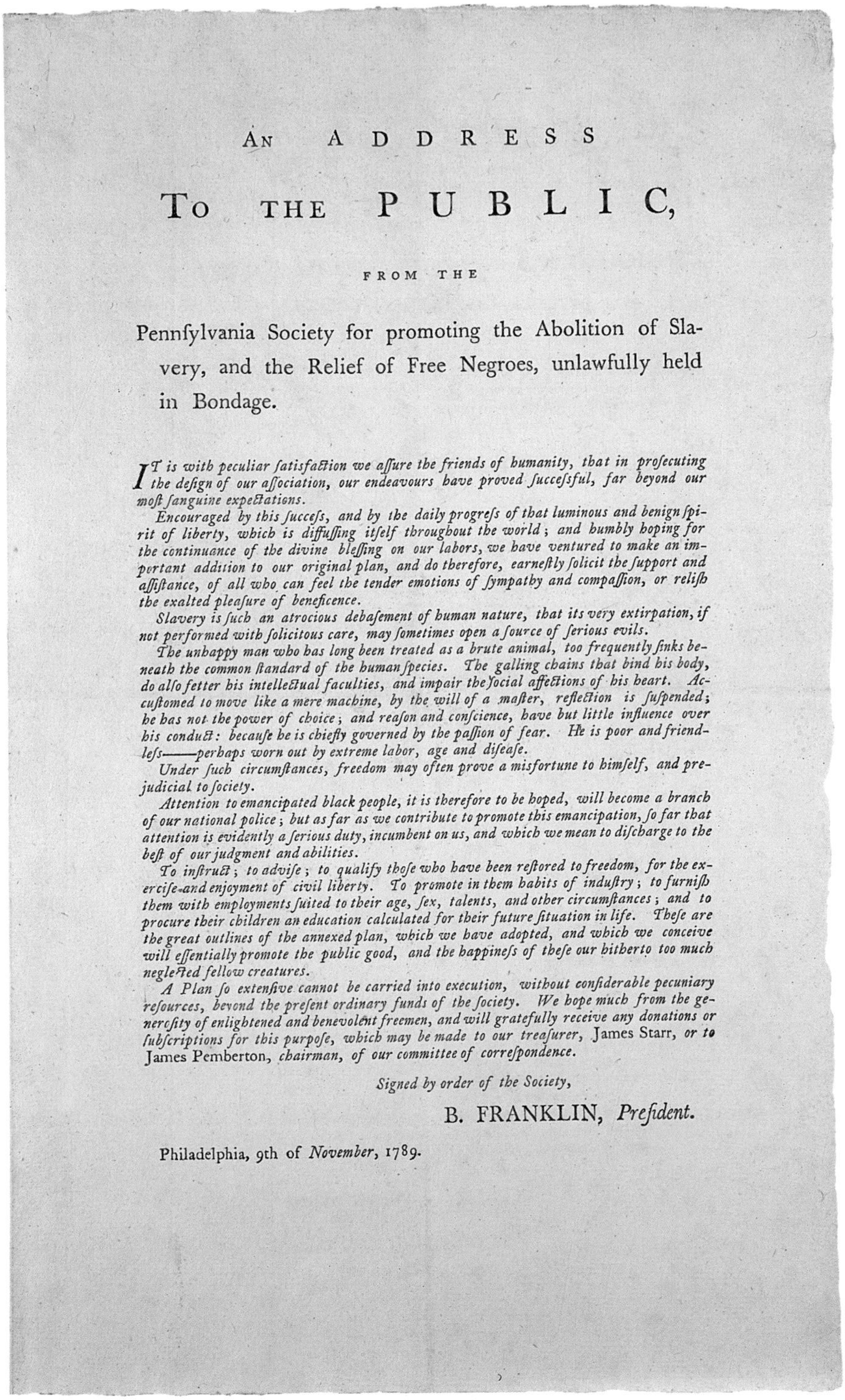

Fig. 8.13 Title page of An Address To the Public, *from the Pennsylvania Society for promoting the Abolition of Slavery . . . , signed B. Franklin, President, November 9, 1789. As president of the society, Franklin wrote this address as an appeal for money to help emancipated blacks become self-supporting.*

An Address

To the PUBLIC,

FROM THE

Pennsylvania Society for promoting the Abolition of Slavery, and the Relief of Free Negroes, unlawfully held in Bondage.

IT is with peculiar satisfaction we assure the friends of humanity, that in prosecuting the design of our association, our endeavours have proved successful, far beyond our most sanguine expectations.

Encouraged by this success, and by the daily progress of that luminous and benign spirit of liberty, which is diffusing itself throughout the world; and humbly hoping for the continuance of the divine blessing on our labors, we have ventured to make an important addition to our original plan, and do therefore, earnestly solicit the support and assistance, of all who can feel the tender emotions of sympathy and compassion, or relish the exalted pleasure of beneficence.

Slavery is such an atrocious debasement of human nature, that its very extirpation, if not performed with solicitous care, may sometimes open a source of serious evils.

The unhappy man who has long been treated as a brute animal, too frequently sinks beneath the common standard of the human species. The galling chains that bind his body, do also fetter his intellectual faculties, and impair the social affections of his heart. Accustomed to move like a mere machine, by the will of a master, reflection is suspended; he has not the power of choice; and reason and conscience, have but little influence over his conduct: because he is chiefly governed by the passion of fear. He is poor and friendless——perhaps worn out by extreme labor, age and disease.

Under such circumstances, freedom may often prove a misfortune to himself, and prejudicial to society.

Attention to emancipated black people, it is therefore to be hoped, will become a branch of our national police; but as far as we contribute to promote this emancipation, so far that attention is evidently a serious duty, incumbent on us, and which we mean to discharge to the best of our judgment and abilities.

To instruct; to advise; to qualify those who have been restored to freedom, for the exercise and enjoyment of civil liberty. To promote in them habits of industry; to furnish them with employments suited to their age, sex, talents, and other circumstances; and to procure their children an education calculated for their future situation in life. These are the great outlines of the annexed plan, which we have adopted, and which we conceive will essentially promote the public good, and the happiness of these our hitherto too much neglected fellow creatures.

A Plan so extensive cannot be carried into execution, without considerable pecuniary resources, beyond the present ordinary funds of the society. We hope much from the generosity of enlightened and benevolent freemen, and will gratefully receive any donations or subscriptions for this purpose, which may be made to our treasurer, James Starr, or to James Pemberton, chairman, of our committee of correspondence.

Signed by order of the Society,

B. FRANKLIN, President.

Philadelphia, 9th of November, 1789.

But in the end, Franklin's abolitionism remains something of an enigma, replete with questions, contradictions, inconsistencies. Some have argued that Franklin's apparent antislavery energy was little more than the backwater of his wife's commitment to the cause. Yet in the final weeks of his life, he adopted passionate postures on behalf of abolition. In February 1790 he presented a petition to the first U.S. Congress, calling on that body to "devise means for removing this Inconsistency [slavery] from the Character of the American People" because "equal liberty was originally the Portion, & is still the Birthright of all men" (fig. 8.15), a bold plea that would seem to show him as a champion of black rights, one who might have sympathized with artist Samuel Jennings's depiction of black people sitting at the feet of *Liberty Displaying the Arts and Sciences* (fig. 8.16).[31]

Fig. 8.14 Front page of Banneker's Almanack, and Ephemeris for the Year of our Lord 1793, *[1792]. Banneker, an astronomer, imagined that his almanac would combine scientific data with his own antiracist arguments. The renowned Philadelphia astronomer and clockmaker David Rittenhouse called the work a "very extraordinary performance."*

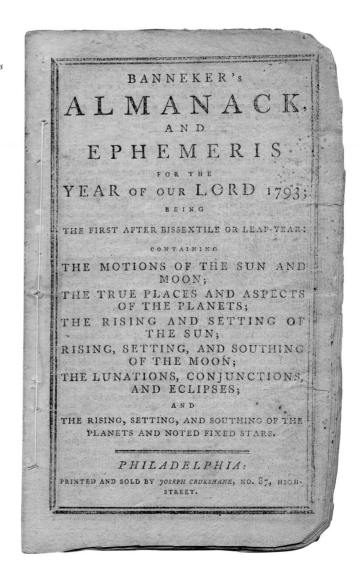

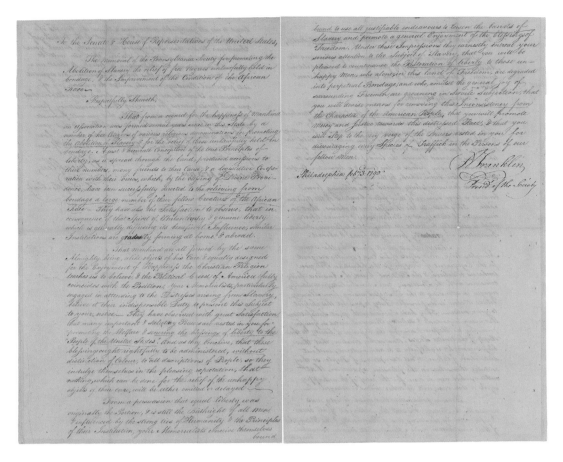

It is tempting to see Franklin in this light, especially because when James Jackson, the congressional representative from Georgia, responded to the petition with a diatribe against abolitionists and Quakers, Franklin was inspired to pen his last published work: an attack on slaveholders that has been called "a whole-hearted defense of the Quaker humanitarianism." In this essay, a letter to the editor of the *Federal Gazette,* Franklin employed a technique he had perfected over a lifetime: affecting another persona. Adopting the voice of "Sidi Mehemet Ibrahim," an Algerian Muslim prince, he exposed the absurdity of enslaving people because of their race or religion. But how is this final statement to be understood in the context of his many years of waffling and timidity on the subject of slavery? It was clearly motivated by Franklin's personal anger at Jackson. Was the Franklin who had used slavery to lash out against Britain in 1772 now using the same strategy to retaliate against the Georgian's attacks on his friends and family? Was he taking advantage of the serendipitous opportunity to stake out the high moral ground while embarrassing a bitter opponent? One historian argued that this essay was the result of failing health and pain medication; it was not attributed to the ailing Franklin until later ab-

olitionists needed his name to buttress their cause. The fact that there is no evidence that Franklin ever made friends with a black person gives cause to raise such a question. [32] Apparently new insights did not alter his behavior toward the black people surrounding him.

One chronicler describes Franklin as having "brought [antislavery] into the marketplace of ideas only to leave it there."[33] But such an interpretation takes little account of the complexity of race and slavery in early America—and the legacy they leave in the world today. For even as he implored his government to recognize that "equal liberty . . . is the Birthright of all men," Franklin, confounded by the magnitude of the American struggle with race, class, and culture, appeared to have no workable plan in mind and little framework for modeling a society where equal liberty is the birthright of all. Perhaps this, too, gives him resonance in our own time (fig. 8.17).

Fig. 8.17 Charles Willson Peale, Portrait of Benjamin Franklin, 1785. This is believed to be the last life portrait of Franklin, made when he was eighty-one years old, serving as "governor" of Pennsylvania, and attending sessions of the Constitutional Convention.

Afterword

The End of His Pragmatism

EDMUND S. MORGAN

Pragmatism is the word most commonly used to describe Franklin's way of dealing with the world. We don't mean by it an adherence to the philosophy of Charles Sanders Peirce or William James, from which the modern word probably derived (it was not in Franklin's vocabulary). We mean, I think, simply a willingness to compromise in pursuit of some goal, a willingness not to insist on some abstract principle in transactions with other people, a willingness to make concessions. A prime example would be Franklin's best-known contribution to the proceedings of the 1787 convention that created the federal Constitution, the so-called Great Compromise, which he proposed as a way to break the deadlock over representation between the small states and the large. The states would be represented equally in the Senate and in proportion to population in the House of Representatives.

This compromise went against Franklin's own beliefs. He would have preferred a single national representative assembly based strictly on population or, failing that, a bicameral legislature in which the members of both houses were apportioned that way. From the time when the states first joined in the Continental Congress, Franklin had objected to voting by state: he thought it ridiculous for a state the size of Rhode Island or Delaware to have the same share in making decisions as Virginia or Pennsylvania. He did not prevail in the Continental Congress or in the Constitutional Convention, but he and those who thought like him at least got half of what they wanted or, rather, more than half. They got the union, first of the colonies, then of the states. Like Abraham Lincoln after them, they put the union first, ahead of goals that could not in any case have been reached without it. Franklin's pragmatism meant putting first things first, accepting half a loaf if he could not get the whole, and ungrudgingly accepting nothing at all if that was the price of carrying on an enterprise he believed in.

Franklin learned his pragmatism in Philadelphia before he ever had need or opportunity to apply it on a continental or global scale. Putting first things first in his printing business doubtless contributed to the success that enabled him to retire at the age of forty-two, but his retirement is only one sign of the fact that he already had goals that he put ahead of making money. As he told his mother in 1750, "I would rather have it said, *he lived usefully*, than, *He died rich*."[1] It will be admitted that he succeeded in that goal, and his success was the result of a personal philosophy in which putting first things first often meant putting himself last. He organized a whole array of societies for improving life in Philadelphia: a fire company, an insurance company, a library, a hospital, a university. In these initiatives, guided by the insights into human psychology that he put in the mouth of "Poor Richard," he learned to lead from the rear. As the instigator of so many projects for public benefit, he found it most effective to present them as coming from other people. He employed the same technique on a larger scale when his colony's government failed to arm Pennsylvania against the threatened wartime invasion by the French in 1747. He organized a militia and raised money for fortifications while making it all seem to be the spontaneous work of other leading citizens. In his militia he served as a common soldier, declining any position of command. Pragmatism was not just a willingness to compromise, it was an art.

By "the end of his pragmatism" I intend both the common meanings of the word *end:* end as a goal or purpose and end as the place where something stops. Where did Franklin's pragmatism end, stop? For what goals was Franklin willing to compromise, and where did he draw a line and say, No compromise, or No further compromise? The answer is not easy, for there were many goals, many principles he believed in but did not pursue or struggle to attain. He believed in free trade among nations. He believed that there should be an international law embodied in treaties to forbid privateering and also to forbid nations at war from interfering with the peaceful activities of farmers, sailors, and merchants. These were beliefs he did not hold lightly; as the principal U.S. negotiator in the treaty that ended the War for Independence he made

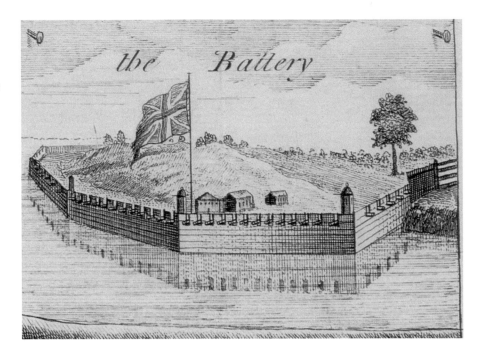

Fig. A.2 George Heap, Association Battery, 1755. Funds raised through Franklin's lottery contributed to the construction of this fort, built just outside Philadelphia on the Delaware River.

an effort to secure their recognition. But he was pragmatic. He did not draw a line and say, No treaty without them. In early life Franklin had a plan for an international party of virtue, whose members would further goals like these. He was going to write a book on the art of virtue that would be a kind of manifesto for an international movement. He was still thinking about it in the 1780s, but he never did write it. I think it is fair to say that Franklin recognized that his major goals for the good of mankind in general were unattainable, that even small steps toward them would be too small to be worth fighting for. He was not Don Quixote, and he would not waste his time breaking lances with the guardians of the status quo in contests he could not win.

But there were occasions when he dug in his heels and refused to make concessions, occasions when his goal was nonnegotiable, when defeat was preferable to compromise, when his pragmatism came to an end, a stop. One of these was in his campaign to substitute royal government for proprietary government in Pennsylvania. The campaign had begun in the Pennsylvania Assembly's attempt to tax the tax-exempt lands of the Penn family. Frustrated

Fig. A.3 (Opposite) An Essay of a Declaration of Rights, Brought in by the Committee appointed for that Purpose, and now under the Consideration of the Convention of the State of Pennsylvania, *1776, with handwritten annotations by Franklin.*

AN *ESSAY* of a DECLARATION of RIGHTS,

Brought in by the Committee appointed for that Purpose, and now under
the Consideration of the CONVENTION of the State of *Pennsylvania*.

1. THAT all Men are born equally free and independant, and have certain natural, inherent and unalienable Rights, amongst which are the enjoying and defending Life
and Liberty, acquiring, possessing and protecting Property, and pursuing and obtaining Happiness and Safety.

2. That all Men have a natural and unalienable Right to worship almighty GOD according to the Dictates of their own Consciences and Understandings: And that no Man ought
or of Right can be compelled to attend any Place of Religious Worship, or support or maintain any Worship Place or Ministry, contrary to, or against his own free Will and Consent.
Nor can any Man be justly deprived or abridged of any Civil Right as a Citizen, on account
of his peculiar Mode of religious Worship. And that no Authority can or ought to be vested
in, or assumed by, any Power whatever that shall in any Case interfere with, or in any Manner controul, the Right of Conscience in the free Exercise of religious Worship.

3. That the People of this State have the sole exclusive and inherent Right of governing
and regulating the internal Police of the same.

4. That all Power being originally inherent in, and consequently derived from, the People,
therefore all Officers of Government, whether Legislative or Executive, are their Trustees
and Servants, and at all Times accountable to them.

5. That Government is or ought to be instituted for the common Benefit, Protection and
Security of the People, Nation or Community; and that a Majority of the Community hath
an indubitable, unalienable and indefeasible Right to reform, alter or abolish it in such a
Manner as shall be by that Majority judged most conducive to the Public Weal.

6. That those who are employed in the Legislative and Executive Business of the State
may be restrained from Oppression, by feeling and participating the common Burthens, the
People have a Right, at such Periods as they may think proper, to reduce their Public Officers to a private Station, return them into that Body from which they were originally taken,
and supply the Vacancies by certain and regular Elections: But that the having served in any
Office, ought not in all Cases to disqualify the Persons for being re-elected.

7. That all Elections ought to be free, and that all Men having an evident, permanent
and common Interest with, and Attachment to, the Community, have a Right to elect Officers, or be elected into Office.

8. That all private Property, being protected by the State, ought to pay its just Proportion
towards the Expence of that Protection; but that no Part of a Man's Property can be taken
from him, or applied to Public Uses, without his own Consent, or that of his legal Representatives: Nor are the People bound by any Laws but such as they have, in like Manner, assented to, for their common Good.

9. That in all Criminal Prosecutions a Man hath a Right to be heard by Council, to demand the Cause and Nature of his Accusation, to be confronted with the Accusers or Witnesses, to call for Evidence in his Favour, and a speedy public Trial by an impartial Jury of
the Country, without whose unanimous Consent he cannot be found guilty, nor can he be
compelled to give Evidence against himself, nor can any Man be justly deprived of his Liberty, except by the Laws of the Land, or the Judgment of his Peers.

10. That the People have a Right to hold themselves, their Houses, Papers and Possessions free
from Search or Seizure, and therefore

10. That Warrants without Oaths or Affirmations first made, affording a sufficient Foundation for them, and whereby any Officer or Messenger may be commanded or required to
search suspected Places, or to seize any Person or Persons his or their Property not particularly described, are contrary to that Right, and ought not to be granted.

11. That in Controversies respecting Property, and in Suits between Man and Man, the
Parties have a Right to Trial by Jury, which ought to be held sacred.

12. That the People have a Right to Freedom of Speech, and writing and publishing their
Sentiments, therefore the Freedom of the Press ought not to be restrained.

13. That the People have a Right to bear Arms for the Defence of themselves and the
State, and as standing Armies in the Time of Peace are dangerous to Liberty, they ought
not to be kept up: And that the Military should be kept under strict Subordination to, and
governed by, the Civil Power.

14. That a frequent Recurrence to fundamental Principles, and a firm Adherence to
Justice, Moderation, Temperance and Frugality are absolutely necessary to preserve the Bless-
ings of Liberty, and keep a Government free, the People have therefore a Right to exact a
due and constant Regard to these Points from their Officers and Representatives.

15. That all Men have a natural inherent Right of Emigration from one State to any
other that will receive them, or for the Forming a new State in vacant or purchased Countries whenever they find that thereby they may promote their own Happiness.

16. That an enormous Proportion of Property vested in a few Individuals is dangerous to
the Rights, and destructive of the Common Happiness, of Mankind; and therefore every
free State hath a Right by its Laws to discourage the Possession of such Property.

vacant Countries, or such as they can purchase,

by the veto of the Penns' appointed governor (the Penns themselves remained in England), the Assembly sent Franklin to England in 1757 to persuade the British government to require the Penns to allow the taxation. Franklin failed in this mission, or rather won a very limited right to tax a portion of the Penn lands. He returned to Pennsylvania in 1764, determined on what he and his political allies may have had in mind from the beginning, a revocation of the Penn family's authority over the colony in favor of direct royal control. Franklin and his allies dominated the Pennsylvania Assembly, and the Assembly sent him back to England with his desired petition for royal government. But it was not a popular move in Pennsylvania and not likely to succeed in England. It did not succeed, and it was unrealistic to think it ever could have. In this case I think Franklin had already achieved a pragmatic halfway measure in making some of the Penn lands taxable. His new goal, the destruction of the Penns' authority, could not be reached pragmatically. It was nonnegotiable.

We have to ask why he thought it was a good idea anyhow. We cannot rule out the role of personal feelings. By the time he began his campaign Franklin had developed a bitter hatred toward the principal proprietor, Thomas Penn, and Penn returned the favor. He had seen Franklin's organization of a militia to protect the colony as a threat to his authority, a "Military Common Wealth." He wished that Franklin would take his role as tribune of the people somewhere else. When the two finally met in England, Franklin came away with "a more cordial and thorough Contempt for him than I ever before felt for any Man living."[2] Personal feelings may have raised the stakes in the contest, but Franklin's eagerness to bring down the Penns had deeper roots, as will become evident if we consider another case in which his pragmatism ended.

The two cases are closely linked though they may seem at odds with each other. During the colonists' quarrel with the mother country, which was just beginning when Franklin returned to England with his petition for royal government, he became the unofficial spokesman for the colonists in their protests against the British Parliament's attempt to tax them. As will be seen, he came to view Parliament's exercise of authority in America in the same way that he viewed the Penn family's, as an unacceptable interposition of other Englishmen between the king and his American subjects. As Franklin developed this view, his pragmatism was at first very much in evidence. He did not himself believe in the natural rights that the colonists kept affirming, and he hoped to work out a compromise, as in effect he did for a time. Largely through his efforts Parliament repealed the Stamp Act while at the same time asserting in the Declaratory Act that it had a right to pass such an act.

FRANKLIN S'OPPOSE AUX TAXES

en 1766.

Dessiné par le Jeune   Gravé par David

Fig. A.4 David[?] after LeJeune[?],
Franklin s'oppose aux taxes en
1766, *n.d. This French engraving
of Franklin's testimony to the House
of Commons shows Franklin in a
toga, implicitly comparing him to
a Roman orator.*

The Declaratory Act was not Franklin's idea, but he was content to have Parliament claim the right, provided it was not exercised. In succeeding years, as Parliament again exercised that right in the Townshend Acts of 1767 and the Tea Act of 1773, he did his best to excuse and defend the colonists' declarations and manifestos and to minimize the violence that accompanied them. At the same time, in letters home he urged the colonists to calm down, avoid the confrontations that were giving them a bad name in England, and be patient until the mother country changed its policies, as he was urging it to do at every opportunity. His hope was that the British would recognize the need to adjust their policies to the reality of colonial opposition before the opposition hardened to the point of no return, the point of withdrawing from the empire.

His hopes were frustrated, of course, though only because the British proved blind to the realities of the situation. Again, his frustration may have been aggravated by personal feelings about the people he had to deal with. Lord Hillsborough, secretary of state for the colonies from 1768 to 1772, he described as "proud, supercilious, extreamly conceited, . . . fond of every one that can stoop to flatter him, and inimical to all that dare tell him disagreeable Truths." Lord Dartmouth, who succeeded Hillsborough, was effusive in expressions of goodwill but no more capable than the other great lords of comprehending what was going on in North America. The men governing Great Britain and the empire, Franklin concluded at last, had "scarce Discretion enough to govern a Herd of Swine."[3]

By the time he left England, late in 1774, his pragmatic efforts to save the empire had reached an end. From that time forward he knew that independence was the only way Americans could gain the rights they claimed and would never give up. He waited for other Americans to catch up, as the Continental Congress made pragmatic efforts to save the empire in petitions to the king that he knew were useless. But in July 1776, in the document he helped to draft, independence became nonnegotiable. After his colleagues in Congress sent him as their envoy to France he gave a frosty answer to all British overtures to win the colonies back. There was now no room for pragmatism, no room for concessions, no halfway house on the road to independence. But what had been the end, in the sense of purpose, of his pragmatic efforts to smooth relations between Britain and the colonies before they reached the point of no return?

Franklin has been called a reluctant revolutionary, and so he was—reluctant to break up the empire. But that label is a little misleading, for he was never a reluctant American. Throughout his public career, whether he was

OBSERVATIONS concerning the Increafe of Mankind, Peopling of Countries, &c.

1. Tables of the Proportion of Marriages toBirths, of Deaths to Births, of Marriages to the Numbers of Inhabitants, &c. form'd on Obfervaions made upon the Bills of Mortality, Chriftnings, &c. of populous Cities, will not fuit Countries ; nor will Tables form'd on Obfervations made on full fettled oldCountries, as *Europe*, fuit new Countries, as *America*.

2. For People increafe in Proportion to the Number of Marriages, and that is greater in Proportion to the Eafe and Convenience of fupporting a Family. When Families can be eafily fupported, more Perfons marry, and earlier in Life.

3. In Cities, where all Trades, Occupations and Offices are full, many delay marrying, till they can fee how to bear the Charges of a Family ; which Charges

B   are

Fig. A.5 Title page of Benjamin Franklin, "Observations concerning the Increase of Mankind . . . ," in William Clarke, Observations On the late and present Conduct of the French: with Regard to their Encroachments upon the British Colonies in North America. Together with remarks on the importance of these colonies to Great-Britain, *1755.*

Fig. A.6 Jean-Antoine Houdon, Portrait bust of Benjamin Franklin, 1779. That Houdon, the leading portrait sculptor of the eighteenth century, chose Franklin as a subject is testimony to Franklin's celebrity status in France. Though not taken from life, this well-known likeness is considered accurate because Houdon and Franklin were acquaintances.

making compromises or stubbornly refusing to, the end, the goal, of his pragmatism was a vision that others only gradually learned to share and none ever fully shared. Franklin's vision, his ultimate goal, first began to take shape in an essay he wrote in 1751, but did not publish until 1755, entitled "Observations concerning the Increase of Mankind, Peopling of Countries, &c."[4] The immediate occasion for it may have been the British Iron Act of 1750, limiting iron manufacturing in the colonies. Most Americans at that time, and right through their quarrel with the British Parliament over taxation, had taken care not to object to the restrictions imposed by Parliament on American manufacturing.

There was no public outcry against the Iron Act when it was passed. Even the Declaration of Independence, in its catalogue of tyrannical British actions, made no mention of the limitations placed on colonial trade and manufactures. Franklin objected to them in 1751 because they would inhibit a growth that he saw as the most significant development in modern history.

The growth that he foresaw in the immediate future was not a growth of iron manufacturing or of anything else that would compete with British products. It was a growth in the number of Americans, who would for the foreseeable future become customers for those products. British policy, he argued, should take account of something that the policy makers had not noticed, namely, the increase of population in America from causes unique to new countries. To understand the impact of Franklin's argument and its implications both for him and for the American future, it has to be seen in the context of a continuing discussion in print among writers of the time on British economic policy.[5]

It was a basic premise of the discussion that a country's prosperity and strength were to be measured by the size of its population. Anything that increased population was good; anything that decreased it was bad. Immigration was good; emigration was bad. Another premise was that the population within a settled country could be increased only by adding manufacturing enterprises and the laborers engaged in them—at the lowest possible wage that would keep them alive. Colonies in this formula were by nature bad because the loss of people emigrating to them weakened the mother country by that much. But it could be argued, and was, that if the colonists could be required to buy all their manufactures from the mother country, their trade would make up for the loss in numbers at home by expanding the number of laborers needed to supply them. Colonies could be, in effect, foreign countries whose economies you could control, as England had been doing all along with the American colonies in the Navigation Acts of the seventeenth century and in the acts forbidding or penalizing colonial manufactures: the Woollen Act of 1699, the Hat Act of 1732, and the Iron Act just passed.

Some writers, but by no means all, were persuaded by this reasoning. Many continued to regard colonies as more of a burden than a benefit to England's population. Franklin entered the discussion with a new slant on the sources of population increase. The argument of his essay was that population in new countries, that is, America, did not depend on the same forces that governed population in old, urbanized countries like England. Americans occupied a continent originally peopled by natives who could maintain only the numbers that a life of hunting and gathering could support (a misconception about Indian economies but not about their post-Columbian numbers). The English settlers by farming the land could grow in numbers as fast as they could marry and have children, which they did at an early age in large families. Sustained only by farming the abundant land, they doubled their numbers every twenty-five years. It was foolish and needless for the English (and irritating to the Americans, or at least to Franklin) to limit manufacturing in America because Americans were too busy farming to spend their time on any but the crudest manufactures. They bought English goods in quantities that grew with their numbers and would continue to do so as they continued to grow, and thus would enable the English manufacturing population to grow. It was also foolish to allow immigration to English colonies from other countries, foolish to admit the Germans who were swarming to Pennsylvania and the Africans who were dragged forcibly to the southern colonies. America should be an extension of England, peopled by the prolific American Englishmen already there.

This was an argument, on the surface, against restricting American manufactures. But it seemed to make the restriction more needless than harmful. At the same time it advertised a fact that could make uneasy the writers and policy makers who measured a country's wealth and greatness by the size of its population. Some 80,000 Englishmen, Franklin estimated, had peopled the colonies in the seventeenth century. They were now more than a million. "This Million doubling, suppose but once in 25 Years, will in another Century be more than the People of England, and the greatest Number of Englishmen will be on this Side the Water."[6] And he went on to rhapsodize about the great accession of power to the British Empire, including the ominous fact that the number of American privateers in the war with France just concluded (the War of the Austrian Succession) exceeded both in men and guns the entire British navy in Queen Elizabeth's day, the navy, he did not need to say, that defeated the Spanish Armada.

Franklin was undoubtedly sincere in his exultation over the new power that American Englishmen were bringing to England, not to mention the new customers they were bringing to English merchants and manufacturers. This was more than a mathematical calculation. It was an expression of the pride in his country's future that sustained him in his pragmatic efforts to guide the British to a peaceful acceptance of that future. He could not have been unaware of the implications of his prediction that in another century there would be more Englishmen in America than in England. Modern readers are a little shocked by the ethnocentrism of his appeal against Africans and Germans. But contemporary readers must have noticed that this was based on his identification of Americans as Englishmen. The American colonies were not a foreign country that you could control. They were English and would soon outnumber their brothers and sisters in England.

He reprinted the essay at the end of his famous Canada Pamphlet of 1760 (*The Interest of Great Britain Considered*), in which he argued for the retention of Canada rather than the French West Indies in the peace that would conclude the Seven Years' War (the French and Indian War). The conquest and retention of Canada would open a vast new territory to be peopled not by a needless immigration from England but by American Englishmen as they proliferated and spread over the continent. They would bring to "the British name and nation a stability and permanency that no man acquainted with history durst have hoped for, 'till our American possessions opened the pleasing prospect."[7]

Note that he says "name and nation." Franklin was developing a vision of the empire in which North America, with its immense territory and limitless natural resources, would be the center of "the greatest Political Structure Human Wisdom ever yet erected." As he said to his Scottish friend Lord Kames in 1760, after finishing the Canada Pamphlet, "I have long been of Opinion, that the Foundations of the future Grandeur and Stability of the British Empire, lie in America."[8] He did not say, then or later, that he had plans for transferring the government of the empire to the center of its power and population. But when his *Observations Concerning the Increase of Mankind* landed among the writers who had been discussing population as the measure of a country's strength, they were not slow to draw the inference that Franklin's objective was to bring the government where the people were.

Josiah Tucker, dean of Gloucester Cathedral, had been an ardent proponent of laws to encourage foreign immigration to England as a means of increasing population. In the reverse of Franklin's argument against allowing the non-English to people America, Tucker argued for laws to make naturalization easier for foreign immigrants to England. He viewed colonies as a burden, and a dangerous burden at that. They were a drain on the population of the mother country. They were not a foreign country under your control but one you could not control, one that might in the end control you. Franklin, he believed, was the man who meant to bring that about. In 1767 in a conversation with Lord Shelburne, then in charge of colonial matters, about a paper Shelburne had written anonymously advocating settlements in the Ohio Valley, Tucker remarked "that he was sure that paper was drawn up by Dr. Franklin, he saw him in every paragraph; adding that Dr. Franklin wanted to remove the seat of government to America; that, says he, is his constant plan."[9]

It was not, in fact, Franklin's plan, but it could very well have been his unspoken prediction. In pressing the colonists' case against parliamentary taxation in the 1760s and 1770s Franklin was arguing simply for their recognition as Englishmen, the full equals of Englishmen in England, united with them in allegiance to the same king. His campaign against the Penns can be seen as the first application in practical politics of the view of the British Empire that he had adumbrated in his essay on population growth. It was an empire of Englishmen, divided into many kingdoms: England, Scotland, Ireland, Pennsylvania, Virginia, Massachusetts, and so on. The king's government in each of his kingdoms was conducted by representative assemblies of the people under the direction of royal appointees. Pennsylvania (along with Maryland) was an anomaly, where the king's authority had been mistakenly entrusted to the family of one of his private subjects, a kind of imperium in imperio. That needed correcting. No subject should stand between the king and his other subjects as the Penn family did in Pennsylvania. Much worse was the interposition of the British Parliament between the king and his other subjects in all the American colonies. The campaign for removing the authority of the Penns in Pennsylvania was a dress rehearsal for removing the authority of Parliament anywhere outside Great Britain.

The Penns, Franklin and his allies contended, were "private subjects" like everyone else in Pennsylvania and should be required to obey the same laws and pay the same taxes as everyone else. More important, they should not be given powers that properly belonged only to the king, powers that placed them between the king and other subjects. After the king's Privy Council finally rejected Franklin's petition for royal government in 1766, his ally in Pennsylvania, Joseph Galloway, warned Franklin that his countrymen would never "be easy under a Government which Admits of the Intervention of a Private Subject between their Sovereign and them."[10] By this time Franklin, a little ahead of other Americans, had decided that the authority of Parliament extended only to Great Britain: the colonies had their own parliaments and were joined to one another and to Great Britain only by allegiance to the king. Other Americans may have reached that position from a belief in natural and constitutional rights. For Franklin it was a matter of colonists being Englishmen united in equality before the king.

Franklin's stubborn and fruitless demand for royal government in Pennsylvania did not arise from oppression by the proprietary government, which actually gave more power to the colony's representative assembly than was the case in existing royal colonies like Massachusetts and Virginia. What Franklin objected to was placing the Pennsylvania colonists on a different footing from other Englishmen. Similarly, what he objected to in parliamentary taxation was not the burden, which in the attempted statutes would have been small, but Parliament's usurpation of the king's authority over his subjects in America. The expressed devotion to the king was scarcely a prostration before the throne. It was a way of displacing Parliament from its already anachronistic place at the top of an empire that would soon be, properly speaking, American. And the equality of subjects meant more, at least for Franklin, than an equality of rights. It meant an equality that would deflate the air of condescension he had to suffer in the officials he had to deal with, all of them his intellectual inferiors, who could treat him and his constituents as supplicants.

As early as 1754, when he was preparing to attend the Albany Congress, Franklin had confided to a friend in London, Peter Collinson, his opinion that "Britain and her Colonies should be considered as one Whole, and not as different States with separate Interests." As the colonies' quarrel over taxation developed, Franklin dreamed of a consolidation of the empire under a new written constitution that would treat Americans the same as Englishmen in England. At first he thought of simply admitting American representatives to Parliament. When he realized that this was not practicable, he was willing to settle for making American legislative assemblies equal to Parliament. He would still have preferred a general reorganization of the empire, a union of Great Britain and the colonies on the equal terms that the word *union* implied. In 1767 he confided his hopes to Lord Kames, with whom he could be more open than in public statements. Such a union, he explained, would actually benefit Britain more than America by preserving for the mother country an equal place in an empire that must soon be principally American. America had resources far outweighing what the British Isles possessed. It was bound to "become a great Country, populous and mighty; and will in a less time than is generally conceiv'd be able to shake off any Shackles that may be impos'd on her, and perhaps place them on the Imposers. In the mean Time, every act of Oppression will sour their Tempers . . . and hasten their final Revolt."[11]

Franklin continued to hope that British statesmen would recognize the opportunity they had for preserving their empire by ceasing to treat the colonies as a foreign country they could control. The only alternative if they continued on their course was for America to become a foreign country indeed, beyond their control. The longer he viewed at firsthand the way the British ran their empire, the more he despaired of his attempts to save it for them. In Pennsylvania his friend Galloway, without Franklin's firsthand experience, worked on a plan for the union they had both wanted. When the Continental Congress met in 1774 and Galloway presented them with his plan, the Congress rejected it, and so, when he learned of it, did Franklin. America, treated as a foreign country, had become one, and Franklin did not wish to see its future inhibited any longer by connection with a people so blind to its future importance. "When I consider," he wrote Galloway, "the extream Corruption prevalent among all Orders of Men in this old rotten State, . . . I cannot but apprehend more Mischief than Benefit from a closer Union."[12]

The vision that had guided Franklin's pragmatism continued to guide him in the years ahead. He still had many good friends in England, but they had no more power than he to lift the blinders from the king's ministers. He regretted, as he told them, that this hopes for allowing England to remain a part of the great American future had been destroyed "by the mangling hands of a few blundering ministers." But America's growth to greatness, he assured his friends, could not be stopped: "God will protect and prosper it: You will only exclude yourselves from any share in it."[13]

The greatness that Franklin envisioned for America embraced the whole continent but was not to be measured merely by the huge population he predicted. It was to be found in "the greatest Political Structure Human Wisdom ever yet erected." Independence had become a necessary step toward that goal. The peace treaty that ended the Revolutionary War, with boundaries short of Canada, Louisiana, and Florida, was another step, the Constitution of 1787 yet another. Each step had been worth taking, worth whatever compromises and concessions it had required. But they all stopped well short of the great political structure he predicted. His vision of that structure had itself grown. He had long since found reason to repent of his expressed wish to exclude the German immigrants from a share in it, if only because they had become a force to be reckoned with in Pennsylvania politics. And at some time after he returned to Philadelphia he joined his friends there in a wish to give Africans a share. There had never been a chance that the Constitutional Convention of 1787 would abolish slavery. But in one of the last acts of his public career he put his name to a petition to the new Congress for the national abolition of slavery; and just before he died he penned one of his most effective satirical pieces, mocking the reasons offered in Congress for rejecting the petition.

It may be worth asking, then, how the great political structure of his vision would have differed from what Americans actually got and now have in place. Franklin never set out a plan for his ideal state, as he never got around to writing his treatise on the art of virtue. But we know that his model for the United States, besides abolishing slavery, would have given the separate states no power as states in the national government. There would have been no president with the powers that office now carries. Even with slavery still established in the South, southern states would not have had the extra power that the three-fifths clause of the Constitution gave them, and the people of the small states today would not have the extra power that the Senate and the electoral college give them.

From a few letters to friends we know that Franklin would have given far fewer privileges to private property and especially to large accumulations of property than the Constitution and the courts have accorded them. He regarded property as "the Creature of publick Convention," and believed that the public, therefore, through its governing bodies, should have the power "of limiting the Quantity and the Uses of it." This was a long-standing belief with him. As early as 1750 he had given his opinion "that what we have above what we can use, is not properly *ours,* tho' we possess it."[14] He was probably the author of a provision of the Pennsylvania Constitution of 1776 limiting the accumulation of property, a provision that did not survive in the final document, as his proposals for the U.S. Constitution did not survive discussion in the convention. His great political structure would have embodied a much more egalitarian society than the United States has ever seen. But Franklin did get as much as was pragmatically possible. The result has prevailed through many challenges. His vision remains unfulfilled, itself a challenge to Americans who still search for a better world.

Notes

Abbreviations

The following short titles and abbreviations are used in the notes.

APS	American Philosophical Society
Autobiography	*Benjamin Franklin's Autobiography*
Diary of John Adams	*The Diary and Autobiography of John Adams*
PBF	*The Papers of Benjamin Franklin*
Reappraising Franklin	J. A. Leo Lemay, ed., *Reappraising Benjamin Franklin: A Bicentennial Perspective*
Writings	Benjamin Franklin, *Writings,* ed. J. A. Leo Lemay
Smyth	*The Writings of Benjamin Franklin,* ed. Albert Henry Smyth

 Chapter 1. The Life of Benjamin Franklin

1. In 1752 Great Britain adopted the Gregorian calendar, a revision of the Julian calendar, and dropped eleven days, skipping from Wednesday, September 2, to Thursday, September 14. Under the Julian calendar, the new year had begun on March 25. Therefore, before 1752, when giving dates from January 1 to March 25, a year will be given with a slash (e.g., 1705/6), indicating that under the Julian calendar, the year was reckoned 1705 but is by the Gregorian calendar identified as 1706. Thus Franklin's birthdate was January 6, 1705 (according to the Julian calendar), or January 17, 1706 (according to the Gregorian calendar).

2. *Autobiography,* 6–7.

3. Ibid., 7.

4. Ibid., 12.

5. Ibid., 10, 12

6. Ibid., 15; *Writings,* 43–56; "Dingo," *New-England Courant,* July 15, 1723.

7. *Autobiography,* 15; Silence Dogood, no. 5, May 28, 1722, *PBF* 1: 19.

8. *Autobiography,* 14–15; Silence Dogood, no. 5, May 28, 1722, *PBF* 1: 19; and *New-England Courant,* July 15, 1723.

9. *Autobiography,* 20.

10. Ibid. On this passage and its resonance in American literature, see James H. Justus, "Arthur Mervyn, American," *American Literature* 42 (1970): 304–24; A. B. England, "Robin Molineux and the Young Ben Franklin: A Reconsideration," *American Studies* 6 (1972): 181–88; Denis M. Murphy, "Poor Robin and Shrewd Ben: Hawthorne's Kinsman," *Studies in Short Fiction* 15 (1978): 185–90; Leo B. Levy, "Henry James and the Image of Franklin," *Southern Review* 16 (1980): 552–59; and Floyd C. Watkins, "Fitzgerald's Jay Gatsby and Young Ben Franklin," *New England Quarterly* 27 (1954): 249–52.

11. *Autobiography*, 33.

12. *Oxford Dictionary of National Biography*, s.v. "Mandeville, Bernard."

13. *Autobiography*, 35–36.

14. Ibid., 36–37.

15. Ibid., 53.

16. *Pennsylvania Gazette*, March 13, 1729; *Autobiography*, 54; John Wise, *Vindication of the Government of New England Churches* (Boston: Allen, 1717), 39; John Wise, *A Word of Comfort to a Melancholy Country* (Boston: James Franklin, 1721), 33.

17. Benjamin Franklin to Abiah Franklin, April 12, 1750, *PBF* 3: 474n1.

18. *Pennsylvania Gazette*, June 27, 1734.

19. See Krider, "Benjamin Franklin's Science," in this volume.

20. "Felons and Rattlesnakes," May 9, 1751, *Pennsylvania Gazette*, *PBF* 4: 130–33; "Observations Concerning the Increase of Mankind," 1755, *PBF* 4: 225–34; *Papers of John Adams*, 1: 5 and n1.

21. "Short hints towards a Scheme for a General Union of the British Colonies on the Continent," [June 28, 1754], *PBF* 5: 361; "The Albany Plan of Union," July 10, 1754, *PBF* 5: 374–92.

22. Franklin to William Shirley, December 4, 1754, *PBF* 5: 444; Franklin to William Shirley, December 22, 1754, *PBF* 5: 451; and Max Farrand, ed., *The Records of the Federal Convention of 1787*, 4 vols. (New Haven: Yale University Press, rev. ed. 1966), 3: 540n1.

23. *Poor Richard's Almanack*, 1758, *PBF* 7: 347, 348–49.

24. May 9, 1759, *PBF* 8: 340–56; Anne Reynolds Phillips, "Expressions of Cultural Nationalism in Early American Magazines" (Ph.D. diss., Brown University, 1953), 37–39. Phillips knew the pseudonymous essay only from its reprinting in the *New American Magazine* 1 (1759): 607–13.

25. *Letters of David Hume*, 2: 269.

26. *Autobiography*, 145; Order in Council, September 2, 1760, *PBF* 9: 207n4.

27. "Election Results in Philadelphia County," 1764, *PBF* 11: 390–91.

28. "Examination before the Committee of the Whole of the House of Commons," February 13, 1755, *PBF* 13: 142.

29. "Remarks on Judge Foster's Argument in Favor of the Right of Impressing Seamen," before September 17, 1781, *PBF* 35: 500; for the date of composition, see *Pennsylvania Magazine of History and Biography* 126 (2002): 327–40, at 328. For Franklin's references to America's growing strength, see *The Interest of Great Britain Considered*, 1760, *PBF* 9: 90–91; Franklin to Thomas Cushing, January 5, 1773, *PBF* 20: 10. Jan Ingenhousz referred to Franklin's prediction of independence for America "made me 12 or 13 years ago" (Ingenhousz to Franklin, December 14, 1777, *PBF* 25: 288); Franklin to Lord Kames, February 25, 1767, *PBF* 14: 67–69; Franklin praised the prediction of Jacques Barbeu-Dubourg that America would achieve independence in a letter to P. S. du Pont de Nemours (June 15, 1772, *PBF* 19: 178). Joseph Priestley recorded that Franklin "dreaded the war, and often said that, if the difference should come to an open rupture, it would be a war of *ten years*, and he should not live to see the end of it. . . . That the issue would be favourable to America, he never doubted. The English, he used to say, may take all our great towns, but that will not give them possession of the country" (Priest-

ley, *Autobiography*, ed. Jack Lindsay [Teaneck, N.J.: Farleigh Dickinson University Press. 1970], 117–30).

30. Franklin to Thomas Cushing, January 5, 1773, *PBF* 20: 10.

31. *PBF* 20: 515.

32. Priestley, *Autobiography,* 117.

33. *Diary of John Adams,* 1: 253; "Song: 'The King's Own Regulars,'" November 27, 1775, *PBF* 22: 274–77; "'Bradshaw's Epitaph': A Hoax Attributed to Franklin," December 14, 1775, *PBF* 22, 303–4.

34. *Diary of John Adams,* 3: 422.

35. Franklin to Emma Thompson, February 8, 1777, *PBF* 23: 298.

36. *Works of John Adams,* 1: 659; Aldridge, *Benjamin Franklin and His French Contemporaries,* 124.

37. *Writings,* 917; Franklin in *New York Journal,* September 8, 1777, cited in Moore, *Diary of the American Revolution,* 1: 389–90.

38. Franklin to Madame Brillon: "The Ephemera," *PBF* 27: 430–35; Franklin to Madame Helvétius, "The Elysian Fields," ca. January 1, 1780, *PBF* 35: 322–27.

39. Continental Congress Instructions, June 15, 1781, *PBF* 35: 167; Franklin, "Notes for a conversation with Oswald," on or before April 19, 1782, *PBF* 37: 171; Franklin to John Adams, April 20, 1782, *PBF* 37: 178.

40. Oswald's notes on Franklin's terms for peace, July 10, 1782, *PBF* 37: 599–600.

41. Franklin to Joseph Banks, August 30, 1783, *Writings,* 1075; Aldridge, *Franklin and His French Contemporaries,* 188; *Information to those who would remove to america,* February 1784, *Writings,* 976–77.

42. Smyth 9: 318; "Maritime Observations," Smyth 9: 372–413.

43. Farrand, *Records of the Federal Convention,* 1: 488 (see also 4: 132); 1: 523, 526; 2:13.

44. Barbara B. Oberg, "'Plain, insinuating, persuasive': Benjamin Franklin's Final Speech to the Constitutional Convention of 1787," in *Reappraising Franklin,* 175–92.

45. Franklin to Elizabeth Partridge, November 25, 1788, Smyth 9: 683.

46. Bowling, *Petition Histories and Nonlegislative Official Documents,* 314–38, quotation on 316. Jackson's speech of March 16 appeared in the *Federal Gazette,* March 22, 1790, and Franklin's rejoinder of March 23 appeared there on March 25, 1790 (quotation near the end).

47. Smyth 10: 69; *Poor Richard's Almanack,* 1737, *PBF* 2: 171 (cf. Cotton Mather, *Bonifacius,* ed. David Levin [Cambridge: Harvard University Press, 1966], 24).

 Chapter 2. Benjamin Franklin, Printer

Portions of this essay were previously published, in earlier form, in "The Book Trade in the Middle Colonies, 1680–1720," in *The Colonial Book in the Atlantic World,* ed. Hugh Amory and David D. Hall (Worcester, Mass.: American Antiquarian Society/ New York: Cambridge University Press, 2000), and are used with permission.

1. Green, "Book Trade in the Middle Colonies," 199–223.

2. Thomas, *History of Printing in America*, 110–12, 215–26, 232, 234–42.

3. Massachusetts, General Court, *A Journal of the House of Representatives* (Boston: B. Green and S. Kneeland, 1722), 60; *Autobiography*, 17.

4. *Autobiography*, 21–22, 112–13. If Franklin's recollection that Keimer had not yet printed anything was correct, he could not have arrived in October as he says in the *Autobiography*, since the Friends' Monthly Meeting denounced Keimer's first imprint *A Parable* (no copy known) in September.

5. *Autobiography*, 21–22; *Samuel Keimer's "Elegy on the Death of Aquila Rose."*

6. *Autobiography*, 23, 31–33.

7. Tolles, *Logan and the Culture of Provincial America*, 113–14, 124–26; Nash, *Quakers and Politics*, 332–35; Haugaard, "William Keith," 1710–56. It is also possible that at the last minute Keith realized that he had no credit to give. Franklin's friend Thomas Denham said as much, though he cannot have known all the facts. It later emerged that to secure his governorship, Keith had gone deeply in debt to a number of London merchants, including the king's printer, the very sort of man he would have asked to give credit to Franklin in the book trade. For Keith's debts see *The Case of the Heir at Law and Executrix of the Late Proprietor of Pennsylvania* (Philadelphia, 1726), probably published by Andrew Hamilton.

8. Miller, *Franklin's Philadelphia Printing*, 1–2.

9. *Autobiography*, 49, 50. Keimer printed a pamphlet that is now lost but which was evidently some kind of reply to the "Busy-Body" papers called *A Touch of the Times* (cf. Charles Evans, *American Bibliography: A Chronological Dictionary of All Books, Pamphlets, and Periodical Publications Printed in the United States . . . to 1820*, 14 vols. [New York: Peter Smith, 1903–59], no. 3174). The pamphlet's imprint read, "New Printing Office," Franklin's address, and instructed the hawkers to get it there. Franklin issued a disclaimer in the *Philadelphia Mercury* on April 24, 1729.

10. *Autobiography*, 53, 54. It seems that Franklin misremembered the fact that Bradford printed the money that year, but Franklin got the job of printing the next issue in 1731 and was paid a hundred pounds for it. But his point remains valid, that the contract was a reward for his services. For an explanation of the political and economic context of the *Modest Enquiry*, see *PBF* 1: 139–141.

11. *Autobiography*, 50–51, 80.

12. Ibid., 79.

13. *Account Books Kept by Benjamin Franklin* shows that Franklin sent a thousand almanacs a year or more to Jonas Green in Annapolis, James Parker in New York, his sister in Newport, and Lewis Timothy's widow in Charleston; smaller quantities were sent to two booksellers and a binder in Boston.

14. *Autobiography*, 54. For a catalogue of Franklin's job printing see Miller, *Franklin's Philadelphia Printing*, Appendix A, 54.

15. Miller, *Franklin's Philadelphia Printing*; Wroth, *Colonial Printer*, 181. In the nine years from 1730 (the year Franklin took over the Pennsylvania government printing) to 1738, Bradford produced only 32 books and pamphlets, not counting his newspaper and an annual flurry of four to six almanacs. Franklin produced 118 imprints in the same years, not counting newspapers and almanacs.

16. *Autobiography*, 51, 55, 85.

17. Miller, *Franklin's Philadelphia Printing*, xxxvii.

18. *Autobiography*, 63.

19. The discussion that follows summarizes my article "Benjamin Franklin as Publisher and Bookseller," in *Reappraising Franklin*, 98–114. A full-sized book is one made up of more than ten full sheets of standard-sized paper. Depending on how the sheets were folded and gathered, a book of ten sheets would contain 40 pages in folio, 80 pages in quarto, 160 pages in octavo, or 240 pages in duodecimo. Since paper was the most expensive element in bookmaking, the amount used is an accurate gauge of the expense and risk involved in any given publication.

20. *Autobiography*, 18.

21. The evidence for a Philadelphia Testament is summarized in Miller, *Franklin's Philadelphia Printing*, 368. See also Thomas, *History of Printing*, 103–4, 120–21; and Lydenberg, "Problem of the Pre-1776 Bible."

22. The contract is reprinted in *PBF* 2: 341.

23. See Frasca, "Franklin's Printing Network" and "From Apprentice to Journeyman to Partner."

24. The contract between Franklin and Hall is printed in *PBF* 3: 263–67. Between 1748 and his death in 1772, Hall imported more than £30,000 worth of books and stationery from Strahan alone, plus some twenty thousand Bibles and three tons of other books from Strahan's Edinburgh associates Hamilton and Balfour. When Hall took over Franklin's stock of books and stationery in 1748, it was valued at only £681. Hall's gross income from printing during the years he ran Franklin's shop, including the *Pennsylvania Gazette*, ten thousand almanacs a year, and all the government printing, was only about £28,000 Pennsylvania currency, on which he received only half the profit. See the Franklin-Hall account, *PBF* 13: 97. For the books Hall published, see Green, "Franklin as Publisher and Bookseller," 106–7, 110.

25. *PBF* 1: 111.

Chapter 3. Benjamin Franklin, Civic Improver

I thank Richard Dunn and John C. Van Horne for their useful suggestions for this essay.

1. *Autobiography*, 20.

2. Latrobe, *Correspondence*, 3: 76. Although Franklin's precise actions and route are unknown, the details concerning his life, vignettes about the people, and descriptions of the city's streets and structures in this chapter are factual. To avoid burdensome prose in this essay, I have intentionally used assertive rather than conditional language to describe Franklin's activities.

3. On the economic structure of Philadelphia, see Smith, *"Lower Sort,"* chap. 3.

4. *Pennsylvania Gazette*, November 25, 1736. The Assembly declined to act on the 1723 petition since it would be "injurious to the rights and privileges of those who keep negroes." White workers lodged similar complaints several years later. See Scharf and Westcott, *History of Philadelphia*, 1: 163–65. Franklin as "Runaway": *Autobiography*, 21. On slaves attempting to gain their freedom through escape, see Smith and Wojtowicz, *Blacks Who Stole Themselves*. Emma Lapsansky-Werner's chapter in this volume explores Franklin's attitudes toward slavery.

5. *Autobiography*, 20. The initial locations of the Junto and the Library are indicated

in the *Pennsylvania Gazette,* April 26, 1733, and in the *Autobiography,* 63. Bryant's bakery is described in the *Pennsylvania Gazette,* June 28, 1733.

6. Scharf and Westcott, *History of Philadelphia,* 1: 163.

7. Watson, *Annals of Philadelphia in the Olden Time,* 1: 101–3; *Pennsylvania Gazette,* July 16 and November 5, 1730.

8. Scharf and Westcott, *History of Philadelphia,* 1: 163–64, 188.

9. The announcement of the meeting of the Philadelphia Contributionship, the first fire insurance company in America, is in the *Pennsylvania Gazette,* April 9, 1753. Sabbath regulations and information about street paving are reported in Scharf and Westcott, *History of Philadelphia,* 1: 163, 188–89. Robert Venable made the "Filthy-dirty" remark, as quoted in Watson, *Annals of Philadelphia,* 1: 101. The notice of the drowned man is in the *Pennsylvania Gazette,* November 5, 1730.

10. *Autobiography,* 53. On the American Philosophical Society see Jackson, *Encyclopedia of Philadelphia,* 1: 70. On the ravages of smallpox see Smith, "Death and Life in a Colonial Immigrant City." Many Britishers had speculated wildly in the South Sea Company, a business that monopolized trade in the South Seas. However, its directors employed shady means to inflate stock prices, and the speculative frenzy crashed in 1720, shaking the imperial economy and the British government. On Philadelphia's economic problems, see Scharf and Westcott, *History of Philadelphia,* 1: 163–64; and Nash, *Urban Crucible,* chap. 5.

11. Isaacson, *Franklin,* 55–57. The club's original name is identified in Jackson, *Encyclopedia of Philadelphia,* 2: 796. Shakespeare is (mis)quoted in Watson, *Annals of Philadelphia,* 1: 175. The Franklin quote is from a "Silence Dogood" letter in the *New-England Courant,* April 2, 1722.

12. Franklin describes in his autobiography how many of his early ambitions were thwarted (*Autobiography,* 5–10, quote on 7). Significantly, Franklin borrowed funds from two members of the Junto to buy out his partner and become the sole proprietor of the newspaper and printing press. See also Wright, *Franklin of Philadelphia,* 36–37.

13. *Autobiography,* 7. See also Hawke, *Franklin,* 30–31.

14. Franklin, "Observation on my Reading of History at Library," May 9, 1731, *PBF* 1: 192–93; Isaacson, *Franklin,* 59; Hawke, *Franklin,* 30–31. Two excellent analyses of Franklin's philanthropic philosophy, on which this essay draws heavily, are John C. Van Horne, "Collective Benevolence and the Common Good in Franklin's Philanthropy," and Michael Zuckerman, "Doing Good While Doing Well: Benevolence and Self-Interest in Franklin's *Autobiography,*" both in *Reappraising Franklin,* 425–40 and 441–51, respectively.

15. *Autobiography,* 57, 63.

16. *Pennsylvania Gazette,* April 26, 1733. The library was most likely located in Pewter Platter Alley (subsequently Church Street); Jackson, *Encyclopedia of Philadelphia,* 2: 840; "Athens of America": *Pennsylvania Gazette,* May 31, 1733; "godly approval": Isaacson, *Franklin,* 103; Wright, *Franklin,* 38–39; and Hawke, *Franklin,* 51–52.

17. *Autobiography,* 57, 63. Wright, *Franklin,* 38–39; and Hawke, *Franklin,* 51–52.

18. *Autobiography,* 81; Hawke, *Franklin,* 52.

19. *Pennsylvania Gazette,* April 30, 1730, and December 20, 1733.

20. *Pennsylvania Gazette,* April 30, 1730, December 20, 1733, and February 4, 1735.

21. Franklin, "On Protection of Towns from Fire," *Pennsylvania Gazette*, February 4, 1735, *PBF* 2: 14; *Autobiography*, 87; *Pennsylvania Gazette*, February 4, 1735; and Hawke, *Franklin*, 52–53.

22. *Pennsylvania Gazette*, December 30, 1736. See also *Pennsylvania Gazette*, May 28, 1730.

23. Smith, "Death and Life," 876; Lopez and Herbert, *Private Franklin*, 37.

24. *A Proposal for Promoting Useful Knowledge among the British Plantations in America*, *PBF* 2: 380–83.

25. Franklin to Cadwallader Colden, August 15, 1745, *PBF* 3: 36. See also Brands, *First American*, 168–71.

26. *Autobiography*, 34; Franklin, *Modest Enquiry into the Nature and Necessity of a Paper-Currency*, *PBF* 1: 139–57; Franklin to William Strahan, June 2, 1750, *PBF* 3: 479. On Franklin's formation of the militia and advocacy of the election of officers, see Lopez and Herbert, *Private Franklin*, 52; and Isaacson, *Franklin*, 123–26. Franklin was clearly acutely aware of the amounts of money he spent: three pennies for bread on his first day in Philadelphia (*Autobiography*, 20), eighteen pence for food for a week in the city (29), three shillings and sixpence for weekly lodging in London (33), fifty pounds (Pennsylvania currency) as the annual income he earned as a merchant's clerk (40), and twenty-four pounds as the annual rent he paid for his first print shop.

27. Benjamin Franklin to Abiah Franklin, April 12, 1750, *PBF* 3: 475; Franklin to William Strahan, June 2, 1750, *PBF* 3: 479; and *Poor Richard's Almanack*, 1737, *PBF* 2: 165; art historian Wayne Craven quoted in Isaacson, *Franklin*, 128. See also Morgan, *Benjamin Franklin*, 25, 29, 44.

28. *Proposals Relating to the Education of Youth in Pensilvania*, *PBF* 3: 397a.

29. Isaacson, *Franklin*, 146–47; Brands, *First American*, 662.

30. *PBF* 5: 285; *Autobiography*, 104. See also Wright, *Franklin*, 91.

31. *Autobiography*, 103–4.

32. Smith, *"Lower Sort,"* 37–39.

33. A map of the city is available in *Philadelphia 1787* (Philadelphia: Friends of Independence National Historical Park, 1986).

 Chapter 4. Benjamin Franklin at Home

1. Even though Franklin's correspondence is filled with references to his home in Franklin Court (razed in 1812), the historical architects of the National Park Service were unwilling to reconstruct the building in the 1970s because of insufficient physical evidence concerning details of its construction and finished appearance. In 1969, when the staff at Independence National Historical Park, where Franklin Court is located, were considering reconstructing the house, they assigned Charles Dorman, as curator, to do a study of the furnishings. The result, "The Furnishings of Franklin Court, 1765–1790: A Preliminary Study," like all Dorman's scholarship, is thorough and insightful, and many of the furnishings described in this essay were included in his report. Franklin left London for a brief period between 1762 and 1764, when he returned to Pennsylvania to carry out political duties.

2. Carlton, "Notes from the Franklin Institute Museum," 315. An advertisement

in the *Pennsylvania Packet* announced the auction of "Mr. B. Franklin's house-hold & kitchen furnishings, at his lodgings," on October 21, 1790. Two years later Dunlap's *American Daily Advertiser* of May 21, 1792, listed the sale of "Furniture . . . at the House of the late Doctor Franklin, in Franklin-Court, Market Street." A letter from Franklin's grandson Benjamin Franklin Bache to his father on January 10, 1793, lists £438 income from the sale of furniture (Castle-Bache Collection, Reel 2, APS). Other sales were held on April 24, 1799, and June 22, 1809.

3. Benjamin Franklin to Deborah Franklin, August 1765, *PBF* 12: 251.

4. The first of these was *Mon Cher Papa*, followed by *The Private Franklin* (with Eugenia W. Herbert), and *My Life with Benjamin Franklin*.

5. *Autobiography,* 20, 34, 41.

6. Some scholars have suggested that William Franklin may have been Deborah's child, born out of wedlock, but more recent writers doubt this assumption.

7. Sellers, *Benjamin Franklin in Portraiture*, 11. Sellers argues that the portrait of Franky is, in fact, "the first portrait of Benjamin Franklin," as he probably sat for the picture. With the son who bore a strong resemblance to him dead, Franklin may have posed for the unknown artist so that he might have a starting point for the picture.

8. Benjamin Franklin to Deborah Franklin, June 10, 1758, *PBF* 8: 91. Franklin sent Sally a second pair of buckles in August 1768, as mentioned in his letter to her husband, Richard Bache, dated August 13, 1768 (*PBF* 15: 186).

9. Sally and Richard Bache had eight children: Benjamin Franklin (1769–98); William (1773–1814); Sarah (1775–76); Elizabeth (1777–1820), who married John Edmund Harwood; Louis (1779–1819); Deborah (1780–1865), who married William John Duane; Richard (1784–1848); and Sarah (1788–1863), who married Thomas Sargeant. For more on the Hoppner portraits, see Baetjer and Dobkin, "Benjamin Franklin's Daughter."

10. *Autobiography,* 64–65.

11. Ibid., 71, 65.

12. See James Fairbairn et al., *Fairbairn's Book of Crests of the Families of Great Britain and Ireland,* 2 vols. (Edinburgh: T. C. and E. C. Jack, 1892), 2: pl. 139, fig. 97.

13. Josiah Franklin to Benjamin Franklin, May 26, 1739, *PBF* 2: 229.

14. Franklin to Sally Bache, January 26, 1784, quoted in Isaacson, *Franklin,* 422.

15. Most of the items included in this essay have strong family provenance or a history of Franklin ownership since early in the nineteenth century; their provenance is therefore accepted as reliable.

16. Solomon Fussell, Ledger, 1738–51, Stephen Collins Papers, Manuscript Division, Library of Congress.

17. One of these timepieces belonged in Franklin's library and one was listed as "on the stairs" in his inventory. Other executors of Franklin's will were Henry Hill, John Jay, and Francis Hopkinson.

18. *Autobiography,* 144–45; Benjamin Franklin to Deborah Franklin, April 5, 1757, *PBF* 7: 175. David Hall carried on for Franklin as his partner in his Philadelphia printing concerns, but Deborah managed their personal finances to a large extent.

19. Benjamin Franklin to Deborah Franklin, February 19, 1757, *PBF* 7:367. With Franklin were his son William and his two slaves, Peter and King.

20. Benjamin Franklin to Deborah Franklin, February 19, 1757, *PBF* 7: 383.

21. Ibid. A "Dish, Porcelain. English (Bow), about 1755," was part of the Metropolitan Museum of Art exhibition *Benjamin Franklin and His Circle* (1936). See the exhibition catalogue: Metropolitan Museum of Art, *Benjamin Franklin and His Circle,* 140.

22. Cyril Williams-Wood, *English Transfer-Printed Pottery and Porcelain* (London: Faber and Faber, 1981), 76–91. Previously these coffee cups were thought to have been of German manufacture, a gift from Franklin's friend Madame Helvétius. But recent scholars have identified the mark as the "pseudo-Meissen variant type" used by Worcester around 1770–75.

23. Benjamin Franklin to Deborah Franklin, February 19, 1757, *PBF* 7: 383.

24. Benjamin Franklin to Deborah Franklin, November 22, 1757, *PBF* 7: 272. Franklin later wrote to Deborah, "Yours is at the Painters, who is to copy it, and do me of the same Size" (Benjamin Franklin to Deborah Franklin, June 10, 1758, *PBF* 8: 90). During the British occupation of Philadelphia, Richard and Sally Bache moved out of the city, taking with them "all the valuable things, mohoginy excepted" (Sarah Franklin to Benjamin Franklin, February 23, 1777, *PBF* 23: 361).

25. Benjamin Franklin to Deborah Franklin, February 19, 1757, *PBF* 7: 383. Perhaps he delayed this purchase, as he paid £19.9.0 to "Jeffery's for knives and spoons." This probably refers to Thomas Jeffrys, in Cockspur Street near Charing Cross. Benjamin Franklin to William Franklin, October 5, 1768, *PBF* 15: 224–25. Franklin also speaks of this illustrious guest in his *Autobiography,* 64.

26. Lopez and Herbert, *Private Franklin,* 114.

27. Benjamin Franklin to Deborah Franklin, February 14, 1765, *PBF* 12: 62.

28. Benjamin Franklin to Deborah Franklin, August 1765, *PBF* 12: 250; Benjamin Franklin to Deborah Franklin, July 13, 1765, *PBF* 12: 62. For information about the building fabric and room descriptions of Franklin's house, see Contributionship for the Insurance of Houses from Loss by Fire, Survey no. 1148, in William E. Lingelbach, "Old Philadelphia: Redevelopment and Conservation," APS *Proceedings* 93 (1949), 193. For a history of Franklin Court see Riley, "Franklin's Home." No printed views or other depictions of Franklin's home exist.

29. Benjamin Franklin to Deborah Franklin, [August 1765], *PBF* 12: 251; Deborah Franklin to Benjamin Franklin, [October 6–13? 1765], *PBF* 12: 294, 298.

30. Deborah Franklin to Benjamin Franklin, [October 6–13? 1765], *PBF* 12: 292–96.

31. Benjamin Franklin to Deborah Franklin, June 22, 1767, *PBF* 14: 194–95. The papier maché ornaments, when gilded, were meant to look like wood carvings.

32. Benjamin Franklin to Deborah Franklin, August 25, 1766, *PBF* 13: 388. Deborah Franklin to Benjamin Franklin, [October 6–13? 1765], *PBF* 12: 292. Benjamin Franklin to Deborah Franklin, April 6, 1766, *PBF* 13: 233.

33. Franklin Papers, vol. 66, fol. 145 a, MS, APS; Deborah Franklin to Benjamin Franklin, [October 6–13? 1765], *PBF* 12: 294. Later Franklin urged Deborah to move all the papers out of the great chest to the garret. Benjamin Franklin to Deborah Franklin, August 25, 1766, *PBF* 13: 388.

34. Benjamin Franklin to Deborah Franklin, April 6, 1766, *PBF* 13: 233. Sarah Bache to Benjamin Franklin, October 30, 1773, *PBF* 20: 453. Benjamin Franklin to Deborah Franklin, March 21, 1769, *PBF* 16: 68.

35. "In Favr of Mayhew for a Writing Table £10.0," June 1772. Franklin's Journal in London (1764–76), MS, APS. For more on the copy press, see *PBF* 33: 115–18.

36. Benjamin Franklin to Deborah Franklin, July 4, 1771, *PBF* 18: 162. The mate to this tea caddy was sold at the Stan V. Henckels auction of the effects of Mrs. Elizabeth Duane Davis, June 6, 1924.

37. *Journals of the Continental Congress,* 247 (September 13, 1775); Benjamin Franklin to Richard Bache, October 19[–24], 1775, *PBF* 22: 241.

38. Franklin to Margaret Stevenson, January 25, 1779, *PBF* 28: 422. For more on Franklin's residence in Passy see Meredith Martindale, "Benjamin Franklin's Residence in France: The Hôtel de Valentinois in Passy,"*Antiques* 112, no. 2 (August 1977), 262–73.

39. Charles G. Dorman, Curator, Independent National Historic Park, to Mrs. Claude Lopez, April 9, 1974, INHP Archives. See, for example, the entry "The Tapissier for 3 mos. Hire of Furniture as per Acc't.," May 2, 1779, in Account of Monies Received from Benjamin Franklin Esquire (For the purpose of paying the Family Expenses), (1779–82), MS, APS.

40. Sellers, *Franklin in Portraiture,* 214. Letter from Madame Herbaut de Marcenay to Franklin, August 22, 1778, *PBF* 27: 288. Carmontelle's painting was engraved by François-Denis Née in 1781 and was widely circulated with an inscription by Nogaret, "On l'a vu disarmer les Tirans et les Dieux" (He has been seen disarming the Tyrants and the Gods). Franklin's informal attire apparently delighted his French admirers.

41. This set of chairs was formerly thought to have been made in France, but wood analysis, X-rays, and expert opinion all suggest an English origin. Made "in the French taste," the chairs would have been equally acceptable in England and in France.

42. According to ceramics historian Susan Detweiler, so plentiful were these products, in fact, that the pattern is sometimes called the "Angoulême sprig," even though other Parisian factories used the design as well ("French Porcelain on Federal Tables," *American Ceramics Circle Bulletin* 3 [1982], 96–98); Clark et Cie, Bill for Tableware, June 3, 1780, *PBF* 32: 468. See Lopez, *My Life with Franklin,* 140–47.

43. Detweiler, "French Porcelain," 91.

44. "A Letter from Dr. Benjamin Franklin to Mr. Alphonsus Le Roy . . . containing sundry Maritime Observations," August 1785, in APS, *Transactions,* vol. 2 (1786), 322.

45. Franklin to Jane Mecom, September 21, 1786, *Letters of Franklin and Mecom,* 282–83.

46. A short article by Waldo Hopkins describing the chair and its history appeared in *American Collector* (March 1941), 5.

47. *Writings,* 1116.

48. William Parker Cutler and Julia Perkins Cutler, *Life, Journals and Correspondence of Rev. Manasseh Cutler, LL.D., by His Grandchildren* (Cincinnati: R. Clarke, 1888), 1: 267–70.

49. Inventory of the Estate of Dr. Benjamin Franklin, 1790/189, Register of Wills Archive, Philadelphia, Pennsylvania.

50. *Diaries of George Washington,* 5: 183, quoted in Merritt Ierley, *The Comforts of Home: The American House and the Evolution of Modern Convenience* (New York: Three Rivers Press, 1999), 151; Col. Robert Carr, "Personal Recollections of Benjamin Franklin," *History Magazine,* 2d ser., 4 (1868): 59–60.

51. Postscript of a letter from Franklin to Jane Mecom, May 30, 1787, in Sotheby Parke Bernet, *Fine Printed and Manuscript Americana and European Historical Manuscripts* (May 23, 1984), Sale 5187, Lot 130.

52. Lopez, *Benjamin Franklin's Good House,* 49.

53. Postscript of a letter from Franklin to Jane Mecom, May 30, 1787.

 Chapter 5. Benjamin Franklin's Science

1. *Poor Richard's Almanack,* 1747, *PBF* 3: 104; *Poor Richard's Almanack,* 1742, *PBF* 2: 339–40; Franklin to Jacques Barbeu-Dubourg, March, 1773, *PBF* 20: 131–33 (translation in Smyth 5: 542–45); *Autobiography,* 38–39; Franklin to Oliver Neave, [before 1769], *PBF* 15: 295–98.

2. *The Art of Procuring Pleasant Dreams,* [1786], in Goodman, *Ingenious Dr. Franklin,* 35–40; Benjamin Franklin to John Franklin, December 8, 1752, *PBF* 4: 385–87; Franklin to Benjamin Vaughan, July 31, 1786, in Goodman, *Ingenious Dr. Franklin,* 29–32.

3. Franklin to George Whatley, May 23, 1875, in *Writings,* 1109–10.

4. *Poor Richard Improved,* 1751, *PBF* 4: 91.

5. Edmund Berkeley and Dorothy Smith Berkeley, *The Life and Travels of John Bartram* (Tallahassee: University Presses of Florida, 1982), 245–46. The name of the tree was misspelled on Bartram's print. "Alatamaha" should read Altamaha, after the river in coastal Georgia where the tree was first found.

6. Benjamin Franklin to Peter Franklin, May 7, 1760, *PBF* 9: 106–7; Franklin to George Croghan, August 5, 1767, *PBF* 14: 221–22.

7. *Physical and Meteorological Observations, Conjectures, and Suppositions,* 1751, *PBF* 4: 235–43. Certain aspects of Franklin's model parallel what George Hadley described in the *Philosophical Transactions of the Royal Society of London* 39 (1735–36): 58–62. For developments after Franklin, see James Rodger Fleming, *Meteorology in America, 1800–1870* (Baltimore: Johns Hopkins University Press, 1990), 136–40.

8. Franklin to Alexander Small, May 12, 1760, *PBF* 9: 110–12; see also Gisela Kutzbach, *The Thermal Theory of Cyclones* (Boston: American Meteorological Society, 1979), 63–117.

9. Franklin to John Perkins, February 4, 1753, *PBF* 4: 429–42. Franklin's description anticipated a convective theory of storms by Herman von Helmholtz in 1876, including the "bath tub" analogy; see Kutzbach, *Thermal Theory,* 96–99.

10. Franklin to Anthony Todd, October 29, 1768, *PBF* 15: 246–48; Smyth 9: 405–13.

11. Franklin to John Pringle, December 1, 1762, *PBF* 10: 158–60; Franklin to William Brownrigg, November 7, 1773, *PBF* 20: 463–74; Tanford, *Franklin Stilled the Waves,* 227.

12. Franklin to Sir John Pringle, May 10, 1768, *PBF* 15: 115–18.

13. Benjamin Franklin, "Meteorological Imaginations and Conjectures," May 1784, in Smyth 9: 215–18; Haraldur Sigurdsson, "Volcanic Pollution and Climate: The 1783 Laki Eruption," *Eos. Transactions—American Geophysical Union* 63 (1982): 601–2.

14. Cohen, *Franklin's Science,* 185–93; Hindle, *Pursuit of Science in Revolutionary America,* 146–65.

15. *A Modest Enquiry into the Nature and Necessity of a Paper-Currency,* 1729, *PBF* 1: 139–57; *Autobiography,* 40.

16. *An Account of the New Invented Pennsylvanian Fire-Places . . . ,* 1744, *PBF* 2: 419–46; Samuel Y. Edgerton, Jr., "Supplement: The Franklin Stove," in Cohen, *Franklin's Science,* 199–211; Cohen, *Franklin's Science,* 159–171; Franklin to Jan Ingenhousz, August 18, 1785, in APS, *Transactions,* vol. 2 (1786), 4–5.

17. James Ferguson, *Select Mechanical Exercises: Showing How to Construct Different Clocks, Orreries, and Sun-Dials, on Plain and Easy Principles* (London, 1778), *PBF* 8: 216–20.

18. Franklin to Peter Collinson, 1752? *PBF* 4: 392–96; for further comments on the properties of Franklin's magic squares and circles, see Franklin to Collinson, 1752? *PBF* 4: 399–403, and Franklin to John Canton, May 29, 1765, *PBF* 12: 146–349.

19. Cohen, *Franklin and Newton* and *Franklin's Experiments;* Heilbron, *Electricity in the Seventeenth and Eighteenth Centuries,* 309–402; Heilbron, *Elements of Early Modern Physics;* 159–240; Cohen, *Franklin's Science,* 66–109.

20. Lemay, *Ebenezer Kinnersley,* 54–59.

21. Franklin to Peter Collinson, May 25, 1747, *PBF* 3: 126–35.

22. Franklin to Peter Collinson, July 28, 1747, *PBF* 3: 156–64.

23. Franklin to Peter Collinson, April 29, 1749, *PBF* 3: 352–65.

24. Franklin to John Mitchell, April 29, 1749, *PBF* 3: 365–76.

25. Franklin to Peter Collinson, July 29, 1750, *PBF* 4: 19.

26. Ibid., 19–20.

27. Lemay, *Ebenezer Kinnersley,* 62–81.

28. Thomas-François Dalibard, *Mémoire,* May 13, 1752, *PBF* 4: 303.

29. Priestley, *History and Present State of Electricity,* 179–80.

30. Cohen, *Franklin's Experiments,* 21–56; Cohen, *Franklin and Newton,* 481–514; Heilbron, *Electricity in the Seventeenth and Eighteenth Centuries,* 324–43; Cohen, *Franklin's Science,* 66–109.

31. Franklin to Peter Collinson, September 1753, *PBF* 5: 71.

32. *Poor Richard Improved,* 1753, *PBF* 4: 408–9. See also headnote to "The Kite Experiment," [1752], *PBF* 4: 360–66.

33. Lemay, *Ebenezer Kinnersley,* 78; Franklin to Cadwallader Colden, April 12, 1753, *PBF* 4: 463; Cohen, *Franklin's Science,* 118–58.

34. Ebenezer Kinnersley to Franklin, March 12, 1761, *PBF* 9: 282–93.

35. Franklin to Ebenezer Kinnersley, with Associated Papers, February 20, 1762, *PBF* 10: 37–59.

36. Ibid., 50–51.

37. Ibid., 55–59.

38. Franklin to Marsilio Landriani, October 14, 1787, in Smyth 9: 618.

39. Principles of lightning protection are described by E. Philip Krider and Martin A. Uman, "Cloud to Ground Lightning, Lightning Protection, and Lightning Test Standards," in *Wiley Encyclopedia of Electrical and Electronics Engineering,* 24 vols. (New York: John Wiley and Sons, 1999), 11: 350–57. Franklin's improvements in the construction of protective rods are described in Franklin to Ebenezer Kinnersley, with Associated Papers, February 20, 1762, *PBF* 10: 50–51. Current methods used worldwide are described in R. H. Golde, *Lightning Protection* (New York: Chemical, 1975); *Lightning Protection Code,* National Fire Protection Association 780 (Quincy, Mass.: National Fire Protection Association, 1997); *Installations de paratonnerres,* NF C 17–100 (Paris: Norme Française, 1987); *Code of Practice for Protection of Structures Against Lightning,* British Standard 6651 (London: British Standards Association, 1999); and National Standard of the People's Republic of China, *Design Code for Lightning Protection of Structures,* GB 50057–94 (Beijing: Ministry of Machinery Industries, Institute of Project Planning and Research, 1994).

40. *Works of John Adams,* 1: 660–62.

41. Cohen, *Franklin's Science,* 1–13. See also Cohen, *Benjamin Franklin: Scientist and Statesman;* Hale and Hale, *Franklin in France,* 1: 69–83; Aldridge, *Franklin and His French Contemporaries,* 21–38, 59–73; Lopez, *Mon Cher Papa,* 179–87.

Chapter 6. Benjamin Franklin, Pragmatic Visionary

1. *Autobiography,* 13–14.
2. *Plain Truth, PBF* 3: 180–204.
3. For quotations see Middlekauff, *Benjamin Franklin,* 38–39, and the sources cited there.
4. Franklin to John Fothergill, March 14, 1764, *PBF* 11: 103–4.
5. Franklin to Mary Stevenson, March 25, 1763, *PBF* 10: 232.
6. Franklin to Samuel Cooper, February 5, 1771, *PBF* 18: 24.
7. Examination before the Committee of the Whole of the House of Commons, February 13, 1766, *PBF* 13: 159.
8. The Final Hearing before the Privy Council . . . For the Removal of Hutchinson and Oliver, January 29, 1774, *PBF* 21: 48–49.
9. Franklin to Thomas Cushing, February 15[–19?], 1774, *PBF* 21: 93–94.
10. *Diary of John Adams,* 2: 369.
11. The Continental Congress: Instructions to Benjamin Franklin, Silas Deane, and Arthur Lee, *PBF* 22: 628.
12. Franklin to Arthur Lee, March 21, 1777, *PBF* 23: 511.
13. Bemis, *Diplomacy of the American Revolution,* 114n4.
14. Benjamin Franklin, Notes for a Conversation with Oswald, *PBF* 37: 171.
15. Franklin to Richard Oswald, July 12, 1782, *PBF* 37: 623.
16. Journal of the Peace Negotiations, *PBF* 37: 341–42.

Chapter 7. The Printer at Passy

1. *PBF* volumes 23 through 38 bring Franklin's life up to January 20, 1783, the date of the signing of the preliminary peace agreement with Britain. Adams's quip is in *Diary of John Adams,* 4: 118.

2. *Diary of John Adams,* 4: 118.

3. McMurtrie, *History of Printing,* 2: 53; Wroth, "Benjamin Franklin: The Printer at Work," 125; McMurtrie, *Benjamin Franklin, Typefounder,* 6. In *A History of Printing,* McMurtrie goes on to say that Franklin produced "leaflets and broadsides, chiefly intended to divert himself and his friends." In this he echoed John Clyde Oswald's, *Benjamin Franklin, Printer,* 162, and *History of Printing: Its Development through Five Hundred Years.* By contrast, the biographer Carl Van Doren summarized the function of the press briefly and for the most part accurately in *Benjamin Franklin,* 661.

4. Livingston, *Franklin and His Press at Passy,* 8.

5. William Temple Franklin, *Memoirs of the Life and Writings of Franklin,* 1: 337.

6. This essay summarizes part of a book-length study of the Passy press currently in preparation. Some of the information, as noted below, has appeared in the annotation of *The Papers of Benjamin Franklin.*

7. Jean-Baptiste Le Roy to Franklin, June 23, [1777], *PBF* 24: 214–15; Lefebvre de Longeville to Franklin, May 7, 1778, *PBF* 26: 171, and 29: 114–16.

8. Franklin to Elizabeth Partridge, October 11, 1779, *PBF* 30: 514; Jonathan Trumbull to Franklin, May 30, 1778, *PBF* 26: 547.

9. Simon-Pierre Fournier le jeune to Franklin, February 10, 1779, *PBF* 28: 505.

10. Letter of Credence for Franklin as Minister Plenipotentiary to France, [October 21, 1778], *PBF* 27: 596–97; Franklin's Diary of Correspondence, [February 12–March 2, 1779], *PBF* 28: 509; headnote to "Petition of the Letter Z," [after February 12, 1779?], *PBF* 28: 517.

11. "Hemery fondeur en Caractere rue st jaque ché monsieur Canon Cordonié vis à vis monsieur dépré," *PBF* 28: 586n.

12. Ibid.; *PBF* 33: xxviii; Augustin-Martin Lottin, *Catalogue chronologique des libraires et des libraires-imprimeurs de Paris . . .* (Paris, 1789), 241; Marius Audin, *Les livrets typographiques des fonderies françaises créées avant 1800* (Paris, 1933; reprint, Amsterdam: Gérard Th. van Heusden, 1964), 102.

13. Cash Book, June 13, 1778, to October 19, 1780, Franklin Collection, APS; Hémery's Account of the Fonts Cast at Passy, [July 22, 1780], *PBF* 33: 102–5; Account of the Contents of the 34 Boxes of Printing Letters, &c Cast at Passy, January 27, 1781[–June 21, 1785], *PBF* 34: 321–25.

14. The complicated story of the *Lafayette* and its cargo is summarized in Lopez, *My Life with Franklin,* 129–39.

15. Livingston, *Franklin and His Press at Passy,* 105.

16. James Mosley identified this type for me and supplied me with references to the romain du roi. Mosley retired as Librarian of the St. Bride Printing Library in London and is currently visiting professor in the department of typography and graphic communication at the University of Reading. See his essay, "Les

caractères de l'Imprimerie royal" in *Le romain du roi, la typographie au service de l'Etat* (Lyon: Musée de l'Imprimerie, 2002), 33–80.

17. Franklin to Fournier le jeune, May 4, 1780, *PBF* 32: 350; see also the headnote and annotation to Fournier le jeune to Franklin, September 16, 1779, *PBF* 30: 346–48. The title "Le Franklin" appears on Fournier's preliminary proof sheet, reproduced for the first time in *PBF* 32, facing p. 363. A subsequent proof sheet printed by Philippe-Denis Pierres is illustrated in Livingston, *Franklin and His Press at Passy,* facing p. 197. Another is illustrated in *PBF* 30, facing p. 347.

18. Jean-François Fournier fils to Franklin, October 24, 1778, *PBF* 27: 618.

19. This description is a condensed version of the headnote in *PBF* 29: 726–27.

20. John Torpey, *The Invention of the Passport: Surveillance, Citizenship and the State* (Cambridge: Cambridge University Press, 2000), 21.

21. List of Persons to Whom Passes Have Been Given, [January 5–October 3, 1782], *PBF* 36: 378–80.

22. Franklin paid 36 livres for the woodblock on December 3, 1780: William Temple Franklin's Accounts, March 15, 1779, to February 12, 1782, Franklin Collection, APS.

23. The story of Franklin's order is told in a headnote in *PBF* 30: 609–12. Franklin directed his banker to pay the stationer, James Woodmason, in May 1780, though the paper would not arrive for another several months: Franklin to Ferdinand Grand, May 30, 1780, *PBF* 32: 441–42; French Loan Certificate, *PBF* 30: 345–46.

24. Many of these forms are illustrated in Livingston, *Franklin and His Press at Passy.*

25. Franklin and Lafayette had once drawn up a "List of British Cruelties" to serve as subject matter for a set of thirty-five prints illustrating British atrocities that Congress wanted engraved for a children's schoolbook: *PBF* 29: 590–93. For Franklin's discussions with Oswald see Franklin's Notes for a Conversation with Oswald, on or before April 19, 1782, *PBF* 37: 169–72; Franklin's Journal of the Peace Negotiations, May 9–July 1, 1782, *PBF* 37: 295–97.

26. "Supplement to the Boston Independent Chronicle," *PBF* 37: 184–96.

27. See the headnote of "Supplement to the Boston Independent Chronicle," ibid., 184–86.

28. Pierre-André Gargaz, *Conciliateur de toutes les nations d'Europe, ou Projet de paix perpétuelle entre tous les souverains de l'Europe & leurs voisins* (Passy: Benjamin Franklin, 1782). This work is discussed and translated in George Simpson Eddy, *A Project of Universal and Perpetual Peace . . .* (New York: G. S. Eddy, 1922). See also *PBF* 37: 611–14. Jacques Barbeu-Dubourg, *Petit code de la raison humaine . . .* (Passy, 1782; reprint, Paris, 1789), vi.

29. All the songs Franklin wrote, as well as a drinking song in his honor written by Morellet, are reprinted with music in Ellen R. Cohn, "Benjamin Franklin and Traditional Music," in *Reappraising Franklin*, 290–318. On Franklin's chess habits, see the headnote to "The Morals of Chess," *PBF* 29: 750–53. The best and most comprehensive portrayal of Franklin's social life in France is Lopez, *Mon Cher Papa.*

30. One copy of the collected bagatelles is at the Yale University Library, the other

is at the Bibliothèque nationale. The quote from "Information to Those Who Would Remove to America" can be found in *Writings*, 977.

31. Franklin to Elizabeth Partridge, October 11, 1779, *PBF* 30: 514.

 Chapter 8. At the End, an Abolitionist?

1. See *Reappraising Franklin*. "Reappraising Franklin" has long been a national—indeed international—pastime, as evidenced by the array of contributors and the dense bibliography of this volume.

2. Wood, *Americanization of Franklin*, ix. On lost papers see *PBF* 1: xxi–xxiii. Eight recent biographies form the backbone of my argument here. All reflect the premise set forth by Arthur S. Pitt in 1943 that ardent abolitionism was Franklin's final posture, yet our evidence for understanding this position is sketchy at best. See Pitt's "Franklin and the Quaker Movement Against Slavery."

3. *Autobiography,* 12.

4. Waldstreicher, *Runaway America*, 33, 35; Srodes, *Franklin, the Essential Founding Father*, 14–15.

5. Waldstreicher, *Runaway America*, 24–25.

6. On Franklin as runaway, see ibid., 4; as slaveowner, see John C. Van Horne, "Collective Benevolence and the Common Good in Franklin's Philanthropy," in *Reappraising Franklin,* 433; Waldstreicher, *Runaway America,* xii, 25–26; Morgan, *Benjamin Franklin,* 105–6; Srodes, *Franklin, the Essential Founding Father,* 120. Benjamin Franklin to Deborah Franklin, June 27, 1760, *PBF* 9: 174.

7. Morgan, *Benjamin Franklin,* 105–6; *PBF* 9: 174.

8. *Observations Concerning the Increase of Mankind, PBF* 4: 231, quoted in Campbell, *Recovering Franklin,* 246, to support his argument that though Franklin had not yet come to sympathize with slaves, his humanitarian principles would inevitably bring him to do so.

9. *Observations Concerning the Increase of Mankind, PBF* 4: 234. Winthrop Jordan in *White over Black: American Attitudes Toward the Negro, 1550–1812* (Chapel Hill: University of North Carolina Press, 1968) was the first to discuss Linnaeus's writings on race; since then many scholars have followed in Jordan's footsteps.

10. *Observations Concerning the Increase of Mankind, PBF* 4: 234; Cadwallader Colden to Franklin, February 13, 1754, *PBF* 5: 197.

11. Mather, quoted in Waldstreicher, *Runaway America,* 35–36; Tryon, quoted in ibid., 66–67.

12. Soderlund, *Quakers and Slavery,* 15–16.

13. "A Conversation on Slavery," *The Public Advertiser* (January 30, 1770), *PBF* 17: 41; *Observations Concerning the Increase of Mankind, PBF* 4: 227.

14. *The Interest of Great Britain Considered,* 1760, *PBF* 9: 62; Franklin to James Read, November 2, 1755, *PBF* 6: 235; *Observations Concerning the Increase of Mankind, PBF,* 4: 234; *A Plan for Settling Two Western Colonies,* [1754], *PBF* 5: 458.

15. Waldstreicher, *Runaway America,* 193. A full treatment of Woolman's life and writings can be found in *The Journal and Major Essays of John Woolman,* ed.

Phillips P. Moulton (Richmond, Ind.: Friends United Press, 1989). On the Associates of Doctor Bray, see Van Horne, "Collective Benevolence," 433–35.

16. Franklin to John Waring, December 17, 1763, *PBF* 10: 396; Franklin to John Waring, January 3, 1758, *PBF* 7: 356; Waldstreicher, *Runaway America,* 194–95; Franklin to John Waring, February 17, 1758, *PBF* 7: 378.

17. Franklin to John Lining, June 17, 1758, *PBF* 8: 111; "Minute of the Associates of the Late Dr. Bray," January 17, 1760, *PBF* 9: 20.

18. Franklin to John Waring, December 17, 1763, *PBF* 10: 396; *A Narrative of the late Massacres,* 1764, *PBF* 11: 66; Franklin to Richard Jackson, February 11, 1764, *PBF* 11: 76.

19. Morgan, *Benjamin Franklin,* 156; *London Chronicle,* June 18–20, 1772, *PBF* 19: 188.

20. Campbell, *Recovering Franklin,* 245; Brands, *First American,* 701–2.

21. Waldstreicher, *Runaway America,* 202–3.

22. Franklin to Deborah Franklin, [March 28? 1760], *PBF* 9: 38; Marginalia, in *The True Constitutional Means . . .* (1769), *PBF* 16: 289; "Franklin and Lafayette's List of Prints to Illustrate British Cruelties" [ca. May 1779], *PBF* 29: 591; Franklin to Benjamin Vaughan, July 10, 1782, *PBF* 37: 459.

23. See Jordan, *White over Black.*

24. See, for example, Franklin to Anthony Benezet, August 22, 1772, *PBF* 19: 269. Poem quoted in Sidney Kaplan, *The Black Presence in the Era of the American Revolution* (Amherst: University of Massachusetts Press, 1989), 179. For a good short biography of Wheatley, see Henry Louis Gates, *The Trials of Phillis Wheatley: America's First Black Poet and Her Encounters with the Founding Fathers* (New York: Basic, 2003). On Franklin's sheltering of Montague, see *PBF* 35: 454.

25. On the size of the black community see Smith, *"Lower Sort,"* 156–58. Many of the events of Allen's life are chronicled in Nash, *Forging Freedom,* Emma Jones Lapsansky, *Neighborhoods in Transition: William Penn's Dream and Urban Reality, 1780–1854* (Westport, Conn.: Garland, 1994), and Carol V. George, *Segregated Sabbaths: Richard Allen and the Emergence of Independent Black Churches, 1760–1840* (New York: Oxford University Press, 1973).

26. See Srodes, *Franklin, the Essential Founding Father,* 280; Pitt, "Franklin and the Quaker Movement Against Slavery," 25–26; Thomas E. Drake, *Quakers and Slavery in America* (New Haven: Yale University Press, 1950), 79.

27. Bacon, *History of the Pennsylvania Society for Promoting the Abolition of Slavery,* 3; Jenny Uglow, *The Lunar Men: The Friends Who Made the Future, 1730–1810* (London: Faber, 2002), 411–12.

28. "An Address to the Public from the Pennsylvania Society for Promoting the Abolition of Slavery . . . ," November 9, 1789, *Writings,* 1154, 1155; Srodes, *Franklin, the Essential Founding Father,* 381.

29. Franklin to Samuel Elbert, December 16, 1787, in Smyth 9: 625; "An Address to the Public from the Pennsylvania Society for Promoting the Abolition of Slavery," *Writings,* 1155.

30. See Henry Louis Gates and Evelyn Brooks Higginbotham, eds., *African American Lives* (New York: Oxford University Press, 2004), 45.

31. Waldstreicher, *Runaway America,* 194; Memorial of the Pennsylvania Abolition Society, February 3, 1790, manuscript, National Archives, Washington, D.C.

32. Pitt, "Franklin and the Quaker Movement Against Slavery," 27, 28–29; Wright, *Franklin of Philadelphia,* 344; "Sidi Mehemet Ibrahim on the Slave Trade, To the Editor of the Federal Gazette," March 23, 1790, *Writings,* 1157–60; Waldstreicher, *Runaway America,* 238.

33. Waldstreicher, *Runaway America,* 83.

Afterword. The End of His Pragmatism

1. *PBF* 3: 475.
2. Ibid., 3: 186n8; 7: 362.
3. Ibid., 18: 122; 21: 583.
4. Ibid., 4: 225–34.
5. For a detailed account of this discussion see Edgar S. Furniss, *The Position of the Laborer in a System of Nationalism* (New York: A. M. Kelley, 1965).
6. *PBF* 4: 233.
7. *The Interest of Great Britain Considered,* 1760, *PBF* 9: 47–100; quote on p. 78.
8. *PBF* 9: 5.
9. Ibid., 14: 325.
10. Ibid., 13: 292.
11. Ibid., 5: 332; 14: 69–70.
12. Ibid., 21: 509.
13. Ibid., 22: 217.
14. *Writings,* 1081–82; *PBF* 3: 479.

Bibliography

Writings by Benjamin Franklin

Account Books Kept by Benjamin Franklin. Vol. 2: *Ledger "D" 1739–1747.* Notes by
    George Simpson Eddy. New York: Columbia University Press, 1929.
Benjamin Franklin's Autobiography. Ed. J. A. Leo Lemay and P. M. Zall. New York:
    Norton, 1986.
Cash Book, June 13, 1778, to October 19, 1780. Franklin Papers. American Philosophi-
    cal Society.
Journal Kept During His Residence in London (1764–76). Hays Catalogue, Pt. 1.
    American Philosophical Society.
Letters of Benjamin Franklin and Jane Mecom, The. Ed. Carl Van Doren. Memoirs of
    the American Philosophical Society, vol. 27. [Princeton]: Published for the Ameri-
    can Philosophical Society by Princeton University Press, 1950.
Modest Enquiry into the Nature and Necessity of a Paper-Currency, A. Philadelphia:
    New Printing-Office, 1729.
Papers of Benjamin Franklin, The. Ed. Leonard W. Labaree et al. 37 vols. to date.
    New Haven: Yale University Press, 1959– .
Works of Benjamin Franklin, The. Ed. Jared Sparks. 10 vols. Boston: Hilliard, Gray,
    1836–40.
Writings. Ed. J. A. Leo Lemay. New York: Library of America, 1987.
Writings of Benjamin Franklin, The. Ed. Albert Henry Smyth. 10 vols. New York:
    Macmillan, 1905–7.

Writings About Benjamin Franklin

Adams, John. *Diary and Autobiography of John Adams.* Ed. L. H. Butterfield. 4 vols.
    Cambridge: Harvard University Press, 1961.
———. *Papers of John Adams.* Ed. Robert J. Taylor et al. Cambridge: Harvard Univer-
    sity Press, 1977– .
———. *The Works of John Adams.* Ed. Charles Francis Adams. 10 vols. Boston: Little,
    Brown, 1850–56.
Aldridge, Alfred Owen. *Benjamin Franklin and His French Contemporaries.* New
    York: New York University Press, 1957.
Asimov, Isaac. *The Kite That Won the Revolution.* Boston: Houghton Mifflin, 1963.
Bacon, Margaret Hope. *History of the Pennsylvania Society for Promoting the Abolition
    of Slavery, the Relief of Negroes Unlawfully Held in Bondage, and for Improving the
    Condition of the African Race.* Philadelphia: Pennsylvania Abolition Society, 1959.
Baetjer, Katharine, with Josephine Dobkin. "Benjamin Franklin's Daughter." *Metro-
    politan Museum Journal* 38 (2003): 169–80.

Bemis, Samuel Flagg. *The Diplomacy of the American Revolution.* 1935; Bloomington: Indiana University Press, 1957.

Bowling, Kenneth R., et al., eds. *Petition Histories and Nonlegislative Official Documents.* Vol. 8 of *Documentary History of the First Federal Congress of the United States of America, March 4, 1789–March 3, 1791.* Ed. Linda Grant Depauw et al. Baltimore: Johns Hopkins University Press, 1998.

Brands, H. W. *The First American: The Life and Times of Benjamin Franklin.* New York: Doubleday, 2000.

Campbell, James. *Recovering Benjamin Franklin: An Exploration of a Life of Science and Service.* Chicago: Open Court, 1999.

Carleton, A. C. "Notes from the Franklin Institute Museum: Franklin Bible." *Journal of the Franklin Institute,* October 1954, 315.

Carr, Robert. "Personal Recollections of Benjamin Franklin." *History Magazine* 2d ser., 4 (August 1868): 59–60.

Clark, Ronald W. *Benjamin Franklin: A Biography.* New York: Random House, 1983.

Cohen, I. Bernard. *Benjamin Franklin: Scientist and Statesman.* New York: Scribner's, 1972.

———. *Benjamin Franklin's Experiments.* Cambridge: Harvard University Press, 1941.

———. *Benjamin Franklin's Science.* Cambridge: Harvard University Press, 1990.

———. *Franklin and Newton.* Philadelphia: American Philosophical Society, 1956.

Cohn, Ellen R. "Benjamin Franklin and Traditional Music." In *Reappraising Benjamin Franklin: A Bicentennial Perspective,* ed. J. A. Leo Lemay, 290–318. Newark: University of Delaware Press, 1993.

Dorman, Charles. "The Furnishings of Franklin Court, 1765–1790: A Preliminary Study." Report prepared for Independence National Historical Park, 1969.

Dull, Jonathan R. *A Diplomatic History of the American Revolution.* New Haven: Yale University Press, 1985.

———. *Franklin the Diplomat: The French Mission.* Philadelphia: American Philosophical Society, 1982.

Edgerton, Samuel Y., Jr. "Supplement: The Franklin Stove." In *Benjamin Franklin's Science,* by I. Bernard Cohen, 199–211. Cambridge: Harvard University Press, 1990.

Franklin, William Temple. Accounts, March 15, 1779, to February 12, 1782. William Temple Franklin Papers. American Philosophical Society.

Franklin, William Temple, ed. *Memoirs of the Life and Writings of Benjamin Franklin, L.L.D., F.R.S., &c.* Quarto ed. 3 vols. London: Printed for Henry Colburn, 1818.

Frasca, Ralph. "Benjamin Franklin's Printing Network." *American Journalism* 5 (1988): 145–58.

———. "From Apprentice to Journeyman to Partner: Benjamin Franklin's Workers and the Growth of the Early American Printing Trade." *Pennsylvania Magazine of History and Biography* 114 (1990): 235–37.

Fussell, Solomon. Ledger, 1738–51. Stephen Collins Papers. Manuscript Division, Library of Congress.

Goodman, Nathan G. *The Ingenious Dr. Franklin.* Philadelphia: University of Pennsylvania Press, 1931.

Green, James N. "Benjamin Franklin as Publisher and Bookseller." In *Reappraising Benjamin Franklin: A Bicentennial Perspective*, ed. J.A. Leo Lemay, 98–114. Newark: University of Delaware Press, 1993.

———. "The Book Trade in the Middle Colonies, 1680–1720." In *The Colonial Book in the Atlantic World*, ed. Hugh Amory and David D. Hall, 199–223. Worcester, Mass.: American Antiquarian Society/New York: Cambridge University Press, 2000.

Hadley, George. "Concerning the Cause of the General Trade-Winds." *Philosophical Transactions of the Royal Society of London* 39 (1735–36): 58–62.

Hale, Edward E., and Edward E. Hale, Jr. *Franklin in France*. 2 vols. Boston: Roberts Brothers, 1887–88.

Hanna, William. *Benjamin Franklin and Pennsylvania Politics*. Stanford: Stanford University Press, 1964.

Haugaard, David. "Sir William Keith." In *Lawmaking and Legislators in Pennsylvania: A Biographical Dictionary*, ed. Craig W. Horle, vol. 2. Philadelphia: University of Pennsylvania Press, 1997.

Hawke, David Freeman. *Franklin*. New York: Harper and Row, 1976.

Heilbron, John L. *Electricity in the Seventeenth and Eighteenth Centuries*. Berkeley: University of California Press, 1979.

———. *Elements of Early Modern Physics*. Berkeley: University of California Press, 1982.

Hindle, Brooke. *The Pursuit of Science in Revolutionary America, 1735–1789*. Chapel Hill: University of North Carolina Press, 1956.

Hopkins, Waldo. "Armchair from Benjamin Franklin's Library." *American Collector* 10, no. 2 (1941): 5.

Hume, David. *Letters of David Hume*. Ed. J. Y. T. Greig. 2 vols. Oxford: Clarendon, 1932.

Hutson, James. *Pennsylvania Politics, 1746–1770*. Princeton: Princeton University Press, 1972.

Isaacson, Walter. *Benjamin Franklin: An American Life*. New York: Simon and Schuster, 2003.

Jackson, Joseph. *Encyclopedia of Philadelphia*. 2 vols. Harrisburg: National Association Telegraph Building, 1931.

Journals of the Continental Congress, 1774–1789, vol. 2. Washington, D. C.: U. S. Government Printing Office, 1905.

Kaplan, Sidney. *The Black Presence in the Era of the American Revolution*. Amherst: University of Massachusetts Press, 1989.

Latrobe, Benjamin Henry. *The Correspondence and Miscellaneous Papers of Benjamin Henry Latrobe*. Ed. John C. Van Horne et al. 3 vols. New Haven: Yale University Press, 1984–88.

Lemay, J. A. Leo. *Ebenezer Kinnersley*. Philadelphia: University of Pennsylvania Press, 1964.

———. "John Mercer and the Stamp Act in Virginia, 1764–1765." *Virginia Magazine of History and Biography* 91 (1983): 3–38.

Lemay, J. A. Leo, ed. *Reappraising Benjamin Franklin: A Bicentennial Perspective*. Newark: University of Delaware Press, 1993.

Livingston, Luther S. *Franklin and His Press at Passy*. New York: Grolier Club, 1914.

Lopez, Claude-Anne. *Benjamin Franklin's Good House.* Washington, D.C.: National Park Service, 1981.

——. *Mon Cher Papa: Franklin and the Ladies of Paris.* 2d ed. New Haven: Yale University Press, 1990.

——. *My Life with Benjamin Franklin.* New Haven: Yale University Press, 2000.

Lopez, Claude-Anne, and Eugenia W. Herbert. *The Private Franklin: The Man and His Family.* New York: Norton, 1975.

Lydenberg, Harry Miller. "The Problem of the Pre-1776 Bible." *Papers of the Bibliographical Society of America* 48 (1954): 183–94.

McMurtrie, Douglas C. *Benjamin Franklin, Typefounder.* New York: Privately printed, 1925.

——. *A History of Printing in the United States.* 2 vols. New York: Bowker, 1936.

Metropolitan Museum of Art. *Benjamin Franklin and His Circle.* Exh. cat. New York: Plantin Press, 1936.

Middlekauff, Robert. *Benjamin Franklin and His Enemies.* Berkeley: University of California Press, 1996.

Miller, C. William. *Benjamin Franklin's Philadelphia Printing: A Descriptive Bibliography.* Philadelphia: American Philosophical Society, 1974.

Moore, Frank. *Diary of the American Revolution.* 2 vols. Hartford: J. B. Burr, 1876.

Morgan, Edmund S. *Benjamin Franklin.* New Haven: Yale University Press, 2002.

Morris, Richard. *The Peacemakers: The Great Powers and American Independence.* New York: Harper and Row, 1965.

Nash, Gary B. *Forging Freedom: The Formation of Philadelphia's Black Community, 1720–1840.* Cambridge: Harvard University Press, 1988.

——. *Quakers and Politics: Pennsylvania, 1681–1726.* Princeton: Princeton University Press, 1968.

——. *The Urban Crucible: Social Change, Political Consciousness, and the Origins of the American Revolution.* Cambridge: Harvard University Press, 1979.

Oswald, John Clyde. *Benjamin Franklin, Printer.* New York: Doubleday, 1917.

——. *A History of Printing: Its Development Through Five Hundred Years.* New York: Appleton, 1928.

Pitt, Arthur S. "Franklin and the Quaker Movement Against Slavery." *Bulletin of Friends Historical Association* 32, no. 1 (Spring 1943): 13–31.

Priestley, Joseph. *Autobiography.* Ed. Jack Lindsey. Teaneck, N. J.: Fairleigh Dickinson University Press, 1971.

——. *History and Present State of Electricity, with Original Experiments.* London: Printed for J. Dodsley, J. Johnson, B. Davenport, and T. Cadell, 1767.

Riley, Edward M. "Franklin's Home." *Transactions of the American Philosophical Society* 33 (1933): 148–60.

Samuel Keimer's "Elegy on the Death of Aquila Rose," Benjamin Franklin's First Known Philadelphia Printing Job, 1723. Philadelphia: Carmen Valentino Rare Books and Manuscripts, Catalogue Fifty, 2000.

Scharf, J. Thomas, and Thompson Westcott. *A History of Philadelphia.* 3 vols. Philadelphia: Pawson and Nicholson, 1886.

Sellers, Charles Coleman. *Benjamin Franklin in Portraiture.* New Haven: Yale University Press, 1962.

Sewall, Samuel. *Diary of Samuel Sewall, 1674–1729.* 3 vols. Boston: Massachusetts Historical Society, 1878–82 [vols. 5–7, series 5, of the Collections of the Massachusetts Historical Society].

Smith, Adam. *An Inquiry into the Nature and Causes of the Wealth of Nations.* Ed. W. B. Todd. 2 vols. Indianapolis: Liberty Classics, 1981.

Smith, Billy G. "Death and Life in a Colonial Immigrant City: A Demographic Analysis of Philadelphia." *Journal of Economic History* 37 (1977): 863–89.

———. *The "Lower Sort": Philadelphia's Laboring People, 1750–1800.* Ithaca: Cornell University Press, 1990.

Smith, Billy G., and Richard Wojtowicz. *Blacks Who Stole Themselves: Advertisements for Runaways in the "Pennsylvania Gazette," 1728–1790.* Philadelphia: University of Pennsylvania Press, 1989.

Soderlund, Jean. *Quakers and Slavery: A Divided Spirit.* Princeton: Princeton University Press, 1985.

Srodes, James. *Franklin, the Essential Founding Father.* Washington, D.C.: Regnery, 2002.

Tanford, Charles. *Ben Franklin Stilled the Waves.* Durham, N. C.: Duke University Press, 1989.

Thomas, Isaiah. *The History of Printing in America.* Barre, Mass.: Imprint Society, 1970.

Tolles, Frederick B. *James Logan and the Culture of Provincial America.* Boston: Little, Brown, 1957.

Tully, Alan. *William Penn's Legacy: Politics and Social Structure in Provincial Pennsylvania, 1726–1755.* Baltimore: Johns Hopkins University Press, 1977.

Uglow, Jenny. *The Lunar Men: The Friends Who Made the Future, 1730–1810.* London: Faber, 2002.

Van Doren, Carl. *Benjamin Franklin.* New York: Garden City Publishing, 1941.

Waldstreicher, David. *Runaway America: Benjamin Franklin, Slavery, and the American Revolution.* New York: Hill and Wang, 2004.

Washington, George. *The Diaries of George Washington.* Ed. Donald Jackson and Dorothy Twohig. 6 vols. Charlottesville: University of Virginia Press, 1976–79.

Watson, John F. *Annals of Philadelphia and Pennsylvania in the Olden Time.* 2 vols. Philadelphia: Lippincott, 1870.

Wood, Gordon S. *The Americanization of Benjamin Franklin.* New York: Penguin, 2004.

Wright, Esmond. *Franklin of Philadelphia.* Cambridge: Harvard University Press, 1986.

Wroth, Lawrence C. "Benjamin Franklin: The Printer at Work." *Journal of the Franklin Institute* 234, no. 2 (1942): 105–32.

———. *The Colonial Printer.* Portland, Maine: Southworth-Anthoensen Press, 1938.

Zirkle, Conway. "Benjamin Franklin, Thomas Malthus and the United States Census." *Isis* 48 (1957): 58–62.

Contributors

Ellen R. Cohn is editor-in-chief of *The Papers of Benjamin Franklin* and senior research scholar, Department of History, Yale University.

Richard S. Dunn is co-executive officer of the American Philosophical Society. He taught history at the University of Pennsylvania. His publications include *Puritans and Yankees* (1962), *Sugar and Slaves* (1972), *The Papers of William Penn* (1981–1987), co-edited with Mary Maples Dunn, and *The Journal of John Winthrop* (1997), co-edited with Laetitia Yeandle.

James N. Green is librarian of the Library Company of Philadelphia. He is on the editorial board of the multivolume *History of the Book in America,* published by the American Antiquarian Society.

Walter Isaacson is the president of the Aspen Institute, a former chairman of CNN, and a former managing editor of *Time* magazine. His books include *Benjamin Franklin: An American Life* (2003).

E. Philip Krider is professor of atmospheric sciences at the Institute of Atmospheric Physics at the University of Arizona. He is the author or co-author of more than 130 scientific papers and 8 patents and is a fellow of the American Geophysical Union and the American Meteorological Society.

Emma J. Lapsansky-Werner is professor of history and curator of special collections at Haverford College. She is the co-editor of *Quaker Aesthetics* (2003) and the author of the forthcoming *Back to Africa*.

J. A. Leo Lemay is H. F. du Pont Winterthur Professor of English at the University of Delaware. He is the author of *The Canon of Benjamin Franklin: New Attributions and Reconsiderations* (1986) and editor of the Library of America's *Benjamin Franklin, Writings* (1987). The first two volumes of his *Life of Benjamin Franklin* will be published in 2005.

Robert Middlekauff is Preston Hotchkis Professor of American History Emeritus at the University of California, Berkeley. He is the author of *Benjamin Franklin and His Enemies* (1996).

Edmund S. Morgan is Sterling Professor of History Emeritus at Yale University. The author of more than a dozen books, including *Benjamin Franklin* (2002), he was awarded the National Humanities Medal in 2000.

Rosalind Remer is a historian who has written on printing and publishing in early America. She is executive director of the Benjamin Franklin Tercentenary.

Billy G. Smith is the Michael P. Malone Professor of History at Montana State University. His books include *Life in Early Philadelphia: Documents from the Revolutionary and Early National Periods* (1995) and *Down and Out in Early America* (2004).

Page Talbott is associate director and chief curator of the Benjamin Franklin Tercentenary. Her books include *Classical Savannah: Fine and Decorative Arts, 1800–1840* (1995), *The Philadelphia Ten: A Women's Artist Group, 1917–1945* (1998), and *Philadelphia's Cultural Landscape: The Sartain Family Legacy* (2000).

John C. Van Horne is director of the Library Company of Philadelphia and a member of the board of the Benjamin Franklin Tercentenary. He was formerly editor of *The Papers of Benjamin Henry Latrobe*.

Acknowledgments

A great many individuals and institutions have had a hand in ensuring the success of the Tercentenary. Some provided funds, some ideas, and some their time and talents. All deserve special mention here.

Generous funders made the Tercentenary's extensive programming and exhibition-related activities possible. The Tercentenary's board of directors and members of the Benjamin Franklin Tercentenary Federal Commission are enormously grateful to The Pew Charitable Trusts, the John Templeton Foundation, the Commonwealth of Pennsylvania, the Annenberg Foundation, the National Endowment for the Humanities and Department of the Interior, the Florence Gould Foundation, the Barra Foundation, Mr. and Mrs. Po Chung, the Lenfest Foundations, and the McLean Contributionship. In addition, for invaluable in-kind support, the Tercentenary is grateful to Samuel T. Freeman and Company. The following individuals were especially helpful throughout the multiyear project: Rebecca Rimel, Marian Godfrey, and Gregory Rowe of The Pew Charitable Trusts; Dr. John Templeton, Arthur Schwartz, Kimon Sargeant, and Pamela Thompson of the Templeton Foundation; Governor Edward G. Rendell; Pennsylvania House Speaker John Purzel; Wayne Spilove and Barbara Franco of the Pennsylvania Historical and Museum Commission; Marcella Reis of the Philadelphia Workforce Development Corporation; Mrs. Walter Annenberg, Gail Levin, and Gillian Norris Szanto of the Annenberg Foundation; John Young of the Florence Gould Foundation; Mary Bomar and Dennis Reidenbach of Independence National Historical Park; Robert L. McNeil, Jr., Gail H. Fahrner, and William Harral III of the Barra Foundation; Edward Resovsky of the University of Pennsylvania; Mr. and Mrs. H. F. (Gerry) Lenfest and Bruce Melgary of the Lenfest Foundations; Sandra McLean of the McLean Contributionship; David Donaldson, David Bloom, Gary Eichelberger, Samuel M. Freeman II, and Lynda Cain of Samuel T. Freeman and Company.

Staff members at the five Tercentenary consortium institutions collaborated in numerous ways. From the American Philosophical Society we thank Robert Cox, Mary Maples Dunn, Roy Goodman, Martin Levitt, Valerie Lutz, Sue Ann Prince, Mary Teeling, Annie Westcott, and Katie Wood; from The Franklin Institute, John Alviti, Irene Coffey, Cheryl Desmond, Philip Hammer, Rosalyn McPherson, Derrick Pitts, Steve Snyder, and Sean Woods; from the Library Company of Philadelphia, James N. Green, Kate Norton, Charlene Peacock, and Nicole Scalessa; from the Philadelphia Museum of Art, Kathleen Foster, John Ittman, Rian Deurenberg, David DeMuzio, Danielle Rice, Shannon N. Schuler, Irene Taurins, Dean Walker, and Suzi Wells; and from the University of Pennsylvania, Richard R. Beeman, Peter Conn, Lynne Farrington, Jacqueline Jacovini, Mark Lloyd, Alison McGhie, Daniel Richter, Michael Ryan, and Michael Zuckerman.

Others at a variety of institutions were also of great help in the planning stages: Georgia B. Barnhill, American Antiquarian Society, Worcester, Mass.; Jeffrey Ray, the Atwater Kent Museum of Philadelphia; Joel Fry and Bill LeFevre, Bartram's Garden, Philadelphia; Ellen Kuhfeld and David Rhees, the Bakken Library and Museum of Electricity, Minneapolis; Marcia Balisciano, Sir Bob and Lady Reid, and Anne Prescott Keigher, the Benjamin Franklin House, 36 Craven Street, London; Rainey Tisdale, The Bostonian Society; Matthew Shaw, the British Library, London; Nian-Sheng Huang, California State University, Channel Islands; Sarah Nichols and Elizabeth Agro Hansen, Carnegie Museum of Art, Pittsburgh; Lisa Porter, Cheekwood Botanical Garden and Museum of Art, Nashville, Tenn.; Donald Smith, Christ Church Preservation Trust, Philadelphia; Andrew Brunk, Dean Failey, and Donald Johnston, Christie's; Melissa Hough and Sue Levy, CIGNA Museum and Art Collection, Philadelphia; Neil Handley, College of Optometrists, London; Margaret Lyman, Edward Morman, and the late Gretchen Worden, College of Physicians of Philadelphia and Mütter Museum; Cary Carson and Ronald Hurst, Colonial Williamsburg Foundation, Virginia; Jocelyn Wilk, Columbia University; Carol Smith, the Contributionship Companies, Philadelphia; Michael Kammen, Cornell University; Hervé Aaron, Didier Aaron et Cie, Paris; John Fry, Christopher Raab, and Ann Steiner, Franklin and Marshall College, Lancaster, Pa.; Lori Blount, Alyce Bodine, William Lang, Linda Pitts, and James R. DeWalt, the Free Library of Philadelphia; Kathy DeLuca, Friends of Franklin; Marjorie Cohn and Sandra Grindlay, Harvard University Art Museums, Cambridge, Mass.; Lee Arnold, Mickey Herr, Tamara Miller, David Moltke-Hansen, and Kathryn Wilson, Historical Society of Pennsylvania, Philadelphia; Jack P. Greene, Johns Hopkins University; Mary Robertson and David Zeidberg, the Huntington Library, San Marino, Calif.; Frances Delmar, Karie Diethorn, Doris Devine Fanelli, Robert Giannini, Sue Glennon, Steve Sitarski, and Karen Stevens, Independence National Historical Park, Philadelphia; Jim Hutson, Tambra Johnson, and Rachel Waldron, Library of Congress, Washington, D.C.; Laura Libert, Kenneth McCarty, and Glenys Waldman, Masonic Library and Museum of Pennsylvania, Philadelphia; Anne Bentley, Massachusetts Historical Society, Boston; Katharine Baetjer, Nancy Britton, Morrison Heckscher, Danielle Kisluk-Grosheide, Jeffrey Munger, and Frances Redding Wallace, The Metropolitan Museum of Art, New York; Eugénie Angéles, Anne Doppfer, and Jacques Perot, Musée National de la Coopération Franco-américaine; James Zeender, National Archives, Washington, D.C.; Hilary Anderson, National Heritage Museum, Lexington, Mass.; Brandon Brame Fortune and Wendy Wick Reaves, National Portrait Gallery, Washington, D.C.; Lucy Peltz and David McNeff, National Portrait Gallery, London; David Burnhauser and Margaret Hofer, New-York Historical Society; Judith Magee, Natural History Museum, London; Douglas Hamilton and Nigel Rigby, National Maritime Museum, Greenwich, England; Ellen R. Cohn and Kate M. Ohno, the Papers of Benjamin Franklin, Yale University, New Haven, Conn.; Robert Harman and Gale Rawson, Pennsylvania Academy of the Fine Arts, Philadelphia; Stacey Peeples, Pennsylvania Hospital, Philadelphia; Carla Mulford, Penn State University, University Park, Pa.; Bruce James, Public Printer of the United States, and Andy Sherman, Maria Robinson and Bob Tapella of the U. S. Government Printing Office; Elizabeth Fuller, Judy Guston, and Karen Schoenewaldt, Rosenbach Museum and Library, Philadelphia; Geoff Botting, Royal Society of Arts, London; Anne Grocock and Ian Snowley, Royal Society of Medicine, London; James Holloway and Anne Steinberg, Scottish National Portrait Gallery, Edinburgh; Caroline Archer, St. Bride Library,

London; Beatrice Hulsberg, State Museum of Pennsylvania, Harrisburg; James Mc-Clellan, Stevens Institute of Technology, Hoboken, N.J.; Michael Conforti and Monique Le Blanc, Sterling and Francine Clark Art Institute, Williamstown, Mass.; Jamie Day, Transylvania University, Lexington, Ky.; Gail Serfaty and Lynn Turner, Diplomatic Reception Rooms, U.S. Department of State, Washington, D.C.; James Cheevers and Donald Leonard, U.S. Naval Academy Museum, Annapolis, Md.; E. Philip Krider, University of Arizona, Tucson; J. A. Leo Lemay, University of Delaware, Newark; Gillian Wakely, University of Pennsylvania Museum, Philadelphia; Scott Houting and Michelle Ortwein, Valley Forge National Historical Park, Pa.; Xavier Salomon, Château de Versailles; Mark Anderson, Kate Cooney, Linda Eaton, Grace Eleazer, Leslie Grigsby, Patricia Halfpenny, Gregory Landrey, Michael Podmaniczki, Neville Thompson, and Anne Verplanck, Winterthur Museum, Garden and Library, Wilmington, Del.; Ellen Cordes, Beinecke Rare Book and Manuscript Library, Yale University, New Haven, Conn. Thanks also go to the following individuals: Penelope Batcheler, Katherine Eustace, Jonathan Fairbanks, Meredith Martindale Frappier, Lee-Ann Grunwald, Letitia Roberts, and Gail Winkler.

The following individuals from the host institutions for the exhibition have been true partners in the exhibition's development. The Tercentenary would like to express thanks to Gordon Jones and Kay Buckham of the Atlanta History Center, Georgia; Ken Cashion, Marianne Reynolds, and Bonnie Downing of the Denver Museum of Nature and Science, Colorado; Robert Archibald, Nicola Longford, and Whitney Watson of the Missouri Historical Society, St. Louis; Thierry Lalande, Anne-Catherine Hauglustaine, and Daniel Thoulouze of the Musée des Arts et Métiers, Paris; Aimée Fontaine, Jean-Marc Léri, and Christophe Léribault of the Musée Carnavalet, Paris; and Phil Castellano, Steve Frank, Richard Stengel, and Beth Twiss-Garrity of the National Constitution Center, Philadelphia.

Tercentenary partnerships with French institutions have been forged with the generous help of the Embassy of the United States in Paris, led by the enthusiastic support of Ambassador Howard H. Leach, Renée M. Earle, Minister-Counselor for Public Affairs, and Katja Graisse, Cultural Affairs Specialist. Furthering the aim of Franco-American relations and building on Franklin's own historical efforts to forge a long-lasting friendship between the two nations, Jean-David Levitte, Ambassador of France to the United States, provided help and encouragement throughout the project. On both sides of the ocean David Maxey and Jacques Friedmann lent a hand toward achieving a trans-Atlantic Franklin celebration, as did Danielle Easton Thomas, Honorary French Consul in Philadelphia.

The Tercentenary has had especially enthusiastic, competent, and hard-working staff members, consultants, and interns in Anne Brandt, Sherry Bufano, Laura Carey, Melissa Clemmer, Dana Devon, Ellen Epstein, Christina Freeman, Lori Geisinger, Katie Gould, Peter Grollman, Connie Hershey, Kathy Hill, Patti Jeppson, Brent Kissel, Andrew Krause, Susan Taylor Leduc, Susan Lee, Geoff Manaugh, Allison McBride, Rose McManus, Emily Rome, Mike Rosenstein, Lisa Rudy, Dave Rupp, Lori Scherr, Kate Snider, Nicola Twilley, Christine Van Horne, and Steve Weintraub.

The exhibition designers did a splendid job of rendering Franklin's life and accomplishments in three dimensions: Barbara Fahs Charles, Robert Staples, David Gelles, Judy Cheng, Matt Duffy, and Mary Wolff at Staples and Charles produced the exhibition design; Fred Brink, Philip Clendaniel, Salvatore Raciti, Stewart Smith, and Beth Sternheimer of a More Perfect Union developed the media interactive elements of the exhibition; Danny Rozin created the technology that makes "See Yourself in Franklin" possible; Ken Hopkins, Mike Slayton, Caleb Donat, and Kyoji Nakano of Proto Productions fabricated the exhibition; and Jan Adkins of Jan Adkins Studio brainstormed creatively.

Thanks also go to Bart Marable and Paco Link of Terra Incognita, the Tercentenary Web-site developer; Robert Borghese and Daniel J. Remer, who provided legal counsel; congressional staffers Catherine Graham in Sen. Joseph Biden's office and Emily Pfeiffer in Rep. Michael Castle's office, and Heather Fitzgerald in the White House Office on Commissions for help with the Franklin Commemorative Coin Bill and the establishment of the federal commission.

The Tercentenary is grateful to Yale University Press for its interest and faith in this book and for the sensitive and expert editing of the manuscript, led by acquisitions editor Lauren Shapiro and manuscript editor Susan Laity. The handsome design of this book is the work of Sonia Shannon. Steve Colca provided assistance throughout.

The team at the Greater Philadelphia Tourism and Marketing Corporation—the Tercentenary's marketing partner—includes President Meryl Levitz, Paula Butler, Sharon Rossi, Sarah Monk, Keren Ini, Cara Schneider, and Cathy McVey, and the Tercentenary also worked closely with Susan Hamilton at the Philadelphia Convention and Visitors Bureau.

Peter Harholdt produced the majority of the photography for the exhibition and for this volume, supplemented by the photography of Will Brown for the Library Company, and Frank Margeson for the American Philosophical Society.

Conservation of objects in the exhibition was supervised by Rolf Kat of Philadelphia's Conservation Center for Art and Historic Artifacts (CCAHA). Ingrid Bogel and Lee Price of the Conservation Center aided in the preparation of the "Save America's Treasures" grant that has underwritten much of the conservation. Most works on paper were conserved at CCAHA by Kim Andrews, Rondi Barricelli, Susan M. Bing, Theresa Cho, Soyeon Choi, Heather Godlewski, Joan A. Irving, Jilliann Herrick, Richard Homer, Anna C. Yates Krain, Keith Jameson, Barbara E. Lemmen, Glen A. Ruzicka, Mary Schobert, Shelly Smith, Britt Stadig, Laura Wahl, and Morgan Zinsmeister. Artifacts in other media were conserved by independent conservators Kory Berrett, Catherine Coho, Steven Erisoty, Thomas Heller, and Virginia Whelan. In addition, conservators at partner institutions treated works in their collections: Anne Downey and Denise Carbone of the American Philosophical Society; Jennifer Woods Rosner, Andrea Krupp, and Alice Austin of the Library Company of Philadelphia; and the Conservation Department of the Philadelphia Museum of Art.

Many more institutions and individuals are contributing to the diverse array of Benjamin Franklin Tercentennial programming that will complement the themes and extend the reach of the exhibition, and the Tercentenary staff, board members, and federal commission are proud and grateful to be working with each one of them.

Illustration Credits

Fig. I.1 Sheet of one hundred Franklin half-cent stamps, signed by postal officials and others, 1938
Paper, 10¼ × 8⅞ in. (26 × 22.5 cm)
Frankliniana Collection, The Franklin Institute, Inc., Philadelphia
Photo: Courtesy of The Franklin Institute, Inc., Philadelphia

Fig. I.2 Red Grooms
Dr. Franklin's Profile, 1982
Ink and watercolor on paper, 42 × 29½ in. unframed, 50 × 37¼ in. framed (107 × 75 cm unframed, 127 × 95 cm framed)
Philadelphia Museum of Art, Purchased with the Alice Newton Osborn Fund, 1982
Photo: Philadelphia Museum of Art

Fig. I.3 Attributed to Samuel Skillin
Portrait bust of Benjamin Franklin, ca. 1777–85
Wood and plaster covering, 29 × 14¾ × 10 in. (73.7 × 37.5 × 25.4 cm)
Frankliniana Collection, The Franklin Institute, Inc., Philadelphia

Fig. I.4 Figurine of Benjamin Franklin, mid-nineteenth century
Bronze, 15 × 16 × 7 in. (38.1 × 40.6 × 17.8 cm)
American Philosophical Society, Philadelphia
Photo: American Philosophical Society, Philadelphia

Fig. I.5 *Poor Richard Illustrated. Lessons for the Young and Old on Industry, Temperance, Frugality &c. by Benjamin Franklin* from *Our Home and Fireside Magazine: Gift Plate Supplement* (Portland, Maine: Hallett, 1873–88)
Paper, 18⅝ × 23½ in. (47.5 × 59.7 cm)
American Philosophical Society, Philadelphia
Photo: American Philosophical Society, Philadelphia

Fig. I.6 Berlinwork portrait of Benjamin Franklin, ca. 1850
Painted canvas, wool, and gold thread, 34¾ × 29 in. framed (88.3 × 73.7 cm)
Private collection

Fig. I.7 William Overend Geller after André-Edouard, Baron Jolly
Franklin at the Court of France, 1853
Engraving (artist's proof), 43 × 54 in. framed (109.2 × 137.1 cm)
Collection Stuart E. Karu

Fig. I.8 Abbé Jean Richard Claude de Saint-Non after Jean-Honoré Fragonard
Le Docteur Francklin couronné par la Liberté, 1778
Aquatint, 9½ × 8 in. (24.1 × 20.3 cm)
Collection Stuart E. Karu

Fig. I.9 Snuffbox with portrait print of Franklin, Voltaire, and Rousseau, late eighteenth century
Horn, satinwood, gilt, engraving on paper, and glass, 1 × 3 in. (2.5 × 7.6 cm)
Masonic Library and Museum of Pennsylvania, Philadelphia

Fig. I.10 Jean-Baptiste Nini after a drawing by Anne Vallayer-Coster
Portrait medallion of Benjamin Franklin, 1779
Terra cotta, 11 × 11 × 2 in. framed (27.9 × 27.9 × 5 cm)
Collection Stuart E. Karu

Fig. I.11 Samuel J. Formica
Looking to the Future, 2003
Oil on canvas, 84 × 60 in. (203.2 × 152.4 cm)
Collection Samuel J. Formica, on loan to The Franklin Institute, Philadelphia
Samuel J. Formica, copyright © 2003, Philadelphia

Fig. I.12 *The Art of Making Money Plenty in every Man's Pocket; by Doctor Franklin* (New York and Hartford: E. B. and E. C. Kellogg, ca. 1847)
Lithograph, 14 × 11 in. (35.6 × 27.9 cm)
Collection Stuart E. Karu

Fig. I.13 Benjamin West
Benjamin Franklin Drawing Electricity from the Sky, ca. 1816
Oil on slate, 13⅓ × 10 in. (34 × 26 cm)
Philadelphia Museum of Art, Mr. and Mrs. Wharton Sinkler Collection
Photo: Philadelphia Museum of Art

Fig. I.14 Title page of Jacques Gibelin, trans., *Mémoires de la vie privée De Benjamin Franklin, écrits par lui-méme* (Paris: Buisson, 1791)
Book, 7¾ × 4⅞ in. (21.5 × 14 cm)
Collection Stuart E. Karu

Fig. I.15 Bookplate of the Library Company of Philadelphia (Philadelphia: Benjamin Franklin, ca. 1740)
Printed paper, ⅞ × 2½ in. (2.2 × 6.4 cm)
Library Company of Philadelphia

Fig. I.16 Quart whisky flask with portrait of Benjamin Franklin, ca. 1820–38, made by Kensington Glass Works (American)
Aquamarine nonlead glass, 8 × 6 × 3 in. (20 × 15 × 8 cm)
Collection Stuart E. Karu

Fig. I.17 "Oraison Funèbre de M. Franklin par L'Abbé Fauchet," in *Le Panthéon des philantropes, ou, L'école de la révolution; almanach . . .* (Paris: Janet, [1792])
Wood engraving in pamphlet, 3⅛ × 2 in. (6 × 5 cm)

Franklin Collection, Yale University Library, New Haven, Conn.
Photo: Yale University Library

Fig. 1.1 John Bonner
The Town of Boston in New England, 1722
Engraving, 17 × 23¼ in. (43 × 59 cm)
I. N. Phelps Stokes Collection, Miriam and Ira D. Wallach Division of
    Art, Prints and Photographs, The New York Public Library, Astor,
    Lenox and Tilden Foundations
Photo: The New York Public Library

Fig. 1.2 The First King's Chapel in the Boston Grammar (Latin)
    School, ca. 1810
Wood engraving, 3¼ × 3 in. (8.3 × 7.6 cm)
The Bostonian Society
Courtesy of The Bostonian Society/Old State House
Photo: The Bostonian Society

Fig. 1.3 Frontispiece and title page of Antoine Arnauld and Pierre
    Nicole, *Logic; or, the Art of Thinking . . . By Mr. Ozell* (London:
    William Taylor, 1717)
Book, 7 × 4¼ in. (17.8 × 10.8 cm)
Library Company of Philadelphia
Photo: Library Company of Philadelphia

Fig. 1.4 Front page of Joseph Addison and Richard Steele, *The
    Spectator*, number 124, July 23, 1711 (London, 1711)
Newspaper, 13 × 8½ in. (33 × 21.6 cm)
Library Company of Philadelphia
Photo: Library Company of Philadelphia

Fig. 1.5 Peter Pelham
Cottonus Matherus (portrait print of Cotton Mather), 1727
Mezzotint, 12 × 9¼ in. (35.6 × 25.4 cm)
National Portrait Gallery, Smithsonian Institution, Washington,
    D.C.
Photo: National Portrait Gallery, Smithsonian Institution, Washington,
    D.C.

Fig. 1.6 Nathaniel Emmons
Portrait of Samuel Sewall, 1728
Oil on canvas, 49⅓ × 40⅓ in. (125.3 × 102.3 cm)
Massachusetts Historical Society, Boston
Courtesy of the Massachusetts Historical Society, Boston
Photo: David Bohl, Boston

Fig. 1.7 Front page of the *Pennsylvania Gazette,* January 6–13, 1736/37
    (Philadelphia: Benjamin Franklin, 1737)
Newspaper, 11¾ × 7⅝ in. (30 × 19.5 cm)
Walter J. and Leonore Annenberg Rare Book and Manuscript Library,
    University of Pennsylvania, Philadelphia

Fig. 1.8 Title page of James Anderson, *The Constitutions of the Free-
    Masons* (Philadelphia: [Benjamin Franklin], 1734)
Book, 8¼ × 6⅛ in. (21 × 15.5 cm)
Walter J. and Leonore Annenberg Rare Book and Manuscript Library,
    University of Pennsylvania, Philadelphia

Fig. 1.9 "Lion's Mouth" box, ca. 1750
Painted tin, 11⅜ × 7¾ × 5½ in. (29 × 19.7 × 14 cm)

Library Company of Philadelphia
Photo: Library Company of Philadelphia

Fig. 1.10 Whale oil street lamp, ca. 1800
Tin and glass, 23 × 14¼ × 14¼ in. (58.4 × 36.2 × 36.2 cm)
Atwater Kent Museum of Philadelphia
Courtesy of The Historical Society of Pennsylvania Collection,
    Atwater Kent Museum of Philadelphia

Fig. 1.11 Milepost
Stone, 55½ × 13½ × 5½ in. (141 × 34.3 × 14 cm)
Atwater Kent Museum of Philadelphia
Courtesy of the Atwater Kent Museum of Philadelphia

Fig. 1.12 Joseph Breintnall, Page of a book of nature prints of leaves,
    ca. 1731–44
Ink on paper, 12¼ × 15⅜ in. (31.1 × 39.1 cm)
Library Company of Philadelphia
Photo: Library Company of Philadelphia

Fig. 1.13 James Turner after Lewis Evans
Illustration of the parts of the "Franklin Stove" from Benjamin
    Franklin, *An Account Of the New Invented Pennsylvanian Fire-
    Places . . .* (Philadelphia: Benjamin Franklin, 1744)
Engraving, 8 × 10 in. (20 × 25 cm)
Library Company of Philadelphia

Fig. 1.14 "The Waggoneer and Hercules" cartoon from *Plain Truth;
    or, Serious considerations on the present state of the city of Phila-
    delphia, and province of Pennsylvania. By a tradesman of
    Philadelphia* (Philadelphia: Benjamin Franklin, 1747)
Pamphlet, 7½ × 4⅜ in. (19.1 × 11.2 cm)
Library Company of Philadelphia

Fig. 1.15 Signatures of subscribers to the "Constitutions of the Publick
    Academy, in the City of Philadelphia," 1749
Bound manuscript, 12⅜ × 8¼ in. (31.5 × 21 cm)
University of Pennsylvania Archives and Records Center, Philadelphia

Fig. 1.16 Benjamin Franklin, Draft of the cornerstone inscription for
    the Pennsylvania Hospital, 1755
Manuscript, 8 × 7 in. (20.3 × 17.8 cm)
Pennsylvania Hospital Historic Collections, Philadelphia
Courtesy of the Pennsylvania Hospital Historic Collections,
    Philadelphia

Fig. 1.17 Benjamin Franklin to James Alexander and Cadwallader
    Colden
"Short hints towards a scheme for uniting the Northern Colonies"
    (Draft of the Albany Plan of Union), June 8, 1754
Manuscript, 13 × 8 in. (33 × 20.3 cm)
Collection of The New-York Historical Society
Photo: The New-York Historical Society

Fig. 1.18 Postmaster's bill (Philadelphia: Benjamin Franklin, 1745?)
Printed paper, 3¼ × 8½ in. (8.3 × 21.6 cm)
American Philosophical Society, Philadelphia
Photo: American Philosophical Society

Fig. 1.19 Benjamin Franklin, *The Way to Wealth* (Philadelphia: Daniel
    Humphreys, ca. 1785)

Broadside, 24½ × 16¾ in. framed (62.2 × 42.5 cm)
Collection Michael Zinman

Fig. 1.20 Gilbert Stuart
Portrait of John Fothergill, 1781
Oil on canvas, 35⅝ × 27¾ in. (90.5 × 70.5 cm)
The Pennsylvania Academy of the Fine Arts, Philadelphia
Courtesy of the Pennsylvania Academy of the Fine Arts, Philadelphia,
    Annual Membership Fund
Photo: Pennsylvania Academy of the Fine Arts

Fig. 1.21 Attributed to Ralph Wood
Staffordshire statuette of Benjamin Franklin, ca. 1762–72
Porcelain, 13½ × 5½ × 5½ in. (34.3 × 14 × 14 cm)
American Philosophical Society, Philadelphia

Fig. 1.22 David Martin
Portrait of Benjamin Franklin, 1767
Oil on canvas, 49½ × 39½ in. (125.7 × 100.3 cm)
Pennsylvania Academy of the Fine Arts, Philadelphia
Courtesy of the Pennsylvania Academy of the Fine Arts, Philadelphia,
    Gift of Maria McKean Allen and Phebe Warren Downes through
    the bequest of their mother Elizabeth Wharton McKean
Photo: Pennsylvania Academy of the Fine Arts

Fig. 1.23 "MAGNA Britannia: her Colonies REDUC'D," designed by
    Benjamin Franklin (London: printer unknown, ca. 1766)
Printed on Pro Patria paper, 5 × 3⅛ in. (12.5 × 7.9 cm)
Library Company of Philadelphia
Photo: Library Company of Philadelphia

Fig. 1.24 Augustin de Saint-Aubin after Charles-Nicholas Cochin
Benjamin Franklin (portrait print), 1777
Engraving, 7⅞ × 5⅞ in. (20 × 14.8 cm)
Collection Stuart E. Karu

Fig. 1.25 Marguerite Gérard after Jean-Honoré Fragonard
Au génie de Franklin (To the genius of Franklin), ca. 1778
Etching, 19 × 14½ in. (48.3 × 36.8 cm)
Bibliothèque nationale de France, Paris
Photo: Bibliothèque nationale de France

Fig. 1.26 Page 99 of Benjamin Franklin's autobiography manuscript,
    ca. 1771–89
Manuscript, 12⅜ × 8 in. (31.3 × 20.3 cm)
The Huntington Library, San Marino, Calif.
Photo: The Huntington Library

Fig. 1.27 Masonic sash, ca. 1782
Silk with gold and silver thread, sequins, beads and crystal,
    26⅓ × 4⅓ in. (66.8 × 11 cm)
Masonic Library and Museum of Pennsylvania, Philadelphia

Fig. 1.28 Joseph Sansom
Silhouette of Benjamin Franklin, ca. 1790
Ink on paper in book
The Winterthur Library, Garden and Museum
Courtesy of The Winterthur Library, Joseph Downs Collection of
    Manuscripts and Printed Ephemera, Winterthur, Del.
Photo: The Winterthur Library

Fig. 2.1 Title page of Richard Saunders [Benjamin Franklin], Poor
    Richard, 1733: An Almanack For the Year of Christ 1733 . . .
    (Philadelphia: Benjamin Franklin, [1732])
Pamphlet, 7 × 4 × ⅛ in. (17.8 × 10.2 × 0.3 cm)
Rosenbach Museum and Library, Philadelphia

Fig. 2.2 James Franklin's printing press, ca. 1716–17
Wood and metal, 83 × 35 × 62 in. (211 × 90 × 157 cm)
From the Collections of the Newport Historical Society (L93.54). On
    loan from the Massachusetts Charitable Mechanics Association
Photo: John W. Corbett, Newport, R.I.

Fig. 2.3 Front page of The New-England Courant, with Silence Dogood
    letter, issue 35, March 26–April 2, 1722 (Boston: James Franklin,
    1722)
Newspaper, 12¼ × 7⅝ in. (31.2 × 19.2 cm)
Massachusetts Historical Society, Boston
Courtesy of the Massachusetts Historical Society, Boston
Photo: Massachusetts Historical Society

Fig. 2.4 George Heap
The East Prospect of the City of Philadelphia, in the Province of
    Pennsylvania, 1755
Engraving, 6¼ × 19½ in. (15.9 × 49.5 cm)
CIGNA Museum and Art Collection, Philadelphia
Photo: Joseph Painter

Fig. 2.5 L'Opération de la casse (Composing room), in Denis Diderot
    et al., Encyclopédie, ou Dictionnaire raisonné des sciences, des arts
    et des métiers, 1761–89
Engraving, 5¼ × 8 in. (13.3 × 20.3 cm)
Library Company of Philadelphia
Photo: Library Company of Philadelphia

Fig. 2.6 Composing stick (American), 1740–60
Wood and metal, 8¼ × 2 × ⅝ in. (21 × 5.1 × 1.5 cm)
Atwater Kent Museum of Philadelphia
Courtesy of The Historical Society of Pennsylvania Collection,
    Atwater Kent Museum of Philadelphia

Fig. 2.7 Ink balls, eighteenth century
Wood and leather, 10⅞ × 8¾ × 8¾ in. and 8⅝ × 7 × 7 in. (25.4 × 20.3
    × 20.3 cm and 20.3 × 17.8 × 17.8 cm)
Frankliniana Collection, The Franklin Institute, Inc., Philadelphia

Fig. 2.8 Attributed to Gustavus Hesselius
Portrait of James Logan, ca. 1728–35
Oil on canvas, 31½ × 25½ in. (80 × 64.8 cm)
Atwater Kent Museum of Philadelphia
Courtesy of The Historical Society of Pennsylvania Collection,
    Atwater Kent Museum of Philadelphia
Photo: Atwater Kent Museum of Philadelphia

Fig. 2.9 Front page of the Pennsylvania Gazette, May 2, 1745
    (Philadelphia: Benjamin Franklin, 1745)
Newspaper, 13 × 8 in. (30 × 20.5 cm)
Walter J. and Leonore Annenberg Rare Book and Manuscript Library,
    University of Pennsylvania, Philadelphia

Fig. 2.10 Title page of Benjamin Franklin, *A Modest Enquiry into the Nature and Necessity of a Paper-Currency* (Philadelphia: [Franklin and Meredith] at the New Printing Office, 1729)
Pamphlet, 7¼ × 4½ in. (18.4 × 11.4 cm)
Library Company of Philadelphia
Photo: Library Company of Philadelphia

Fig. 2.11 Colonial currency: 15 shilling note, Pennnsylvania (Philadelphia: Franklin and Hall, 1757); 20 shilling note, Delaware (Philadelphia: Franklin and Hall, 1758); and 5 pound note, Pennsylvania (Philadelphia: Franklin and Hall, 1759)
Leaf-printed paper, 3⅞ × 2¾ in. each (9.8 × 7 cm)
Frankliniana Collection, The Franklin Institute, Inc., Philadelphia

Fig. 2.12 Title page of Richard Saunders [Benjamin Franklin], *Poor Richard improved . . .* (Philadelphia: Benjamin Franklin, [1757])
Pamphlet, 6¾ × 4½ (17.1 × 11.4 cm)
The Historical Society of Pennsylvania
Courtesy of The Historical Society of Pennsylvania, Philadelphia

Fig. 2.13 H. S. Grimm and J. Macky
Caricature of Benjamin Franklin, 1789
Engraving, 7⅞ × 4⅞ in. (20 × 12.5 cm)
Walter J. and Leonore Annenberg Rare Book and Manuscript Library, University of Pennsylvania, Philadelphia

Fig. 2.14 Front page of *The General Magazine, and Historical Chronicle, For all the British Plantations in America* (Philadelphia: Benjamin Franklin, 1741)
Printed paper, 7 × 4 × 1 in. (17.8 × 10.2 × 2.5 cm)
The Historical Society of Pennsylvania, Philadelphia
Courtesy of The Historical Society of Pennsylvania, Philadelphia

Fig. 2.15 Bill of lading (Philadelphia: Benjamin Franklin, ca. 1740–48)
Printed paper, 4⅝ × 9⅝ in. (11.9 × 24.3 cm)
American Philosophical Society, Philadelphia
Photo: American Philosophical Society, Philadelphia

Fig. 2.16 General Loan Office of Pennsylvania, blank mortgage bond (Philadelphia: Benjamin Franklin, 1729)
Printed paper, 12¾ × 8 in. (32 × 20 cm)
Library Company of Philadelphia
Photo: Library Company of Philadelphia

Fig. 2.17 Title page of George Webb, *Batchelors-Hall; a Poem* (Philadelphia: Benjamin Franklin, 1731)
Pamphlet, 12⅜ × 7¾ in. (31.4 × 19.7)
American Philosophical Society, Philadelphia
Photo: American Philosophical Society

Fig. 2.18 Unknown artist, Cartoon of a post rider from the newspaper *Boston Post-Boy* (Boston: Ellis Huske, 1750–54)
Woodcut, 1⅞ × 2 in. (4.5 × 5 cm)
American Antiquarian Society, Worcester, Mass.
Courtesy of the American Antiquarian Society, Worcester, Mass.
Photo: American Antiquarian Society

Fig. 2.19 Benjamin Franklin and Deborah Franklin, Shop book, 1735–39
Manuscript book, 15 × 6¼ in. (38.2 × 15.7 cm)

American Philosophical Society, Philadelphia
Photo: American Philosophical Society

Fig. 2.20 Title page of James Logan, trans., *M. T. Cicero's Cato Major, or his Discourse of Old-Age . . .* (Philadelphia: Benjamin Franklin, 1744)
Book, 8⅜ × 5½ in. (21.3 × 13.9 cm)
Rosenbach Museum and Library, Philadelphia

Fig. 2.21 Title page of Samuel Richardson, *Pamela: or, Virtue Rewarded* (Philadelphia: Benjamin Franklin, 1742–43)
Book, 6⅝ × 4 in. (16.8 × 10.2 cm)
American Antiquarian Society, Worcester, Mass.
Courtesy of the American Antiquarian Society, Worcester, Mass.
Photo: American Antiquarian Society

Fig. 2.22 Title page of John Bunyan, *The Pilgrim's Progress* (London: Printed for W.P., 1702)
Book, 3½ × 6 × ½ in. (9 × 14.8 × 1.3 cm)
Print Collection, Miriam and Ira D. Wallach Division of Art, Prints and Photographs, The New York Public Library, Astor, Lenox and Tilden Foundations
Photo: The New York Public Library

Fig. 2.23 Title page of Lewis Evans, *Geographical, Historical, Political, Philosophical and Mechanical Essays: The First, Containing an Analysis Of a General Map of the Middle British Colonies in America . . .*, 2d ed. (Philadelphia: Franklin and Hall, 1755)
Book, 10 × 7⅜ in. (25.4 × 18.7 cm)
The Library of The Franklin Institute, Inc., Philadelphia

Fig. 2.24 Benjamin Franklin, *Directions to the Deputy Post-Masters, for keeping their Accounts* (Philadelphia, 1753?)
Printed paper, 20⅞ × 16⅜ in. (53 × 41.6 cm)
The Historical Society of Pennsylvania, Philadelphia
Courtesy of The Historical Society of Pennsylvania, Philadelphia

Fig. 2.25 Joshua Reynolds
Portrait of William Strahan, 1783
Oil on canvas, 36 × 28 in. (91.4 × 71.1 cm)
National Portrait Gallery, London
Photo: National Portrait Gallery, London

Fig. 2.26 James McArdell after Benjamin Wilson
B. Franklin of Philadelphia (portrait print), 1761
Mezzotint, 21 × 17 in. framed (53.3 × 43.1 cm)
Collection Stuart E. Karu

Fig. 2.27 Benjamin Franklin, Epitaph, 1728
Manuscript, 9 × 7¼ in. (22.5 cm × 18.5 cm)
Beinecke Rare Book and Manuscript Library, Yale University, New Haven, Conn.
Photo: Beinecke Rare Book and Manuscript Library

Fig. 3.1 Peter Cooper
The South East Prospect of The City of Philadelphia, ca. 1718
Oil on canvas, 28 × 94 in. (71.1 × 238.8 cm)
Library Company of Philadelphia
Photo: Library Company of Philadelphia

Fig. 3.2 *To the Mayor Recorder Aldermen Common Council and Freemen of Philadelphia. This Plan of the improved part of the City surveyed and laid down by the late Nicholas Scull, Esqr. . . .* (Map of Philadelphia) (Philadelphia: Matthew Clarkson and Mary Biddle, 1762)
American Philosophical Society, Philadelphia
Photo: American Philosophical Society

Fig. 3.3 William L. Breton
London Coffee House, ca. 1830
Lithograph, 5¾ × 9 in. (14.6 × 22.9 cm)
Library Company of Philadelphia
Photo: Library Company of Philadelphia

Fig. 3.4 David Rent Etter
Franklin with Loaf of Bread, ca. 1830
Oil on panel, 25 × 13¾ in. (64 × 35 cm)
CIGNA Museum and Art Collection, Philadelphia
Photo: Joseph Painter

Fig. 3.5 Unknown artist
Stone Prison at Philadelphia, 1728, ca. 1830
Lithograph, 5¼ × 7½ in. (13.3 × 19 cm)
The Historical Society of Pennsylvania, Philadelphia
Courtesy of The Historical Society of Pennsylvania, Philadelphia
Photo: The Historical Society of Pennsylvania

Fig. 3.6 William Birch and Thomas Birch
High Street, From the Country Market-place Philadelphia, 1798
Engraving, 15¾ × 18 in. (40 × 45.7 cm)
The Historical Society of Pennsylvania, Philadelphia
Courtesy of The Historical Society of Pennsylvania, Philadelphia

Fig. 3.7 Nicholas Scull and George Heap
A Map of Philadelphia and Parts Adjacent, 1753
Engraving, 13½ × 11¾ in. (34.3 × 29.8 cm)
Library Company of Philadelphia
Photo: Library Company of Philadelphia

Fig. 3.8 James Morris's subscription receipt for the Library Company (Philadelphia: Benjamin Franklin, 1732)
Printed paper, 9¾ × 7½ in. (24.8 × 19.1 cm)
Library Company of Philadelphia
Photo: Library Company of Philadelphia

Fig. 3.9 Title page of Francis Hopkinson, copied after Joseph Breintnall and Benjamin Franklin, *A Book of Minutes, containing An Account of the Proceedings of the Directors of the Library Company of Philadelphia, Beginning November 8th, 1731, taken by the Secretary to the Company, Vol: 1st,* 1759
Manuscript book, 13 × 8½ in. (33 × 21.6 cm)
Library Company of Philadelphia

Fig. 3.10 Philip Syng, Jr.
Seal of the Library Company, ca. 1731-33
Brass, 1½ in. diameter (3.8 cm)
Library Company of Philadelphia

Fig. 3.11 Title page of *A Catalogue of Books belonging to the Library Company of Philadelphia* (Philadelphia: Benjamin Franklin, 1741)

Book, 6⅛ × 4 in. (15.6 × 10 cm)
Library Company of Philadelphia
Photo: Library Company of Philadelphia

Fig. 3.12 Rattle (American), nineteenth century
Wood and brass, 7½ × 6 × 2¼ in. (19.1 × 15.2 × 5.7 cm)
CIGNA Museum and Art Collection, Philadelphia
Photo: Joseph Painter

Fig. 3.13 Full-sized side-crank hand pumper, 1753
Wood and nickel, 49½ × 88 × 39¾ in. (125.7 × 223.5 × 100.9 cm)
CIGNA Museum and Art Collection, Philadelphia
Photo: Joseph Painter

Fig. 3.14 Fire bucket inscribed "Library Company of Philadelphia," late eighteenth–early nineteenth century
Leather, 18 × 9¾ × 9¾ in. (45.7 × 24.8 × 24.8 cm)
Library Company of Philadelphia

Fig. 3.15 Salvage bag inscribed "John Coburn PHIL AD" (American), late eighteenth century
Canvas, 44 × 25½ in. (111.8 × 64.8 cm)
CIGNA Museum and Art Collection, Philadelphia
Photo: CIGNA Museum and Art Collection

Fig. 3.16 Fire warden's staff (American), nineteenth century
Wood, 48 in. long (121.9 cm)
CIGNA Museum and Art Collection, Philadelphia
Photo: Joseph Painter

Fig. 3.17 Fire ax (American), ca. 1865
Wood and iron, 14 × 35¼ × 8⅝ in. (35.6 × 89.5 × 21.8 cm)
CIGNA Museum and Art Collection, Philadelphia
Photo: Joseph Painter

Fig. 3.18 Fire hook (American), nineteenth century
Wood and iron, 65½ in. long (166.4 cm)
CIGNA Museum and Art Collection, Philadelphia
Photo: Joseph Painter

Fig. 3.19 Scene depicting firefighting in the eighteenth century from an insurance policy issued by the Insurance Company of North America, 1828
Engraving, 5 × 9 in. (12.7 × 22.9 cm)
CIGNA Museum and Art Collection, Philadelphia
Photo: CIGNA Museum and Art Collection

Fig. 3.20 *Articles of the Union Fire-Company, of Philadelphia*, 1794
Printed document, 18 × 13 in. (46 × 33 cm)
Courtesy of The Historical Society of Pennsylvania, Philadelphia

Fig. 3.21 Page of the minute book of the Union Fire Company, 1736-85
Manuscript book, 13 × 8½ in. (33 × 21.6 cm)
Library Company of Philadelphia

Fig. 3.22 John Stow
Philadelphia Contributionship fire mark, 1752–53
Wood and lead, 12⅞ × 12¼ in. (32.8 × 31.1 cm)
CIGNA Museum and Art Collection, Philadelphia
Photo: Joseph Painter

Fig. 3.23 Membership certificate for the American Philosophical Society, signed by Benjamin Franklin, 1786
Printed document, 9 × 13½ in. (22.9 × 34.3 cm)
CIGNA Museum and Art Collection, Philadelphia
Photo: Joseph Painter

Fig. 3.24 Robert Feke
Portrait of Benjamin Franklin, ca. 1738–46
Oil on canvas, 50¼ × 40⅛ in. (127.4 × 101.9 cm)
Harvard University, Cambridge, Mass.
Courtesy of the Harvard University Portrait Collection, Bequest of Dr. John Collins Warren, 1856, Cambridge, Mass.
Photo: Katya Kallsen

Fig. 3.25 Title page of Benjamin Franklin, *Proposals Relating to the Education of Youth in Pensilvania* (Philadelphia: Benjamin Franklin, 1749)
Pamphlet, 7½ × 5 in. (19.1 × 12.7 cm)
Library Company of Philadelphia

Fig. 3.26 First page of "Account of School Money . . ." (tuition book) belonging to the Philadelphia Academy, 1751–57
Manuscript book, 12⅝ × 7⅞ in. (32 × 20 cm)
University of Pennsylvania Archives and Records Center, Philadelphia

Fig. 3.27 William L. Breton after Pierre Eugène Du Simitière
The Old Academy Buildings in 4th Street as originally constructed, ca. 1830
Watercolor, 6 × 7¾ in. (15.2 × 19.7 cm)
The Historical Society of Pennsylvania, Philadelphia
Courtesy of The Historical Society of Pennsylvania, Philadelphia

Fig. 3.28 William Marchant after Gilbert Stuart
Provost William Smith, 1871
Oil on canvas, 42½ × 57 in. (107.9 × 144.8 cm)
The University of Pennsylvania Art Collection, Philadelphia
Courtesy of The University of Pennsylvania Art Collection

Fig. 3.29 List of financial subscribers to Franklin College (subsequently Franklin and Marshall College), 1786–88
Paper, 8¼ × 13½ in. (21 × 34 cm)
Archives and Special Collections, Franklin and Marshall College, Lancaster, Pa.
Courtesy of Archives and Special Collections, Franklin and Marshall College, Lancaster, Pa.
Photo: Franklin and Marshall College Library

Fig. 3.30 Title page of Benjamin Franklin, *Some Account of the Pennsylvania Hospital* . . . (Philadelphia: Franklin and Hall, 1754)
Book, 9⅝ × 7⅝ in. (24.4 × 19.4 cm)
Courtesy of the Pennsylvania Hospital Historic Collections, Philadelphia

Fig. 3.31 Henry Steeper and John Dawkins
A South-East Prospect of the Pensylvania Hospital with the Elevation of the intended Plan, 1755
Copperplate engraving, 10 × 14 in. (25 × 35 cm)
Library Company of Philadelphia
Photo: Library Company of Philadelphia

Fig. 3.32 Unknown artist
Rendering of the Franklin block of Market Street, ca. 1949
Watercolor, 14 × 18 in. (35.6 × 45.7 cm)
Independence National Historical Park, Philadelphia

Fig. 3.33 William Birch and Thomas Birch
Back of the State House, Philadelphia, 1799
Engraving, 15¾ × 18 in. (40 × 45.7 cm)
The Historical Society of Pennsylvania, Philadelphia
Courtesy of The Historical Society of Pennsylvania, Philadelphia

Fig. 4.1 36 Craven Street, London, 2004
Photograph
Courtesy of The Friends of Benjamin Franklin House, US

Fig. 4.2 Mather Brown
Portrait of William Franklin, ca. 1790
Oil on canvas, 30 × 25 in. (76.2 × 63.5 cm)
Private collection
Photo: Private collection

Fig. 4.3 Attributed to Samuel Johnson
Portrait of Francis Folger Franklin, ca. 1736
Oil on canvas, 33 × 25 in. (83.8 × 63.5 cm)
Private collection

Fig. 4.4 Shoe buckles given by Benjamin Franklin to his daughter Sally (French), ca. 1758
Silver, paste, silk
Collection of The New-York Historical Society, Gift of Dr. Abram Joseph Abeloff, 1942, 1942.234a-c
Photo: The New-York Historical Society

Fig. 4.5 John Hoppner
Portrait of Sarah "Sally" Franklin Bache, 1793
Oil on canvas, 30 × 24¾ in. (76.5 × 63.2 cm)
The Metropolitan Museum of Art, Catharine Lorillard Wolfe Collection, Wolfe Fund, 1901. (01.20)
Photo: ©1998 The Metropolitan Museum of Art, New York

Fig. 4.6 Famille Rose bowl (Chinese), ca. 1760–70
Hard-paste porcelain, 3⅞ × 9⅜ × 9⅜ in. (9.9 × 23.8 × 23.8 cm)
Frankliniana Collection, The Franklin Institute, Inc., Philadelphia

Fig. 4.7 Elias Cachart
Spoon, 1771-72
Silver, ¾ × 6⅞ × 1⅜ in. (1.9 × 17.5 × 3.5 cm)
Walter J. and Leonore Annenberg Rare Book and Manuscript Library, University of Pennsylvania, Philadelphia, gift of the Class of 1904. Purchased by Col. William Hoopes at the sale of the effects of Mrs. Elizabeth Duane Davis, June 6, 1924.

Fig. 4.8 Philip Syng, Jr.
Baptismal bowl for Sally Franklin, engraved "D. EVANS to S. FRANKLIN," ca. 1743
Silver, 2½ × 5¾ × 5¾ in. (6.5 × 14.5 × 14.5 cm)
Private collection

Fig. 4.9 Elias Boudinot
Tankard, 1733–52

Silver, 8¼ × 5¼ × 8½ in. (21.1 × 13.3 × 21.6 cm)
Frankliniana Collection, The Franklin Institute, Inc., Philadelphia

Fig. 4.10 Detail of marrow spoon, English, ca. 1770
Silver, 8⅛ in. long (20.7 cm)
Private collection
Photo: David Heald

Fig. 4.11 Detail of fig. 4.12

Fig. 4.12 Fish slice (probably English), ca. 1760–70
Silver and wood, 1¾ × 4⅛ × 13⅜ in. (4.6 × 10.5 × 34 cm)
Frankliniana Collection, The Franklin Institute, Inc., Philadelphia

Fig. 4.13 Attributed to Solomon Fussell
Side chair (Philadelphia), ca. 1748
Walnut and spruce, 41¾ × 21¼ × 21 in. (10 × 54 cm)
Philadelphia Museum of Art, Promised gift of Robert L. McNeil, Jr.
Photo: Graydon Wood

Fig. 4.14 Armchair (Philadelphia), ca. 1750–70
Walnut, 38⅛ × 30¼ × 21 (97 × 76.8 × 53.3 cm)
Frankliniana Collection, The Franklin Institute, Inc., Philadelphia,
    Gift of Mrs. A. Boissevain, in memory of her mother Mary
    Chickering Nichols

Fig. 4.15 Attributed to William Savery
Dressing table (Philadelphia), ca. 1745–55
Curly maple, poplar, white cedar, and brass, 30 × 35½ × 22 in.
    (76.2 × 90.2 × 55.9 cm)
Collection of Jay Robert Stiefel, Philadelphia
Photo: Philadelphia Museum of Art

Fig. 4.16 Attributed to William Savery, probably after a design by
    Benjamin Franklin
Four-sided music stand (Philadelphia), ca. 1770
Walnut, pine, and iron, 41½ × 28 × 28 in. (105.4 × 71.1 × 71.1 cm)
Atwater Kent Museum of Philadelphia
Courtesy of The Historical Society of Pennsylvania Collection,
    Atwater Kent Museum of Philadelphia
Photo: Atwater Kent Museum of Philadelphia

Fig. 4.17 Tilt-top table and firescreen (Philadelphia), ca. 1740–70,
    possibly designed by Benjamin Franklin
Walnut, 26½ × 30 × 19 in. (67.3 × 76.2 × 48.3 cm)
The Metropolitan Museum of Art, Gift of Mrs. Alfred Mueller, 1956
    (56.221)
Photo: © 2004 The Metropolitan Museum of Art, New York

Fig. 4.18 Edward Duffield
Tall case clock (Philadelphia), ca. 1750
Wood, 82½ × 16 × 9½ in. (209.6 × 40.6 × 24.1 cm)
American Philosophical Society, Philadelphia

Fig. 4.19 Unknown artist (English)
Portrait of Polly Stevenson, ca. 1765
Pastel, 9½ × 7½ in. (24.1 × 19.1 cm)
Theodore E. Wiederseim
Photo: Courtesy of Theodore E. Wiederseim

Fig. 4.20 Benjamin Franklin's handwritten calling card from when he
    lived in England, ca. 1757–75
Paper, 4⅞ × 5¾ × 3⅜ in. framed (12.5 × 14.7 × 1.9 cm)
Masonic Library and Museum of Pennsylvania, Philadelphia

Fig. 4.21 Pieces from a tea service (lidded teapot, lidded sugar bowl,
    lidded creamer) (Worcester), 1770
Earthenware: creamer, 5 in. high, covered (12.7 cm); sugar bowl, 4½ in.
    high, covered (10.8 cm); teapot, 7½ in. high, covered (19 cm)
Carnegie Museum of Art, Pittsburgh

Fig. 4.22 Twelve-piece tea service (Worcester), ca. 1765–75
Hard-paste porcelain, gilt: cups 3 × 3½ × 2¾ in. (7.6 × 9.9 × 7cm);
    saucers 5⅛ × 1 in. (13.2 × 2.5 cm); case 5½ × 17½ × 11¾ in.
    (14 × 44.5 × 15.2 cm)
Frankliniana Collection, The Franklin Institute, Inc., Philadelphia

Fig. 4.23 Benjamin Wilson after an unknown American artist
Portrait of Deborah Franklin, ca. 1758–59
Oil on canvas, 29¾ × 24⅞ in. (75.6 × 63.2 cm)
American Philosophical Society, Philadelphia
Photo: American Philosophical Society

Fig. 4.24 Benjamin Wilson
Portrait of Benjamin Franklin, ca. 1760
Oil on canvas, 50 × 40 in. (127 × 101.6 cm)
Diplomatic Reception Rooms, U.S. Department of State, Washington,
    D.C.; Gift of A. H. Meyer, 1967
Photo: Will Brown

Fig. 4.25 Benjamin Franklin
Sketch of table seating at dinner with the king of Denmark, 1768
Ink on paper, 9⅛ × 11⅓ in. (23 × 28.8 cm)
American Philosophical Society, Philadelphia
Photo: American Philosophical Society

Fig. 4.26 Floor plan of the first floor of the Franklin house in
    Philadelphia, ca. 1765, possibly sketched by Benjamin Franklin
Ink on paper, 12 × 7⅔ in. (30.3 × 19.5 cm)
American Philosophical Society, Philadelphia
Photo: American Philosophical Society, Philadelphia

Fig. 4.27 Marble-top mixing table (Philadelphia), ca. 1750–60
Mahogany, 28 × 32¾ × 21 in. (71 × 83 × 53.5 cm)
Private collection
Photo: Courtesy of Sotheby's

Fig. 4.28 Side chair (Philadelphia), ca. 1765
Walnut, 40¼ in. high (102.2 cm)
Private collection
Photo: Courtesy of Sotheby's

Fig. 4.29 High chest (Philadelphia), ca. 1765–75
Mahogany, 97¾ × 45½ × 23 in. (248.3 × 115.6 × 58.4 cm)
Colonial Williamsburg Foundation, Virginia, Gift of Mr. and Mrs.
    Joseph H. Hennage
Photo: Colonial Williamsburg Foundation

Fig. 4.30 John Mayhew
Flat-top or "partner's" desk, ca. 1770–85

Mahogany, brass, and steel, 28⅝ × 61⅜ × 28½ in. (72.5 × 155.8 × 72.4 cm)
Walter J. and Leonore Annenberg Rare Book and Manuscript Library, University of Pennsylvania, Philadelphia

Fig. 4.31 Robert Gurney and Thomas Cook
Tankard, ca. 1750
Silver, 7¾ × 5½ × 5½ in. (19.7 × 13.8 × 13.8 cm)
Atwater Kent Museum of Philadelphia
Courtesy of The Historical Society of Pennsylvania Collection, Atwater Kent Museum of Philadelphia

Fig. 4.32 Tea caddy (English), 1771
Sheffield plate, 3⅞ × 3⅝ × 2⅝ in. (9.9 × 9.1 × 6.7 cm)
Independence National Historical Park, Philadelphia

Fig. 4.33 Attributed to Alexis Nicolas Perignon, Sr.
The Potager of the Chateau de Valentinois, Passy, ca. 1775–80
Gouache on linen, 7¾ × 11⅜ in. (19.5 × 28.7 cm) (oval)
Didier Aaron et Cie, Paris
Courtesy Didier Aaron et Cie, Paris

Fig. 4.34 Louis Carrogis de Carmontelle
Portrait of Benjamin Franklin in an armchair, ca. 1780–81
Ink, crayon, and watercolor on paper, 12 × 7½ in. (30.5 × 19.1 cm)
National Portrait Gallery, Smithsonian Institution, Washington, D.C., Bequest of Mrs. Herbert Clark Hoover, Washington, D.C.
Photo: National Portrait Gallery

Fig. 4.35 Armchair (English), ca. 1765
Mahogany, beech, silk damask (modern), 35 × 26 × 22 in. (88.9 × 66 × 55.9 cm)
Independence National Historical Park, Philadelphia

Fig. 4.36 Antoine Guérhard and Christophe Dihl, Manufacture d'Angoulême
Pieces from a tea service with Chantilly sprig pattern: teapot, cup with handle, cup without handle (tea bowl), saucers, 1784
Porcelain, cup 3½ in. diameter (9 cm); saucer 5⅜ in. diameter (14 cm); teapot 5¾ × 8¼ × 3⅞ in. (14.6 × 21 × 9.8 cm)
Cups and saucers: Carnegie Museum of Art, Pittsburgh. Teapot: Walter J. and Leonore Annenberg Rare Book and Manuscript Library, University of Pennsylvania, Philadelphia

Fig. 4.37 Probably from the Faubourg Saint-Denis porcelain factory
Spirit barrel, ca. 1780
Hard-paste porcelain and wood, 8⅜ × 7 × 7 in. (21.3 × 17.8 × 17.8 cm)
Atwater Kent Museum of Philadelphia
Courtesy of The Historical Society of Pennsylvania Collection, Atwater Kent Museum of Philadelphia

Fig. 4.38 François Joubert and François-Nicholas Rousseau
Spirit Lamp, ca. 1775–81
Silver and wood, 4⅛ × 7¼ × 4¾ (10.6 × 18.4 × 12.1 cm)
Atwater Kent Museum of Philadelphia
Courtesy of The Historical Society of Pennsylvania Collection, Atwater Kent Museum of Philadelphia, Gift of Lawrence Wainwright, 1972

Fig. 4.39 Armchair (London or Philadelphia), ca. 1770
Mahogany and leather, 47 × 29¼ × 25½ in. (119.3 × 74.3 × 64.8 cm)
Columbia University Archives, Columbiana Library, New York
Photo: Gavin Ashworth

Fig. 4.40 Library chair with folding steps (London or Philadelphia), 1760–80, possibly designed by Benjamin Franklin
Mahogany, leather, and steel, 50 × 27½ × 34¼ in. (127 × 69.9 × 87 cm)
American Philosophical Society, Philadelphia

Fig. 4.41 Sketches of long-arm pole designed by Benjamin Franklin, from "Description of an Instrument for Taking Down Books from High Shelves," 1786, in Jared Sparks, *The Works of Benjamin Franklin* (Boston: Hilliard, Gray, 1836–40), 6: 563
Library Company of Philadelphia

Fig. 4.42 Charles Willson Peale
Illustration of Mr. Cram's fan chair, 1786
Ink on paper, 8⅛ × 10 in. (20.5 × 25.2 cm)
American Philosophical Society, Philadelphia
Photo: American Philosophical Society

Fig. 5.1 Illustration depicting movement and method of swimming (crawl) from M. Thévenot, *L'Art de nager démontré par figures: Avec des Avis pour se baigner utilement* (Paris, 1696)
Engraving, 2⅜ × 3½ in. (6 × 9 cm)
Department of Printing and Graphic Arts, Houghton Library, Harvard University, Cambridge, Mass., Typ 615.96.831
Photo: Harvard University, Houghton Library

Fig. 5.2 Bifocals, after 1784, design suggested by Benjamin Franklin
Metal, 4⅞ × 4½ in. (12.4 × 11.4 cm)
Frankliniana Collection, The Franklin Institute, Inc., Philadelphia

Fig. 5.3 Benjamin Franklin
Sketch of bifocal lenses from a letter to George Whatley, May 23, 1785
Manuscript, 12⅝ × 7¾ in. (32 × 19.7 cm)
Library of Congress, Washington, D.C.
Photo: Library of Congress, Washington, D.C.

Fig. 5.4 Compound monocular microscope with accessories, ca. 1750, made in London by John Cuff
Brass on a wooden base, 13½ in. high on a 6⅝ in. square base (34.3 cm; 16.8 cm)
Billings Microscope Collection, National Museum of Health and Medicine, Armed Forces Institute of Pathology, Washington, D.C.
Photo: National Museum of Health and Medicine, Washington, D.C.

Fig. 5.5 James Trenchard after William Bartram
Franklinia alatamaha, ca. 1786
Engraving, 12 × 9¾ in. (30.5 × 24.8)
American Philosophical Society, Philadelphia
Photo: American Philosophical Society

Fig. 5.6 J. S. Miller
Portrait print of Peter Collinson, 1770
Line engraving, 8⅛ × 6¼ in. (20.6 × 15.9 cm)
The Burndy Library, Dibner Institute for the History of Science and Technology, Cambridge, Mass.
Photo: The Burndy Library

Fig. 5.7 John Bartram
Map of the Allegheny Ridge, ca. 1745–47
Ink on paper, 12¼ × 15 in. (31.1 × 38.1 cm)
American Philosophical Society, Philadelphia
Photo: American Philosophical Society

Fig. 5.8 Illustration of a mastodon tooth fossil from *Philosophical Transactions of the Royal Society,* vol. 57, pt. 1 (London, 1768)
Engraving, 9⅛ × 11⅝ in. (23 × 29.5 cm)
American Philosophical Society, Philadelphia
Photo: American Philosophical Society

Fig. 5.9 Mastodon tooth fossil
Fossilized stone, 3¼ × 3⅜ in. (8.3 × 8.6 cm)
Independence National Historical Park, Philadelphia

Fig. 5.10 James Poupard after Georges-Louis Le Rouge
A Chart of The Gulf Stream, from Benjamin Franklin, "Maritime Observations," in APS, *Transactions* 2 (1786)
Engraving, 8 × 10 in. (20.3 × 25.5 cm)
American Philosophical Society, Philadelphia
Photo: American Philosophical Society

Fig. 5.11 Charles Willson Peale
Portrait of David Rittenhouse, 1772
Oil on canvas, 30 × 25 in. (76.2 × 63.5 cm)
University of Pennsylvania Art Collection, Philadelphia
Courtesy of the University of Pennsylvania Art Collection, Philadelphia

Fig. 5.12 Astronomical transit telescope, ca. 1769, built by David Rittenhouse
Brass, 34 × 20¾ × 25¼ in. (86.4 × 52.7 × 64.1 cm)
American Philosophical Society, Philadelphia

Fig. 5.13 Unknown artist
Joseph Priestley, L.L.D. F.R.S. (portrait print) (London: J. Walker, 1782)
Engraving, 11 × 7½ in. (28 × 19 cm)
SSPL/The Image Works, Woodstock, N.Y.
© SSPL/The Image Works, Inc.
Photo: © SSPL/The Image Works, Inc.

Fig. 5.14 V. Vitold Rola Piekarski
Lavoisier dans son laboratoire, 1888
Engraving, 6⅛ × 9⅜ in. (15.5 × 24 cm)
Walter J. and Leonore Annenberg Rare Book and Manuscript Library, University of Pennsylvania, Edgar Fahs Smith Memorial Collection

Fig. 5.15 Edward Nairne, Thermometer, ca. 1760.
Walnut, glass, and metal, 21 × 2¼ × 1⅜ in. (53.3 × 5.7 × 3.5 cm)
Atwater Kent Museum of Philadelphia
Courtesy of The Historical Society of Pennsylvania Collection, Atwater Kent Museum of Philadelphia

Fig. 5.16 George Adams, Double-acting pneumatic air pump, ca. 1740–70
Wood, glass, brass, with two glass bell jars, 30 × 12⅞ × 26 in. (76.2 × 32.8 × 66.1 cm); base, 20⅛ × 18¾ × 18⅞ in. (51.2 × 47.7 × 48 cm)
Collections of Independence National Historical Park, Philadelphia

Fig. 5.17 Front page of Benjamin Franklin, *An Account Of the New Invented Pennsylvanian Fire-Places . . .* (Philadelphia: Benjamin Franklin, 1744)
Pamphlet, 8 × 5 in. (20.3 × 12.7 cm)
Library Company of Philadelphia

Fig. 5.18 James Turner after Lewis Evans
"Profile of the Chimney and Fire-Place" from Benjamin Franklin, *An Account Of the New Invented Pennsylvanian Fire-Places . . .* (Philadelphia: Benjamin Franklin, 1744)
Woodcut in pamphlet, unfolded page 8⅛ × 16⅜ (20.6 × 41.6 cm)
Library Company of Philadelphia

Fig. 5.19 Odometer, ca. 1763, possibly designed by Benjamin Franklin
Iron, brass and paint, 1⅝ × 6⅞ × 4¼ in. (4.1 × 17.5 × 10.8 cm)
Frankliniana Collection, The Franklin Institute, Inc., Philadelphia

Fig. 5.20 J. Lodge
Diagrams of three-wheel clock from James Ferguson, *Select Mechanical Exercises: Showing How to Construct Different Clocks, Orreries, and Sun-Dials, on Plain and Easy Principles,* 2d ed. (London, 1778)
Engraving, 7¾ × 6 in. (20 × 15 cm)
Franklin Collection, Yale University Library, New Haven, Conn.
Photo: Yale University Library

Fig. 5.21 Benjamin Franklin
Magic square, Canton Papers, vol. 2, ca. 1765
Pen and ink, 13 × 8 in. (32 × 20.5 cm)
The Royal Society, London
Photo: © The Royal Society, London

Fig. 5.22 Benjamin Franklin
A Magic Circle of Circles, Canton Papers, vol. 2, ca. 1765
Pen and ink, 8.3 × 13.3 in. (21.2 × 34 cm)
The Royal Society, London
Photo: © The Royal Society, London

Fig. 5.23 After John Vanderbank
Miniature portrait of Isaac Newton, after 1725
Watercolor on ivory, 1¼ × 1⅛ in. (3.2 × 2.9 cm)
American Philosophical Society, Philadelphia
Photo: American Philosophical Society

Fig. 5.24 Robert Feke
Portrait of Thomas Hopkinson, 1746
Oil on canvas, 49¾ × 39⅝ in. (126.4 × 101 cm)
Smithsonian American Art Museum, George Buchanan Coale Collection, Washington, D.C.
Photo: Smithsonian American Art Museum

Fig. 5.25 Title page of Benjamin Franklin, *Experiments and Observations on Electricity . . .* (London: E. Cave, 1751)
Book, 9¼ × 7 ×½ in. (23 × 18 × 1 cm)
The Library of The Franklin Institute, Inc., Philadelphia

Fig. 5.26 Electrical apparatus (Philadelphia), ca. 1742–47
Walnut and iron, 59 × 28 × 24 in. (149.8 × 71.1 × 61 cm)
Library Company of Philadelphia
Photo: David A. Gentry

Fig. 5.27 Static electricity tube (English), ca. 1747
Glass, 30½ × 2 × 2 in. (77.5 × 5.1 × 5.1 cm)
Frankliniana Collection, The Franklin Institute, Inc., Philadelphia

Fig. 5.28 Bells attached to a Leyden jar capacitor, late eighteenth
    century
Metal and wood, 11⅝ × 5¾ × 15½ in. (29.5 × 14.6 × 39.4 cm)
Courtesy of the Bakken Library and Museum of Electricity,
    Minneapolis
Photo: Bakken Library and Museum of Electricity

Fig. 5.29 "Electrical Battery" of Leyden jars, ca. 1760–69
Glass, metal, and wood, 14 × 18 × 13 in. (35.6 × 45.7 × 33 cm)
American Philosophical Society, Philadelphia

Fig. 5.30 Thomas Jefferys after Lewis Evans's original sketch
Illustration of a sentry box from Benjamin Franklin, *Experiments and
    Observations on Electricity . . .* (London: E. Cave, 1751), fig. 9,
    following p. 72
Engraving in book, 9¼ × 7 ×½ in. (23 × 18 × 1 cm)
The Library of The Franklin Institute, Inc., Philadelphia

Fig. 5.31 Model of a "thunder house," late eighteenth century
Wood and metal, 14⅝ × 8⅝ × 16⅛ in. (37.1 × 21.8 × 40.9 cm)
Courtesy of the Bakken Library and Museum of Electricity,
    Minneapolis
Photo: Bakken Library and Museum of Electricity

Fig. 5.32 Broadside advertising Ebenezer Kinnersley's lecture tour,
    March 16, 1752
Broadside, 13 × 8¾ in. (33 × 22.2 cm)
Rosenbach Museum and Library, Philadelphia

Fig. 5.33 Diagram of the apparatus that Thomas-François Dalibard
    used in an experiment at Marly-la-Ville, France, from Dalibard's
    translation of Benjamin Franklin, *Experiments and Observations
    on Electricity . . .*, 2d ed. (Paris: Chez Durand, 1756)
The Burndy Library, Dibner Institute for the History of Science and
    Technology, Cambridge, Mass.
Photo: The Burndy Library

Fig. 5.34 Illustration of the Annual Medal of the Royal Society
    (Copley Medal) from *The Gentleman's Magazine*, December 1753
    (London, 1753)
Engraving, 5 × 8 in. (12.7 × 20.3 cm)
The Library of The Franklin Institute, Inc., Philadelphia
Photo: Courtesy of the Library of The Franklin Institute

Fig. 5.35 Edward Fisher after Mason Chamberlin
Benjamin Franklin of Philadelphia, L.L.D., F.R.S., 1763
Mezzotint, 15 × 11 in. (38 × 28 cm)
Collection Stuart E. Karu

Fig. 5.36 Unknown artist
A View of the State House in Philadelphia (now Independence Hall)
    from *The Gentleman's Magazine*, September 1752 (London, 1752)
Engraving with later hand-coloring, 5 × 8 in. (12.7 × 20.3 cm)
Courtesy of E. Philip Krider
Photo: Courtesy of E. Philip Krider

Fig. 5.37 Jacques de LaJoue
Portrait of Abbé Nollet, mid-eighteenth century
Oil on canvas, 21¼ × 17⅜ in. (54 × 44 cm)
Musée Carnavalet, Paris
© Photothèque des Musees de la Ville de Paris
Photo: Lifermann

Fig. 5.38 Top portion of a lightning rod, ca. 1756
Iron, 12½ × 1½ × 1¼ in. (31.7 × 3.8 × 3.2 cm)
Frankliniana Collection, The Franklin Institute, Inc., Philadelphia

Fig. 6.1 Page of *Minutes of Conferences, held with the Indians at Easton*
    (in a portfolio of four treaties) (Philadelphia: Franklin and Hall,
    1757)
Book, 14¾ × 9⅞ in. (37.5 × 25.1 cm)
Walter J. and Leonore Annenberg Rare Book and Manuscript Library,
    University of Pennsylvania, Philadelphia

Fig. 6.2 Daniel Smith and Robert Sharp
Milk jug, 1765
Silver, 5 × 5⅜ × 2¾ in. (12.7 × 13.7 × 7 cm)
Sterling and Francine Clark Art Institute, Williamstown, Mass.

Fig. 6.3 Association for Defense, Second Philadelphia lottery ticket
    (Philadelphia: Benjamin Franklin, 1748)
Printed document, 5⅜ × 2⅜ in. (13.7 × 6 cm)
Rosenbach Museum and Library, Philadelphia

Fig. 6.4 "Join, or Die" cartoon from the *Pennsylvania Gazette*, May 9,
    1754 (Philadelphia: Benjamin Franklin, 1754)
Woodcut, 2 × 2⅞ in. (5.1 × 7.3 cm)
Library Company of Philadelphia
Photo: Library Company of Philadelphia

Fig. 6.5 Attributed to Henry Dawkins
The Paxton Expedition (Philadelphia, 1764)
Engraving, 9¼ × 13¾ in. (23.5 × 35 cm)
Library Company of Philadelphia
Photo: Library Company of Philadelphia

Fig. 6.6 Front page of Benjamin Franklin, *A Narrative of the late
    Massacres, in Lancaster County, of a Number of Indians . . .*
    (Philadelphia: Benjamin Franklin, 1764)
Pamphlet, 7½ × 5 in. (19.1 × 12.7 cm)
Library Company of Philadelphia

Fig. 6.7 Mason Chamberlin
Portrait of Benjamin Franklin, 1762
Oil on canvas, 50⅜ × 40¾ in. (128.2 × 103.5 cm)
Philadelphia Museum of Art, Gift of Mr. and Mrs. Wharton Sinkler,
    1956
Photo: Philadelphia Museum of Art

Fig. 6.8 Paper embossed with tax stamp, 1765
Paper, 8 × 6 in. (20.3 × 15.2 cm)
Library Company of Philadelphia

Fig. 6.9 Front page of *The Pennsylvania Journal; and Weekly
    Advertiser*, no. 1195, October 31, 1765 (Philadelphia: William and
    Thomas Bradford, 1765)

Newspaper, 17¼ × 12 × 2 in. (43.8 × 30.5 × 5.1 cm)
The Historical Society of Pennsylvania, Philadelphia
Courtesy of The Historical Society of Pennsylvania, Philadelphia

Fig. 6.10 Title page of *The Examination of Doctor Benjamin Franklin
. . . relating to the Repeal of the Stamp-Act, &c.* (Philadelphia: Hall
and Sellers, 1766)
Printed paper, 8 × 5¼ in. (20.3 × 13.3 cm)
Library Company of Philadelphia
Photo: Library Company of Philadelphia

Fig. 6.11 Attributed to Benjamin Wilson
The Repeal, Or the Funeral of Miss Ame-Stamp (London, 1766)
Engraving, 10¾ × 17¾ in. (27 × 45 cm)
Library Company of Philadelphia
Photo: Library Company of Philadelphia

Fig. 6.12 Mather Brown
Portrait of Alexander Wedderburn, 1st earl of Rosslyn, 1791
Oil on canvas, 50 × 40⅛ in. (127 × 101.9 cm)
The Scottish National Portrait Gallery, Edinburgh
Photo: The Scottish National Portrait Gallery

Fig. 6.13 Robert Whitechurch after Christian Schussele
Franklin Before the Lords in Council, 1774, 1859
Engraving, 41 × 50 in. framed (104.1 × 127 cm)
Collection Stuart E. Karu

Fig. 6.14 François Dumont
Snuffbox with portrait of Benjamin Franklin, 1779
Watercolor on ivory and tortoise, 2⅜ in. diameter (6 cm)
Collection Stuart E. Karu

Fig. 6.15 Jean-Antoine Houdon
Portrait bust of Thomas Jefferson, 1787
Plaster, 29 in. high (73.7 cm)
American Philosophical Society, Philadelphia
Photo: American Philosophical Society

Fig. 6.16 Begun by Robert Edge Pine and finished by Edward Savage
Congress Voting Independence, ca. 1784–1801
Oil on canvas, 25 × 32½ in. framed (63.5 × 82.6 cm)
Atwater Kent Museum of Philadelphia
Courtesy of The Historical Society of Pennsylvania Collection,
Atwater Kent Museum of Philadelphia
Photo: Historical Society of Pennsylvania

Fig. 6.17 "Original Rough draught" of the Declaration of
Independence, June 1776
Manuscript, 12½ × 8 (31.9 × 20.3 cm)
Library of Congress, Washington, D.C.
Photo: Library of Congress

Fig. 6.18 Etienne Palliere
Allegory of the Franco-American Alliance, ca. 1778
Watercolor, 26½ × 32¾ in. framed (67.3 × 83.2 cm)
Collection Stuart E. Karu

Fig. 6.19 Louis Sicardy
Miniature portrait of Louis XVI, 1784

Watercolor on ivory with gold and glass, 2 × 1¾ in. (5.1 × 4.4 cm)
American Philosophical Society, Philadelphia
Photo: American Philosophical Society

Fig. 6.20 Mather Brown
Portrait of John Adams, 1788
Oil on canvas, 35½ × 28 in. (90.2 × 71.3 cm)
Boston Athenaeum
Photo: Boston Athenaeum

Fig. 6.21 Hubert Robert
The Departure of Lafayette for America in 1777, ca. 1800
Oil on canvas, 25 × 68 in. (63 × 173 cm)
Musée de la Cooperation Franco-américaine, Blérancourt
Photo: Gerard Blot, Réunion des Musées Nationaux/Art Resource, N.Y.

Fig. 6.22 After Antoine-François Callet
Portrait of Charles Gravier, comte de Vergennes, ca. 1781
Oil on canvas, 31 × 24 in. (oval) (78.8 × 61 cm)
Châteaux de Versailles et de Trianon, Versailles
Photo: J. Schormans, Réunion des Musees Nationaux/Art Resource,
N.Y.

Fig. 6.23 Front page of *Treaty of Alliance Eventual and Defensive,
between His Most Christian Majesty Louis the Sixteenth, King of
France and Navarre, and the Thirteen United States Of America*
(Treaty of Amity) (Philadelphia: John Dunlap, 1778)
Pamphlet, 10½ × 8⅓ in. (26.8 × 21.2 cm)
American Philosophical Society, Philadelphia
Photo: American Philosophical Society

Fig. 6.24 First page of Congressional order for supplies, July 1779
Manuscript, 13¼ × 16¼ in. (open folio) (33.7 × 41.3 cm)
The Historical Society of Pennsylvania, Philadelphia
Courtesy of The Historical Society of Pennsylvania, Philadelphia
Photo: Historical Society of Pennsylvania

Fig. 6.25 John Wallis
*The United States of America laid down From the best Authorities,
Agreeable to the Peace of 1783* (London, 1783)
Hand-colored engraving and ink, 19½ × 23⅜ in. (49.5 × 59.4 cm)
The Historical Society of Pennsylvania, Philadelphia
Courtesy of The Historical Society of Pennsylvania, Philadelphia

Fig. 6.26 Benjamin West
*American Commissioners of the Preliminary Peace Negotiations with
Great Britain,* 1783–84
Oil on canvas, 28⅜ × 36⅓ in. (72.1 × 92.3 cm)
Winterthur Museum, Garden and Library, Winterthur, Del., gift of
Henry Francis du Pont
Photo: Courtesy of Winterthur Museum

Fig. 6.27 Attributed to Jacques-Louis David
Portrait of Benjamin Franklin, n.d.
Pen and ink, 4⅝ × 4 in. (11.7 × 10.2 cm)
Rosenbach Museum and Library, Philadelphia

Fig. 6.28 Title page of *The Definitive Treaty between Great Britain, and
the United States of America, Signed at Paris, the 3d day of September
1783* (Treaty of Paris) (Passy, 1783)

Book, 7⅞ × 5 in. (20.1 × 12.7 cm)
American Philosophical Society, Philadelphia
Photo: American Philosophical Society

Fig. 6.29 Anton Van Ysendyck
Proclamation of the Treaty of Paris, ca. 1827
Oil on canvas, 31 × 57 in. (78.7 × 61 cm)
Châteaux de Versailles et de Trianon, Versailles
Photo: Gerard Blot, Réunion des Musées Nationaux/Art Resource, N.Y.

Fig. 6.30 U.S. Constitution, 1787
Printed document with handwritten annotations, 16⅛ × 9⅞ in. (40.8 × 25 cm)
American Philosophical Society, Philadelphia
Photo: American Philosophical Society

Fig. 6.31 Fugio penny, 1787
Brass and copper, 1⅛ in. diameter (2.8 cm)
Masonic Library and Museum of Pennsylvania, Philadelphia

Fig. 7.1 Joseph Siffred Duplessis
Portrait of Benjamin Franklin, 1778
Oil on canvas, 28½ × 23 in. (oval) (72.4 × 58.4 cm)
The Metropolitan Museum of Art, Friedsam Collection, Bequest of Michael Friedsam, 1931. (32.100.132)
Photo: © 1981 The Metropolitan Museum of Art, New York

Fig. 7.2 John Trumbull
Miniature portrait of William Temple Franklin, 1790
Watercolor on ivory, 3⅝ × 3⅛ in. (oval)
Yale University Art Gallery, Trumbull Collection, New Haven, Conn.
Photo: Yale University Art Gallery

Fig. 7.3 Anne-Rosalie Boquet Filleul
Portrait of Benjamin Franklin, 1778 or 1779
Oil on canvas, 35 × 27½ in. (47½ × 41½ in. framed) (89 × 70 cm [121 × 105 cm])
Private collection

Fig. 7.4 "Depense journaliere du Vin pendant le mois de 7bre. 1782" (Chart of daily wine consumption for the month of September 1782)
Single sheet, 11 × 14 in. (28 × 36 cm)
American Philosophical Society, Philadelphia
Photo: American Philosophical Society

Fig. 7.5 Attributed to Alexis Nicolas Pérignon, Sr.
View of the Château de Valentinois, Passy, ca. 1775–80
Gouache on linen, 7¾ × 11⅜ in. (oval) (19.5 × 28.7 cm)
Didier Aaron et Cie, Paris
Courtesy Didier Aaron et Cie, Paris
Photo: Didier Aaron et Cie

Fig. 7.6 Type matrices (French), probably made by Claude Mozet, ca. 1740
Brass, approximately 2 × 1 in. per piece (5.1 × 2.5 cm)
Massachusetts Historical Society, Boston
Courtesy of the Massachusetts Historical Society, Boston
Photo: Massachusetts Historical Society

Fig. 7.7 Type ladle (probably American), ca. 1785
Walnut and iron, ⅞ × 8¼ × 1½ in. (2.2 × 21 × 3.8 cm)
Frankliniana Collection, The Franklin Institute, Inc., Philadelphia

Fig. 7.8 Pierre-Simon Fournier le jeune
"Fourneau à fondre les Lettres" (Typefoundry), plate 2 in Fournier, *Manuel typographique,* vol. 1 (Paris: [1764])
Engraving in book, 7¾ × 6⅛ in. (plate) (20 × 16 cm)
Library Company of Philadelphia
Photo: Library Company of Philadelphia

Fig. 7.9 Page of Benjamin Franklin's cash book, headed "Passy, December 4, 1779"
Bound manuscript, 8 × 6⅛ in. (20.4 × 15.5 cm)
American Philosophical Society, Philadelphia
Photo: American Philosophical Society

Fig. 7.10 Invitation to a celebration of the anniversary of the Declaration of American Independence, July 5, 1779 (Passy: Benjamin Franklin, 1779)
Single sheet, 9 × 7¼ in. (22.9 × 18.2 cm)
American Philosophical Society, Philadelphia
Photo: American Philosophical Society

Fig. 7.11 Blank passport (Passy: Benjamin Franklin, ca. 1780)
Single sheet, 14¼ × 9½ in. (36.2 × 24.1 cm)
Walter J. and Leonore Annenberg Rare Book and Manuscript Library, University of Pennsylvania, Philadelphia

Fig. 7.12 Passport for William Rawle and Benjamin[?] Walker, May 8, 1782 (Passy: Benjamin Franklin, 1782)
Single sheet, 16 × 10¼ in. (40.6 × 26 cm)
The Historical Society of Pennsylvania, Philadelphia
Courtesy of The Historical Society of Pennsylvania, Philadelphia
Photo: Historical Society of Pennsylvania

Fig. 7.13 George Peter Alexander Healy
Franklin Urging the Claims of the American Colonies Before Louis XVI, ca. 1847
Oil on canvas, 24 × 36 in. (61 × 91.4 cm)
American Philosophical Society, Philadelphia
Photo: American Philosophical Society

Fig. 7.14 French loan certificate, no. 12, August 15, 1781 (Passy: Benjamin Franklin, 1781)
Printed document, 10¾ × 8⅜ in. (27.3 × 21.3 cm)
American Philosophical Society, Philadelphia
Photo: American Philosophical Society

Fig. 7.15 Promissory notes signed by John Hindman, September 25, 1781 (Passy: Benjamin Franklin, 1781)
Printed paper, 9¼ × 7¼ in. (23.3 × 18.2 cm)
American Philosophical Society, Philadelphia
Photo: American Philosophical Society

Fig. 7.16 Benjamin Franklin, *Supplement to the Boston Independent Chronicle,* March 1782 (Passy: Benjamin Franklin, 1782)
Single sheet, 15½ × 9½ in. (39.5 × 24 cm)
American Philosophical Society, Philadelphia
Photo: American Philosophical Society

Fig. 7.17 Title page of Pierre André Gargaz, *Conciliateur . . . ou Projet de paix perpétuelle . . .* (Passy: Benjamin Franklin, 1782)
Book, 6½ × 3¾ in. (16.5 × 9.5 cm)
The Historical Society of Pennsylvania, Philadelphia
Courtesy of The Historical Society of Pennsylvania, Philadelphia
Photo: Historical Society of Pennsylvania

Fig. 7.18 Set of stencils in a box, 1781, made by Bery
Walnut and brass, 12½ × 10 × 3½ in. (31.8 × 25.4 × 8.9 cm)
American Philosophical Society, Philadelphia
Photo: American Philosophical Society

Fig. 7.19 Anne Louise Boivin d'Hardancourt Brillon de Jouy, "Marche des insurgents," 1778
Manuscript sheet music, 11⅞ × 9⅜ in. (30 × 23.3 cm)
American Philosophical Society, Philadelphia
Photo: American Philosophical Society

Fig. 7.20 Charles James
Glass armonica, ca. 1761–62
Wood, brass, glass, cork, and iron, 35¾ × 45 × 12 in. (90.8 × 114.3 × 30.3 cm)
Frankliniana Collection, The Franklin Institute, Inc., Philadelphia

Fig. 7.21 William Temple Franklin
"Three Positions of the Elbow," from M. Lemontey, ed., *Mémoires de l'abbé Morellet . . .* , 2 vols. (Paris, 1821)
Engraving, 7⅝ × 4¾ in. (19.4 × 12 cm)
American Philosophical Society, Philadelphia
Photo: American Philosophical Society

Fig. 7.22 Chess set, ca. 1750–80
Pearwood, 3⅝ in. (pawn height) (9.2 cm)
American Philosophical Society, Philadelphia

Fig. 7.23 Louis-Michel van Loo
Portrait of Madame Helvétius, 1755
Oil on canvas, 74⅖ × 51⅗ in. (189 × 131 cm)
Private collection

Fig. 7.24 First page of the corrected draft of Benjamin Franklin, "Dialogue entre la Goutte & M. F." (Dialogue between the gout and Mr. Franklin), 1780
Manuscript, 12¼ × 8¼ in. (31.2 × 21 cm)
American Philosophical Society, Philadelphia
Photo: American Philosophical Society

Fig. 7.25 Title page of Benjamin Franklin, *Dialogue entre La Goutte et M. F.* (Passy: Benjamin Franklin, 1781?)
Pamphlet, 4¼ × 7 in. (10.8 × 17.2 cm)
Beinecke Rare Book and Manuscript Library, Yale University, New Haven, Conn.
Photo: Beinecke Rare Book and Manuscript Library

Fig. 7.26 Title page of Benjamin Franklin, *Information to those who would remove to america* (Passy: Benjamin Franklin, 1784)
Pamphlet, 6⅓ × 4⅛ in. (16 × 10.5 cm)
American Philosophical Society, Philadelphia

Fig. 7.27 Title page of Louis-Alexandre, duc de La Roche-Guyon et de La Rochefoucauld, trans., *Constitutions des Treize États-Unis de l'amérique* (Paris: Pierres and Pissot, 1783)
Book, 10¼ × 8 in. (26 × 20.5 cm)
American Philosophical Society, Philadelphia
Photo: American Philosophical Society

Fig. 7.28 Benjamin Franklin
Sketch of the Great Seal of the United States, 1784–85
Manuscript, image: 1¾ × 2 (4.4 × 5.1 cm)
Library of Congress, Washington, D.C.

Fig. 8.1 Pierre Eugène Du Simitière
Musiciens d'un Calinda, ca. 1760
Watercolor, 9⅝ × 7⅝ in. (24 × 19 cm)
Library Company of Philadelphia
Photo: Library Company of Philadelphia

Fig. 8.2 Title page of Samuel Sewall, *The Selling of Joseph: A Memorial* (Boston: Bartholomew Green and John Allen, 1700)
Book, 11 × 7 in. (27.5 × 18.2 cm)
Massachusetts Historical Society, Boston
Courtesy of the Massachusetts Historical Society, Boston
Photo: Massachusetts Historical Society

Fig. 8.3 Page of the *Pennsylvania Gazette,* May 2, 1745 (Philadelphia: Benjamin Franklin, 1745)
Newspaper, 11⅘ × 8¹⁄₁₀ in. (30 × 20.5 cm)
Walter J. and Leonore Annenberg Rare Book and Manuscript Library, University of Pennsylvania, Philadelphia

Fig. 8.4 Attributed to John Lewis Krimmel (formerly attributed to Pavel Petrovich Svinin)
Worldly Folk Questioning Chimney Sweeps and Their Master Before Christ Church, Philadelphia, 1811–ca. 1813
Watercolor and graphite on white laid paper, 9½ × 6⅞ in. (24 × 17.4 cm)
The Metropolitan Museum of Art, Rogers Fund, 1942 (42.95.15)
Photo: © 1989 The Metropolitan Museum of Art, New York

Fig. 8.5 [?] Mackenzie after an unknown American artist
Alice ([London]: T. Hurst, 1803)
Stipple engraving, 5¾ × 3½ in. (14.7 × 9 cm)
Library Company of Philadelphia
Photo: Library Company of Philadelphia

Fig. 8.6 Title page of Ralph Sandiford, *A Brief Examination of the Practice of the Times . . .* (Philadelphia: Printed for the Author [by Benjamin Franklin and Hugh Meredith], 1729)
Pamphlet, 6½ × 4 in. (16.5 × 10.2 cm)
Library Company of Philadelphia

Fig. 8.7 Title page of Benjamin Lay, *All Slave-Keepers That keep the Innocent in Bondage . . .* (Philadelphia: Printed for the Author [by Benjamin Franklin], 1737)
Book, 6 × 3¾ in. (15.2 × 9.5 cm)
Walter J. and Leonore Annenberg Rare Book & Manuscript Library, University of Pennsylvania, Philadelphia

Fig. 8.8 Unknown artist
Phillis Wheatley, Negro Servant . . . (portrait print) from Phillis
    Wheatley, *Poems on Various Subjects, Religious and Moral,* 1773
Engraving, 4 × 5 in (10.16 × 12.7 cm).
Library of Congress, Washington, D.C.
Photo: Library of Congress

Fig. 8.9 Unknown artist
Rev. Richard Allen (portrait print) (Philadelphia: J. Dainty, 1813)
Stipple engraving, 11½ × 8¼ in. (29.2 × 21 cm)
Library Company of Philadelphia
Photo: Library Company of Philadelphia

Fig. 8.10 Pitcher with silhouette of Absalom Jones, ca. 1808
Earthenware, 8⁷⁄₁₆ in. high (21.5 cm)
National Portrait Gallery, Smithsonian Institution; gift of Sidney
    Kaplan, Washington, D.C.
Photo: National Portrait Gallery

Fig. 8.11 Title page of "The Constitution and Minutes of the
    Pennsylvania Society for promoting the Abolition of Slavery . . . ,"
    April 23, 1787
Manuscript, 13 × 8 in. (33 × 20.3 cm)
The Historical Society of Pennsylvania, Philadelphia
Courtesy of The Historical Society of Pennsylvania, Philadelphia

Fig. 8.12 Josiah Wedgwood
Am I Not a Man and a Brother? ca. 1787
Jasperware, 1¼ × 1⅛ in. (oval) (3.2 × 2.9 cm)
American Philosophical Society, Philadelphia
Photo: American Philosophical Society

Fig. 8.13 Title page of *An Address To the Public, from the Pennsylvania
    Society for promoting the Abolition of Slavery* . . . (Philadelphia:
    Francis Bailey, [1789])
Broadside, 13½ × 8¼ in. (34.3 × 21 cm)
Library Company of Philadelphia

Fig. 8.14 Front page of *Banneker's Almanack, and Ephemeris for the
    Year of our Lord 1793* (Philadelphia: Joseph Crukshank, [1792])
Pamphlet, 6½ × 4 in. (17 × 10 cm)
Haverford College Library, Haverford, Pa.
Photo: Haverford College Library

Fig. 8.15 Benjamin Franklin, Petition from the Pennsylvania Society for
    Promoting the Abolition of Slavery to the U.S. Congress, February
    3, 1790
Manuscript, 15 × 9¼ in. (38.1 × 23.5 cm)
National Archives and Records Administration, Washington, D.C.
Courtesy of the National Archives and Records Administration,
    Washington, D.C.
Photo: National Archives and Records Administration

Fig. 8.16 Samuel Jennings
Liberty Displaying the Arts and Sciences, 1792

Oil on canvas, 60¼ × 74 in. (153 × 188 cm)
Library Company of Philadelphia
Photo: Library Company of Philadelphia

Fig. 8.17 Charles Willson Peale
Portrait of Benjamin Franklin, 1785
Oil on canvas, 23⅛ × 19 in. (58.7 × 48.4 cm)
Pennsylvania Academy of the Fine Arts, Philadelphia, Bequest of
    Mrs. Sarah Harrison (The Joseph Harrison, Jr. Collection)
Photo: Pennsylvania Academy of the Fine Arts

Fig. A.1 Charles Washington Wright
Benjamin Franklin, the Fireman, ca. 1850
Oil on canvas, 29½ × 24½ in. (75 × 62.2 cm)
CIGNA Museum and Art Collection, Philadelphia
Photo: Joseph Painter

Fig. A.2 George Heap
Association Battery, detail of *The East Prospect of the City of
    Philadelphia, in the Province of Pennsylvania,* 1755
Engraving, 6¼ × 19½ in. (15.9 × 49.5 cm)
CIGNA Museum and Art Collection, Philadelphia

Fig. A.3 *An Essay of a Declaration of Rights, Brought in by the
    Committee appointed for that Purpose, and now under the
    Consideration of the Convention of the State of Pennsylvania*
    (Philadelphia: John Dunlap, 1776)
Broadside, 14⅛ × 8⅞ in. (36 × 22.7 cm)
Library Company of Philadelphia

Fig. A.4 David[?] After LeJeune[?]
Franklin s'oppose aux taxes en 1766, n.d.
Engraving, 6 × 3½ in. (15.2 × 8.9 cm)
American Philosophical Society, Philadelphia
Photo: American Philosophical Society

Fig. A.5 Title page of Benjamin Franklin, "Observations concerning
    the Increase of Mankind . . . ," in William Clarke, *Observations
    On the late and present Conduct of the French: with Regard to
    their Encroachments upon the British Colonies in North America.
    Together with remarks on the importance of these colonies to Great-
    Britain* (Boston: S. Kneeland, 1755)
Book, 7⅛ × 4½ in. (18 × 11.5 cm)
Library Company of Philadelphia

Fig. A.6 Jean-Antoine Houdon
Portrait Bust of Benjamin Franklin, 1779
Marble, 21 × 13½ × 10 in. (53.3 × 34.3 × 25.4 cm)
Philadelphia Museum of Art, purchased with funds from the Barra
    Foundation, the Henry P. McIlhenny Fund in memory of Frances P.
    McIlhenny, funds bequeathed by Walter E. Stait, the Fiske Kimball
    Fund, the Women's Committee of the Philadelphia Museum of Art,
    and by donors to the Fund for Franklin
Photo: Graydon Wood, 1999, Philadelphia

Chronology

1706 Benjamin Franklin born in Boston, January 17 (January 6, 1705, Old Style), into a devout Puritan family.

1714 Attends Boston Latin school.

1715 Attends Brownell's school.

1716 Begins working at father's candle shop.

1718 Apprenticed to brother James, a printer.

1722 Writes "Silence Dogood" essays.

1723 Runs away to Philadelphia. Works as printer for Samuel Keimer.

1724 Moves to London; finds work as printer.

1725 Writes *A Dissertation on Liberty and Necessity, Pleasure and Pain*. In Philadelphia, sweetheart Deborah Read marries John Rogers.

1726 Returns to Philadelphia. Works as clerk for Thomas Denham, merchant.

1727 Rejoins Keimer's print shop. Founds Junto, a self-improvement society, which meets every Friday night.

1728 Borrows money and opens his own print shop with Hugh Meredith.

1729 Writes "Busy-Body" essays. Buys failing *Pennsylvania Gazette*. Around this time illegitimate son William is born.

1730 Enters into common-law marriage with Deborah (Read) Rogers.

1731 Joins Freemasons. Founds Library Company of Philadelphia.

1732 Son Francis ("Frankie") Folger is born. Launches *Poor Richard's Almanack*.

1736 Becomes clerk of Pennsylvania Assembly. Forms Union Fire Company. Son Francis dies of smallpox.

1737 Becomes postmaster of Philadelphia.

1739 Becomes friends with the English evangelist George Whitefield.

1741 Launches *General Magazine*, which fails. Around this time designs Franklin stove, making improvements over the next several years.

1743 Daughter Sarah (Sally) is born. Founds American Philosophical Society.

1745 The English merchant and scientist Peter Collinson sends electricity pamphlets and glass tube.

1746 Performs electricity experiments over the summer.

1747 Writes *Plain Truth* and hoax "The Speech of Miss Polly Baker." Forms Associator companies (voluntary militia) to defend Pennsylvania.

1748 Retires from printing business, forming partnership with his foreman David Hall.

1749 Writes proposal for the Philadelphia Academy (later the University of Pennsylvania). Designs and advocates lightning rods.

1750 Devises experiment to prove lightning is electrical in nature.

1751 Electricity writings published in London, with the help of Peter Collinson.

Elected to Pennsylvania Assembly. Proposes starting a hospital (later the Pennsylvania Hospital) using matching public and private funds.

1752 Performs kite experiment proving lightning is electrical.

1753 Receives honorary Masters degrees from Harvard and Yale. Appointed joint deputy postmaster general of North America. Awarded Copley Medal of the Royal Society of London.

1754 French and Indian War begins. Designs first political cartoon urging union of colonies, "Join, or die." Drafts Albany Plan of Union.

1755 Arranges supplies for General Braddock during Indian campaign. Persuades Assembly to pass militia bill. Quarrels with the proprietors over the militia.

1756 Elected a member of the Royal Society of London and corresponding member of the Royal Society of Arts. Helps pass bills to establish night watchmen and street lighting in Philadelphia.

1757 Leaves for London as agent of the Pennsylvania Assembly. Writes *Way to Wealth* and last *Poor Richard's Almanack*. Takes lodgings at the Craven Street home of Margaret Stevenson.

1758 Invents damper for stoves or chimneys. Visits Ecton with William to research ancestry.

1759 Receives honorary Doctor of Laws degree from University of Saint Andrews. Visits northern England and Scotland; meets the Scots intellectuals David Hume, Adam Smith, William Robertson, and Lord Kames. British and American troops capture Quebec.

1760 Writes *The Interest of Great Britain Considered* (Canada Pamphlet), urging Britain to acquire Canada. Privy Council gives him partial victory in fight with Penns. Travels in England with William; meets Samuel Johnson.

1761 Travels to Flanders and Holland with William.

1762 Invents glass armonica. Returns to Philadelphia. William marries Elizabeth Downes in London, is made royal governor of New Jersey.

1763 Begins new Market Street house. Undertakes postal inspection trip from Virginia to New England. French and Indian War ends.

1764 Writes *A Narrative of the late Massacres* against the Paxton Boys. Defeated in bitter Assembly election. Returns to London as agent of Pennsylvania Assembly.

1765 Stamp Act passes. Writes "The Grand Leap of the Whale." Colonists refuse to use stamps; massive nonimportation begins.

1766 Testifies against Stamp Act in Parliament. Act repealed. Partnership with David Hall expires. Tours Germany.

1767 Townshend duties imposed. Travels to France. Daughter Sarah marries Richard Bache.

1768 Wages press crusade in London on behalf of the colonies. Appointed agent of Georgia Assembly. Prints maps of Atlantic showing the course of the Gulf Stream.

1769 Appointed agent of New Jersey House of Representatives. Second visit to France.

1770 Townshend duties repealed on everything except tea. Elected agent of Massachusetts House of Representatives.

1771 Showdown with earl of Hillsborough over credentials as agent for the Massachusetts lower house. Begins *Autobiography*. Visits Ireland and Scotland. Meets son-in-law Bache.

1772 Secretly sends purloined Hutchinson letters to Boston. Elected foreign associate of the French Academy.

1773 Writes parodies "Rules by Which a Great Empire May Be Reduced to a Small One" and "An Edict by the King of Prussia." Experiments with oil to calm water. Boston Tea Party.

1774 Showdown with the Privy Council in the Cockpit over Hutchinson letters. Dismissed as postmaster. Coercive Acts passed. Begins peace discussions with both Lord Chatham and Lord Howe. Wife Deborah dies.

1775 Returns to Philadelphia. Battles of Lexington and Concord. Elected to Second Continental Congress. Proposes first Articles of Confederation.

1776 William removed as royal governor and imprisoned in Connecticut. Undertakes Canada mission. Helps draft and signs Declaration of Independence. Meets with Lord Howe on Staten Island. Elected one of three commissioners to France, sailing with grandsons William Temple Franklin and Benjamin Franklin Bache. Meets secretly with the French minister Vergennes to arrange French loans for America.

1777 Receives promise of two million livres from the French government. Settles in Passy, fêted throughout Paris.

1778 Reports grant of six million livres for year; by end of Revolution has secured twenty million livres. Arranges Treaties of Alliance and Commerce with France. Becomes sole minister plenipotentiary to France. William released from captivity; he moves to loyalist New York.

1779 Attends the salons of Mesdames Brillon and Helvétius.

1780 John Adams arrives in Paris as commissioner to negotiate peace with Britain; Franklin helps get him dismissed after Adams insults the French. Rejects surrendering American claims to the Mississippi in exchange for Spanish aid. British capture Charleston.

1781 Congress appoints Franklin, Adams, John Jay, and Henry Laurens peace commissioners. Cornwallis surrenders at Yorktown.

1782 Along with Adams and Jay negotiates peace treaty with Britain. William returns to London.

1783 Witnesses two of the first manned balloon flights. Signs Treaty of Paris, making peace with Great Britain.

1784 Writes part 2 of *Autobiography*. Mary (Polly) Stevenson visits Passy.

1785 Describes invention of bifocals in letter to the London merchant George Whatly. Last meeting with William. Returns to Philadelphia. Elected president of Supreme Executive Council of Pennsylvania (in effect, governor).

1786 Builds addition to Market Street house. Designs instrument for taking down books from high shelves.

1787 Serves as Pennsylvania delegate to Constitutional Convention. Elected president of Pennsylvania Society for Promoting the Abolition of Slavery.

1788 Writes part 3 of *Autobiography*. Ends service as president of Pennsylvania Council.

1790 Dies April 17 at age eighty-four.

Index

198, 230; allegorical and historical, French, *8, 9, 46, 47,* 220, 221, *305; on decorative objects, 10, 15, 216;* as diplomat to France, *8, 198, 220, 221, 230, 254;* figurines, *5, 39;* with fur cap, *5, 46, 220,* 221; portrait busts, *5,* 298, *308;* portraits, American, *96, 112,* 113, *297;* portraits, English, *16, 40, 41, 86, 143, 192,* 208, *209;* portraits, French, 152, *153, 230, 236, 237–38, 239,* 326n40

Franklin, Benjamin, inventions of: bifocals, 49, 163–64, *165;* catheter, 163–64; chair with concealed ladder, 51, *157, 158;* chair with writing arm, 51; clock (three-wheel), 39, 178, *179;* copperplate press, 176; copy press, 149, 160; electrical battery, 185, *186 (see also* electricity); glass armonica, 39, 136, 143, 158, *263,* 263–64; hot water system (bath), 160; long-arm pole, 51, 158, *158,* 160; music stand, four-sided, 136, *136;* nature printing, 29, *29, 67,* 176; odometer (three-wheel), 178, *179;* rocking chair with fan, 51, 158, *159,* 160; salting lumber (to preserve), 48; stove and fireplace improvements, 29–30, *30,* 39, *177,* 177–78, *178;* street lamp, 28, *28;* swimming paddles, 163; tilt-top table/firescreen, 136, *136. See also* lightning rod

Franklin, Benjamin, postmaster: artifacts of, *29, 35, 83, 179;* of North America (1753), *34, 36, 44, 75,* 85, 178; of Philadelphia (1737), 29, 75–76, 178

Franklin, Benjamin, printer in Passy, *261,* 262–63; and bagatelles, 48, *237, 240, 248, 265, 267, 268;* and Fournier's type, 243, 247, 253; and loan certificates, 248, 254–56, *255;* and passports, 133, 250–54, *251,*

252, 256, 331n22; press at, 237–38, 249–62, 257, *260;* printing for new nation, 241, 268–71; printing type at, 238, 240–41, *244,* 245–49, 253–54, *255,* 256; typefoundry at, 241–42, *245,* 245–48, *247*

Franklin, Benjamin, printer in Philadelphia, 58, *61, 177;* as editor, 69–72; epitaph of, 87, 89; and *General Magazine, and Historical Chronicle, 71,* 74; integrated business of, 5, 72–76, 85–86; as job printer, 69–71, 72, *73, 74, 202;* and Keimer, 23–27, 60–63, 66–67, 320n9; and Keith, 23–24, 63–65, 320n7; open-press policy of, 69, 71–72; and paper currency, 26, 29, *67,* 68–69, 75, 176, 320n10; as paper merchant, 29, 31, 76; as printer to Pennsylvania Assembly, 27, 55, 75, 200, 320n15; and printing partnerships, 5, 28, 85 *(see also* Hall, David; Meredith, Hugh); prints antislavery tracts, 282–83, *284;* as publisher, 76–82, *78, 80,* 321n19; rivalry with Bradford, 55–57, 69, 72, 75–76, 79–81, 320n10, 320n15; role as second printer, 55–80; shop of, 28–29, 76, *77,* 131, 137. See also *Pennsylvania Gazette*

Franklin, Benjamin, scientific interests of: aurora borealis, 48–49; botany, *166,* 166–67; fossils and geology, *167,* 167–68, *168;* Gulf Stream, *170,* 170–72; health and exercise, 163–64, *164;* heating technology, 32, 177–78; maritime topics, 51, 271, *271;* oil and water, 172; scientific instruments, *162,* 165, *165, 175,* 176; ship speeds in canals, 173–74; smallpox inoculation, *21,* 91, 99, 108–10, 123, 164; transits of Mercury and Venus, 172, 174–76; volcanoes, 174; weather and climate, 168–69, 174; wind and whirlwinds, 169–70. *See also* electricity

Franklin, Benjamin, writings of: *Account Of the New Invented Pennsylvanian Fire-Places . . . , 30,* 176–78, *177, 178; Address to the Public, from the Pennsylvania Society for promoting the Abolition of Slavery . . . ,* 293; "Articles of Confederation" (1775), 44, 217; *Art of Procuring Pleasant Dreams,* 164; *Art of Swimming, Made Safe . . . ,* 164; *Bagatelles,* 265; "Bradshaw's Epitaph," 44–45; "Busy-Body," 26–27, 67; "Causes of the American Discontents before 1768," 43; "Defense of the Americans," 38, 40; "Dialogue Between the Gout and Mr. Franklin," 265, *267, 268; Directions to the Deputy Post-Masters,* 82, *83; Dissertation on Liberty and Necessity, Pleasure and Pain,* 24; "Edict by the King of Prussia," 43; "Elysian Fields," 48; "Ephemera," 48; Epitaph, 87, *88,* 89; *Experiments and Observations on Electricity,* 174, 182–88, *184, 187,* 195–96; "Grand Leap of the Whale over Niagara Falls," 43; "The Handsome and the Deformed Leg" 265; *Information to those who would remove to america,* 49, 265, *267, 269; Interest of Great Britain Considered* (Canada Pamphlet), 39, 311; "Jakes on Our Tables," 33, 38–39; "King's Own Regulars," 44; "Maritime Observations," *170,* 271, *271; Modest Enquiry into the Nature and Necessity of a Paper-Currency,* 26–27, 66, 68–69, 176; "Morals of Chess," 265; *Narrative of the late Massacres,* 40, 204, *207;* "Observations concerning the Increase of Mankind . . . ," 33, 43, 281–82, *307,* 308–312; petition from PAS, *295; Physical and Meteorological Observations, Conjectures, and Suppositions,* 168; *Plain Truth,* 31, *31,* 201;